THE BRAHMS-KELLER CORRESPONDENCE

THE
Brahms-Keller
Correspondence

Edited by
GEORGE S. BOZARTH
in collaboration with
Wiltrud Martin

Published by the
University of Nebraska Press
LINCOLN AND LONDON
in cooperation with the
Library of Congress
Music Division

⊛ The paper in this book meets the minimum requirements of
American National Standard for Information Sciences –
Permanence of Paper for Printed Library Materials,
ANSI z39.48-1984.

Library of Congress Cataloging in Publication Data

The Brahms-Keller correspondence / edited by George S.
Bozarth in collaboration with Wiltrud Martin.

p.   cm.

Includes bibliographical references (p.) and index.

ISBN 0-8032-1238-0 (alk. paper)

1. Brahms, Johannes, 1833–1897 – Correspondence.
2. Keller, Robert, d. 1891 – Correspondence. 3. Composers –
Germany – Correspondence. 4. Editors – Germany –
Correspondence.

I. Bozarth, ML410.B8A4 1996 780'.92'2–dc20 [B]

95-16158 CIP MN

For Donald L. Leavitt,
Chief of the Music Division,
The Library of Congress
(1929–86)

Contents

Contents

Plates

Abbreviations

In the commentary and notes, references to letters published in the *Johannes Brahms Briefwechsel* are cited as (volume: pages), and references to letters published in Kurt Stephenson, ed., *Johannes Brahms und Fritz Simrock: Weg einer Freundschaft: Briefe des Verlegers an den Komponisten* are given as (*no.* plus letter number). Cross references to letters in the present volume are made as (item number).

Other abbreviated references to published correspondence used in the commentary include the following:

Billroth
Otto Gottlieb-Billroth, ed., *Billroth und Brahms im Briefwechsel* (1935)

Schumann
Berthold Litzmann, ed., *Clara Schumann–Johannes Brahms Briefe* (1927)

Stockhausen
Julia Wirth, ed., *Julius Stockhausen: Der Sänger des deutschen Liedes* (1927)

References to the *Johannes Brahms sämtliche Werke*, edited by Eusebius Mandyczewski and Hans Gál (1926–28), are given as *Brahms Werke*. For further information on these publications, see the bibliography.

In transcribing the letters, common words abbreviated by Brahms and Keller have been left in their shortened form: *erhalten* (*erh.*), *für* (*f.*), *statt* (*st.*), *und* (*u.*), *letzt* (*l.*), and *vorletzt* (*vorl.*) as well as forms of *der, die,* and *das* (*d.*). The musical terms *Partitur* (*P.* and *Part.*), *Pause* (*P.*), *Takt* (*T.*), and *Zeile* (*Z.*), when abbreviated, have also been left in their shortened forms. The missing portions of other abbreviated words have been added in brackets and abbreviation periods have been suppressed.

Preface

In the early 1980s word reached the Library of Congress about a cache of Brahms manuscripts in private hands in Massachusetts soon to come on the market. Inquiries revealed the significance of these holdings. Prime among the musical scores were handwritten copies of Brahms's long-lost *Kyrie* and *Missa canonica,* WoO 17 and 18, two products of the composer's studies in counterpoint during the mid-1850s heretofore known only from the correspondence. The collection also contained a dated autograph manuscript of *Klosterfräulein,* Op. 61 No. 1, that established this duet as one of Brahms's earliest extant works, composed at least twenty-one years before its publication; the engravers' models for Brahms's first two opuses of songs—the *Gesänge,* Opp. 3 and 6 (published in 1853)—sources crucial for the preparation of a critical edition of these youthful works but unavailable to Eusebius Mandyczewski and Hans Gál when they prepared the *Johannes Brahms sämtliche Werke* (1926–28); and vocal parts in Brahms's hand for the *Ave Maria,* Op. 12, and the first two of the *Drei geistliche Chöre,* Op. 37. All these manuscripts were originally part of the personal collection of Julius Otto Grimm, a composer and conductor whom Brahms met in Leipzig in November 1853 and who became a lifelong friend.[1] Also preserved in the Massachusetts collection were a large number of unpublished letters, the most substantial and important group consisting of correspondence between Brahms and Robert Keller, the editor who oversaw the publication of Brahms's works by the firm of N. Simrock in Berlin from the early 1870s until his death in 1891.[2]

This impressive collection went on the auction block with J. A. Stargardt in Marburg in 1981–82.[3] The mass movements and the Op. 6 songs were acquired by the Gesellschaft der Musikfreunde in Vienna; the Op. 3 songs, the duet *Klosterfräulein,* and the Brahms-Keller correspondence went to the Gertrude Clarke Whittall Collection of the Library of Congress.[4]

Published in the present volume, in transcription and translation, are the complete Brahms-Keller materials in the Library of Congress, consisting of eighteen letters, fourteen postcards, and a copy of an additional postcard, all from Brahms to Keller; drafts in Keller's hand of four letters to Brahms; two letters from Fritz Simrock to Keller; an envelope for a missing letter from Brahms to Keller (25 May 1890); an annotated list of possible keys for the transposed edition of the songs Opp. 69–72; Keller's draft of a foreword to Simrock's Brahms *Thematisches Verzeichniss* (1887), with comments added by Brahms; and a single sheet and a manuscript of twenty-eight pages detailing potential corrections of the first edition of the Third Symphony, prepared by Keller and annotated by Brahms. Supplementing these documents are eight letters and two postcards from Keller to Brahms that were part of Brahms's estate and are preserved in the archive of the Gesellschaft der Musikfreunde in Vienna (Sign. Brahms-Korrespondenz 180; drafts of three of these letters are among the Library of Congress materials) and two letters from Keller to Joseph Joachim owned by the Staatliches Institut für Musikforschung, Preußischer Kulturbesitz, in Berlin.

In 1917 and 1919 the Deutsche Brahms-Gesellschaft (Berlin) published 939 letters from Brahms to the music publisher Peter Joseph Simrock (1792–1868) and his son and business successor Fritz Simrock (1837–1901). Edited by Max Kalbeck, this correspondence appeared as volumes 9–12 of the *Johannes Brahms Briefwechsel*. The other side of this exchange remained unknown until 1961, when Kurt Stephenson released 156 of Fritz Simrock's letters to Brahms in his book *Johannes Brahms und Fritz Simrock: Weg einer Freundschaft: Briefe des Verlegers an den Komponisten*. The publication of the letters between Brahms and Robert Keller now supplies the final link in the extant communications between Brahms and his foremost publishing house.[5]

The earliest letter in the Brahms-Keller correspondence dates from 28 September 1877, the latest from 30 May 1890. During this period of nearly thirteen years Robert Keller assisted Brahms with the publication of all four of his symphonies, the D Major Violin Concerto, the Second Piano Concerto, several important chamber works, and numerous keyboard pieces, choral compositions, and Lieder. Discussion of many of these works appears in the correspondence, as Brahms and Keller strive together to ensure accurate musical texts. The letters also touch on Keller's piano arrangements of Brahms's music and on his preparation of the first edition of the Brahms *Thematisches Verzeichniss*.

Little is known about the provenance of the Brahms-Keller correspondence after Keller's death in 1891. The letters very likely first passed into the hands of his sister-in-law and sole heir, Minna Günther (see the introduction); by circa 1920 they were in the possession of Diplom-Ingenieur Phil. Elkan in Berlin, as reported by Max Friedlaender, who examined the two postcards from Brahms to Keller concerning the song *Therese*, Op. 86 No. 1 (items 12 and 13).[6] It has not been possible to confirm the circumstances under which the correspondence subsequently passed into the Massachusetts collection. According to Kenneth W. Rendell, the manuscript dealer who initially represented the Massachusetts family in the early 1980s, the Brahms manuscripts and letters were found in a trunk that came from Holland in the 1930s and was thought to contain only family papers. The Brahms materials were discovered after the family moved from New York to Cape Cod. The family could only speculate that their father, who by then had died, had purchased the manuscripts early in the century.

A few words about the transcriptions and translations are in order. Brahms's indentation, or lack of it, for paragraphs has been preserved in the transcriptions, but in the translations all paragraphs have been indented. When revisions occur in the original text, both original and final readings are given in the transcriptions, but only the final one is translated. Words left incomplete owing to haste in writing (*di* for *die*, *Si* for *Sie*, *i* for *in*, etc.) have been completed in the transcriptions, without editorial indication, but abbreviated words have been completed only when the meaning is unclear (a list of common abbreviations is given at the front of this book). When abbreviated words have been completed, the period has been deleted. Missing punctuation has been added silently, and $\bar{m}$ and $\bar{n}$ have been rendered *mm* and *nn*. All other editorial additions and emendations have been placed in brackets. Passages underlined one or more times in the original documents have been underscored in the same manner in the transcriptions but printed in italic type in the translations. Passages written in roman (rather than German gothic) script in the original documents have been rendered in italic type in the transcriptions.

Introductory remarks and commentary have been provided for the letters, to elucidate their contents and to place them within the context of Brahms's correspondence with Fritz Simrock and others. Six appendixes follow the main text. A discussion of the two handwritten inventories that accompany the letters owned by the Library of Congress and of the several numbering systems that have been applied to these letters appears in appendix A. Appendix B explains the basis for dating the undated items, and appendix C provides information about the types of papers used for the letters. Appendix D comprises a transcription and translation of Keller's twenty-eight-page compilation of potential corrections for the Third Symphony. Transcriptions and translations of two letters from Robert Keller to Joseph Joachim are presented in appendix E. Appendix F catalogs Keller's numerous arrangements of works by Brahms and others.

The preparation of this volume was a collaborative effort. The initial transcriptions and translations were made by Wiltrud Martin, who acquired her expertise at deciphering Brahms's often difficult handwriting through several years of work as a research assistant to Margit McCorkle's Brahms Cataloguing Project at the University of British Columbia. I provided the prefatory material, commentary, and appendixes and also edited the transcriptions and revised the translations. The final readings for the translations were achieved by consensus.

An Arts and Humanities Research Professorship from the Graduate School Research Fund at the University of Washington provided time for me to work on this project, and a subvention from the same fund helped to underwrite the publication of this book. Special thanks are due to Arnhild Dietz and Dr. Imogen Fellinger, who tracked down most of the biographical information on Robert Keller drawn from archival sources in Berlin; to Dr. Fellinger for calling the Keller-Joachim letters to my attention, and to the Staatliches Institut für Musikforschung, Preußischer Kulturbesitz, Berlin West, for allowing publication of these letters; to James Pruett, Elizabeth Auman, and the staff of the Music Division of the Library of Congress and to Dr. Otto Biba and the late Peter Riethus of the archives of the Gesellschaft der Musikfreunde for permitting the use of their collections' manuscript and printed sources and for their kind assistance with numerous aspects of this project; to the Pierpont Morgan Library in New York, the Brahms Archive of the Staats- und Universitätsbibliothek in Hamburg, the Abteilung Musik und darstellende Kunst of the Hochschulbibliothek, Hochschule der Kunst in Berlin, and the Oesterreichische National-bibliothek and the Stadt- und Landesbibliothek in Vienna for allowing examination of Brahms manuscripts and editions in their collections and for answering inquiries about these sources; to the Muzeum České hudby in Prague for providing photocopies of Keller's letters and postcards to Dvořák; to Dr. Michael Struck of the Wissenschaftliche Arbeitsstelle of the *Johannes-Brahms-Gesamtausgabe* (Kiel) for providing photocopies of early Brahms editions and for assisting with numerous inquiries; to G. Henle Verlag, Munich, for lending photocopies of manuscripts in private possession in Germany; to Professors David Brodbeck and Walter Frisch for offering helpful suggestions on the manuscript of this book; to Kenneth W. Rendell for information concerning the provenance of the Brahms-Keller correspondence; to Professor William Horne for verifying information about sources in Vienna; to Professor David Kappy for his consultations on matters of notation for the French horn; to Professor Nelda Murri, director of the Drug Information Center, and Professor Keith Benson of the Department of Medical History and Ethics at the University of Washington for their assistance in interpreting the symptoms and treatment of Keller's final illness; to Ben Kohn for his research assistance and scrutiny of translations; to Thane Lewis, who assisted with typesetting and proofreading; to Sydney Keegan, who prepared the index; and to my wife, Tamara Friedman, who graciously shared her husband and home with Brahms and Keller for the duration of this project.

This volume is dedicated to the memory of Donald L. Leavitt (1929–86), head of the Music Division of the Library of Congress from 1978 until 1986 and a staunch supporter and friend of Brahms scholarship. Don's importance to this field is little known by most, for such was the way he worked. Preferring to be the "man behind the scenes," he was always ready to suggest and encourage but seldom to be found when credit was being distributed. It was his idea to hold an international Brahms conference at the Library of Congress during the sesquicentennial year 1983 and his planning that made it possible for the conferees and for Washington's music lovers to enjoy on this occasion a series of concerts by some of the world's finest performers. It was also during Don's tenure that, in anticipation of the sesquicentennial festivities, the Music Division found the means to enrich its already important collection of Brahms music manuscripts and letters through the acquisition of the Brahms-Keller correspondence and the manuscripts of *Klosterfräulein* and the six *Gesänge*, Op. 3.

GEORGE S. BOZARTH
Seattle, January 1995

Introduction

Anyone who has experienced the rigors of publishing knows the value of a first-rate editor. It was in this capacity that Robert Keller served Johannes Brahms for two decades. With diligence and devotion he ushered the master's works into print, first by checking for inconsistencies within and variants among the manuscript sources submitted for scores, parts, and keyboard arrangements, then by assisting with the proofreading of the new editions. Benefiting from Keller's scrutiny were those compositions issued by the N. Simrock Verlag in Berlin from circa 1871, the year of the earliest reference to Keller as proofreader of a Brahms work, to 1891, the year of Keller's death—that is, roughly from the *Schicksalslied*, Op. 54, to the G Major String Quintet, Op. 111. In addition, Keller was responsible for preparing solo piano versions of eighty-six of Brahms's songs, vocal duets, and choral pieces, and keyboard arrangements of thirty-one of his choral, chamber, and orchestral compositions.

To read the correspondence between Brahms and his able assistant is to witness a relationship of mutual respect and, as the years passed, increasing friendship, to experience the excitement of an ardent admirer as he came to know the composer's latest works (sometimes literally part by part), and to gain an appreciation of the labors that went into the process of trying to achieve accurate texts for these masterpieces. Brahms emerges in these dealings as frank and demanding but appreciative, often good humored, and ever sensitive to the feelings of his collaborator; for his part, Keller was a dedicated Brahmsian who viewed his work as a mission but endeared himself through diligent application rather than flattering words. Read together with the correspondence between Brahms and Fritz Simrock, the extant letters between Brahms and Keller permit a reconstruction, often in considerable detail, of the editorial process; viewed in conjunction with other materials documenting Keller's life and times in Berlin, the correspondence provides a rare glimpse of a freelance musician at work in the flourishing capital of Bismarckian Germany.

Robert Keller was born in the village of Harpersdorf in the Goldberg district of Lower Silesia, southwest of Liegnitz (Legnica), on 6 January 1828.[1]

Located in the hill country of the Riesengebirge between Goldberg and Löwenberg, Harpersdorf was a parish town with a castle and, by 1850, a population of 1,710.[2] In the early Middle Ages, gold had been found on the ridges of the Riesengebirge. A wealth of other minerals was subsequently mined throughout this realm of the legendary Rübezahl, "the Silesian sprite who haunts the forest and reigns over subterranean regions"[3] (and the subject of a well-known painting by Moritz von Schwind and a fairy-tale opera once envisioned by Gustav Mahler). To the east of Harpersdorf, around Liegnitz and in the plain of the River Oder, the good, arable land supported a thriving agricultural economy.

Until the population transfers after the Second World War, the majority of the inhabitants of this area were German and Protestant. The larger cities of Lower Silesia—Görlitz, Liegnitz, and Breslau—had been important for their textile industries since the eighteenth century, and during the nineteenth century the region became notable for manufacturing. A sense of the language and character of the workers who populated the rural Silesia of Keller's youth, of the conflicts between tradition and the dawning industrial age during his formative years, was vividly conveyed by Gerhart Hauptmann (1862–1946), Silesia's preeminent playwright, in the controversial drama *Die Weber* (*The Weavers*, 1892), set in his grandfather's generation of the 1840s. The archetypal German Silesian has been described as "hard-working, hospitable, kind, open-minded, honest, full of deep feeling, somewhat dreamy, deliberate, and often slow in decisive actions," with a respect for authority, "a healthy loyalty to tradition," and a "joy of living"[4]—traits many of which Keller demonstrates in his relationship with Brahms.

Reporting his occupation simply as "musician," Robert Keller first appeared in the published directories of his adopted city of Berlin in 1855.[5] During the next thirteen years, he lived in at least four different buildings, all located in the Louisenstadt district, south of the center of the city—at Alte Jacobstraße 16 (1855), Alexandrinenstraße 27 (1856–61), Dresdenerstraße 121 (1863), and Ritterstraße 99 (1887).[6] Judging from a map of Berlin prepared in 1850, on which a structure appears only at the Alte Jacobstraße address, most of Keller's residences were in buildings of relatively new construction, erected to accommodate Berlin's rapid population growth during the middle years of the century.[7] Keller's coresidents in these buildings were members of either the minor ranks of the government or the skilled working class. In 1856, for instance, his neighbors at Alexandrinenstraße 27 were a strap maker (who owned the building and may have had a shop on the ground floor), a law clerk (*Kanzlist*), a retired second lieutenant of noble birth, a gilder (*Vergolder*), two shoemakers, an umbrella maker, a cabinetmaker (*Tischler*), another musician, and two widows. Residing at Keller's first three addresses and changing residences at the same time as he did was a widow Günther. Very likely, Keller was her *Untermieter.*

Directly to the west of the Louisenstadt lay the Friedrichstadt, the commercial district in which the offices of N. Simrock Verlag were located. In response to the growing economic and political importance of Berlin, the twenty-five-year-old Fritz Simrock (1839–1901), son of the Bonn music publisher Peter Joseph Simrock (1792–1868) and nephew of the poet and philologist Karl Simrock, had taken over the firm of Robert Timm and Company in 1864 and opened the Simrock'sche Musikhandlung at Jägerstraße 18. Between 1867 and 1870, he issued music in both Bonn and Berlin. In mid-1870, two years after his father's death, he closed the Bonn offices and moved his entire operation to Berlin, taking up business quarters at Friedrichstraße 171, a location situated prominently on the southwest corner of the Friedrichstraße and the Französischestraße.[8]

Once a residential boulevard, the Friedrichstraße had become a shopping street for the well-to-do and the main thoroughfare traversing the business and financial district of Berlin. Located just two blocks south of the grand boulevard Unter den Linden, Simrock's offices were in "one of the most lively quarters of the new imperial city" (9:14), within walking distance of the Schauspielhaus, the opera, the university, the Königliche Bibliothek, the Königliche Akademie, and the Singakademie.[9]

By 1873 Keller had moved out of the old city to an apartment block on the Steglitzerstraße, a newly developed area south of the Tiergarten along the Potsdamerstraße, a few blocks beyond the Landwehr-Canal and one block north of the present-day Kurfürstenstraße. In 1850 this street was still in open country; by 1875 it was lined with apartment buildings. The pressure of Berlin's rapidly increasing population during these twenty-five years (rising from 418,690 to 962,970),[10] together with the rampant financial speculation that followed the creation of the Second Reich in 1871 and the injection into the German economy of five billion francs in reparations from the Franco-Prussian War, caused a significant rise in rental prices within the old city and the construction of new residential buildings outside the city gates. Grim, crowded *Mietskasernen* (rental barracks) were erected to the north, east, and south to accommodate Berlin's burgeoning working class; the bourgeoisie relocated to the west of the old city.

Keller remained on the Steglitzerstraße (now the Pohlstraße) for the rest of his life, living first at 71/III (1873–77), then at 1/IV (1878–83) and 72/IV (1884–87), and finally returning to 1/IV (1888–91). At Steg-litzerstraße 71 the owner of the building was a "painter of historical topics" (*Geschichtsmaler*), and Keller's neighbors included two other painters as well as a private secretary (*Geheimer Sekretär*), a greengrocer, a wine retailer, a baker, and three businessmen. In 1882 Keller shared Steglitzerstraße 1, located at the intersection with the Flottwellstraße and overlooking the tracks of the Potsdam-Magdeburger railroad, with a silver worker, a painter, a tailor, a shoemaker, a proofreader (*Korrektor*), a teacher, a businessman, a masonry foreman, a master mason/contractor (*Mauermeister*), a railway construction contractor (*Eisenbahn Baumeister*), two first lieutenants on ac-tive service, and two widows. Two years later his neighbors at Steglitzer-straße 72 included a banker (*Banquier*), a stockbroker, two businessmen, a teacher, a music dealer (named Dörffel, perhaps the Balduin Dörffel who also worked for Simrock), a retired captain, a woman taking in board-ers (*Pensionat*), and a widow. One discerns a gradual improvement in the economic level of Keller's coinhabitants that may indicate a comparable improvement in his own financial well-being; one should also note, how-ever, that all four of his residences were on less expensive (albeit sunnier) upper floors. Although his reasons for moving frequently are unknown, his migrations about the Steglitzerstraße should be viewed within the con-text of a neighborhood in constant flux. For instance, of the sixteen oc-cupants of Steglitzerstraße 1 listed in the 1878 city directory, only three were still to be found living there when the 1882 directory was prepared.

A few blocks north of the Steglitzerstraße, on a street overlooking the Landwehr-Canal with its rows of chestnut and willow trees, one encoun-tered a residence on a much grander scale—the Simrocks' home at Am Carlsbad 3. While the pace of activity in most sections of Bismarckian Ber-lin had quickened considerably, certain areas of *der alte Westen,* especially around the Tiergarten, retained the slower rhythm of preimperial days. The neighborhood situated between the Tiergarten and the canal was fa-vored by the educated and the wealthy members of the middle class (the *Bildungsbürgertum* and the *Besitzbürgertum*).[11] Max Kalbeck described the Simrock home as "a museum" of fine old furniture and carpets, its walls hung with paintings and engravings by the contemporary artists Arnold Böcklin, Max Klinger, and Franz von Lenbach (including Böcklin's *Triton and Nereide, Pan and Dryads, Autumnal Thoughts, The Isle of the Dead,* and *Saint Anthony Preaching to the Fishes* and one of Lenbach's many portraits of Bismarck) (9:14). In this setting Simrock's wife, Clara (1839–1928), held her salon, entertaining the finest artists, composers, and performers of the day, among them Böcklin, Max Bruch, Antonín Dvořák, Anton Rubinstein,

Pablo de Sarasate, Clara Schumann, Julius Stockhausen, Georg Henschel, Richard Mühlfeld, and, of course, Brahms.[12]

The Berlin directory for 1856, like the one for the previous year, listed Keller simply as a *Musiker* (musician), but by 1858 he was cited as a *Musiklehrer* (music teacher), to which appellation was added *und Korrektor* starting in 1880.[13] Actually, Keller's editorial activities for N. Simrock had begun several years before: the earliest reference in the Brahms-Simrock correspondence to Keller serving as proofreader occurs in the autumn of 1871, in a letter from Brahms to Fritz Simrock concerning the *Schicksalslied*, Op. 54 (26 November 1871; 9:107).[14] By 1881 Keller was working in a similar capacity for the Berlin music publisher Bote & Bock (appendix E, item 1). In 1873 he made his first keyboard arrangement of a Brahms composition—a two-piano, eight-hand version of the first two volumes of the Hungarian Dances, WoO 1 (9:144). From the same year stem his first transcriptions for Simrock of works by other composers—thirteen overtures by Auber, Beethoven, Boieldieu, Cherubini, Gluck, and Mozart, also arranged for two pianos, eight hands (see appendix F). Two years later Keller completed four-hand arrangements of Brahms's E Minor Violoncello Sonata, Op. 38, and the Horn Trio, Op. 40, the first of many such arrangements that he would prepare over the next decade and a half. In the 1880s Keller also worked as an arranger for Bote & Bock, Ries & Erler, and Carl Paez in Berlin, J. Rieter-Biedermann in Leipzig, and Schmidt in Heilbronn, preparing transcriptions of chamber and orchestral music for four-hand piano.

From a cumulative register of faculty at the Stern Conservatory published in 1899 we learn that Robert Keller began teaching piano at this prominent Berlin music school on 1 September 1862 (no date is given for the end of his tenure); he is also cited on two lists of prominent graduates of the institution. Founded in 1850 as the Berliner Musikschule by Julius Stern, A. B. Marx, and Theodor Kullak, the conservatory was renamed in 1857 after the departure of Marx and Kullak and remained under the direction of Stern until his death in 1883. On a staff roster for November 1875, Keller is cited as a member of the piano faculty for the Conservatory's Elementar-Klavier- und Violinschule; he is also listed as a *Musiklehrer am Stern'schen Konservatorium und privat* in the *Berlin Addreß-Buch* for 1876.[15]

Virtually nothing is known of Keller's personal life during his early years in Berlin. From his later correspondence with Brahms one would deduce that he was a bachelor. No greetings to or from a wife are offered, we learn that he spent his Swiss vacations in the company of male colleagues from

Berlin, and in 1889 Brahms invited Keller and his *Freundin* to an evening at the Ascanischer Hof in Berlin (item 47). The announcement of Keller's death in the *Königlich privilegirte Berlinische Zeitung* (19 June 1891), however, implies that he might once have been married: placed by a Minna Günther, the notice informs the public of the demise of "my dear brother-in-law, the music teacher Robert Keller" (*mein lieber Schwager, der Musiklehrer Robert Keller*). Moreover, the *Todten-Register* of the Zwölf-Apostel-Kirchhof records as Keller's sole heir "a sister-in-law of legal age" (*eine majorenne Schwägerin*). A sister-in-law with a surname other than one's own, in addition to being the sister of one's wife, could be the wife of a half-brother or the remarried wife of a deceased brother. But Günther is also the name of the widow with whom Keller shared his initial three addresses in Berlin (in the city directory for 1860 she is cited more fully as "Günther, A., née Voigt, proprietress of a studio for gilding and painting" [*Günther, A. geb. Voigt, Inhaberin eines Ateliers für Vergolderei und Malerei*]). Keller's reason for changing apartments with the widow Günther could have been that he had married one of her daughters, who may have been deceased by the time Brahms came to know him. (Berlin directories did not list women, unless they were widows or owned a business.) Keller's infatuation with a certain Fräulein Köckert from Geneva, who charmed him with her singing of Brahms Lieder but married another (items 37–41, 50), and the great enjoyment he took in "cooking and keeping house *à trois*" with his friend Raif and "a young lady" while hiking in the Swiss Alps (item 43) would appear in a different light were he not, like Brahms, a lifelong bachelor. Nonetheless, as men essentially on their own, composer and editor had much in common.

Even though Brahms had been corresponding with Keller since 1871 and visited Berlin at least five times during the 1870s, he still had not met his loyal assistant in person when, on 31 August 1879, he wrote Simrock: "If I should come to Berlin again, then don't forget that we [should] go to [see] Keller; I always forget to do so when I am there, and I really must meet the diligent man" (10:128–29). The late date of Brahms's first personal encounter with Robert Keller was due to the nature of Keller's employment with Simrock: in contrast to assistants like Balduin Dörffel, who worked in Simrock's offices and would have received a regular salary,[16] Keller undertook his editorial activities "freelance" in his own residence. Brahms's letters to Keller sent via Simrock were remailed to Keller. Therefore, when visiting the firm of N. Simrock on the Friedrichstraße, Brahms would not necessarily have encountered Keller.

Although little specific information is at hand concerning Keller's fees from Simrock, his income from teaching, editing, and arranging seems to have secured for him a comfortable, if modest, existence. (As late as 1890, he still linked his ability to take a summer vacation in Switzerland with the income that he expected from his arrangements of Brahms's works [item 50].) Brahms appreciated Keller's position and tried to guarantee that he not receive too little for his services. In 1882, for example, Brahms instructed Simrock to pay Keller 50 Marks for his assistance with organizing the *51 Uebungen,* but Keller would accept only half that amount for work that must have taken a good number of hours (10:207; no. 128). Two years later, Dvořák asked Simrock to pay Keller 24 Marks for his editorial assistance with the Hussite Overture, Op. 67.[17] At this time Simrock marketed the orchestral score for Brahms's Second Piano Concerto, Op. 83, for 30 Marks and each volume of his Lieder, Opp. 84–86, for 4 Marks.[18] For his work as an arranger, Keller would have been more generously rewarded, perhaps at a level approaching Brahms's remuneration for his own arrangements: in 1873 Simrock paid Brahms the equivalent of 1,020 Marks for his four-hand arrangement of the two String Quartets, Op. 51 (as well as an additional 798 Marks for sale of the French rights; no. 24), and 600 Marks for his four-hand rendition of the *Triumphlied,* Op. 55.[19] (Brahms's honoraria for the two string quartets and the *Triumphlied* in all countries totaled 3,798 Marks and 2,210 Marks, respectively.) In contrast, 25 to 30 Marks was a good salary for a member of the Berlin proletariat for a full week's work.[20] Keller openly acknowledged that he owed to Brahms's praise of his editorial work the security of his position with Simrock, who he felt paid him decently and "to whom cheaper workers may often enough offer their services" (item 7).

Yet Keller viewed his editorial work as more than a source of income. His mission, as he saw it, was to relieve the composer, as much as possible, of the task of correcting, "which is draining for a creative spirit and cripples new endeavors" (item 7). His reward was the experience of dealing with the works themselves, of being able to admire their beauty and their craftsmanship at close hand (items 7, 29). Such was his devotion to the task that, after expending a monumental effort compiling a list of potential revisions for the score and parts of the Third Symphony that ran to twenty-eight closely written pages (appendix D), he could term the inventory "a small private pleasure for me . . . by which . . . I believe I declare my keen and ardent interest in your work of art far better than through flattering words and enthusiastic exclamations" (item 19).

An attitude like this was certain to endear Keller to Brahms. In general he had only words of praise for Keller's editorial efforts on his behalf.

Concerning Keller's assistance with the first edition of the *Gesang der Parzen*, Op. 89, for instance, he informed Simrock: "I am deeply indebted to Herr Keller, as quite often before. . . . Yes, you see, where would you and your copyist be were it not for Keller!! . . . To Herr Keller my very best thanks" (19 November 1882; 11:7–8). After Keller's death, a decline in publishing standards at Simrock's was apparent. "Your Smetana [pieces], which are quite nice and joyful, have just arrived!" Brahms wrote to Simrock in 1894, "but, but, you have to provide for a replacement for Keller! On the first page a mere 13 sharps are missing.—Even though further on it is not quite as bad—it dampens the spirit when something looks so slovenly" (12:159–60). Simrock's editions of Brahms's own piano pieces, Opp. 116–19, issued in 1892 and 1893, likewise reveal declining standards.[21]

Keller's editorial markings can be seen in the extant engraver's models for Brahms's orchestral works, entered in a neat, precise hand, typically in red ink. When preparing an orchestral score for the engraver, Keller would indicate which abbreviated passages should be written out in full, add dynamics and articulation where they were missing in certain parts, clarify imprecisely drawn slurs, rewrite unclear passages, add cautionary accidentals, and, when working with a copyist's manuscript rather than an autograph, correct errors in rhythm and pitch. When opportunity allowed, Keller also scrutinized the orchestral parts and keyboard reductions before they were sent to the engraver (see item 2). Once the score, parts, and reductions had been engraved, Keller assisted with the task of proofreading. The inventory of corrections that he prepared for the Third Symphony (appendix D) amply demonstrates his sharp eye for detail.

For Lieder, solo piano music, and chamber music, a different procedure was followed. None of the extant engraver's models available for examination reveals editorial intervention by Keller. The manuscripts that Brahms submitted were sent on to the engraver after receiving limited scrutiny from Fritz Simrock himself. Keller's involvement began only with the reading of page proofs.

Only once did Brahms register a sharp rebuke to Keller on editorial matters. In the process of preparing the first editions of the Academic Festival and Tragic Overtures, Opp. 80 and 81, Keller apparently attempted to institute certain new notational practices to which Brahms took vigorous exception in the postscript to a letter to Simrock:

Wait! On the next page, a few words for Herr Keller.
    Namely, I see with horror that Herr Keller takes notice of Härtel-Brißler notions. Among these:

1. That they discard the two-voice nature of the winds (and even the horns). In *unisono* these must always be engraved doubly [i.e., with separate stems]; only quite rarely (with too much figuration) may one permit oneself the *a due.*

2. (Easily happens with me too.) They write even *divisi* violins without providing the notes with tails from above and below! Godless!

3. Tempo markings (*rit., a tempo,* etc.) are used too sparingly and [printed] too small, which is highly unpleasant for the conductor. Everything of this nature (especially *stringendo, rit., a tempo*) should always be quite large, [and] be at the top, the bottom, and next to the strings—at the very least!

In the overtures I have just put NB. . . . But in principle, I ask, where it is possible, without special effort, that you restore the long-accustomed and better!!!! (10 May 1881; 10:174–75)

The "Härtel-Brißler notions" that Brahms condemned were the editorial practices espoused by Friedrich Ferdinand Brißler (1818–93), Keller's counterpart at Breitkopf & Härtel in Leipzig, against whom Brahms had tilted his spear the previous year with regard to Breitkopf's edition of Robert Schumann's B♭ Major Symphony, Op. 38, scheduled for publication in the Schumann *Gesamtausgabe:*

Today I am returning R. Schumann's B flat major Symphony and the rest—with the urgent request to delay the edition further.

The new score has become more disagreeable to the eye and more impractical for use due to the various unexpected, as well as incomprehensible instructions of Herr Brißler.

Once before, on the occasion of the new edition of Schumann's early piano pieces, I urgently requested that Herr Brißler might respect the original [and] indicate his recommendations before the engraving, even when they concern superficialities and apparently minor details, so that the respective editor involved can say "yes" or "no."

In those fantastic pieces, I could understand that the notation, which was eccentric, departing often from the norm, aroused Herr Brißler's opposition. But Schumann wrote an orchestral score in precisely the same manner as Mozart and Beethoven before him and we after him. To what and to whom does Herr Brißler refer for those ideas and innovations that contradict all standard practice, that are so illogical and unmusical?

I need not deal with specific cases, since the majority of them are mentioned in the enclosed letter of Herr [Hermann] Levi. . . . If Schumann or anyone occasionally departs from the rule or the norm, then he has his reasons, and we and Herr Brißler have only to take care to appreciate and respect them. (23 September 1880; 14:309–11)

The one specific offense that Brahms cited in this letter was Brißler's use of an unnecessary accidental sign with notes tied over a barline. In a contemporaneous letter to Julius Otto Grimm, he specified other Brißler "stupidities"—the same ones that Keller would dare to adopt the following year: "The notes of the horns and trumpet must always be stemmed from above and below, other instruments [too], if they are *divisi*, etc.; often rehearsal letters, etc., etc., belong thrice on the page, namely, again for the first violin. . . . I get really angry . . . about certain doctored-up scores" (26 November 1880; 4:136). Brahms's protest was lost on Brißler. "With regard to the symphony," he lamented to Clara Schumann, "the only thing that can be said is that the Härtels have given no proper or direct answer to the letter from Levi and me, but instead [have made] an indirect reply through this copy—in which absolutely no notice has been taken of the letter; on the contrary, Brißler has touched up everything as usual. . . . Well now—take it or leave it?"[22] In contrast, Keller took heed of Brahms's complaints and reverted to the notational practices of the composer.

Keller's editorial assistance to Brahms extended beyond proofreading. In certain cases he was entrusted with the preparation of manuscripts that served as models for the engravers, in order to save time and ensure accuracy, even though, as he once informed Brahms (item 10), his rates were significantly higher than those of a professional copyist. Letters from Simrock to Brahms and extant manuscripts establish that Keller prepared the engraver's models for the vocal parts of the Motet, Op. 74 No. 1 (no. 76), the transposed editions of the *Gesänge*, Opp. 69–72 (no. 83; Brahms Institut, Lübeck), and possibly the transposed editions of the *Lieder*, Opp. 84–86 (no. 124). Brahms also turned to Keller for assistance with the "dreadful" task of putting order to the piano exercises that he had developed over the years. Brahms drew on Keller's pedagogical expertise to classify the exercises and his knowledge of the étude literature to avoid inadvertently publishing as Brahms's own any exercises composed by others (items 9–11, 14–16). In his expressions of appreciation for all these services Brahms was unstinting.

Quite another matter were Robert Keller's arrangements of Brahms's works. In the nineteenth century, keyboard reductions of orchestral works and piano arrangements of chamber music played a role much like engravings and photographic reproductions of paintings: while rendering the works less colorful, both transfers of medium facilitated wide dissemination to an art-loving public when access to the originals was limited. Keller likened such keyboard versions to drawings that could give the impatient public a foretaste of a new orchestral work and allow it after hearing a performance "to investigate the fine lines of the drawing while the magnificent color of the whole is still fresh in their minds and to delight in the abundance of attractive and ingenious details that are simply impossible to grasp in their entirety during the first exciting hearing of the original" (item 27). Moreover, with a piano in every respectable bourgeois residence, the potential for profits from keyboard arrangements was enormous.

Brahms took on himself the responsibility for preparing nearly two dozen keyboard arrangements of his own works, recasting the Third and Fourth Symphonies for two pianos and most of the orchestral and chamber music for four-hand piano.[23] When Keller suggested that Brahms disliked transcriptions, the composer took strong exception (item 45). His arrangements for two pianos and four hands, as also his original works for these forces (the Sonata in F Minor, Op. 34*bis*, and the Haydn Variations, Op. 56*b;* the Schumann Variations, Op. 23, the Waltzes, Op. 39, and the Hungarian Dances, WoO 1), attest to a special affinity for these media. His motivation for preparing these versions, no doubt, was to make sure that his music would be represented well in the form in which it would be reaching its broadest audience.[24]

In arrangements of his instrumental works for other keyboard combinations—solo piano; two piano, four hands; and two piano, six and eight hands—Brahms entertained little interest. The only solo-piano arrangement that he made of one of his own works was a two-hand rendition of the Variations from the Sextet in G Major, Op. 18, prepared as a birthday gift for Clara Schumann in 1860 (and subsequently performed in concert by both Frau Schumann and Brahms). Of Keller's two-hand arrangements of the first two symphonies, Brahms wrote Simrock: "You must know better than I whether such an arrangement for girls' boarding school is necessary! I would have considered a two-hand arrangement interesting only if an extraordinary virtuoso did it. Somewhat like how Liszt did the Beethoven symphonies" (March 1880; 10:143). Brahms viewed such arrangements as financial rather than musical matters; in communicating to Simrock his reaction to Keller's two-hand versions of the Academic Festival and Tragic Overtures, Opp. 80 and 81, he summarized his opinion of such dealings:

> An additional word concerning the two-hand overtures, which I will enclose soon. It is purely business; you must know whether it is necessary and desired. K. is a splendid man [*vortrefflicher Mann*] and does everything so diligently and neatly that one cannot find fault. But do I need to tell you that a two-hand arrangement by him shows the Philistine and cannot be of interest to any player who is the least bit gifted? Similar things by [Hans von] Bülow or [Theodor] Kirchner (cf., arrangements by Liszt) immediately have a different appearance. I wanted to alter [Keller's arrangements], but that will not work; one can only start over again.
>
> So do what business demands—but do not use me to hurt dear Keller! (19 September 1881; 10:187)[25]

Fleißig was Brahms's typical appellation for a Keller arrangement, *fleißig und hübsch* if it had turned out better than usual. On occasion, Brahms attempted to spur Keller on to a somewhat less literal rendition:

> [The four-hand arrangement of the C Minor Piano Quartet] Op. 60 we will leave to Herr Keller—he must have something to do as well. I only ask him not to be shy! Light, brisk, leaving out all that is possible, etc. (21 December 1876; 10:21)

> I have suggested a very little bit how I might find the piano reduction [of the Violin Concerto, Op. 77] more practical, in case this is comprehensible to Herr K[eller] and he still wants to expend some effort on it. He is, however, much too shy and should act as if I did not exist, treat everything completely unimpeded—just so it sounds really well for 4 hands and is playable! (12 December 1879; 10:139)

> The greatest fear I could have about your work [a transcription of the String Sextet in B♭ Major, Op. 18, for solo piano] is that it is too reverent, not lively and free enough! (17 November 1888; item 45)[26]

In these remarks one is reminded of Arnold Schoenberg's lament about the quality of the typical keyboard transcription: "Most authors of modern piano reductions limit their achievement to transposing each of the voices in the score for piano, placing them one on top of the other. These arrangers are like a cook who, instead of a meal, has the ingredients served that are to go into it."[27]

At first Brahms was willing to look at Keller's arrangements before they were published (see 10:62, 138, 142). But, as time passed, he came to know what to expect and tried to withdraw himself entirely from the process, particularly when, as in the case of Keller's four-hand arrangement of the *Gesang der Parzen,* Op. 89, he could not understand why such an arrangement had been made in the first place: "That I must also return the four-hand Keller is hard. Why do you do this to me? Just by glancing at the first page I can see what an orderly, diligent man he is—but play it, I cannot!? Besides, who will actually play it? That person may just as well play it with two hands!?" (11 October 1882; 10:224).

With the Third Symphony, the issue of Keller's pedestrian arrangements came to a head. Brahms had made a two-piano version of this work himself, but he wanted the two-hand and four-hand arrangements prepared by someone else: "Could Kirchner possibly do the two-hand arrangement? Or, at least, the one for 2 hands, which he would surely do more elegantly and tastefully than our good Keller?" (10 April 1884; 11:56). But Keller apparently had planned on undertaking the arrangement himself and was disturbed that the project might be assigned to someone else. "Concerning arrangements, I have, of course, said nothing!" Brahms replied to Simrock. "You know what I think of Keller; I would feel very sorry for you if you lost the able [*tüchtigen*] man. (With two-hand arrangements a little of the Philistine reveals itself—but that may even be rather good for business.)" (19 April 1884; 11:58).

When Keller's four-hand arrangement of the Third Symphony arrived at Brahms's summer retreat in Mürzzuschlag in September, the composer acknowledged it good-naturedly: "The *Kattermäng* [Brahms's humorous spelling of the French *quatre-main*] came—but no pretty girl to play it with!" (27 September 1884; 11:72). Inspection of the reduction, however, put him in a foul mood: "Have I not asked you often enough not to send me any arrangements for proofreading! Herr Keller can share with you— if he wants to—the enclosed letter [to him]" (8 October 1884; 11:73). But of his own volition Simrock opened the letter Brahms had enclosed, and the fat was in the fire. Brahms's letter, in which the composer had tried to muster as much diplomacy as possible, is published herein, together with Simrock's note of apology to Keller and request for an extraordinary Saturday morning meeting at his home, Keller's masterful response to Brahms, and Brahms's reply (items 21–24). In the end, Brahms made a number of revisions in the four-hand arrangement, all of which Keller cordially accepted.

Brahms's critique of the Third Symphony arrangement may well have proved instructive for Keller, for with his last two arrangements of symphonic works Keller was finally able to please Brahms. In response to requests for two-piano versions of the First and Second Symphonies, Brahms had written to Simrock on 7 January 1888 requesting Theodor Kirchner's services: "My first two symphonies have *not* appeared for 2 pianos and for 4 hands? I am often asked about that. *In case* such an edition is necessary or intended, I ask very much that you let it be prepared by Kirchner (if I don't do it)—not by Keller. You know how much I like the good man—but this he cannot do, and you will surely find a white lie: that Kirchner did it on his own, or whatever!!?" (11:170)

As noted earlier, Brahms had prepared two-piano transcriptions of the Third and Fourth Symphonies himself, and it is clear that he took special interest in the quality of the two-piano versions of the First and Second Symphonies. But, when informed two years later that Keller had done the arrangements, Brahms's personal feelings intervened:

> As things and circumstances stand, I ask simply that you accept the Keller arrangements. You know that I have all possible sympathy for the good, dear fellow [*guten lieben Mann*]—[you know] just as well, of course, that this does not extend to his arrangements. *For this reason* I have recommended to you in special cases that Kirchner be commissioned, before Herr Keller could come into question. For a two-hand [actually, two-piano] arrangement of the first two symphonies, though, I have expressly offered myself, because often the wish for this has been expressed to me. But you replied that there was no demand for this and no prospect of sales. Since you commissioned neither me nor Kirchner, and Keller has the work finished, I can only wish for its acceptance. I would very much like to see them, *after* you have bought them. On purpose I will not say anything further here about K's manner of arranging—since unfortunately I must ask you to deal discreetly with my written remarks and—honestly! (2 May 1890; 12:21–22)

In this instance, however, Brahms was surprised to find the quality of Keller's work greatly improved:

> I am rather pleased that I had the arrangement by Keller sent to me; I had no displeasure in it, but genuine joy. Not only are they set in a touchingly diligent manner, but they are also pleasing to the ear and skillfully done. My fingers would rather play differently—but otherwise I have nothing to desire and alter in his very good work. (30 May 1890; 12:23–24)

Tell me when I *must* send the symphonies; there probably is no hurry.
I so enjoy having them here, and they so nicely keep me from com-
posing—! (2 July 1890; 12:24)

Just today my package maker left for Oberammergau, and I must ask
you to be patient for 8 days. Moreover, Keller needs to have the symphonies temporarily, because of a few suggestions [I've made].
Should I send them to him in due course, and where? (7 July 1890;
12:25)

The helpful suggestions which Brahms had denied Keller before the Third
Symphony affair were now offered without special ado. Keller's gratitude
for Brahms's approbation, so long in coming, is recorded in his final extant
letter to Brahms (item 50).

As Simrock's chief editor, Keller did not confine his duties to works by
Brahms. From 1879 on, one finds numerous references to Keller in the
published letters from Dvořák to Simrock; furthermore, five pieces of unpublished correspondence from Keller to Dvořák are extant.[28] The services
rendered to Dvořák were much the same as those provided to Brahms—
playing through new works for Fritz Simrock, editing, proofreading, and
preparing the occasional engraver's model. In Dvořák's case, however, Simrock also sought Keller's assessment of the composer's works before de-
ciding to accept them for publication.

Dvořák's String Sextet in A Major, Op. 48, and String Quartet in E♭
Major, Op. 51, the first works by the Czech composer published by Simrock, are the subject of the earliest extant letter from Keller to Dvořák.
Writing from Berlin on 26 May 1879, Keller expressed his pleasure that
Dvořák had accepted his suggestions concerning the String Quartet and,
for the most part, had made the requested changes. He then proceeded
with a ten-point critique of the voice leading in the Sextet and the structure
of the first and second movements of this work. A comparison of this letter
with Dvořák's autograph manuscript (Národní muzeum, Prague) and the
Simrock edition reveals that the composer paid heed to a number of Keller's suggestions. Indeed, the final form of the Dumka movement matches
exactly Keller's outline: Dvořák retained the slow Coda but deleted the
third section of the Reprise (comparable to bars 29–71); and, although
he retained the four bars that Keller had suggested he delete from the $\frac{4}{8}$
portion of the central Adagio, he cut six bars from the central $\frac{3}{8}$ section
(called "Adagio" by Keller, "Andante" in the final work). Likewise, while
rejecting the eight-bar retransition to the Poco Allegretto that Keller pro-

posed (to replace bars 113ff.), Dvořák was sensitive to the weakness discerned by Keller in this passage and modified the final bar of his own tenbar retransition (bar 122).

Dvořák was less accepting of Keller's suggestions for modifications in voice leading. None of the alternative readings advanced by Keller was adopted literally. But Keller's objections did prompt the composer to rethink several of these passages. For example, in the first movement, bars 121–27 are pasted over in the autograph. Keller had objected to the "screaming and unresolved dissonances" in this passage and suggested a revised reading for bars 124–27. Dvořák rejected Keller's specific reading but rewrote the passage on his own.

A year later, on 5 May 1880, Keller passed along to Dvořák suggestions for revisions in the first and third of the *Zigeunermelodien,* Op. 55; these ideas were the result of a private trial performance by Amalie Joachim. In the first song Dvořák inserted a second stanza, for the most part in the tonic major, as Frau Joachim had requested, using a poetic text provided by Keller. With a vocal line following closely the melody of the first and third stanzas, this addition increases the proportions of the song and provides modal contrast without disturbing the strophic plan and calm harmonic design necessary to convey the mood of the text. Similarly, to avoid "errors in declamation" Dvořák recast the third song along lines suggested by Frau Joachim and detailed by Keller.

In one instance, however, Keller's proffered advice received a sharp rebuke, communicated in a letter to Fritz Simrock. The work in question was the Violin Concerto, Op. 53, which Dvořák had composed with the initial two movements shorter than usual and joined together. Apparently, Keller advocated recasting the composition with the traditional pause between movements, an unwelcome suggestion:

> I had already written to Keller yesterday. You know that I respect the man and know to appreciate him, but this time he has gone rather too far. The first movement is shortened too much and cannot come to a conclusion on its own; a third of its length would have to be added, and I, to be quite honest, have no desire to do so.
>
> I am thus in complete agreement with your view and Sarasate's that the first two movements can—indeed, must—remain as they are. As concerns the last movement, a few additional cuts could not really do any harm. You will surely hear that.
>
> So please, just tell Keller that I completely agree with your view.

So only the 1st and 2d movements unchanged, a few cuts in the third movement, where the main theme always returns in A major. . . .

My letter from yesterday is in contradiction to the changes made here. I did not want to contradict my dear friend, since I respect him so much, but now he will have to relent on his views. (16 December 1882)[29]

In addition to passing judgment on and editing Dvořák's new compositions (the remaining unpublished letters from Keller to Dvořák document his editorial involvement with the Stabat Mater, Op. 58, and the Sixth Symphony, Op. 60), Keller prepared keyboard arrangements for a number of the composer's piano and chamber works, including the Slavonic Dances, Opp. 46 and 72, the Piano Trio, Op. 65, the Piano Quartet, Op. 87, and the Piano Quintet, Op. 81. As Keller's postcard to Dvořák of 25 July 1879 attests, he was also instrumental in arranging the private trial performance of the E♭ Major Quartet and A Major Sextet that took place at the home of Joseph Joachim on 29 June 1879. Of this occasion the composer wrote his friend Alois Göbl the next day: "I had not been here [in Berlin] for more than a few hours before I had spent among the foremost artists so many happy and agreeable moments that the memory of them will remain with me for the rest of my life. Joachim had been eagerly looking forward to my arrival and held a soirée for me at 7 P.M. at which my new quartet and sextet were performed. How they played everything and with what understanding and enthusiasm, I cannot tell you now."[30] Robert Keller was no doubt among those in attendance.

The other composers whose music Keller arranged for piano include Auber, Beethoven, Bruch, Cherubini, Gluck, Joachim, Mendelssohn, and Mozart. A listing of his keyboard arrangements appears in appendix F.

Robert Keller's letters to Brahms and to Joseph Joachim (see appendix E) provide glimpses of the rich musical life of Wilhelminian Berlin.[31] Established choral societies like the Singakademie (founded in 1791 and directed by Carl Friedrich Zelter, 1800–1832), the Sternscher Gesangverein (1841, Julius Stern; later conducted by Julius Stockhausen and Max Bruch), and the Jähnsscher Gesangverein (1845, F. W. Jähns) vied with newer ensembles like the Bachverein (1862, Wilhelm Rust), the Cäcilienverein (1870), and the Philharmonic Choir (1882, Siegfried Ochs) in the performance of masterpieces from the last three centuries. The early course of the Philharmonic Orchestra, founded in 1882, was guided by a series of conductors with strong Brahmsian sympathies—Franz Wüllner,

Joseph Joachim, and Hans von Bülow—and attracted illustrious guest conductors and soloists. It was at a concert of the Philharmonic Orchestra in 1886 that Keller witnessed a skirmish between Camille Saint-Saëns and the Berlin Wagnerians (item 27). The world's finest soloists were also heard in solo and chamber concerts, both public and private. Clara Schumann and Joseph Joachim organized private chamber concerts; a fine drawing of the Joachim-Schumann duo by the prominent Berlin artist Adolph von Menzel documents one of these performances in 1854. From 1857 to 1878 Frau Schumann lived in Berlin, establishing a residence at 11 Unter den Zelten in 1873.[32] In 1869 Joachim founded the Hochschule für Musik, which under his direction became the preeminent musical institute in Berlin. The year 1869 also saw the creation of the Joachim Quartet, which inaugurated an annual series of public concerts. Keller's enthusiastic reaction to this ensemble's performance of Beethoven's last string quartet is the subject of one of his extant letters to Joachim (appendix E, No. 2).

Brahms enjoyed Berlin and often went there to visit friends and partake of the city's musical offerings. According to the composer Robert Kahn, who encountered Brahms in Berlin on several occasions and had the impression that he seriously considered living there, "the progressive, vigorous musical life of the new capital had a strong attraction for him. . . . 'But I'd take a real beating there,' he once told me. I do not know why he assumed that the Berliners, famous for their quick wit, would abuse him in this manner. He still had many enemies then; he seemed to fear that their hostility and envy might find more drastic and more personal expression there than in *gemütlich* Vienna."[33]

Such feelings may account for why Brahms's concert appearances in Berlin were so few and infrequent.[34] In March 1868 he performed a pair of recitals with the baritone Julius Stockhausen that included both Lieder and works for solo piano. His next appearance was not until January 1882, when he joined Hans von Bülow and the Meiningen Court Orchestra in presenting his two piano concerti at the Singakademie (in the First Piano Concerto, Brahms conducted, and von Bülow played the solo part; for the Second Piano Concerto they exchanged roles).[35] Two years later, in January 1884, Brahms appeared as soloist in his First Piano Concerto and conducted the Academic Festival and Tragic Overtures and the Third Symphony. And, in March 1889, he led the Berlin Philharmonic in performances of the First Piano Concerto (again with von Bülow as soloist), his two overtures, and the Violin Concerto. His next engagement in Berlin was on 8 December 1891, when he conducted the two overtures, the Haydn Variations, and the Fourth Symphony. Four days later he premiered his Clarinet Trio, assisted by Richard Mühlfeld from the Meiningen Court Orchestra and Robert Hausmann of the Joachim Quartet; the Clarinet Quintet received its first performance on the same program, with Mühlfeld joined by the Joachim Quartet. This occasion was commemorated by von Menzel in a drawing of Mühlfeld as a Greek god, with laurel in his hair.[36] In January 1896 Brahms visited Berlin for the last time, to conduct performances of his two piano concerti, both on the same program, with Eugen d'Albert as soloist.

All told, six of Brahms's works received their premieres in Berlin. In addition to the Clarinet Trio and Clarinet Quintet, the Schumann Variations, Op. 9, and the *Clavierstücke*, Op. 76 (von Bülow), the A Minor String Quartet, Op. 51 No. 1 (Joachim Quartet), and the *Zigeunerlieder*, Op. 103 (Amalie Joachim and colleagues), were first heard in public in the German capital.[37] Berlin audiences were regularly treated to Brahms's other works at Joachim's chamber concerts, at solo recitals, and on the programs of the Philharmonic Orchestra, the Cäcilienverein, and the Hochschule für Musik.

Brahms's sojourns to Berlin were not all work. The composer enjoyed visiting the Simrocks' home. On the reverse side of a photograph of himself he registered his comparison of business versus pleasure in Berlin:

Not as usual: Friedrichstr. 171,	but: Am Carlsbad 3
— — — Fritz or Caspar,	— Clara
— — — with annoyance	— in love and grateful
and vexation,	veneration (1889; 9:14)

He delighted in a well-appointed table and the verbal exchange that he found at Adolph von Menzel's; the painter's nephew recalled of Brahms's visit in 1891: "I can truthfully assure you that we have never yet had such fine and enjoyable carousals as those of the December days when you were with us."[38] Less formal gatherings of friends and colleagues, like the evening at the Ascanischer Hof to which Brahms invited Keller in 1889 (item 47), were also to the composer's liking.

One of the high points in Keller's relationship with Brahms was the composer's visit with him in the summer of 1888, while they both were on vacation in Switzerland. That summer Brahms was staying in Hofstetten on the Thunersee, not far from Bern, as he had the two previous years; and Keller was again taking his *Urlaub* in Weesen on the Wallensee, as he had in recent years. In August 1886 Brahms had invited Keller to walk over to Thun to visit him. But Keller had had to decline, pointing out that, while his legs might be up to the trip, his purse was not. Instead, Keller had suggested that Brahms visit Weesen, "an especially charming area, where also grows a rather good grape." Inviting Brahms "amiably [to] descend to the inoffensive musical proletarians" who would treat the master "entirely like one of us and . . . not let you feel your superiority at all," Keller could promise "a bevy of lovely ladies," excellent food and accommodations, and a "very relaxed style of life" (item 30). That year Brahms did not overcome his dislike of traveling about Switzerland in the summer (see item 39), but in 1888, in response to a query from Brahms about his summer plans, Keller offered an additional lure: "a born Brahms singer," a certain Fräulein Köckert from Geneva, whose interpretation of such dramatic songs as *Der Tod, das ist die kühle Nacht* and *Ach, wende diesen Blick* caused "a shudder [to run] up and down your spine," would be in Weesen during the summer (item 37). The temptation proved too great, and during the first week of August Brahms journeyed to Weesen to hear Keller's "dear *Wesen*" (item 40). In his last surviving letter to Brahms, penned two years later, Keller wistfully recalled the visit:

> It makes me proud and happy that you, Herr Doctor, still have such fond memories of the few days you spent in Weesen. Last summer I could not go there, but this summer [the income from arranging] your two symphonies [the First and Second] will make it possible. I doubt, though, that it will be as nice; you and your songs, your accompanying and Frl. Köckert's singing, where are they? *You* are staying in Ischl, which is more than a day-trip away from Weesen, and Frl. Köckert is wielding the ladle as Frau von Hessert and looking after her little girl. But the old mountains are still there and the green lake has not dried up. (Item 50)

Already during the winter of 1890 Keller, then age sixty-two, had experienced serious problems with his health. As he recounted to Brahms (item 50), after a fall, in which he sprained his left hand, a headache had set in that was serious enough for him to seek the advice of both his own doctor and Fritz Simrock's, who diagnosed the pain as "rheumatic and neuralgic in origin." Keller was ordered to rest, apply "all sorts of remedies," including taking phenacitin for severe attacks, avoid cigars and beer, minimize intellectual activity, and take walks.[39] His decline must have been relatively gradual, for he was able to complete the two-piano arrangements of the First and Second Symphonies with which Brahms was so pleased (see above) as well as a two-piano version of selected Hungarian Dances and a four-hand transcription of the revised B Major Piano Trio, Op. 8.

He also guided this trio, as well as the G Major String Quintet, Op. 111, into print (both released by Simrock in February 1891; 12:36, 38). But with the quintet Brahms complained about "very many, so many mistakes" in the proofs that he could not vouch for the quality of his proofreading, although he assumed that Keller was still carefully revising it (4 February 1891; 12:41). Simrock's response has not been preserved, but in it he must have informed Brahms of Keller's deteriorating state, to which Brahms replied: "The news about Keller most deeply [*herzlichst*] disturbs me—if you can report anything comforting, please let me know right away. The poor, good man—and what you will lose with him!" (4 March 1891; 12:42). Two months later he inquired again whether there was "any hope for the poor, good Keller" and then reported to Simrock on the severe illness of his close musical confidant and friend Theodor Billroth, the famous Viennese surgeon (1 May 1891; 12:44). A week later, on his fifty-eighth birthday, Brahms drew up his own last testament, which he sent to Simrock for safekeeping (nos. 159, 160).

Robert Keller died on Tuesday, 16 June 1891, at eleven o'clock in the morning; on the afternoon of Friday, 19 June, he was laid to rest in the old graveyard of the Zwölf-Apostel Kirche, a few blocks from his rooms on the Steglitzerstraße. In the church's *Todten-Register* the cause of death was entered as *Gehirnschlag,* cerebral apoplexy.[40] An announcement of his death was published in the morning edition of the *Königlich privilegirte Berlinische Zeitung* on the day of his burial, and notices of his passing appeared in the *Monatshefte für Musikgeschichte* and the *Allgemeine Musik-Zeitung,* citing his work as a music teacher and arranger of orchestral works for the piano. On 20 June, Brahms sent his condolences to Simrock: "I do not know whether I have written to you since the death of your brother. That was probably in every respect a relief; Keller's death, however, saddens me quite profoundly [*doch ungemein*]. For him I would have wished a peaceful, friendly old age, and he was the type that could have comfortably enjoyed it. I am quite genuinely sorry I shall not see the good man again!" (20 June 1891; 12:46–47).

Final testimony to the composer's regard for his able assistant, as well as evidence of his generosity toward those in need, is provided in a letter from Brahms to Fritz Simrock written on 12 June 1893, two years after Keller's death: "Could you inform me confidentially about Keller's sister [-in-law]? I would still like to give, and it is quite all right, I suppose?" (12:103). The extent of Brahms's largess in this case is unknown.[41]

THE BRAHMS-KELLER CORRESPONDENCE

The First Symphony

Johannes Brahms's earliest extant letter to Robert Keller deals with the correction of galley proofs for the Symphony No. 1 in C Minor, Op. 68, a work of long gestation that was completed in Lichtenthal bei Baden-Baden during the summer of 1876 and taken on tour for trial performances during the concert season of 1876–77.[1] As a result of these performances, Brahms made significant revisions in the work, especially in the second movement.[2] At the end of May he sent the complete score and a set of parts for the first, third, and fourth movements to Simrock; manuscript parts for the second movement were missing, owing to the extensive revisions Brahms had made, and he asked that the engraved parts be prepared directly from the full score. He also suggested that the orchestral parts be compared with the full score, since, as the result of the trial performances, the parts might be more accurate or more fully realized than the score. Variant readings should therefore be indicated with question marks and not automatically accepted (29, 31 May 1877; 10:34–35). (The autograph score of the second and third movements, which served as the engraver's model for the first edition, is preserved in the Mary Flagler Cary Collection at the Pierpont Morgan Library in New York;[3] the manuscripts used as the engraver's models for the first and fourth movements, prepared by the venerable Viennese copyist Franz Hlavaczek and by Joseph Füller, respectively, are owned by the Brahms Institut in Lübeck.)

In mid-June, Brahms began work on the four-hand arrangement of the symphony, which he sent to the publisher at the end of the month (14, 19 June 1877; 10:37, 40–41; the autograph used by the engravers is now owned by the Library of Congress). Further revisions in both the full score and the four-hand arrangement were forwarded to Simrock over the summer (24, 30 June 1877; 10:41–42, 44–45). By 26 July, Fritz Simrock had received proofs from C. G. Röder, the Leipzig firm that did all his engraving, and he informed Brahms that proofs were awaiting correction by Keller, who was away at the time (no. 58). On 7 September, Brahms wrote Simrock from Pörtschach on the Wörthersee (Carinthia), where he was spending the summer months, requesting two sets of proofs of the full score, so that he could enter corrections for the score in one and for the orchestral parts in the other. Three weeks later, on 27 September, Brahms informed Simrock that he planned to send the proofs back the next day and warned him not to rush Keller (10:47; see also 4 June 1877, no. 53; the proofs for this work are no longer extant); on 28 September he posted the proofs to Keller with the following letter:

•◆ 1

JOHANNES BRAHMS TO ROBERT KELLER Lichtenthal bei Baden-Baden, 28 September 1877 (Library of Congress)

Sehr geehrter Herr,

Im Begriff die Revision der Symphonie zurück zu schicken kann ich nicht unterlaßen Ihnen recht von Herzen zu danken für die große Mühe welche Sie an das Werk gewandt haben.

Namentlich bin ich Ihnen natürlich verbunden für die Blaustift= Bemerkungen (nicht allein jene auf S. 48!). Auf eben der Seite laße ich in der Pauke die Triolenbewegung [IV, bar 29], weil diese zu Anfang des nächsten Satzes [bars 30ff.] die Hauptsache ist u. der Paukist es so sicherer faßt.

Die Buchstaben sind für „Vierhänder" wohl unnütz u. doch keine Zierde der Noten.

Um die Herausgabe nicht zu verzögern überlaße ich Ihnen allein in vollstem Vertrauen die Revision der Stimmen. Einige ~~Verschi~~[edenheiten] Abweichungen die vorkommen mögen, namentlich in der Bezeichnung, werden Sie als absichtlich erkennen. So etwa ein überflüßiges *espress.* Auch setze ich wohl dort die verfl. – – – – statt ⌒ oder *dim.* statt ═══ über 2–3 Noten da letztere beiden Bezeichnungen heute von den Geigern durchaus falsch gedeutet werden.

Sollten Sie über irgend etwas in Zweifel sein so werde ich eine Frage schnellstens beantworten.

Für Heute nur nochmals den herzlichsten Dank

Ihres

sehr ergebenen

J. Brahms.

•◆

Dear Sir:

As I am about to return the corrected version of the symphony, I cannot but thank you most sincerely for the great pains you have taken with this work.

In particular, I am indebted to you, of course, for the remarks in blue pencil (not only those on p. 48!). On that very page I will leave the triplet motion in the timpani [IV, bar 29], for this is the main thing at the beginning of the next section [bar 30ff.], and this way the timpanist is more likely to grasp it.

The [rehearsal] letters are, I suppose, superfluous for "four-handers," and certainly do not enhance the appearance of the music.

In order not to delay the publication, I shall entrust the correction of the parts to you with the utmost confidence. You will recognize as intentional certain discrepancies that may occur, especially with regard to performance indications. As, for instance, a superfluous *espress.* There [in the parts] I think I shall also put the damned – – – – instead of ⌢⌢ or *dim.* instead of ═══ over 2–3 notes, since both of the latter indications are generally misinterpreted by violinists today.

Should you be in doubt about anything, I shall answer your questions promptly.

For now, once again my most heartfelt thanks,

Yours very sincerely,

J. Brahms

❦

Keller's markings in "blue pencil" were no doubt made on the proofs, for by this time they had superseded the autograph as the focus of attention. The "triplet motion in the timpani" occurs in the Adagio introduction to the Finale, just before the famous Alphorn passage. Keller had probably queried the change from a simple timpani trill in bar 28 to the measured "triplets" of bar 29, perhaps suggesting that the entire passage be designated with a trill sign and a *rallentando* indication. Brahms viewed his notation of the timpani as crucial for achieving the proper "metrical modulation" between the Adagio and the ensuing Più Andante.[4]

Despite Brahms's resigned acquiescence to having *portamento* indicated in the string parts with dashes rather than dots with slurs (as in piano music), the "damned" dashes were suppressed in the published parts as well as the full score. Two years later the issue of dashes versus dots with slurs arose again, this time in a letter to Joachim about the Violin Concerto, Op. 77:

But by what right, since when, and on what authority, do you violinists write the sign for *portamento* ⌢⌢ where none is indicated? The octave passage in the Rondo [bar 57ff.] you mark ⌢ [see the manuscript part for the solo violin owned by the Library of Congress, p. 17], and I would place sharp staccato markings ⋅⋅ there. Must that be? Until now I have not given in to the violinists, [and] have also not adopted their damned ⌒. Why then should ⌒⋅ mean something different to us than it did to Beethoven? (Mid-May 1879; 6:161–62)

Joachim replied that, since the time of Paganini, Spohr, and Rode, ⌒⋅⋅⋅ had signified to violinists a series of staccato notes all executed on one stroke of the bow:

Since most of the great composers have been (and are) primarily or entirely pianists, a confusion in the present-day manner of designating [*portamento*] is inevitable; for this reason it is advisable to write

portamento for us violinists in the following manner: ♫♫♫. Also

with *legato* it is difficult to distinguish with slurs where it merely means so-and-so-many notes on the same bow or, on the other hand, where it means a division of the groups of notes according to meaning [i.e., articulation]. . . . I always draw the attention of my students to this difference in works originating from piano-playing composers. You too should reflect on this. (Circa 20 May 1870; 6:163–64)

But Brahms remained unconvinced:

With your previous letter you have not cleared up for me the matter of ⌒⋅⋅⋅, etc. You present numerous examples that I would indicate in the same way . . . I would just like to have it proved to me that under certain circumstances you need this questionable designation, something that for the present I do not believe. That confusion is caused, though, by these variant signs and by signs with different meanings I have noticed often enough from the questions of violinists in chamber and orchestral music about the meaning of ⌒⋅⋅⋅, etc.

Brahms then went on to defend using slurs only to indicate articulation (30 May 1879; 6:167–68).[5]

Shortly after posting his letter of 28 September 1877 to Robert Keller, Brahms made two further revisions in the First Symphony, which he sent to Simrock the next day (the addition of the directions *largamente* over the main theme of the Finale, bars 61ff., and *animato* at bar 94—the latter indication appears in the *Brahms Werke;* the former does not [10:49]). In this letter he also complained about the many errors that he had found in the score and the four-hand arrangement and once again warned Simrock not to hurry Keller: "Why should the piece be engraved as badly and slovenly as it is written?! Indeed, it would be desirable to have Keller proofread [the work] again!!!"

The first edition of the Symphony was published in October 1877 (full score, set of orchestral parts, and four-hand arrangement). Additional corrections for the work appear in letters from Brahms to Simrock of 23 November 1877 (mvt. 4, bar 116; 10:58) and December 1877 (mvt. 4, bar 24; 10:61). On the latter occasion Brahms remarked: "I do not look at my symphonies often, but generally I cannot glance through a volume of music without catching an error. (Unfortunately, I do not make proper use of this talent.)" A year later, on 19 December 1878, he requested a clarification in tempo markings: at the end of the first movement the designation should be changed from *Poco sostenuto* to *Meno Allegro*, because "*Poco sostenuto* . . . will be misunderstood and taken at the same tempo as in the introduction" (10:100; see also 30 October 1881, 10:192).

The Second Symphony

The next extant written communication between Brahms and Keller dates from early in the spring of 1878 and concerns the Symphony No. 2 in D Major, Op. 73. Brahms had composed this work in short order during his holiday in Pörtschach am Wörthersee the preceding summer, completing the full score in Baden-Baden during a visit with Clara Schumann in the autumn. The new opus, in a four-hand arrangement, was tried out in November by Brahms and the famous surgeon and avid amateur musician Theodor Billroth (Billroth, 250–51) and again in December by Brahms and the composer Ignaz Brüll, before receiving its orchestral premiere on 30 December 1877 with the Vienna Philharmonic under Hans Richter.[1] Additional performances followed in Leipzig, Amsterdam, The Hague, and Dresden during early 1878, as Brahms continued to polish the work.[2]

On 12 March 1878 Brahms sent Simrock three sources to serve as engraver's models: an autograph manuscript of the full score, to be used for engraving movements 2–4 (referred to as the "Partitur=Manuscript" by Keller, as the "autograph manuscript" in the translation; this source is now owned by Robert Owen Lehman and is on deposit in the Pierpont Morgan Library, New York); a manuscript copy of the first movement prepared by the venerable Viennese copyist Franz Hlavaczek and revised by Brahms (called the "Partitur=Copie" by Keller, the "manuscript copy" in the translation; now in a private collection in Germany); and a set of manuscript orchestral parts (no longer extant). In the letter that accompanied these materials, Brahms observed: "I wanted to correct the parts for you very nicely, but I see that they still must be looked at by expert eyes before they go to the engraver. In which case it is much simpler if Herr Keller carefully compares and corrects them against the score. What was added by the musicians—fingering, bowing, etc.—should naturally be left out, and this time let me read the proofs for the parts" (10:69). Keller undertook the task of comparing the sources, making use of the autograph manuscript of the first movement as well as the manuscript copy. In the following letter he reported the results of his work. (The slurs rendered with broken lines in the first musical example are the blue ones to which Keller refers; Keller first wrote these slurs in ink, then traced over them in blue pencil.)

➤ 2

Robert Keller to Johannes Brahms   Berlin, 27 March 1878
(Archiv der Gesellschaft der Musikfreunde, Vienna)

{Letter folded and addressed to: Herrn *Joh. Brahms.*}

Berlin 27 März 1878.

Hochverehrter Herr!

Bei der Vergleichung von Partitur u. Stimmen Ihrer zweiten Symphonie bin ich auf einige kleine Differenzen gestoßen, deren Ausgleichung ich erbitten möchte.

I. Satz.

1) Bei **E** *(quasi ritenente)* [I, bars 118ff.] u. ebenso im Repetitionstheil [bars 386ff.] steht in den Stimmen des Quartetts die Strichart

die <u>blauen</u> Bogen mit Bleistift; Partitur=Manuskript u. =Copie hat nur Punkte; hat die Bogen vielleicht ein Orchestermitglied hinzugethan oder haben Sie sie selbst eingetragen?

2) Die <u>Trompeten an derselben Stelle</u> haben den Rhythmus

u.s.w. In den Stimmen ist die angebundene Halbe durch ♩ ♩ ersetzt, auch in der Manuscriptpartitur ist mit <u>schwachem</u> Bleistift ♩ ♩ untergeschrieben. Rührt die Aenderung nur von kurzathmigen Trompetern her, oder wird sie von Ihnen gewünscht um das Quartett nicht zu sehr zu verdecken?

3) Buchst. **H** Takt 13–19 [bars 282–88] haben die <u>Hörner u. Tromp.</u> in der Part.=Copie im Part. Manuscr. ist mit Bleistift geändert: welche Lesart soll gelten?

4) Buchst. **L** nach den Flötentriolen [bars 432ff.] bricht die Cantilene des 3$^{\underline{ten}}$ Horns (in E) mit 2 Bogen ab (am

Schluß einer Seite); fehlen angebundene Noten, oder sind die Bogen irthümlich [*sic*] stehen geblieben?

5) Im <u>Finale</u> (diese Ueberschrift hat der IV. Satz in <u>allen Stimmen</u>, soll sie auch in die <u>Partitur</u>?)

bei **E** (S. 13 d. Part.) [bars 122ff.]

hat in der Stimme die
Pauke ein

* $=$ welches in der Part. fehlt, soll es aus der Stimme heraus, oder in die Part. hinein?

*Underlined in blue pencil

6) verte

6) Finale S. 41 d. Part. [bar 381–84] haben die Flöten:

in der Flöte II=Stimme steht: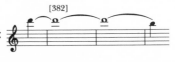

wie ist es richtig?

Mit Freude ergreife ich die Gelegenheit Ihnen, verehrter Meister, meinen Dank (etwas spät) für den liebenswürdigen Brief zu sagen, mit dem Sie mich nach der Correktur Ihrer C moll=Symph. beglückten. Da ich diesmal die Stimmen vor dem Stich zur Revision bekommen habe, so ist es mir möglich gewesen sie so herzustellen, daß die Musiker mit Wollust daraus spielen werden, und alle [added:] schwierigen [then:] Einsätze

{9}

möglichst durch Stichnoten gesichert sind. Auch der manchmal ganz un-
sinnige Schlüsselwechsel (besonders in Fagott II) ist beseitigt.

Mit dem Ausdruck hochachtungsvollster Ergebenheit

Ihr

Robert Keller.

Berlin, 27 March 1878

Dear Sir:

While comparing the score and parts for your second symphony I came
upon several small differences that I would like to ask you to reconcile.

1st Movement

1) At **E** (*quasi ritenente*) [1, bars 118ff.] and also in the repetition of this
section [bars 386ff.] the bowing is indicated in the string parts as

with the *blue* slurs in pencil; the autograph manuscript and the manuscript
copy [pp. 12 and 38 in both sources] only have dots; has perhaps a member of the orchestra added the slurs, or did you enter them yourself?

2) The *trumpets at the same place* have the rhythm

[118]

♩ ♩ ♩ ♩ ♩ ♩ ♩ |etc. In the parts the tied half note is replaced

by ‡ ‡; also in the autograph manuscript ‡ ‡ is written *lightly* in pencil underneath. Does this revision only stem from short-winded trumpeters, or
do you prefer it, so as not to cover the quartet [of strings] too much?

3) At bars 13–19 after letter **H** [bars 282–88], the *horns and trumpets* in

the manuscript copy [p. 29] have ; in the autograph

manuscript this is changed in pencil to Which read-

ing is correct?

4) At letter **L**, after the triplets in the flutes [bars 432ff.], the cantilena of

the 3d horn (in E)  breaks off suddenly

with 2 ties (at the end of a page [after bar 441]); are there tied notes
missing, or were the ties left in by mistake?

5) In the *Finale* (the 4th movement has this heading in *all of the parts;*
should it also appear in the *score?*)

at letter **E** (p. 13 of the [autograph] score) [bars 122ff.]

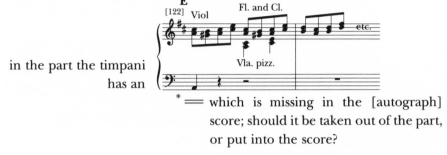

in the part the timpani
has an

* ══ which is missing in the [autograph]
score; should it be taken out of the part,
or put into the score?

*Underlined in blue pencil

6) please turn the page

6) Finale, p. 41 of the [autograph] score [bars 381–84], the flutes have:

in the Flute II part this reads:

What is correct?

With pleasure I take this opportunity, esteemed master, to thank you
(somewhat belatedly) for the kind letter you bestowed upon me after my

editorial work with your C Minor Symphony. Since this time I received the parts to correct before they were engraved, it was possible for me to prepare them so that musicians will really enjoy playing from them and to make sure that all the difficult entrances are introduced with cues. Also, the changes of clefs, which are sometimes quite senseless (especially in the Bassoon II part), have been eliminated.

With most respectful devotion,

Yours,

Robert Keller

◆●

Fritz Simrock forwarded Keller's list of queries to Brahms in a letter of his own in which he reported that the score and parts, "very nicely edited," were being engraved (no. 67). Indeed, in the manuscript copy of the first movement and the autograph manuscript for the other three movements, one finds numerous instances in which Keller supplied performance indications missing for certain instruments and made other refinements to render the score full and complete, all this in addition to his efforts to make the printed parts enjoyable for musicians to use.[3]

In a postscript to his reply to Simrock's letter (3 April 1878), Brahms remarked that he still had to find time to answer Keller's questions (10:71). Later that day, or possibly on the next, he responded to Keller's queries with the following letter:

●◆ 3

JOHANNES BRAHMS TO ROBERT KELLER   Vienna, circa 4 April 1878
(Library of Congress)

{Envelope: Herrn *Rob.Keller.*; added by an unidentified hand, Keller's address: Hier [i.e., Berlin] *Steglitzerstr.* # *1. 4 Tr.* [4th floor], as well as: *Fr*[ei] [i.e., postage paid]}

Geehrtester Herr,

Im Begriff abzureisen kann ich nur in aller Eile für Ihre neue Sorgsamkeit bestens danken u. wie folgt Ihre Fragen beantworten.

bei **E** [I, bar 118ff.] die Geigen nach der Partitur (Punkte.)

die Trompeten [bars 118ff.] keine ⅄ Pausen.

bei **H** [bars 282–88] die Trompeten

die Hörner bei **L** [bars 432ff.] u. die Pauke im *Finale* bei **E** [bars 122ff.] kann ich auswendig nicht bestimmen.

S. 41 hat die 2$\underline{te}$ Flöte [IV, bars 381–84] *d* wohl *d*

Die Ueberschrift *Finale* ist unnöthig.

So dann nochmals besten Dank u. im Sommer werde ich mich weiter Ihrer Arbeit zu freuen haben.

Ihr

sehr ergebener

J. Brahms.

Dear Sir:

As I am just about to leave on a trip, only in great haste can I thank you most kindly for the additional care you have taken, and answer your questions as follows:

at **E** [I, bars 118ff.], the violins according to the score (dots.)

the trumpets [bars 118ff.], *no* ⁊ rests.

at **H** [bars 282–88], the trumpets

about the horns at **L** [bars 432ff.] and the timpani in the Finale at **E** [bars 122ff.], I cannot be sure from memory.

on page 41 [IV, bars 381–84] the 2d flute has *d* [changed to:] probably

has *d*

The heading *Finale* is unnecessary.

Once again, many thanks, and in the summer I shall have further reason to enjoy your work.

Yours

very sincerely,

J. Brahms

Keller entered Brahms's solution to his third query—about the readings for the horns and trumpets after letter **H**—into the manuscript copy of

{13}

the score. For the moment his fourth and fifth questions were left unanswered. Two bars were indeed missing in the third horn's cantilena after rehearsal letter **L** (bars 442–43); the error first came about in the autograph manuscript, where Brahms neglected to continue the horn's melody after a turn of the page, and Hlavaczek perpetuated the error in the manuscript copy. The missing notes were subsequently entered into the manuscript copy and appeared in the first issue of the first edition (Library of Congress). At letter **E** in the Finale, the timpani stroke on A was not retained.

On 9 April, in the company of Theodor Billroth and the composer Carl Goldmark, Brahms left Vienna for a tour of Italy (his first). During the next month Brahms and his friends traveled to Venice, Florence, Perugia, Assisi, Rome, and Naples, returning north to arrive in Pörtschach on 6 May, the day before his forty-third birthday.[4] From there Brahms wrote Simrock requesting two proofs each for the full score and the piano four-hand version of the Second Symphony (May 1878; 10:73). Simrock replied on 14 May by sending Brahms another sheet of queries from Keller—not among the extant Brahms-Keller letters—and promising to forward the proofs soon (no. 68). In this letter Simrock reported that at present the score and parts were receiving their second proofreading and that he would furnish proof copies of the parts for use by the orchestra at Düsseldorf in a performance planned for early June, under the baton of Joseph Joachim (cf. May and 2, 10 June 1878; 6:137–39).

On 3 June Brahms informed Simrock that he had sent the four-hand version of the Second Symphony back to the engraving firm of C. G. Röder in Leipzig and asked that he not allow any further printing to take place, for the full score and piano arrangement still needed editing (10:74); on 15 June, after the Düsseldorf performance, Brahms reiterated his plea, requesting that printing be halted temporarily, for there were "very bad errors everywhere" (10:75). Simrock replied on the eighteenth that he was not allowing the score to be printed and that he awaited corrections from Brahms (no. 69). These corrections arrived on the twenty-fifth, enclosed in a letter from Brahms to Simrock (10:76; see also 30 June 1878, no. 70). Unfortunately, this list of corrections was not published in the *Brahms Briefwechsel*, and its present whereabouts is unknown.

In June Brahms had sent proofs of the score to Otto Dessoff, director of the Hofoper and conductor of the Philharmonic concerts in Vienna, and on 2 July Brahms reported to Simrock an error noticed by Dessoff (a natural missing before C in the first bassoon in bar 364 of the first movement [10:79; see also 26 June 1878, 16:191]). Brahms also noted that, at the first change of tempo in the third movement (bar 33), the proportion indication should read ♩ = ♩ rather than ♩ = ♩ and that, at the second *Presto* (bar 126), the indication ♪ = ♪ should be deleted. The next day brought an additional alteration: Dessoff felt that the direction *Presto non assai* in the third movement was not good Italian, and Brahms offered *Presto ma non assai* and *Presto ma non troppo* as alternatives, suggesting that Simrock consult "a good Italian." Dessoff had not found other engraver's errors, Brahms reported, but it would be a good idea, he advised Simrock, to ask Joachim if he had found any (10:81). On 4 July Simrock wrote that he was forwarding Dessoff's revisions to Röder and thought they would be in time to be taken into account (they were) (no. 72). The first edition of the Second Symphony—in score, parts, and piano four-hand arrangement—was issued in August 1878.

Songs in Transposed Keys

In 1879–80 three of Brahms's publishers issued transposed editions of their most recent volumes of his songs—J. Rieter-Biedermann for Opp. 57–59, C. F. Peters for Op. 63, and N. Simrock for Opp. 69–72—and Breitkopf & Härtel released lower-key editions of Brahms's youthful *Lieder und Gesänge*, Opp. 3 and 7. A first round of publishing transposed editions of Brahms songs had already taken place in 1875–76, when Rieter-Biedermann issued Op. 32 No. 9 and Op. 33 Nos. 1–10 and 12–15 in lower keys and Op. 43 Nos. 1 and 2 in higher keys and Simrock published Opp. 19 and 46–49 in alternative keys (all lower, except Op. 19 Nos. 2–4, Op. 47 No. 3, Op. 48 Nos. 2 and 7, and Op. 49 No. 4, which were transposed higher).[1]

The publication of the *Lieder und Gesänge*, Opp. 57–59, in lower keys was initiated by Rieter-Biedermann near the end of 1877. On 15 December Brahms requested printed copies of the songs in their original keys for the copyist to use, suggesting that the engraver's models for the edition be prepared in Vienna, to eliminate "confusion" (14:283). While proofreading the resulting manuscripts, Brahms altered the accompaniments to render the piano part idiomatic for the lower range. On 1 July 1878 he mailed the manuscripts to Edmund Astor, manager of Rieter-Biedermann, asking, however, that they be carefully proofread against the original editions (14:292–93). (The engraver's models for Opp. 58 and 59, now owned by the Staats- und Universitätsbibliothek in Hamburg, are in the hand of the Viennese copyist Franz Hlavaczek; the present location of the model for Op. 57 is unknown.) On 3 March 1879 Brahms informed Astor that he would take care of reading the proofs, and on 23 April he returned the proofs of Opp. 57 and 58 (and 59?), declaring them "extraordinarily error-free." The transposed editions of Opp. 57 and 58 appeared shortly thereafter, the edition of Op. 59 in 1880.[2]

The firm of C. F. Peters appears to have initiated work on its transposed edition of the *Lieder und Gesänge*, Op. 63, in January 1879. On the fourteenth, Brahms wrote Franz Wüllner requesting that he ask the baritone Georg Henschel which keys he used for the Op. 63 songs (15:92); on the same day Brahms posed this question to Julius Stockhausen (Stockhausen,

452; 18:138). Three days later, having heard about Peters's plans, Fritz Simrock wrote Brahms about issuing the *Gesänge,* Opp. 69–72, in transposed keys. He had already spoken about the project with Amalie Joachim, an alto, and he enclosed with his letter a list of the keys she used, asking that Brahms enter the keys he preferred (no. 82; the list that Simrock prepared was not published with the letter). Keller, Simrock suggested, could oversee the project.

Simrock's letter prompted additional inquiries from Brahms to Stockhausen (14, 21 January 1879; Stockhausen, 452; 18:138–39) and Henschel (this time sent via Julius Otto Grimm [23 January 1879; 4:130]). Brahms also wrote back to Simrock asking whether Keller would copy out the songs himself and suggesting that it would be easier to have them copied in Vienna, since with transpositions into lower keys he always found "a few things to change." But, whoever prepared the copies, he would still want to see them before they were engraved (20 January 1879; 10:103–4). On 25 January Simrock replied that Keller would be making the copies but that Brahms would certainly have an opportunity to see the songs prior to engraving (no. 83).

In answering Brahms's query on 29 January, Stockhausen raised the obvious question—was the edition in lower keys intended for bass, baritone, alto, or mezzo soprano? Nonetheless, he provided a list of possible lower keys (Stockhausen, 452–54; 18:141). Henschel's reply must have reached Brahms at about the same time, for on 5 February he included in a letter to Simrock the following document, which combines Stockhausen's and Henschel's suggestions:

•❯ 4

List of keys recommended by Julius Stockhausen and Georg Henschel, with annotations by Brahms and Keller, for the transposed editions of the *Gesänge,* Opp. 69–72, circa 5 February 1879 (Library of Congress)

{Note: All cancellations and all information in the right-hand column written with blue crayon, unless otherwise indicated.}

		Stockhausen	—	Henschel.	
op.69.	1	~~E~~.	—	~~E~~.	C
	2	~~G~~.	—	~~G~~.	*H moll* [B♭ minor]
	3	~~Des~~ [D♭]	—	~~Des~~ [D♭]	*F dur* [F major]

(4	*Es* [E♭] ~~—~~	~~*F od. Es* [F or E♭]~~)	*G dur* [G major]
5	*F (fis* [F♯]) —	*F.*	*F*
6	*F.*	—	~~*Fis.* [F♯]~~
7	*E.*	—	*Cis* [C♯]	[added after C♯:] *moll* [minor]
8	*A.*	—	*A.*
9	*F.*	—	*F. (fis.* [F♯])

70.	1. *E*	—	~~*Es* [E♭]~~
	2	~~*As* [A♭]~~ —	*As* [A♭]
	3 *As* [A♭]	~~=~~	~~*As* [A♭]~~
	4 *A.*	—	*A.*	? *B* ? [underlined and canceled with pencil]

		St.		H.	
71.	1. *B.* [B♭]	—	~~*H.* [B]~~
	2 *G.*	—	~~*G.*~~
	3 *E.*	—	*Es* [E♭] (*D.*	*Es* [E♭]
	4. *C.*	—	~~*H.* [B]~~	[added after C:] *moll* [minor]
	5 *B* [B♭] (~~*A.*~~) —	*H.* [B] (*B*) [B♭]

72.	1	~~*H.* [B]~~ ~~—~~	(~~*Fis* [F♯], *G*~~	*A moll* [A minor]
	2	(*E.*)	—	*B* [B♭] ———	?
	3	~~(*As* [A♭])~~ ~~—~~	(~~*As* [A♭], *Ges* [G♭]~~)	*B* [B♭]
	4	~~*E.*~~ ~~—~~	~~*E*~~	*A moll* [A minor]
	5	*G.*	—	(~~*G.* (*As* [A♭]~~)

(~~*für Tenor E.*~~) ~~[for tenor E.]~~

[Added by Keller at the end in blue crayon:] [Op.] 72, [No.] 4 lieber nach *E moll* tnp. [transponieren] [better transposed to E minor]

❧

The keys suggested by Stockhausen and Henschel were all lower than the original ones. But, as Simrock pointed out in his reply of 6 February 1879 (no. 84), some of the songs were already in keys suitable for baritones or altos, but too low for sopranos or tenors. Two editions, he felt, were needed, one for high voices, the other for low, with songs either left in their original keys or transposed accordingly. It is likely that Simrock returned the Stockhausen-Henschel list to Brahms at this time and that the composer then added the annotations in blue pencil, giving higher keys for Op. 69 Nos. 2–4 and Op. 72 Nos. 1, 3, and 4, and designating which lower keys should be used for the remaining songs. Brahms probably sent the list back to Simrock on 9 February, together with a letter in which he noted that it was indeed his intention that the low songs be transposed into higher keys and the high songs into lower ones (10:108).

In his letter to Simrock of 5 February, Brahms had agreed that the safest and best solution would be to entrust the task of copying to Keller (10:104; Keller's manuscript copies are preserved at the Brahms Institut in Lübeck.) On 19 April Brahms returned the manuscript copies (or perhaps the proofs?) to Simrock, noting, however, that some of the later songs (probably in Op. 72) had been composed for rather low voices and that it would be more desirable to publish them now in transpositions for higher voice (10:114).

"High" and "low" transposed editions were released for Opp. 69 and 72, "low" editions for Opp. 70 and 71. All the songs were placed in the keys given by Brahms on his list, except for two: Op. 69 No. 1 was raised only a half step, from A minor to B♭ minor, and Op. 72 No. 4 was transposed from F♯ minor down to E minor (as suggested by Keller in his annotation at the end of the list) rather than up to A minor.

The alterations that Brahms made were in those passages of the songs transposed to lower keys where, because of the deeper register, the left hand became less clear. Brahms's emendations included the deletion of the bottom notes from open octaves; the transposition of low chords up an octave; the revoicing of low chords, by moving them into a higher inversion or by thinning notes out of them; and, similarly, the substitution of open octaves for more tightly spaced sonorities. In a few cases he recast entire passages (see, e.g., the extensive revision in *Mädchenfluch*, Op. 69 No. 9). He also altered the right hand of the accompaniment if the transposition created technical problems, as, for instance, in the *Minnelied*, Op. 71 No. 5, when two notes, E–F, both played by the thumb in the original key, became E♭–F♭ in the low key and could no longer be executed in this fashion.

The Violin Concerto and the
Clavierstücke, Op. 76

Three letters from Brahms to Keller and one reply from Keller, all written between July and September 1879, concern the publication of the Violin Concerto in D Major, Op. 77. Keller's letter also touches on errors that he had noticed in the first edition of the *Clavierstücke,* Op. 76.

Brahms had begun work on the Violin Concerto during the preceding summer, while on vacation in Pörtschach am Wörthersee, and in August he had sent an autograph manuscript of the solo violin line for the first movement and the beginning of the third movement to the violinist Joseph Joachim (Staatsbibliothek der Stiftung Preußischer Kulturbesitz, Berlin; 22 August 1878, 6:140–41). The composition was initially conceived in four movements, but in October Brahms reported to Joachim that he was having trouble with the middle movements, an Adagio and a Scherzo (23 October 1878; 6:146); the following month he informed his friend that the two inner movements had been replaced by a single Adagio (6:147). Shortly before this, Brahms had completed the full score (now owned by the Library of Congress), which then served as the copyist's model for a "beautifully written" solo violin part and for a set of orchestral parts (neither source extant).[1]

The concerto received its premiere at the Leipzig Gewandhaus on New Year's Day, 1879, with Joachim as soloist and Brahms conducting. Performances in Budapest and Vienna followed in short order, on 8 and 14 January, with the result that Brahms undertook further refinements in the concerto. After the initial performances Joachim had kept the solo part, and on 21 January Brahms asked him to have a second copy of the part prepared, with some *ossia* readings, so that he could go through it with a "less good" violinist (Hugo Heermann) (6:153). A few days later Brahms sent Joachim the full score and orchestral parts for use during his upcoming English tour, and around 8 February Joachim returned to Brahms the original copy of the violin part, saying that he would retain the newly prepared second manuscript copy (now owned by the Library of Congress).

Brahms completed the violin-piano arrangement by early March and submitted it to Clara Schumann for her opinion (13 March 1879; 10:112). In the months that followed Joachim's return from England, the autograph score and solo violin parts circulated among Brahms, Joachim, and Simrock, as composer and violinist discussed various revisions. The nature of these deliberations can be determined in part from comments in the correspondence (end of March through 26 June 1879; 6:158–72) and from revisions written in the autograph score and in the one extant solo violin part.

Brahms had the score in his possession from mid-April, when he met Joachim in Berlin to discuss the work, until mid-May, when he again lent the score to Joachim, who performed the concerto on 25 May in Amsterdam, and it was during this month that the composer put the finishing touches on the work. Shortly thereafter he began sending Simrock the materials necessary for the publication of the concerto. Manuscripts of the violin-piano arrangement, only recently returned by Frau Schumann (now owned by the Oesterreichische Nationalbibliothek, Vienna; partly in a copyist's hand, partly in Brahms's), and of the solo part (the one preserved in the Library of Congress) were shipped on 9 June. The autograph score followed on 23 June, the day after Joachim returned it to Brahms (10:118, 121–22; see also 12, 27 June 1879, nos. 91 and 92), and the manuscript orchestral parts arrived in Berlin around the same time (no. 92).[2]

At this point, the texts of these four sources still varied from each other. The task of reconciling the readings fell to Keller. In his letter of 22 June to Simrock (10:120–21), Brahms provided guidelines: the solo violin line in the full score should be corrected according to the solo violin part (an annotation on the inside of the front wrapper of the manuscript for the violin-piano arrangement likewise directs that the violin in this arrangement be "corrected according to the enclosed part"), but the orchestral parts must be corrected against the score, and very carefully. Moreover, the *ossia* passages should appear only in the solo violin part and not be included in either the full score or the violin-piano arrangement. The results of Keller's scrutiny can be seen throughout the extant sources, entered in dark red ink.[3] In contrast, his editorial instructions to the engraver are written in light-gray pencil, and other entries raising questions are in blue pencil. (A few further instructions, including the plate number, 8133, were added to the full score in orange-red and blue pencils; the engraver's layout markings are also visible.)

The first exchange concerning the Violin Concerto, however, was prompted, not by problems of variant readings, but rather by a question about how to notate the horns in the orchestral parts. Although the letter containing Keller's query does not survive, Brahms's reply reveals the nature of the problem:

➤ 5

JOHANNES BRAHMS TO ROBERT KELLER Pörtschach am Wörthersee, 6 July 1879 (Library of Congress)

{Envelope: Herrn *R. Keller. Berlin. W. Steglitzerstrasse 1. 4 Tr.* [4th floor]; as well as: Fr[ei] [i.e., postage paid]}

Juni [sic] 79.

Sehr geehrter Herr,

Die fragliche Stelle [II, bar 15] ist in der Partitur richtig notirt, nur bitte ich in die erste Hornstimme statt [♪musical notation♪] [♪] zu setzen. Das darf man vom ersten Hornisten verlangen, vom 2ten aber: [♪musical notation♪]

klingt: [♪musical notation♪]

Sollten Sie es gelegentlich einer Aufführung nicht hören so ist eben der betr[effende] Hornist Schuld u. sein Ventil-Horn.

Ich hatte einst in einer Wiener Orchester=Probe einen großen Streit als ich das [♪musical notation♪] ([♪musical notation♪] von einem tiefen B-Horn verlangte. Da ich indeß nicht zum Nachgeben zu bringen war, mußte schließlich der betr. Musiker zugeben daß er es nur Heute u. auf <u>dem</u> Instrument nicht bringen könne. In der nächsten Probe hatte er dafür gesorgt u. ich mein tiefes *B*.

Für jedes kleine u. große ? bin ich Ihnen sehr dankbar u. wünschte nur, andre Verleger (ich will kein z.B. dazu setzen) erfreuten sich eines so vortrefflichen Correktors wie Hr. Simrock.

Sehr ergeben
<u>J. Brahms</u>

➤

June [*sic*] 1879

Dear Sir:

The passage in question [II, bar 15] is notated correctly in the score, only please put [♪] instead of [♪musical notation♪] in the part for the first horn.

{23}

One may demand that from the first horn player, but from the 2d horn:  will sound: [music]

Should you not hear it in a performance, then it is the fault of that particular horn player and his valve horn.

I once had a big dispute during an orchestra rehearsal in Vienna when

I demanded this [music] ([music] of a low B♭ horn. Since I would not

give in, however, the particular musician finally had to admit that only "today" was he unable to play it, and on *that* instrument. At the next rehearsal he was prepared, and I got my low B♭.

For every small and large ? I am very grateful to you and just wish that other publishers (I don't want to mention any *e.g.*'s) had such an excellent editor as Herr Simrock does.

Very sincerely,
J. Brahms

The autograph score of the Violin Concerto contains a revision in the passage in question, which occurs midway through the transcendental woodwind theme that opens the concerto's Adagio, at the point where the initial melodic phrase returns (bar 15). Brahms originally wrote the first and second horns' sustained Gs two octaves apart:

He subsequently lowered the first horn an octave, writing it in "old" horn notation in bass clef, together with the second horn:

This reading also appears in the published score, with dynamics slightly altered.

Growing up with a father who played the French horn (among other instruments), Brahms would have acquired a thorough knowledge of this instrument early in life. The Trio in E♭ Major for Violin, Waldhorn, and Piano, Op. 40, the four *Gesänge* for Women's Choir, Harp, and Two Horns, Op. 17, and the horn parts in his larger-scale orchestral and choral works all attest to his fascination with and proficiency in writing for horns. Yet, by the late 1870s, his skillful but old-fashioned approach to horn writing, more in the style of his Classical and early Romantic predecessors than of his contemporaries, could lead to difficulties. The incident with the horn player in Vienna illustrates the situation. Having no doubt shown up for rehearsal with his "new" valve horn in F ("*that* instrument," to use Brahms's denigrating expression), the horn player was unable to reach the low B♭ required by Brahms, who had expected the part to be played on a natural horn, which could have reached the low B♭ simply by using the appropriate crook. At the next rehearsal, the Viennese horn player brought along his old natural horn, and Brahms got his low B♭.

In his second letter to Keller concerning the Violin Concerto, Brahms discusses an *ossia* reading for the Finale and the placement of markings for a tempo change in the first movement:

•• 6

JOHANNES BRAHMS TO ROBERT KELLER   Pörtschach am Worthersee, circa 23 August 1879 (Library of Congress)

{Envelope addressed to: <u>Herrn *R. Keller.*</u> Gefälligst mit der beil. Correktur zu übergeben [Please forward with enclosed correction]. *J. Br.*}

Geehrtester Herr,
   Für die Correktur des Concerts habe ich noch recht sehr Ihre freund-liche Hülfe zu erbitten.
Namentlich wünschte ich auf S. 12 der Solostimme [III, bars 21–26] die ursprüngliche Lesart mit dem ossia, fürchte aber dem Stecher die Sache nicht deutlich genug machen zu können.
Auf die Umschlag=Seite des Cl. Auszugs habe ich meine Meinung notirt; hoffentlich ist die Aenderung nicht zu schwierig? In den Cl.=A. müßte dann auch die erste Lesart (nicht das Ossia) kommen.
   Die Wiederholung der Stelle [bars 195ff.] laßen wir wie sie ist.
S. 20 im Cl.=A. u. S. 9 in der Solost: [I, bars 555–59] wissen Sie auch vielleicht besser das *cresc. e poco __ a __ poco __ animato* anzubringen?

Vielleicht: *cresc. ed animato* _____ *poco* _____ *a* _____ | *poco*

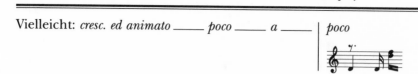

Die 16^{tel} auf der ersten Seite der Solost: [I, bars 82ff.] kommen natürlich auch in die erste Geige des Orchesters.

Ich aber bin wie gewöhnlich Ihnen zu herzlichem Dank verpflichtet.

Ihr

sehr ergebener

J. Brahms.

Dear Sir:

I shall still need quite a bit of your kind assistance with the proofreading of the concerto.

In particular, on p. 12 of the solo violin part [III, bars 21–26] I would like the original reading with the *ossia,* but I am afraid that I cannot make the matter clear enough to the engraver.

I have notated what I want on the wrapper page of the piano reduction; I hope the change is not too difficult to make? The first reading (not the *Ossia*) must then also be put into the piano reduction.

The repeat of this passage [bars 195ff.] we will leave as it is.

On p. 20 in the piano reduction and p. 9 in the solo part [I, bars 555–59]: perhaps you also know a better way to position the *cresc. e poco* _____ *a* _____ *poco* _____ *animato?*

Perhaps: *cresc. ed animato* _____ *poco* _____ *a* _____ | *poco*

The sixteenth notes on the first page of the solo part [I, bars 82ff.] must of course also appear in the first violin part of the orchestra.

I am, however, greatly indebted to you, as usual.

Yours very sincerely,

J. Brahms

The extant manuscript sources reveal that Brahms initially considered providing *ossia* readings for a number of passages in the Finale. Indeed, when laying out the autograph score, he left two staves for the solo violin, to permit the addition of alternative readings. In the end, while allowing the publication of all three *ossia* readings in the first movement, he permitted only one of the seven developed for the Finale—the alternative reading for bars 21–26 cited here. Moreover, the *ossia* readings were published only in the solo violin part.[4] The full *ossia* for bars 21–26 appears on the inside of the back wrapper of the manuscript for the violin-piano arrangement (see plate 1), as Brahms noted in his letter to Keller. In the autograph of the full score, this reading appears as one of Keller's red-ink emendations. The origins of this *ossia* can be seen in the manuscript solo violin part, where, on page 17, Brahms first entered an alternative reading for bars 23–26 at the bottom of the page and subsequently extended it to begin two bars earlier.

Brahms expressed his hope that the addition of this *ossia* to the already engraved solo violin part would not prove too difficult, but, judging from Keller's reply, the alteration necessitated the reengraving of the entire Finale (on six rather than five pages):

•• 7

Robert Keller to Johannes Brahms   Berlin, 27 August 1879
(Archiv der Gesellschaft der Musikfreunde, Vienna)

Berlin 27 August 79.

Hochverehrter Meister!

Gelegentlich der untenfolgenden Anfragen betreffs Ihres Violinconcerts nehme ich freudige Veranlassung, Ihnen einmal meinen herzlichsten Dank zu sagen für die wiederholte Anerkennung meiner für die würdige und correkte Druckstellung Ihrer herrlichen Werke angewandten Bemühungen. Den schönsten Lohn giebt mir ja die Beschäftigung mit diesen Werken selbst; auch honorirt Hr. *Simrock* meine Arbeit anständig; um so mehr muß mich Ihre persönliche Anerkennung erfreuen u. ehren. Zu dem weiß ich sehr wohl, daß meine Stellung bei *Simrock,* dem gewiß billigere Arbeitskräfte oft genug sich anbieten mögen, sich wesentlich durch Ihre günstigen Urtheile über mich so dauernd befestigt hat. Grund genug um mit liebevollster Hingebung Ihnen die für einen schöpferischen Geist austrocknende u. für neue Thaten lahmlegende Correkturarbeit auf ein Minimum zu bringen. Wenn trotzdem Dinge, wie das fehlende ♯ vor *d* (*p.*

4 [No. 1, bar 19]) u. der entsetzliche 𝄞 (*p.* 15 [No. 3, bar 28]) der

Clavierstücke [Op. 76], vorkommen, so darf ich wohl auf die geforderte „Eile" des Verlegers einen kleinen

2

Theil meiner Schuld abwälzen.
Und nun zur Sache.

1) Für das in Cl. A. u. St. recht schwer in schnell übersichtlicher Art anzubringende *cres. e poco a poco animato* am Schluß des 1ten Satzes [bars 555–59] möchte ich vorschlagen:

    cresc. e string. poco a poco – – – – – | *animato.*

Das würde sofort augenfällig sein u. den Zielpunkt genau bezeichnen.

2) Bei dem 2 Mal vorkommenden *tranquillo* [I, bars 312 and 527] habe <u>ich</u> das <u>kleine</u> *t* auf dem Gewissen, und zwar consequent auch in Part. u. Orch. St. — Haben Sie damit eine wirkliche <u>Tempoveränderung</u> gemeint, so muß ich in den sauren Apfel beißen u. werde es mit Temposchrift **„Tranquillo"** machen lassen; ist es aber, (wie ich glaubte) nur eine Mahnung <u>nicht zu eilen</u>, dann ist *tranquillo* das bessere, so wie ja auch das *animato* am Schluß (der Gegensatz dazu) <u>klein</u> gedruckt ist. Es würde mir u. den Stechern lieb sein wenn *tranq.* bleiben könnte. Gegen <u>kleine</u> Schrift und <u>großes</u> *T,* was allerdings leichter zu machen wäre, sträubt sich aber mein besseres Selbst!!

3) Das *ossia* (*p.* 12 d. Solost. [III, bars 21–26]) läßt sich ohne häßlich auffallende Verschiedenheit des Stichs nicht einbringen. Ich habe einen Neustich wenigstens dieser ganzen Platte oder—wie noch besser wäre— eine Vertheilung des Inhalts

3

von *p.* 12–16 [III complete] auf <u>sechs</u> neue Platten beantragt. Ich glaube es wird Herrn *S.* nicht darauf ankommen; denn es würde damit die Stimme sehr an Lesbarkeit gewinnen u. der unangenehme <u>halbe Bogen</u> in der Mitte würde wegfallen. Die für das <u>Umwenden</u> nöthige Eintheilung habe ich für diesen Fall angegeben.

4) Zu einer Vergleichung von Part. u. Cl.-Ausz. wurde mir erst vor Kurzem Gelegenheit, als ich zum ersten Male beides gleichzeitig im Hause hatte. Dabei habe ich folgende größeren u. kleineren Differenzen aufgestöbert, um deren endgültige Entscheidung ich Sie ergebenst bitten möchte. Mit dem Partitur=Abzug wird Ihnen zu diesem Zwecke der Cl. Ausz. noch einmal mit zugehen. Die <u>Stimmen</u> alsdann in Ordnung zu bringen, dürfen Sie getrost mir allein überlassen.

Cl. Ausz.

[In the left margin, before the first entry, in blue crayon:]

p. 3 Syst. v, Takt 1–5   fehlt vielleicht ein $_{8^{va}}$~~ Zeichen? Der
[I, bars 35–39]   Sprung zu dem *gis* hinauf (Takt 6) ist mir
befremdlich.

[The next two entries are canceled, in blue crayon:]

p. 5, I, 4 [bar 81]:   Part. (*p.* 15) hat <u>a</u> statt *b*.

p. 8, IV, 6 [bar 184]:   Part. (*p.* 38) hat <u>h</u> statt *gis*.

p. 9, v, 4 [bar 230]:   steht in d. Part. (*p.* 45) ein Vorschlag

zu , der auch in der Solostimme (wohl
mit Absicht) fehlt, doch wollte ich ihn nicht
eigenmächtig wegbringen. *p.* 18 [bar 473]
ist er wegen der dazwischenliegenden *a*
Saite nöthig.

verte

4
p. 10, IV, 4 [bar 260]:   kann wohl *c* fort, vgl. Part.
(*p.* 51) u. Parallelstelle S. 19 [bar 501]. Von
den Quinten abgesehen kommt die Stimme
<u>*a c h*</u> besser heraus.

10, v, 3 [bar 264]:   Part. (S. 52) hat besser

(vgl. Cl A *p.* 19 [bar 505].)

11, v 2 [bar 290]:   Part. (S. 56) hat <u>c</u> st. *d*.

12, III, 3 [bar 311]:   Part. (S. 60) steht <u>d</u> statt *as*.

(Clav. Ausz. wahrscheinlich richtig!)

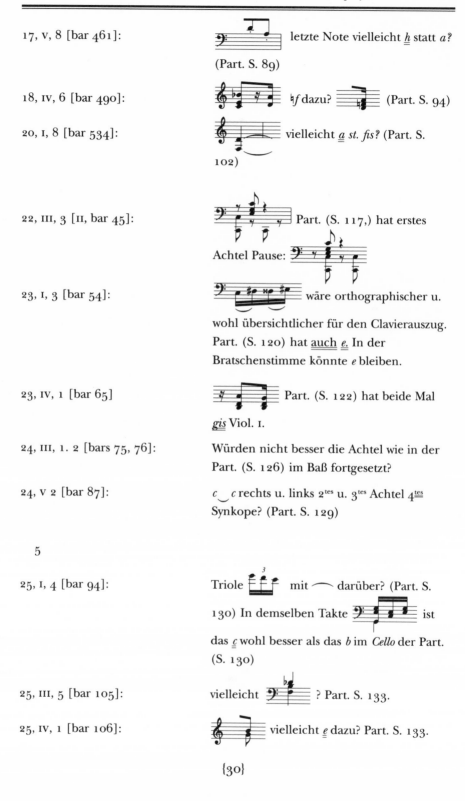

17, v, 8 [bar 461]:   letzte Note vielleicht $\underline{h}$ statt *a*?

(Part. S. 89)

18, iv, 6 [bar 490]: $\natural f$ dazu?   (Part. S. 94)

20, i, 8 [bar 534]:   vielleicht $\underline{a}$ *st. fis*? (Part. S.

102)

22, iii, 3 [ii, bar 45]:   Part. (S. 117,) hat erstes

Achtel Pause:

23, i, 3 [bar 54]:   wäre orthographischer u.

wohl übersichtlicher für den Clavierauszug.
Part. (S. 120) hat <u>auch</u> <u>*e.*</u> In der
Bratschenstimme könnte *e* bleiben.

23, iv, 1 [bar 65]   Part. (S. 122) hat beide Mal

<u>*gis*</u> Viol. 1.

24, iii, 1. 2 [bars 75, 76]:   Würden nicht besser die Achtel wie in der
Part. (S. 126) im Baß fortgesetzt?

24, v 2 [bar 87]: $c \smile c$ rechts u. links 2tes u. 3tes Achtel 4$^{\underline{\text{tes}}}$
Synkope? (Part. S. 129)

5

25, i, 4 [bar 94]:   Triole   mit $\frown$ darüber? (Part. S.

130) In demselben Takte   ist

das $\underline{c}$ wohl besser als das *b* im *Cello* der Part.
(S. 130)

25, iii, 5 [bar 105]:   vielleicht   ? Part. S. 133.

25, iv, 1 [bar 106]:   vielleicht $\underline{e}$ dazu? Part. S. 133.

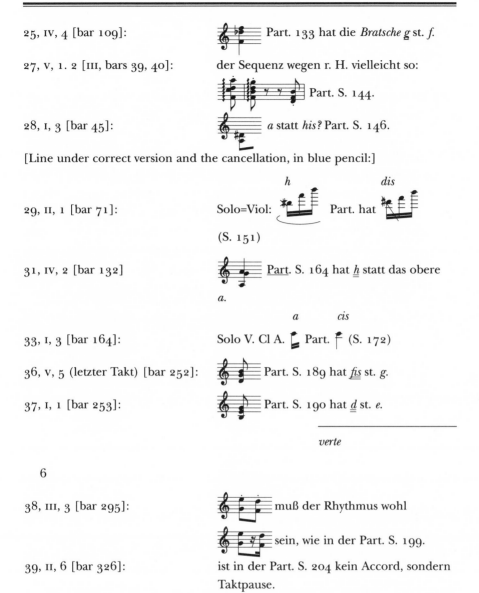

25, IV, 4 [bar 109]:   Part. 133 hat die *Bratsche g* st. *f.*

27, V, 1. 2 [III, bars 39, 40]:   der Sequenz wegen r. H. vielleicht so: Part. S. 144.

28, I, 3 [bar 45]:   *a* statt *his*? Part. S. 146.

[Line under correct version and the cancellation, in blue pencil:]

29, II, 1 [bar 71]:   Solo=Viol: *h*   Part. hat   *dis* (S. 151)

31, IV, 2 [bar 132]   Part. S. 164 hat <u>*h*</u> statt das obere *a.*

33, I, 3 [bar 164]:   Solo V. Cl A. *a*   Part. *cis* (S. 172)

36, V, 5 (letzter Takt) [bar 252]:   Part. S. 189 hat <u>*fis*</u> st. *g.*

37, I, 1 [bar 253]:   Part. S. 190 hat <u>*d*</u> st. *e.*

verte

6

38, III, 3 [bar 295]:   muß der Rhythmus wohl sein, wie in der Part. S. 199.

39, II, 6 [bar 326]:   ist in der Part. S. 204 kein Accord, sondern Taktpause.

Indem ich Sie zum Schluß noch bitte, diese Kleinigkeitskrämerei mir meinem hohen Interesse für das Werk zuzuschreiben, bleibe ich mit hochachtungsvollstem Gruß

Ihr

ergebenster

Robert Keller.

Berlin, 27 August 1879

Dear Sir:

On the occasion of sending the inquiries that follow below concerning your Violin Concerto, I am pleased to take the opportunity to convey to you my heartfelt thanks for your repeated acknowledgment of my efforts to ensure a correct printing that is worthy of your magnificent works. Indeed, my greatest reward is dealing with these works themselves; Herr Simrock also pays me decently for my work; thus there is all the more reason for your personal appreciation to delight and honor me. Also, I know quite well that my position with Simrock, to whom cheaper workers may often enough offer their services, has been established so permanently in large measure thanks to your favorable opinion of me. Reason enough that, with utmost devotion, I should try to reduce to a minimum for you the task of correcting, which is draining for a creative spirit and cripples new endeavors. If, in spite of this, things occur, like the missing ♯

before *D* (p. 4 [No. 1, bar 19]) or the appalling 𝄞 (p. 15 [No. 3, bar 28])

in the *Clavierstücke* [Op. 76], I may perhaps be allowed to shift a small portion of my guilt to the "haste"

2

demanded by the publisher.

And now down to business.

1) For the *cres. e poco a poco animato* at the end of the first movement [bars 555–59], which is rather difficult to position in the piano reduction in a manner that is easy to take in at a glance, I would suggest: *cresc. e string. poco a poco* – – – – – – | *animato.* That would immediately catch the eye and signify the goal of the change precisely.

2) *I* have on my conscience the *lowercase t* that twice occurs for *tranquillo* [I, bars 312 and 527], and, of course, in the score and orchestral parts as well, to be consistent.—If you intended an actual *change of tempo*, then I must bite the sour apple and have it changed to the tempo designation **Tranquillo**; if, however, it is (as I believed) only a reminder *not to rush*, then *tranquillo* is better, just as at the end *animato* (the opposite) is printed *lowercase.* It would please me and the engravers if *tranq.* could remain. My better self resists *lowercase* script and *capital* T, which nevertheless would be easy to do!!

3) The *ossia* (p. 12 of the solo part [III, bars 21–26]) cannot be inserted without unsightly differences in the engraving. I have proposed reengrav-

ing at least this whole plate or—as would be even better—a redistribution of the contents

3

of pp. 12–16 [III complete] onto *six* new plates. I believe it will not matter to Herr Simrock, since the part would be considerably more readable and the unpleasant *half slur* [tie?] in the middle would be eliminated. I have indicated in this case the distribution necessary so that *the page can be turned.*

4) Only recently did I have the opportunity to compare the score with the piano reduction, when, for the first time, I had both of them here at the same time. I then turned up the following major and minor differences, for which I respectfully request your final decision. For this purpose the piano reduction will be sent to you once again, together with the proof of the score. After that you may confidently leave the correcting of the *parts* to me.

Piano reduction

[In the left-hand margin, before the first entry, in blue crayon: ‖]

p. 3, brace v, bars 1–5   An 8va indication is perhaps missing? The
[I, bars 35–39]   leap up to G♯ (bar 6 [bar 40]) seems
     strange.

[The next two entries are canceled, in blue crayon:]

p. 5, I, 4 [bar 81]:   Score (p. 15) has *A* instead of
B♭.

p. 8, IV, 6 [bar 184]:   Score (p. 38) has *B* instead of
G♯.

p. 9, v, 4 [bar 230]:   In the score (p. 45) there is a grace note
     to , which is also missing in the solo part
     (intentionally, I suppose), yet I did not want
     to take it out without checking. On p. 18
     [bar 473] it is necessary because of the A
     string in between.

please turn the page

4

p. 10, IV, 4 [bar 260]: C can probably be taken

out; cf. score (p. 51) and parallel passage,
p. 19 [bar 501]. Apart from the fifths, the
voice *A C B* comes out better.

10, V, 3 [bar 264]: Score (p. 52) should rather

be (cf. piano reduction, p. 19

[bar 505])

11, V 2 [bar 290]: Score (p. 56) has *C* instead of

D.

12, III, 3 [bar 311]: Score (p. 60) has *D* instead

of A♭. (Piano reduction apparently correct!)

17, V, 8 [bar 461]: last note perhaps *B* instead of

A? (score, p. 89)

18, IV, 6 [bar 490]: add ♮F? (score,

p. 94)

20, I, 8 [bar 534]: perhaps *A* instead of F♯?

(score, p. 102)

22, III, 3 [II, bar 45]: Score (p. 117) has an

eighth rest on the first beat:

23, I, 3 [bar 54]: would be better

orthographically and probably easier to read
in the piano reduction. Score (p. 120) has *E*
as well. In the viola part, *E* could remain.

23, IV,1 [bar 65] Score (p. 122) both times has

G♯ in Violin I.

24, III, 1, 2 [bars 75, 76]:

Would it not be better to continue the eighth notes in the bass, as in the score (p. 126)?

24, V, 2 [bar 87]:

C‿C right and left 2d and 3d eighth note, 4th eighth note syncopation? (Score, p. 129)

5

25, I, 4 [bar 94]:

Triplets [♪♪♪] with ⌐ above? (Score, p. 130) In the same bar, [♩♪] C is probably better than B♭ in the cello in the score (p. 130)

25, III, 5 [bar 105]:

Perhaps [♩] ? Score, p. 133.

25, IV, 1 [bar 106]:

[♪] perhaps add *E*? Score, p. 133.

25, IV, 4 [bar 109]:

[♩] Score, p. 133, the viola has *G* instead F.

27, V, 1, 2 [III, bars 39, 40]:

Because of the sequence, perhaps the right hand like this: [chords] Score, p. 144.

28, I, 3 [bar 45]:

[♪] *A* instead of *B♯*? Score, p. 146.

[Line under correct version as well as cancellation, in blue crayon:]

29, II, 1 [bar 71]:

Solo violin: B [notes] Score has D♯ [notes] (p. 151)

31, IV, 2 [bar 132]:

[♪] *Score,* p. 164, has *B* instead of the upper A.

33, I, 3 [bar 164]:

Solo violin, piano reduction, A [note] score C♯ [note] (p. 172)

{35}

36, v, 5 (final bar) [bar 252] ♪♪ Score, p. 189, has *F♯* instead of G.

37, I, 1 [bar 253] ♪♪ Score, p. 190, has *D* instead of E.

please turn the page

6

38, III, 3 [bar 295] ♪♪ the rhythm must probably be

♪♪ , as in the score, p. 199.

39, II, 6 [bar 326] There is no chord in the score, p. 204, but a full bar rest instead.

In closing I ask you to attribute this fussing over petty things to my great interest in the work. I remain, with kindest regards,

Yours

most sincerely,

Robert Keller

❖

The queries included in Keller's letter are those that he labeled *Fragliche Correkturen* (Problematic Corrections) in the draft he made of this letter (Library of Congress). That document also contains a list of *Nothwendige Correkturen* (Necessary Corrections) for the violin-piano arrangement that, in order to minimize the annoyance of corrections for Brahms, he omitted from the queries sent to the composer:

❖

Nothwendige Correkturen.

p. 7 S. III T. 2 [I, bar 136]:	fehlt <u>a tempo</u>
8 I 3 [bar 161]:	1 H: *gis_a*
9 I 6 [bar 198]	Violinst. – fehlt ganze Pause.
9 III 6 [bar 216]	⟨ ⟩ unter *eis eis*)
9 IV 5 [bar 223]	♪ ♪ (Bogen fehlt)

11 II 1 [bar 270]   Viol. d ♮f (Bogen fehlt)

12 III 5 [bar 313]   r H: letztes Viertel ♮f) zusammen abwärts d)

13 III 2 [bar 330]   fehlt ♮ vor *c.* [crossed out by Keller and added in pencil:] ist da!

15 IV 1 [bar 379]   fehlt *poco rit.* (**G** Takt 3 [bar 381]) fehlt *a tempo.*

21 II 5 [II, bar 12] $\overparen{a\ g}\ f$ (Bogen fehlt)

24 III 1 [bar 75]   *calando* (T. 2. [bar 76]) *poco rit.*

25 III 1 [bar 101]   2$\underline{\text{tes}}$ Viertel $<$, (Takt 2 [bar 102]) 1$\underline{\text{tes}}$ Viertel $>$

25 IV 3 [bar 108] $\overline{}$, T. 4 [bar 109] $\overline{}$ vom 2$\underline{\text{ten}}$ Achtel ab.

29 1 1 [III, bar 66]   Baß ♯) vor f) $\begin{smallmatrix}\#\\\#\end{smallmatrix}$ $\begin{smallmatrix}f\\f\end{smallmatrix}$

35 I, 1. [bar 207]   8 hoch ausstechen

37 v, 1 [bar 273]   Solo Viol. *cresc.* unter das 4te–6$\underline{\text{te}}$ Achtel,

39 II 1 [bar 321]   Solo Viol. *cresc.* fehlt.

Necessary Corrections

p. 7, brace III, bar 2 [I, bar 136]   *a tempo* missing

8, I, 3 [bar 161]   l.h.: $G\sharp\ A$

9, I, 6 [bar 198]   Violin part – whole rest missing

9, III, 6 [bar 216] $<\ >$ under $\begin{smallmatrix}E\,\#\\E\,\#\end{smallmatrix}$)

9, IV, 5 [bar 223]   (slur missing)

11, II, 1 [bar 270]   Violin, D ♮F (slur missing)

12, III, 5 [bar 313]   r.h., last quarter note, $\begin{smallmatrix}♮F\\D\end{smallmatrix}$) [stemmed] together, downward

13, III, 2 [bar 330]   Missing ♮ before *C* [crossed out by Keller and added in pencil:] it's there!

15, IV, 1 [bar 379]	Missing *poco rit.* ([rehearsal letter] **G**, bar 3 [bar 381]) missing *a tempo*
21, II, 5 [II, bar 12]	A͡ G F (slur missing)
24, III, 1 [bar 75]	*calando* (bar 2 [bar 76]) *poco rit.*
25, III, 1 [bar 101]	2d quarter note ⤙ , (bar 2 [bar 102]) 1st quarter note ⤚
25, IV, 3 [bar 108]	⤙, bar 4 [bar 109] ⤚ from 2d eighth note on
29, I, 1 [III, bar 66]	Bass ♯♯) before F,F)
35, I, 1 [bar 207]	Engrave up an octave
37, V, 1 [bar 273]	Solo violin, *cresc.* under the 4th–6th eighth notes
39, II, 1 [bar 321]	Solo violin, *cresc.* missing

The errors in the *Clavierstücke* mentioned in item 7 may be two of the three mistakes pointed out by Simrock in a letter (now lost) to Brahms in late March 1879, to which Brahms replied circa 4 April: "I too have seen the three errors you cited in the *Clavierstücke,* and others, also minor" (10:114). It is not surprising that errors should have crept into the first edition, for the engraver's model (extant for Nos. 1–4, private collection, Germany), as copied by Franz Hlavaczek, contained a large number of mistakes, many of which Brahms corrected during his proofreading of that manuscript. (Brahms also made numerous small-scale compositional revisions in the Hlavaczek manuscript.) In this case, it would seem that Keller did not become involved in the editorial process until after the engraving had been done; one finds no corrections or annotations in the engraver's model that can be attributed to him. (Simrock added the titles to the individual pieces, as provided in a letter from Brahms [6 February 1879; 10:106].) The haste demanded by Simrock, then, would have been in comparing the engraver's model with the page proofs, in the process of which Keller overlooked errors in the model that had been perpetuated into the edition.

In his personal copy of the first edition (the *Handexemplar;* Gesellschaft der Musikfreunde, Vienna), Brahms neglected to add the ♯ missing in No. 1, but he did make several other corrections not mentioned by Keller as well as a few minor additions and two major revisions (in Nos. 2 and 7), all of which were taken into account by Eusebius Mandyczewski for his edition of these pieces for the *Brahms Werke* (vol. 14; see his *Revisionsbericht* and also Clara Schumann's critique of these pieces in her letter to Brahms of 7 November 1878 [Schumann, 2:157–59]).

Brahms's reply to Keller's queries about details in the Violin Concerto followed in early September:

•• 8

JOHANNES BRAHMS TO ROBERT KELLER   Pörtschach am Wörthersee, circa 10 September 1879 (Library of Congress)

Sehr geehrter Herr,

Der versprochene Cl-A. ist ausgeblieben; Ihr höchst dankenswerther Brief ist jedoch so ausführlich u. genau daß ich meine Ihn entbehren zu können. Notizen für den Cl.-A. habe ich in die Partitur geschrieben, so, daß Sie nur hiernach auszustreichen haben was die Part. nicht angeht.

Ihr erstes Bedenken geht wohl beiliegende Stelle [1, bars 35ff.] an, die ich dann, wie hier notirt, zu ändern bitte.

Wegen *stringendo, tranquillo etc.* ist mir Alles recht wie Sie es vorschlagen.

So bin ich denn wie gewöhnlich in herzlicher Dankbarkeit

Ihr

ergebener

J. Brahms.

Dear Sir:

The piano reduction you promised to send has failed to appear; but your greatly appreciated letter is so detailed and precise that I think I can do without it. I have written my comments for the piano reduction in the full score, so you only need to cross out what does not have to do with the score.

Your first objection concerns the enclosed passage [I, bars 35ff.], I suppose, which I would like to see changed as notated here.

As far as *stringendo, tranquillo,* etc. are concerned, everything you suggest is fine with me.

Thus I remain, as usual, with sincere thanks,

Yours

truly,

J. Brahms

The proofs for the full score onto which Brahms entered his answers to Keller's inquiries have not survived, but a comparison of the first editions of the full score and the violin-piano arrangement with the engraver's models reveals that most of Keller's suggestions were adopted.

The Fifty-one Exercises
for Piano, Part 1

An exchange of two letters and a postcard between Brahms and Keller during August and September 1880 concerns the organization and preparation of a fair copy of a series of Brahms piano exercises. Additional correspondence, during May and July 1882, documents a subsequent stage of a project that eventually culminated in 1893 with the publication of Brahms's *51 Uebungen für das Pianoforte* (51 Exercises for the Pianoforte), WoO 6. A series of letters between Brahms and Simrock in 1880–81, 1891, and 1893 further elucidates the various phases of this project.

Since the mid-1850s, if not earlier, Brahms had been developing finger exercises for his piano students. Stemming from this period are a sheet of exercises in parallel thirds and sixths, with the ironic title *Fantasiestücke in Callot's kühnster Manier* (Fantasy Pieces in Callot's Most Audacious Manner, a humorous variant of E. T. A. Hoffmann's title for his cycle of essays and stories, the *Fantasiestücke in Callots Manier*[1]), and a pair of leaves containing a variety of exercises, including several for increasing control of the thumbs (New York Public Library).[2] The plaint of the frustrated teacher of beginners is heard in a letter to Clara Schumann from this time:

> I gave the first lesson today to little Miss Weil; tomorrow Frl. Wittgenfels [Anna Wittgenstein] comes.
>
> Etudes by Cramer, Nos. 1 and 2, and a few pieces from Schumann's *Album* [*for the Young*]. How the études and scales reminded me of Hamburg! There is no pleasure in teaching little things to children.
>
> Yes, if I could teach the great works of Bach, Beethoven, Schumann, Schubert, how much I'd enjoy doing that! (25 January 1855; Schumann, 1:64)

The fullest accounts of Brahms as piano teacher come from two of Clara Schumann's pupils, her daughter Eugenie Schumann and the young English pianist Florence May, both of whom Brahms taught in the early 1870s as Frau Schumann's summer replacement. Eugenie recalled in her memoirs: "He was always kind, always patient, and adapted his teaching to my capabilities and the stage of my progress in quite a wonderful way. Also he took a great deal of trouble in the training of my fingers. He had thought about such training and about technique in general much more than my mother, who had surmounted all technical difficulties at an age when one is not yet conscious of them. He made me play a great many exercises, scales, and arpeggios as a matter of course, and he gave special attention to the training of the thumb, which . . . was given a very prominent part in his own playing."[3] Eugenie included in her reminiscences a series of thumb exercises that supplement those in the New York Public Library manuscripts and the *51 Exercises*. Brahms instructed her to practice them with a light thumb, using various rhythmic accentuations, and in various keys, an approach applied to the playing of arpeggios and trills as well:

> I [also] practiced the chromatic scale with the first and third, first and fourth, and first and fifth fingers, and he often made me repeat the two consecutive notes where the thumb was passed under. They were all, in fact, quite simple exercises; but carefully executed, first slowly, then more rapidly, and at last *prestissimo*. I found them extremely helpful for the strengthening, suppleness, and control of the fingers. I also played some of the difficult exercises published later as *Fifty-one Exercises for Pianoforte by Brahms*, in which he did not include the easier and musically less valuable ones.
>
> Brahms as well as my mother was of the opinion that technique, more especially fingering, must be learnt through exercises, so that in the study of pieces attention may be concentrated unhampered upon the spirit of the music.

Florence May underwent a similar course of study. After working for a short period under the tutelage of Clara Schumann, May was turned over to Brahms, who was commissioned to help her correct her technical shortcomings. "He has made a special study of [technique]," Frau Schumann told her pupil, "and can do anything he likes with his fingers on the piano."

> I told him, before beginning my first lesson, of my mechanical difficulties, and asked him to help me. He answered, "Yes, that must come first," and, after hearing me play through a study from Clementi's *Gradus ad Parnassum*, he immediately set to work to loosen and equalize my fingers. Beginning that very day, he gradually put me through an entire course of technical training, showing me how I should best

work, for the attainment of my end, at scales, arpeggi, trills, double notes, and octaves. . . .

He had a great habit of turning a difficult passage round and making me practice it, not as written, but with other accents and in various figures, with the result that when I again tried it as it stood the difficulties had always considerably diminished, and often entirely disappeared.[4]

The immediate impetus for Brahms's effort to put his own technical exercises in order came from his involvement in the preparation of an edition of selected Czerny studies during the spring and early summer of 1880. When Clara Schumann had accepted a position on the faculty of the Frankfurt Conservatory two years earlier, Brahms had advised her "to get hold of a good School of Pianoforte Playing" for her preparatory classes, and soon afterward he had sent her "four volumes of Czerny's, originally published by Diabelli in Vienna."[5] In a letter of 8 July 1880, Frau Schumann informed Brahms that she had examined Czerny's course and found it excellent and that the previous year she had even inquired of the publishing house of C. F. Peters in Leipzig whether they might consider publishing "a small selection of those etudes (finger exercises) which seemed particularly useful."[6] Peters communicated the idea to the publisher August Cranz in Hamburg, who then invited Frau Schumann to prepare such a volume, offering her "a considerable sum" for doing so. Although Frau Schumann had "neither time nor inclination" to undertake the project, her daughters Marie and Eugenie, who had been teaching the preparatory classes for their mother, were interested. But it was the willing participation of Brahms that assured that the project would go forward, as Eugenie Schumann recounted in her memoirs:

When we told Brahms of this [project] the next time we saw him, he said to our mother, "If Marie were to make the selection and I helped her, you would not mind putting your name to it?" She agreed, and work was started without delay. Many annotations and excellent suggestions in Brahms's hand in the second volume show how seriously he took the work, and I had another opportunity of verifying the fact that really great artists excel in faithful attention to the minutest detail. When the work was finished, my mother revised it, and it was subsequently published under the title of *Exercises and Studies from Carl Czerny's Great School of Pianoforte Playing, Op. 500. Selected and edited by Clara Schumann. Published by Aug. Cranz. [Fingerübungen und Studien aus Carl Czerny's grosser Pianoforteschule Op. 500. Ausgewählt und herausgegeben von Clara Schumann* (Leipzig: Aug. Cranz)][7]

With the Czerny project well in hand by August 1880, Brahms turned his attention to organizing his own exercises, a task with which he sought assistance from Robert Keller.

◆◆ 9

JOHANNES BRAHMS TO ROBERT KELLER   Bad Ischl, August 1880
(Library of Congress)

Aug 80

Sehr geehrter Herr,
    Hr. Simrock meint Sie würden <u>vielleicht</u> beifolgende Arbeit für uns in Ordnung bringen. Ich sende Sie [*sic*] Ihnen mit der aufrichtigen Bitte mir aufrichtig zu sagen ob Sie dies können u. mögen.
Vielleicht haben Sie einen geschickteren u. musikalischeren Copisten als ich u. könnten sich von diesem ein gut Theil Mühe abnehmen lassen?
Selbstverständlich sind wir im Voraus einverstanden mit dem, was Sie für die bedeutende Mühe *etc.* berechnen.
    Sehr gern hätte ich sogleich 2 Copieen [*sic*]. Vielleicht läßt es sich machen daß jeder einzelne, in Ordnung gebrachte Bogen, sogleich von einem zweiten Schreiber copirt wird? Diskretion ist selbstverständlich, — daß keiner von den dummen Einfällen gestohlen wird.
Dabei aber eine letzte Bitte. Sie sind vielleicht in der betr[effenden] Litteratur bewandert? In dem Fall möchte ich bitten mir ganz beliebig u. beiläufig Einiges zu äußern, welche der Nummern etwa schon er[schienen] vorhanden u. wo u. bei wem *etc. etc.*
Hoffentlich ist das Manuscript so weit verständlich als nöthig.
Alles, meine ich, braucht nicht ausgeschrieben zu werden. *etc.* in Klammer u. ✗ genügt wohl oft.
Nun bitte ich aber nochmals sich nicht zu genieren wenn Ihnen die Arbeit zu (wie mir) zu entsetzlich ist!
Ich hoffe gelegentlich ein Wort darüber zu hören u. bin in hochachtungsvoller

Ergebenheit
Ischl,   Ihr
Salzkammergut.   *J. Brahms.*
(Salzburgerstr: 51)

◆◆

Aug. 80

Dear Sir:

Herr Simrock believes that you might *perhaps* be willing to bring order for us to the enclosed work. I am sending it to you with the sincere request that you tell me honestly whether you can and want to do this.

Perhaps you have a more skilled and more musical copyist than I do and can have him take over a good deal of the trouble?

It goes without saying that we agree in advance to whatever you may charge for the considerable trouble, etc.

I would very much like to have two copies right away. Perhaps it could be arranged that each page that has been put in order will immediately be copied by a second copyist? Discretion goes without saying—that none of the stupid ideas are stolen.

And now with this, a final request. Perhaps you are better informed about the relevant literature? In that case, I would like to ask you to indicate to me, by and by, which of the numbers may already exist, and where and by whom, etc., etc.

I hope the manuscript is as intelligible as necessary. Not everything, I think, need be written out. *Etc.* in parentheses, and ✗ often may suffice.

But now, once again, I will ask you not to feel embarrassed if the task seems too dreadful to you (as it does to me)!

I hope to hear from you at your convenience, and I remain, with respectful

devotion

yours

Ischl,

Salzkammergut

(Salzburgerstr. 51)

J. *Brahms*

◆◆ 10

ROBERT KELLER TO JOHANNES BRAHMS   Berlin, 30 August 1880
(Archiv der Gesellschaft der Musikfreunde, Vienna)

30 *August* 1880.

Hochgeehrtester Herr!

Ihnen, dem bewunderten Tonmeister zu Liebe habe ich entschlossen in den sauren Apfel gebissen und die mitfolgenden Uebungen in Ordnung gebracht. Nebst der Bitte sie nun genau zu revidiren und das Ihnen nicht Convenirende zur Abänderung für mich anmerken zu wollen, damit ich Alles vollends stichfertig machen kann, möchte ich mir folgende Entgegnungen, Bemerkungen u. Fragen an Sie zu richten erlauben:

Mit einem Copisten Hand in Hand zu arbeiten ging nicht an, da ich einmal keinen kenne (ich schmiere Alles selbst) u. da es wohl auch kaum einen praktischen Vortheil gehabt hätte. S[icherer] Das sicherste war selbst Hand anzulegen. Eine nochmalige Abschrift durch <u>mich</u> würde zu <u>theuer</u> werden; die Copie durch einen Notenschreiber wird ja aber, nachdem Sie meine Arbeit durchgesehen u. ich etwaige Aenderungen nachgetragen, leicht u. schnell zu besorgen sein. — Die Diskretion habe ich gewissenhaft bewahrt. — In der betreffenden Literatur dürfte sich <u>nur Weniges</u> schon vorfinden, es wären dies vor Allem die Nummern 10<u>ab</u> und 22, welche meiner Ansicht nach wegbleiben könnten, da sie erstlich an Schwierigkeit weit hinter den übrigen zurückstehen u. jedenfalls schon

2

bei Czerny, Köhler etc vorkommen, obgleich [added:] ich [then:] den Ort aus Mangel an Material nicht angeben kann. Auch N⁰ 2. 3. 6. 25. 29 bringen glaube ich nichts <u>unbedingt</u> Neues. Die letzte Variante von N⁰ 34 kommt in Clementis *Gradus ad P.[arnassum]* ähnlich vor, wäre aber gleich den vorhergenannten N⁰n ihrer großen <u>Nützlichkeit</u> wegen zu erhalten. — Das Manuscript war mir vollkommen verständlich; wo Zweifel in <u>Kleinigkeiten</u>, vermeintliche Schreibfehler u. dgl. vorkamen, habe ich durch <u>Fragezeichen</u> Ihre gefällige Entscheidung angerufen.

Wegen des <u>Ausschreibens</u> möchte ich aus <u>praktischer</u> Erfahrung rathen, dieses aufs <u>Aeußerste</u> auszudehnen; es wird sonst nicht gespielt. Eine Hälfte <u>kann</u> es nicht transponiren, ♮. die andere ist zu <u>faul</u> dazu; wenn es aber dasteht, dann ist es gut. Ich bin deshalb sogar dafür, die wenigen *etc*s, die ich angebracht (N⁰ 11. 12. 13. 35.) auch noch auszuführen. Ebenso räth die Praxis zu einem bestimmten <u>Abschluß</u> jeder Nummer u. ich möchte Sie ersuchen, da wo ein solcher fehlt, ihn noch anzufügen.

Hingegen könte [*sic*] an Raum nicht unbedeutend gespart werden, wenn die Uebungen in Oktaven (N⁰ 4–10. 22. 26) auf <u>ein</u> System [underneath:] dh. <u>einstimig</u> [*sic*] [then:] mit Fingersatz oben u. unten gebracht würden.

Vielleicht wäre auch eine systematische Anordnung zu empfehlen. Etwa unmaßgeblich in dieser Weise:

Geläufigkeit 1–3. 7–10. 19. 22. 29. 32.

Legato 4–6. 31.

Unabhängigmachung d. Finger 12–18. 20–21. 24–26. 33.

Triller in Octaven 27. Abgleiten der Finger 28.

Fingerwechsel 30.

Accordübung mit weitr Sprung 11. 23. 34. 35.

3

So empfehle ich mich denn Ihrem ferneren gütigen Wohlwollen.
Daß ich oben den *Dr.* vergessen habe, verzeihen Sie mir wohl; es giebt
eben für mich eine ganze Armee von *Drs.*, aber nur Einen Brahms, zu
dessen treuesten Verehrern sich zählt

Ihr

ergebener

Robert Keller

W. Steglitzer Strasse 1.

•◆

30 August 1880

Dear Sir:

Out of respect for you, the admired composer, I have decided to bite
the sour apple and put the enclosed exercises in order. Besides my request
that you revise them carefully now and mark for me everything that does
not suit you, so I can change it and fully prepare everything for engraving,
please permit me to direct the following replies, remarks, and questions
to you:

It was not feasible to work hand in hand with a copyist, since I know of
none (I scribble everything myself) and since there would have been
hardly any practical advantage. It was safest to do it myself. For it to be
copied again by *me* would be too *expensive;* but, once you have checked my
work and I have added any further changes, a copy can be made easily and
quickly by a professional copyist. — I have been scrupulously discreet. —
Only a few might already be found in the relevant literature, particularly
Numbers 10a, b and 22, which could be omitted, I think, since, in the first
place, they fall far short of the others in difficulty, and in any case already

2

appear in Czerny, Köhler, etc., although I cannot cite just where, for lack
of reference material. Also, Nos. 2, 3, 6, 25, and 29 do not, I think, add
anything *entirely* new. The last variant of No. 34 occurs in similar form in
Clementi's *Gradus ad Parnassum,* but it should be retained, just as the
above-mentioned numbers, because of its great *usefulness.* — The manuscript was entirely intelligible to me; where I was in doubt about *details,*
apparent slips of the pen, and the like, I have indicated this with *question
marks* and request your kind decision.

With regard to *writing out in full,* I would like to advise from *practical
experience* that you adopt the most extreme course; otherwise it will not be

played. Half are not *able* to transpose it, the others are too *lazy;* but if it is there, then it is fine. I even advocate that you write out the few *etc*s that I used (Nos. 11, 12, 13, 35). Experience also shows that each number should have a definite *ending,* and I would request that you append one where one is missing.

On the other hand, one could save not an insignificant amount of space by putting the exercises in octaves (Nos. 4–10, 22, 26) on *one* staff, i.e., as a *single voice,* with fingering above and below.

Perhaps a systematic ordering would also be advisable. Perhaps in this fashion, open to correction:

Fluency 1–3, 7–10, 19, 22, 29, 32.

Legato 4–6, 31.

For developing independence of fingers 12–18, 20–21, 24–26, 33.

Trills in octaves 27. Sliding the finger 28.

Finger substitution 30.

Chord exercise with wide leaps 11, 23, 34, 35.

3

Thus I close in the hope of retaining your esteemed goodwill. You will no doubt forgive me for forgetting the Dr. above; for me there is a whole army of Drs., but only one Brahms, among whose most faithful admirers I count

Yours

sincerely,

Robert Keller

W. Steglitzer Strasse 1

❖

In this letter Keller cites thirty-five exercises in all, and his characterizations of two of them are specific enough to identify them as exercises published in the *51 Exercises* of 1893: sliding of the finger (No. 28 = No. 25) and changing of fingers (No. 30 = No. 27). If one also pairs the exercises in octaves listed by Keller with those in the *51 Exercises* (Nos. 4–10, 22, 26 = Nos. 3–8, 20, 24), a pattern begins to emerge, and the remaining exercises of 1880, described more generally by Keller, can then be matched, more or less, with numbers from the *51 Exercises* (see table 1).[8] It would appear that the volume eventually published in 1893 was merely an extension of the collection prepared in 1880, the process of enlargement taking place,

Table 1. 35 Exercises of 1880 vs. *51 Uebungen* of 1893

1880	Description	*1893*
1	Fluency	1
2 or 3	Fluency; nothing new	2
4–5	Legato; in octaves	3–4
6	Legato; in octaves; nothing new	5
7–9	Fluency; in octaves	6–7
10a, b	Fluency; in octaves; already in literature	8a, b
11	Chords with wide leaps; write out transpositions	9
12–13	Independence of fingers; write out transpositions	10
14–18	Independence of fingers	12–16
19	Fluency	17
20–21	Independence of fingers	18–19
22	Fluency; in octaves; already in literature	20
23	Chords with wide leaps	21
24	Independence of fingers	23
25	Independence of fingers; nothing new	22
26	Independence of fingers; in octaves	24
27	Trills in octaves	—
28	Sliding of the finger	25
29	Fluency; nothing new	26
30	Changing of fingers	27
31	Legato	28
32	Fluency	??
33	Independence of fingers	30
34	Chords with wide leaps; compare with Clementi's *Gradus ad Parnassum*	—
35	Chords with wide leaps; write out transpositions	31 or 32?

for the most part, in 1882, when, as we shall see below, Brahms again sought Keller's aid with the project.

A few lines, jotted down quickly on a postcard, register Brahms's appreciation of Keller's assistance with the initial stage of this project.

•• 11

JOHANNES BRAHMS TO ROBERT KELLER   Bad Ischl, 4 September 1880 (Library of Congress)

{Postcard addressed to: Herrn *Robert Keller Berlin. W.;* to the left: *Steglitzer Str:* 1.}

Geehrtester Herr,

Ich bin im Begriff zur Eisenbahn zu gehen, da kommt Ihr Paquet u. ich sage schnell noch meinen herzlichsten, ernstesten Dank für die große Mühe die sie [*sic*] dem Zeug gewidmet haben. Sie wißen, ohne dies [changed to:] ~~daß~~ daß ich's sage, wie sehr ich Ihre Geduld u. Arbeit schätzen muß! Einstweilen nur dies eilige flüchtige Wort des Dankes Ihres ergebenen

J. Brahms.

Dear Sir:

I am about to go to the train, and here comes your packet, and I just quickly want to express my most grateful, most sincere thanks for the great care you have devoted to this stuff. You know, without my saying so, how much I must value your patience and work! For now, only this hasty, cursory note of thanks. Yours sincerely

J. Brahms

Two days later, on 6 September, Brahms wrote Simrock to enlist his aid in seeing that Keller received adequate remuneration for his efforts: "With your letter came one from R. Keller and a copy of the piano exercises about which I spoke to you. Now I ask you quite sincerely to inquire of Herr Keller what he wishes for [this] extremely unpleasant work. You must naturally say that [the work] is for you, and you must encourage him to ask for a lot!!" (10:155). On 9 October, Simrock replied: "For work executed, Keller figures 45 Marks, which I shall debit to your account" (no. 103).

During the autumn of 1880, Brahms must have written to Elizabeth von Herzogenberg, one of his closest musical confidants after Clara Schumann, informing her about his exercises. On 14 December, she reminded him: "Also, don't forget the *melodische Übungsstücke!*" (1:131). Brahms enjoyed her characterization of his entirely unmelodic studies, repeating it in his response of 24 December and upping the ante: "Also [enclosed] are some melodious piano exercises—which are all too obviously influenced by my tender admiration [*Schwärmerei*] for the smiling Professorin's delicate hand and little fingers" (1:132), a reference to their mutual friend Frau Emma Engelmann, an excellent amateur pianist in Utrecht "whose inspired renderings of Brahms's works always gave great pleasure to the composer."[9] On 28 December, Brahms used Frau von Herzogenberg's characterization once again, when thanking her for her reactions: "It was too good of you to remember the melodious finger exercises" (1:134 [trans., 115–16]).

Therese, Op. 86 No. 1

A pair of compositional revisions for the song *Therese,* Op. 86 No. 1 (text by the Swiss poet Gottfried Keller), is the topic of two postcards from Brahms to Robert Keller in April 1882. In the first communication, posted on 23 April, Brahms asked that the first and third phrases of the vocal line be altered in the proofs; with the second postcard, posted five days later, he rescinded the request, with apologies over any trouble he may have caused.

•• 12

JOHANNES BRAHMS TO ROBERT KELLER   Vienna, 23 April 1882
(Library of Congress)

{Postcard addressed to: Herrn *Robert Keller* Adr: Musikverlag *N. Simrock. Berlin. W.*; to the left: 171 Friedrichstr:}

Geehrtester Herr, ich denke m. neuen Lieder sind noch bei Ihnen oder kommen zur ersten Correktur. Wollen Sie gütigst in „*Therese*" die Sing-stimme folgendermaßen ändern

Du   milchjunger   Knabe, wie schaust du mich   an

und:

Alle Ratsherrn in der Stadt u. alle   Weisen der Welt—

Herzlich verbunden für dies u. das

Ihr ergebener
J. Brahms.

••

Dear Sir:

I imagine that my new songs are still with you or are coming to you for first proofreading. Will you kindly change the vocal line in *Therese* as follows:

Du milchjunger Knabe, wie schaust du mich an

and:

Alle Ratsherrn in der Stadt u. alle Weisen der Welt—

Much obliged for this and that,

Yours sincerely,
J. Brahms

⚬ 13

Johannes Brahms to Robert Keller Vienna, 28 April 1882 (Library of Congress)

{Postcard addressed to: Herrn *Robert Keller* (Musikverlag *N. Simrock.*) *Berlin. W.;* to the left: 171 Friedrichstr:}

Geehrtester Herr, ich bitte meine vorige Karte u. Bitte <u>nicht</u> gelten zu laßen. Hoffentlich haben Sie noch keine Correktur, also auch noch keine Mühe davon gehabt! Sonst bitte ich recht sehr zu verzeihen daß Sie mit zu leiden haben wenn ich aus Ärger über ein mißlungenes Produkt confus bin!

Sehr ergeben
Ihr
J. Brahms

⚬

Dear Sir:

Please do *not* pay any attention to my previous postcard and request. I hope you have not yet made the correction, so that it has not yet caused you any inconvenience! If it has, I sincerely ask your pardon for your having to suffer with me when I am all mixed up because of anger over a product that has not turned out well.

Very sincerely

Yours

J. Brahms

❧

The earliest reference to the song *Therese* is an entry on the page for March in Brahms's 1878 pocket calendar book (Stadt- und Landesbibliothek, Vienna), where it is listed on an inventory of ten Lieder, many of which may well have been completed that month.[1] While on holiday at Arnoldstein in the summer of 1878, Elizabeth von Herzogenberg was allowed to make a manuscript copy of the song (24 November 1879; 1:102–3), and it was to Frau von Herzogenberg and her husband, the composer Heinrich von Herzogenberg, that Brahms submitted the alternative readings in April 1882, seeking their opinion:

> I hope you still have a song *Therese?* It would be a special pleasure for me if you could say "yes" to the following reading, and if it seems just right to you. [Then follow the same two passages that Brahms sent to Keller.] I can really add nothing further; the one version is as old as the other—perhaps not so simple and singable. Although this one has been copied and sung more often, I have not accustomed myself to it, and now I am confused.
>
> Sing through the song once again, both of you, and allow the poor youth to languish over it at the piano—and let me know what you think. (1:180)

The readings in the Herzogenbergs' manuscript were no doubt the ones that Brahms finally settled on for the published song:

and

Al-le Rats-herrn in der Stadt und al-le Wei - sen der Welt

On 26 April, Brahms had his reply from Frau von Herzogenberg:

With the best will in the world—and Heinrich feels the same way—I cannot take to the old new version, and I would be very sad if you persisted with it. I find the simpler form . . . with the little counterpoint in the piano to be much more charming than the other jagged version, and to be so much more appropriate in this song, where it is not so much a matter of vocal display [*Stimmenentfaltung*] as of finely sung speech. — Sing for yourself the downward octave leap, in the light manner demanded by the character of the song—how clumsy in comparison with the simple repetition of the three tones!

I do beg you not to meddle any more with the dear little song and to be satisfied with the simpler version! (1:181–82)

Brahms took her advice to heart and immediately wrote Keller withdrawing his first request. On 15 May he informed Frau von Herzogenberg that "it is as wished for with the 'milk-white youth,' that is, according to your wishes" (1:182), and in July 1882 the song was published with the reading she had espoused.[2]

Frau von Herzogenberg defined the issue here as speech simply sung versus vocal display, but Brahms may have viewed the choice as between two types of folk-style melody, one using a narrow range, as if telling a story—the type found in most of his forty-nine *Deutsche Volkslieder,* WoO 33—the other cast in a style imitative of Alpine music (and also many an Austrian Ländler), a touch of local color not out of place in a setting of a *volkstümliche Gedicht* by one of Switzerland's foremost writers of the nineteenth century:

Du milchjunger Knabe,   You beardless boy,
Wie schaust du mich an?   why do you look at me like that?
Was haben deine Augen   What kind of question
Für eine Frage getan!   have your eyes been asking!

Alle Ratsherrn in der Stadt	All the councillors in the town,
Und alle Weisen der Welt	and all the wise men of the world,
Bleiben stumm auf die Frage,	stand mute at the question
Die deine Augen gestellt!	that your eyes asked!
Eine Meermuschel liegt	A seashell lies
Auf dem Schrank meiner Bas':	on top of my aunt's cupboard:
Da halte dein Ohr dran,	hold it to your ear,
Dann hörst du etwas!	then you'll hear something!

That the scene is set in the country is confirmed, not only by the form and the language of the poem, but also by Keller's subsequent alteration of *Meermuschel* to *Schneckhäusel* (snail shell), because, as he told Max Fried-laender, only city children would find a sea shell at their aunt's.[3]

In purely musical terms, the "old new" readings also have merit. With these large leaps present in the melody, each of the three stanzas has a similar beginning, a fitting approach for a strophic poem. Yet by varying each stanza—first by changing the accompaniment, then by shifting the tonal center as well—Brahms was able to underscore the changing content of each stanza and thereby reflect the progress of the poem. A fourth and final appearance of the large leaps occurs for the last line of the third stanza. Its recapitulation here, in the tonic and with the piano again play-ing the introductory material, reinforces the sense of denouement, con-necting enigmatic answer with provocative query.

Thus, a certain amount of structural unity is lost in the version advo-cated by Frau von Herzogenberg and eventually published by Brahms. Indeed, when the large leaps suddenly occur in the third stanza, they seem somewhat arbitrary—one is left to wonder why the style of singing has changed so suddenly. Perhaps it was this inconsistency that caused Brahms to feel that the song had "not turned out well." Yet equally clear are the merits of the simpler setting, with its straightforward communication of this piquant scene.[4]

The Fifty-one Exercises
for Piano, Part 2

During the summer of 1881, Brahms again turned his attention to putting his collection of piano exercises in order. Early in August he wrote Simrock requesting a copy of Robert Eitner's *Hilfsbuch beim Klavierunterrich* (Berlin, 1871) (8 August 1881, 10:182; see also 9 August 1881, no. 117), and on 14 September he informed Simrock that he was thinking of allowing C. F. Peters to publish his own collection (10:184). By the following spring, work on the project had been taken up in earnest. On 12 May 1882 Brahms wrote Simrock:

> Enclosed . . . are a few piano exercises. I am again approaching Herr Keller with the question of whether he would have the patience and (whatever else!) to put some order to these things for me, as he did with the previous ones. I only ask that he not feel at all embarrassed to say "no," if it is tiresome for him, and I also ask him not to demand too little; 50 Marks is too little! Oh, you can settle that favorably with him—if he is at all inclined to do this. . . . I would also be thankful to Herr Keller if he could tell me whether and where he has already seen one or another of the exercises in print! (10:207–8)

Enclosed with this letter was a note from Brahms to Keller and a model page that had been prepared subsequent to the manuscript of thirty-five exercises that Keller had executed for Brahms in 1880 (see items 9–11 above).

➡ 14

Johannes Brahms to Robert Keller   Vienna, circa 12 May 1882
(Library of Congress)

Sehr geehrter Herr,
Ihre vorige Abschrift ist leider durchaus nicht mehr im Stande vorgelegt werden zu können!

Von einer späteren Copie lege ich ein Blatt hier bei, das Ihnen deutlich genug sagen wird wie u. was ich wünsche.

Möglichst viel Platz für meine Bemerkungen, Zusätze, Aenderungen; Abkürzungen, wie sie dem Stecher verständlich sind — weiter fällt mir nichts ein. Nun bin ich Ihnen aber sehr dankbar daß Sie mir die Mühe abnehmen.

Wenn ich versuche derlei auszuschreiben [changed to:] führen, schreibe ich vor Ungeduld u. Langeweile nichts wie falsche Noten u. die Mühe ist ganz vergeblich.

Daher m. unbescheidene Bitte!

> Herzlich verbunden
> Ihr ergebener
> *J. Brahms.*

Dear Sir:

Unfortunately your previous copy is no longer in any condition to be submitted.

I enclose a page from a later copy that will show you clearly enough what I would like and how.

As much space for my remarks, additions, alterations; abbreviations that are comprehensible to the engraver—I can't think of anything else. I am very grateful to you for taking this task off my hands.

If I try to do something like that myself, I write nothing but wrong notes out of impatience and boredom, and the whole effort is completely in vain.

Therefore my immodest request!

> Much obliged,
> Yours sincerely,
> *J. Brahms*

Simrock passed these materials along to Keller with the following cover letter:

◆ 15

FRITZ SIMROCK TO ROBERT KELLER Berlin, 14 May 1882 (Library of Congress)

Letterhead: N. Simrock 171. Friedrichstrasse 171. Berlin. W.

$\frac{14}{5.}$ 82

Lieber Herr *Keller,*

Brahms möchte, daß Sie ihm die beif[olgenden] Clavierübungen wie die vorigen in Ordnung bringen, — natürlich unter Berechung. Auch wünschte er sehr, wenn Sie bei <u>ein</u> od. d. <u>anderen</u> Uebung sagen könnten, <u>daß</u> u. <u>wo</u> sie [*sic*] dieselbe schon gedruckt gesehen haben?

H. Gruß Ihres
<u>F. Simrock</u>

◆●

14 May 1882

Dear Herr Keller,

Brahms would like you to straighten out the enclosed piano exercises for him, as you did with the previous ones—of course for a fee. He would also like very much to know *whether* and *where* you have already seen *one* or the *other* of these exercises in print.

Kind regards,
yours,
F. Simrock

◆●

Occupied as he was with the final stages of overseeing the publication of Brahms's Second Piano Concerto and three volumes of songs, Opp. 84–86, Keller was slow to comply with Brahms's request concerning the additional piano exercises. Near the end of July, Brahms wrote him once again about the project.

◆● 16

JOHANNES BRAHMS TO ROBERT KELLER   Bad Ischl, 24 July 1882 (Library of Congress)

{Postcard addressed to: Herrn *Robert Keller* (durch Hrn. *N. Simrock*) *Berlin, W.;* to the left: 171 Friedrichstr.}

Geehrtester Herr, Ich hätte gern zum 1ten *August* den Ihnen übersandten [added:] Bogen [then:] der Uebungen; für das, was Sie ihm an Neuem beilegen könnten wäre ich Ihnen sehr dankbar. Ist Ihnen aber die Arbeit überhaupt zu entsetzlich, so geniren Sie sich doch nicht, sondern schicken mit Protest zurück?!

Sehr ergeben
J. Brahms.

⇨

Dear Sir:

By the 1st of August I would like to have the page of exercises that I sent you; for any new pages that you may be able to enclose I would be very grateful. If, however, the work seems altogether too dreadful to you, you will not hesitate to send it back with protest, will you?!

Yours sincerely,
J. Brahms

◆•

Sensing that the project might be nearing completion, Simrock began to mount an offensive to secure publication rights to the exercises. On 13 October 1882 he wrote Brahms:

> If you have the exercises ready . . . and want to give them to me (it would, by the way, be horrible if you now did not do so!!) . . . then in all haste immediately pack everything together—and I will make it so cheap that the world will turn somersaults.
>
> Keller has long since received the honorarium of 25 Marks—the amount he requested—and it is charged to your account. . . . (No. 128)

Simrock correctly deduced Brahms's reason for considering Peters as publisher for this collection. The preceding spring Brahms had threatened to allow C. F. Peters to publish his songs, Opp. 84–86, "because they will then be sold so very inexpensively" (11 April 1882; 10:203). Simrock had good reason to worry about losing his monopoly on the publication of Brahms's works. Although Brahms had assigned no works to J. Rieter-Biedermann since 1873 (the *Lieder und Gesänge*, Op. 59), he had given three opuses to C. F. Peters (the nine *Lieder und Gesänge*, Op. 63, and the four vocal Quartets, Op. 64, in 1874 and the choral work *Nänie*, Op. 82, in 1881). Brahms had also allowed Peters to publish six of his piano realizations of Handel vocal duets in 1881. In September 1881, in an attempt to woo Brahms to his firm, Dr. Max Abraham had sent Brahms blank certificates that he could use to name his price for new works (24 September 1881; 14:330).

On 21 October 1882 the worried Simrock received an ambivalent reply: "Regarding the exercises, I finally want to do something serious. It goes without saying that Peters still doesn't know a word about them; I had always thought—because of the inexpensiveness, etc.—that they would be appropriate for [Peters]" (10:226). Taking no chances, Simrock replied firmly on 26 October: "At least send me the exercises *immediately*" (no. 130).

But the project was not to come to fruition in 1882. Indeed, for the next nine years there is little mention of the exercises in the correspondence. On 11 February 1884, Simrock again urged Brahms to send him the collection: "Why are you at present enclosing only the choral songs [the six *Lieder und Romanzen*, Op. 93a]?? . . . The studies should be included and the E-flat Major Trio [a work never published], etc.—no—this laziness!" (no. 134). And on 20 August 1885, he implored Brahms: "When, then, will you surrender regarding the exercises and various other, decidedly indefensible manuscript-positions?? Good Lord—next I will personally have to take the offensive and attack—the starving out [strategy] seems to have its problems?! Good heavens!—Permit me finally to have the joy of engraving [*Stichfreude*] once again!" (no. 144).

Finally, on 10 August 1891 Brahms informed his faithful publisher: "Two things I would like to publish first, about which I am thinking all sorts of things with respect to cheapness, etc. The one item is my famous collection of piano exercises, with which you could leave me in the lurch. The others are canons, from which I will first produce a collection for women's voices, and P[eters], with their practical publication and inexpensiveness, can lead me astray" (12:48). Again the specter of C. F. Peters, to whom Brahms had recently entrusted his six vocal Quartets, Op. 112 (as he informed Simrock later in this same letter), and who did win the rights to the thirteen Canons for Women's Voices, Op. 113 (both published in November 1891). Adding insult to injury, Brahms withheld the exercises from Simrock still another two years. But at long last, on 12 November 1893, Brahms rewarded Simrock for his patience:

I am actually sending here the already fabled and at least 25 years old, highly melodic exercises. Not that you will buy and print them, only that you allow your expert gaze to rest upon them for a moment. In addition to the melodies, you can at best appreciate the bulk (?!), and the title page, which should be very colorful and pretty. I am thinking of all kinds of instruments of torture; from thumbscrews to an iron maiden would be appropriate on it; also perhaps something anatomical and everything in beautiful blood-red and flaming yellow. That would have been such a [publisher's-]number 10,000! Apropos: what then is honored with this [number], since my pieces are already 50 further? The exercises could also appear in 2 volumes, Nos. 1–25 and 25–51. The title would be: *51 Übungen für das Pianoforte von J. B.* No opus number! Also, unfortunately, no famous introduction!

Now tell me, though, quite simply, what you think of the notion of allowing something like this to be printed, and whether you have absolutely no, or even less, desire. The exercises should be engraved *exactly* as in the model, that is, with all abbreviations (bar numbers, etc., etc.). As far as possible: close print and special attention paid to the page turns. (12:107–8)[1]

In the end, as at the beginning, Brahms took a good-humored view of his technical exercises. Needless to say, Simrock accepted the collection. Brahms's *51 Uebungen für das Pianoforte* were issued in two volumes in December 1893 (publisher's numbers 10,062 and 10,065). Unfortunately, publication came too late for Robert Keller to see the fruit of his labors on Brahms's behalf.

The Third Symphony

Brahms's Symphony No. 3 in F Major, Op. 90, which was composed in Wiesbaden during the summer of 1883, received its premiere in Vienna on 2 December 1883, with Hans Richter conducting the Vienna Philharmonic. A triumphal series of first performances under Brahms's direction in cities throughout Germany, Holland, and Hungary culminated with a presentation of the symphony during the Lower Rhenish Music Festival at Düsseldorf early in June, shortly after the publication of the work in full score by N. Simrock.[1]

In the autumn of 1883 Brahms had employed his two regular copyists, Franz Hlavaczek and William Kupfer, to prepare a set of orchestral parts (one per instrumental line; all now lost) from the autograph score (Library of Congress).[2] Additional string parts (now lost) were engraved by Simrock by the end of November to facilitate the performances that soon followed (7 November 1883; 11:38).[3] A manuscript copy of the full score, which subsequently served as the engraver's model (now lost), was also prepared from the autograph score by early December 1883 (6:207).

Brahms did not submit the full score and parts to Simrock until after the final concert of the 1883–84 tour.[4] In a pair of letters to Simrock written during March 1884 he revealed his plans and gave instructions:

> On the 2d of April the symphony will be [performed] in Pest. *Then* I will send you the score and parts. (22 March 1884; 11:52)

> From Pest I will send you the whole ballast. The parts must of course be revised according to the score. (29 March 1884; 11:53–54)

In a letter to Simrock of 4 April, Brahms confirmed that the score and parts had been sent off the day before (11:54). Thus, the engraving and printing of the full score took place in a period of only about six weeks, possibly without the benefit of proofreading by the composer, who left for a tour of Italy on 8 May.[5] The quality of such a hasty enterprise could have been anticipated: the score was rife with errors.

An exchange of six letters, three postcards, and two lists of corrections between Brahms and Keller documents the publication of the full score and Keller's arrangement of the work for four-hand piano from this point on. The first item, a sheet containing a query from Keller about a variant in the score, parts, and two-piano arrangement, probably dates from early in June. Brahms entered his reply directly on the sheet and added three corrections of his own, sending the list, together with a cover letter, back to Keller on 10 June.

➡ 17

CORRECTION SHEET FOR THE THIRD SYMPHONY   early June 1884
(Library of Congress)

Note: The recto of the sheet was prepared by Keller; the comments transcribed in curly brackets ({ }) and the correction in the third example were added by Brahms in blue crayon. The verso is entirely in Brahms's hand, written in lead pencil.

[recto:]
Buchstabe **E** Takt 5. 6. Partitur [I, bars 81–82]:   {richtig}

Für 2 Claviere.   {(auch richtig!}

{66}

Gedruckte Stimmen:

[verso:]

S. 43 der Partitur [I, bar 211] *Bratsche* — Stimme falsch

S. 47. *Bass* u. V=C. [II, bars 34–35]

S. 67 [IV, bar 8] oder (oder und 101 [bar 260]) sind die *Bratschen* falsch

statt wie in der Partitur.

[recto:]
Letter **E**, bars 5, 6, score [I, bars 81–82]   {correct}

for 2 pianos   {(also correct!}

etc.

Printed parts:

{turn the page →}

[verso:]

P. 43 of the score [I, bar 211] Viola — the part is incorrect

P. 47. Bass and cello [II, bars 34–35]

(take out < > in the parts)

P. 67 [IV, bar 8] or (or *and 101* [bar 260]) the violas are incorrect

instead of as in the score.

➻ 18

JOHANNES BRAHMS TO ROBERT KELLER   Vienna, 10 June 1884
(Library of Congress)

{Envelope addressed to: Herrn *Robert Keller. Berlin. W Steglitzerstr. 72. IV.*}

Besten Dank für Ihre freundlichen Worte u. Ihre große Sorgfalt. Die fragliche Stelle ist beide Male richtig; das eine ist für Clavier besser, wie das
andre für Orchester.

Von der Düsseldorfer Aufführung erinnere ich die weiter notirten Fehler in den Stimmen. Leider habe ich sonstige falsche Noten (auch in den
Bläsern) nicht notirt.

Namentlich die Bratschen=Stelle im Finale bitte ich doch gleich in Ordnung bringen zu laßen.

Mit freundlichstem Gruß

Ihr

sehr ergebener

J. Brahms.

➻

Many thanks for your kind words and your great care. The passage in
question is correct in both instances; one is better for the piano, as the
other is better for the orchestra.

From the Düsseldorf performance I remember the errors in the parts
that I've also made note of here. Unfortunately, I did not write down other
wrong notes (in the winds as well).

In particular I request that you have the viola passage in the Finale
straightened out right away.

With kindest regards,

Yours

very sincerely,

J. Brahms

➻

Five days after responding to Keller, Brahms presented his friend Eusebius
Mandyczewski, later archivist of the Gesellschaft der Musikfreunde in Vienna, with a copy of the first edition of the full score containing his hand-

written corrections of a number of errors (Brahms Institut, Lübeck); to
these revisions Mandyczewski subsequently added several of his own. Corrections also appear in the copy of the first edition that Brahms kept for
himself, the so-called *Handexemplar* (Gesellschaft der Musikfreunde, Vienna). The errors that Brahms and Mandyczewski detected were few, however, compared with the number espied by Keller: in mid-July he sent
Brahms twenty-eight closely written pages of queries about the first edition
of the full score, the orchestral parts, and the two-piano version. The text
of Keller's cover letter follows here; the full text of his extensive list of
Correcturen u. Notizen, as annotated by Brahms, appears in appendix D (the
first page of this list is reproduced in plate 2).[6]

◆ 19

Robert Keller to Johannes Brahms   mid-July 1884 (Archiv der
Gesellschaft der Musikfreunde, Vienna)

<u>Herrn *Dr. Johannes Brahms.*</u>

Bei der Anfertigung der verschiedenen Arrangements habe ich mir alles
Fehler= und Zweifelhafte in der [added:] gedruckten [then:] Partitur
Ihrer dritten Symphonie angemerkt, und da dessen eine so große Menge
war, ließ ich mir auch die Orchesterstimmen geben und verglich sie aufs
sorgfältigste mit der Partitur. Es war ein kleines Privatvergnügen für mich,
und es freut mich, Ihnen die Resultate desselben übersenden zu können,
indem ich Ihnen, hochverehrter Meister, damit das lebhafte u. begeisterte
Interesse an Ihrem Kunstwerk thatsächlich besser als mit schmeichler-
ischen Worten und enthusiastischen Ausrufungen kundzugeben ver-
meine.

Da ich bis auf das fehlende Pünktchen über dem *i* in dem Worte *gracioso*
(*Fagott* I p. 2 [I, bar 149]) genau zu Werke gegangen bin, so liegt es mir
durchaus fern, Ihnen zumuthen zu wollen, daß Sie sämmtliche 28 Seiten
Correctur Punkt für Punkt nachsehen sollten (denn [added:] es [then:]
ist so viel selbstverständlich Falsches und so viel Unbedeutendes oder blos
auf die Schönheit u. Egalität des Stiches Bezügliches darunter, womit Sie
nicht behelligt zu werden brauchen); freuen würde es mich aber, wenn
Sie die Güte hätten, die mit <u>Rothstiftkreuzen</u> bezeichneten Stellen, welche
meist eine Anfrage oder einen Zweifel enthalten, zu prüfen und mir gefälligst mit einem <u>ja</u>! oder <u>nein</u>! am Rande Auskunft über Ihren Willen zu

geben; auch die blau unterstrichenen oder mit „?“ oder „Hauptfehler!“ „wichtig“ *etc.* bezeichneten Stellen anzusehen, möchte ich Sie bitten.

verte

Freilich wird der ersten etwas starken Auflage wenig genug davon zu Gute kommen, aber außerdem, daß die 2te Auflage nun gut vorgearbeitet ist, wird sich wohl auch Hr. *Simrock* bewegen lassen, die mit offenbar <u>groben</u> und <u>störenden Notenfehlern</u> behafteten Platten corrigiren u. neu drucken zu lassen. Auch ließe sich auf einem Beibogen ein Verzeichniß der derbsten Fehler zusammenstellen, nach welchem namentlich die Stimmen vor den Aufführung [changed to:] Aufführungen revidiert werden könnten, und besonders deshalb wäre es mir angenehm, wenn Sie mir freundlichst baldigen Bescheid geben könnten, welche Verbesserungen ihnen [*sic*] am nothwendigsten und dringlichsten erscheinen.

Ihrer letzten Anwesenheit in Berlin verdanke ich so glückliche Erinnerungen an Ihre Persönlichkeit und Ihre Kunst, daß es zu meinen lebendigsten Wünschen gehört, dieselben erneut zu sehen, und so grüße ich Sie mit Liebe und Ergebenheit als

> Ihr treuer Correctur=Privat
> *R. Keller.*

Berlin
Mitte *Juli* 84.

●◆

Dr. Johannes Brahms
While preparing the various arrangements, I have marked every inaccuracy and everything that seemed doubtful in the printed score of your Third Symphony, and since there was such a large number, I asked for the orchestral parts as well and compared them most carefully with the score. It was a small private pleasure for me, and it pleases me to be able to send you the results, by which, honored master, I believe I declare my keen and ardent interest in your work of art far better than through flattering words and enthusiastic exclamations.

Since I have worked very thoroughly, even down to the missing dot over the *i* in the word *gracioso* (Bassoon I, p. 2 [I, bar 149]), I certainly do not expect you to check the entire 28 pages of corrections item by item (since so many of the things are obviously wrong and so much is insignificant or merely concerns the beauty and uniformity of the engraving, with which you need not be bothered); I would appreciate it, though, if you would be so good as to check those items marked with *red Xs*, since they generally contain a question or a doubt, and kindly inform me of your intentions with a *yes!* or *no!* in the margin; also, I would like to ask you to have a look at the passages underlined in blue or designated with "?" or "major error," "important," etc.

_____

please turn the page

    Admittedly, this will be of little benefit to the first, rather large printing run, but, aside from being good preparation for the second issue, this will probably also induce Herr Simrock to have those plates corrected and newly printed that contain manifestly *flagrant* and *irritating mistakes in the notes*. One could also compile on a separate sheet a list of the worst mistakes, on the basis of which the parts could be corrected prior to performances, and therefore I would especially appreciate it if you could kindly let me know soon which of the corrections seem most necessary and most urgent to you.

    I owe to your last visit in Berlin such happy memories of you personally and of your art that it is my keenest wish to experience both again, and thus I greet you with fondness and devotion as

Your faithful private corrector,
R. Keller

Berlin
Mid-July 1884

❧

The results of Keller's detailed scrutiny of the printed editions of the Third Symphony testify to his great diligence and acuteness of eye. For Keller, the work was clearly a labor of love, and his care in designating those queries most needful of Brahms's attention and in separating those concerning the score (written in dark brown ink) from those concerning the parts (written in magenta ink) bears witness to his "keen and ardent interest" in Brahms's music. It should be noted, however, that, while Keller was able to find a remarkable number of errors—in pitch, rhythm, articulation, dynamics, and other performance indication—additional errors may have remained undetected, for there is no evidence to suggest that he did more than compare the printed materials with each other. Apparently it did not occur to him to look for variants between the printed editions and their engraver's models, one of the first tasks the editor of a modern "critical" edition would undertake.

Brahms was slow to respond to Keller's document, but, when he did, he was clearly (albeit reticently) appreciative of Keller's efforts on his behalf.

⁜ 20

JOHANNES BRAHMS TO ROBERT KELLER   Mürzzuschlag, 11 September 1884 (Library of Congress)

{Envelope addressed to: Herrn *Robert Keller. Berlin.* W. 35 *Steglitzerstrasse* 72.; on reverse: *J. Brahms.* Mürzzuschlag Steiermark.}

{Note: Both envelope and letter are written in a light purple ink.}

Lieber u. sehr
    geehrter Hr. *Keller,*
    Verzeihen Sie daß Ihre Bögen so spät zurück kommen. Schuld ist einzig daß ich gar so viel u. schön danken wollte u. dies — auch Heute nicht versuche! Sie können sich aber auch wohl ausmalen, eine, wie ganz besondre Freude mir Ihre Sendung war — ich werde Ihnen das einmal in *Berlin* weitläufig beschreiben!
    Natürlich ist sehr zu wünschen daß Hr. Simrock gebührend Notiz davon nimmt u. auch die bisherigen Käufer der S[ymphonie] in den Stand setzt, Ihr Verzeichniß benutzen zu können.
    Mich aber glauben Sie allezeit herzlich u. sehr dankbar u. ergeben.

Ganz Ihr
J. Brahms.

⁜

My dear Herr Keller,
    Excuse my returning your pages so late. The sole blame rests with my wanting to thank you so very much, and this—I will not attempt to do today either! You can well imagine, though, what a very special pleasure your parcel was for me—someday when in Berlin I will give you a detailed account!
    Naturally it is very desirable that Herr Simrock take proper note of this

and also make it possible for all previous buyers of the symphony to be able to use your list.

For my part, believe me always sincere and very grateful and obliged,

Yours truly,

J. Brahms

❧

The annotations that Brahms made directly on Keller's list of possible errors respond to many but not all of Keller's queries; Brahms's attention to these matters seems to have been less than systematic. Nor did he correct in his own copy of the first edition of the score all the errors detected by Keller. Thus, even with such extensive and detailed documentation as Keller's inventory provides, one still does not possess Brahms's full and final wishes concerning the musical text of the Third Symphony. Although Keller's *Correcturen u. Notizen* is an invaluable document for future editors of this work, comparative studies of the texts of all the primary sources will still need to be undertaken.

In September Simrock followed Keller's suggestion, as seconded by Brahms, and issued a list of corrections for the score and parts of the Third Symphony (plate 3). But this three-page corrigenda list treats only a small portion of the passages queried by Keller. (Those entries on Keller's inventory that also appear on Simrock's published list are designated with asterisks in the transcription and translation in appendix D.) Moreover, the published list contains a good number of corrections not present on Keller's inventory. As he revealed in a letter to Brahms of 12 October (see item 23 below), Keller himself was responsible for the preparation of the published list, with which he sought to correct only "the most important and most annoying errors."

As Keller noted in the letter that accompanied his inventory in mid-July, his awareness of inconsistencies in the printed sources for the Third Symphony came about while he was preparing various piano arrangements of the work. Although Brahms made the two-piano reduction, Keller was responsible for the arrangements for two-hand piano, four-hand piano, and two pianos, eight hands, all of which were issued by N. Simrock in 1884. (For his first two symphonies, Brahms had prepared his own four-hand piano reductions, entrusting the two-piano versions to Keller. A complete list of Keller's arrangements of Brahms's works is given in appendix F.)

Brahms's coolness toward Keller's method of making piano arrangements of chamber and orchestral works is discussed in the introduction to the present book. Out of respect for Keller's feelings, Brahms normally shared his opinion only with Fritz Simrock. Typically, when an arrangement was to be assigned, Brahms would urge Simrock to employ Theodor Kirchner rather than Keller. But, if Simrock chose otherwise, Brahms refrained from further interference. In the case of Keller's four-hand arrangement of the Third Symphony, however, Brahms did become involved, much to the personal distress of his publisher.

⊷ 21

Johannes Brahms to Robert Keller Mürzzuschlag, 8 October 1884 (Library of Congress)

{Envelope addressed to: Herrn *Robert Keller*}

Lieber Hr. *Keller,*
            Ich bitte um recht freundlich Gehör!
Ihr Arrangement ist ein vortrefflichstes Zeichen von Fleiß, von Liebe u. Pietät für m. Stück. Alles Mögliche ist daran zu loben — aber — ich hätte es eben anders gemacht! Wie oft habe ich Hrn. Simrock gebeten, mir keine Arrang: zur Ansicht u. Revision zu schicken. Ich habe so meine besondern Ansichten vom Arrangiren, — meine Marotten, wenn Sie wollen, denn die meisten guten Musiker Heute werden auf Ihrer, nicht auf meiner Seite sein. Ich hätte nun, wie gewöhnlich, Ihr Arr: unbesehen zurück geschickt, wenn mich nicht neulich ein Besuch verführt hätte, es durchzuspielen. Nun kann ich nicht umhin, Sie zu fragen u. Sie ernstlich u. ehrlich um ungenirte Antwort zu bitten: Darf ich das Arr. nach m. Geschmack umschreiben? (Es wird meistens den 1ten u. 2 3ten Satz angehen, wenig oder gar nicht den 2ten u. 4ten.) Die erste Bedingung ist, Sie dürfen in keiner Beziehung einen Nachtheil davon haben, auch die neue Mühe nicht umsonst.
Sie brauchen auch keine Notiz von m. Vorschlag zu nehmen u. Hrn S. diesen Brief nicht mitzutheilen *etc.*
Die Schuld trägt ja Hr. S. u. zudem kann ich versprechen daß das Arr: leichter, spielbarer wird — sich also auch besser verkauft!

Ich gehe eben dreister, frecher mit m. Stück um, als Sie d[as] oder ein Andrer kann.

Kurz, jetzt u. hernach können Sie machen was Sie wollen, nur miß verstehen Sie diese Anfrage nicht u. sagen vielleicht ein Wort

Ihrem

herzlich ergebenen

J. Brahms.

⊷

Dear Herr Keller,

I must request your kind attention!

Your arrangement is a most excellent proof of hard work, a token of devotion to and reverence for my piece. A great many aspects of it are praiseworthy—but—I just would have done it differently! How often I have asked Herr Simrock not to send me arrangements for perusal and revision. I have my own particular views on arranging—my whims, if you wish, since most of today's good musicians will be on your side, not mine. I would in this case, as usual, have returned your arrangement without looking at it, had not a visitor recently enticed me to play it through. Now I cannot help but ask you and request that you tell me sincerely and honestly, without the *slightest misgiving:* May I rewrite the arrangement according to my taste? (This would affect mainly the 1st and 3d movements, only slightly or not at all the 2d and 4th.)

My first stipulation is that this must not cause you any disadvantage at all, and also that the additional trouble not be for free.

You also may take no notice of my proposal and not inform Herr Simrock about this letter, etc.

Herr Simrock indeed bears the blame, and I can promise, moreover, that the arrangement will be easier, more playable—and thus will also sell better!

I simply treat my piece less respectfully, more audaciously than you or anyone else can.

In short, now and henceforth you can do whatever you wish, only do not misconstrue this inquiry, and perhaps write me a line,

Yours

most sincerely,

J. Brahms

⊷

Rather than sending this letter directly to Keller, Brahms inserted it into a letter he wrote Simrock, also on 8 October, noting only that "Herr Keller can inform you—if he wants—about the enclosed letter" (11:73–74). Brahms clearly was in a bad mood—"Have I not asked you often enough not to send me arrangements for proofreading!"—and Simrock did not wait for Keller's permission to read Brahms's letter. When penning his letter of explanation to Keller, Simrock reworded Brahms's cautionary remark, omitting the crucial phrase "if he wants."

•❥ 22

Fritz Simrock to Robert Keller   Berlin, 9 or 10 October 1884
(Library of Congress)

Lieber Herr Keller: mir ist etwas Dummes passirt; der einligende Brief von Brahms war <u>so</u> eingelegt, daß ich beim Aufreißen mit dem Falzbein auch das Couvert <u>Ihres</u> Briefes mit aufriß! Nun schreibt Brahms <u>mir</u>: „Herr Keller kann Ihnen d. Inhalt meines Briefes mittheilen."—schreibt aber sonst weiter <u>garnichts</u>—sondern andere Dinge! Ich las also harmlos den an Sie gerichteten Brief! Das <u>schadet aber nicht,</u> Sie wissen ja wie B⁵ ist — —. Sie hätten mir's ja doch sagen müssen! Ja—hätten ich's <u>nicht</u> hingeschickt, wär's besser!! Ich bitte Sie, kommen sie morgen früh (<u>Sonna-bend</u>—um <u>halb</u> 10 Uhr)—zu mir—Carlsbad 3; wir wollen dann <u>zusammen</u> überlegen was wir, vorher was <u>Sie</u> thun u. [added:] was Sie [then:] B⁵ antworten werden? Es ist recht „eklig"! ich schickte sonst stets <u>nur</u> den Stich u. er sagte <u>stets:</u> „es sei nicht nötig"! — <u>Nun</u> sitzt man da! Wir wollen zusammen diplomatisch [along the left margin:] überlegen!

Herzlichst Ihr *Simrock*

•❥

Dear Herr Keller:

Something awkward has happened to me; the enclosed letter from Brahms was inserted in *such a way* that with the paperknife I ripped open the envelope of the letter *to you* as well. Now Brahms writes *to me:* "Herr Keller can inform you of the contents of my letter."—but otherwise tells me *nothing*—goes on to other matters! Thus I innocently read the letter addressed to you! But that *does not matter;* you know how Brahms is — —. You would have had to tell me anyway! Yes—it would have been better had I *not* sent it!! Please do come and see me tomorrow morning (*Saturday—*

at 9:30)—Carlsbad 3; we will then discuss *together* what we, but first of all, what *you* will do and how you will answer Brahms? It is quite "nasty"! I always sent *just* the print and he *always* said: "It is not necessary"! — *Now* what is to be done! We will consider this together diplomatically!

Cordially yours, *Simrock*

◆●

The outcome of the Saturday morning meeting between Simrock and Keller was a letter from Keller to Brahms that is a model of sincerity and tactfulness.[7]

●◆ 23

Robert Keller to Johannes Brahms Berlin, 12 October 1884 (Archiv der Gesellschaft der Musikfreunde, Vienna)

Berlin 12 *Oct.* 84.

Hochverehrter Herr *Doctor*!

Zwei freundliche Briefe habe ich in letzter Zeit von Ihnen erhalten. Ich hätte sofort geantwortet, aber ich mußte doch erst mit Hr. *Simrock* sprechen. Zuerst nun über das Arrangement: Mit tief gefühltem Dank erkenne ich die große Liebenswürdigkeit, mit der Sie mir die Ehre erzeigen, sich in der bewußten Angelegenheit direkt und zuerst an mich zu wenden, trotzdem Sie ja wissen, daß ich darin ohne Herrn S. gar nichts unternehmen kann. Daß Ihre „dritte" einer vierhändigen Bearbeitung für <u>ein</u> Clavier sich sehr widerspenstig zeigt, das haben Sie ja selbst gewißermaßen dokumentirt, indem Sie dieselbe für <u>zwei</u> Claviere setzten; daß ich den Auftrag, das dringende Verlangen der Vierhänder auf <u>einem</u> Clavier zu befriedigen, nach bestem Wissen u. Können in Treue für das Original erfüllt habe, das weiß ich, u. Sie selbst lassen mir ja auch Gerechtigkeit widerfahren, indem Sie sagen, daß Sie mit Ihrem Stück freier umspringen als ich oder ein Anderer darf u. kann; daß die Stellen, die Ihnen am wenigsten in m. Arr. zusagen, sicher diejenigen sind, die mir am meisten Mühe gemacht u. mich doch am wenigsten befriedigt haben, das werden Sie mir auch aufs Wort glauben; — ich kenne die vorhandenen Schwächen m. Arr. ganz genau und möchte nicht einmal behaupten daß ich mit weniger gebundenen Händen viel besseres geleistet haben würde; — wie dürfte ich nun einen Einspruch dagegen erheben, wenn Sie das Arr. umzuschreiben sich die Mühe geben wollen? Ich kann es nur mit <u>Freude</u> begrüßen, wenn Sie Ihr schönes Werk auch dem größeren Publikum in einer Clavierfassung zugänglich machen wollen, wie Sie [changed to:] sie Ihren Intentionen entspricht! Dies Alles habe ich auch Hr. *S.* gesagt u. ihm Ihren Brief zu lesen gegeben, u. er erklärt, daß es ihm in erster Linie darum zu thun sei, Sie in vollem Maße zufrieden zu stellen u. daß die nicht unerheblichen Kosten, die ein theilweiser oder selbst ganzer Neustich ihm verursachen werden, der Erfüllung Ihrer Wünsche nicht hindernd entgegentreten sollen. Damit wäre dieser Punkt erledigt und es ließe sich nur noch die Bitte anfügen, daß Sie durch <u>möglichst</u> baldiges Vornehmen der Umschreibung ein Aequivalent für das pecuniäre Opfer des Verlegers zu geben die Güte hätten, denn das Arr. wird schon längst allseitig dringend verlangt und man weiß sich die Verzögerung des Erscheinens kaum noch anders als durch eine Chikane der (nicht gerade als sehr coulant bekannten) Verlagshandlung zu erklären. — Ich schließe mein Geschwätz über diese Angelegenheit mit der Versicherung daß von einem Mißverstehen Ihrer Anfrage meinerseits nicht die Rede sein kann. Ich habe gewissenhaft gearbeitet, und Sie sowohl als Hr. *Simrock* erkennen dies an; was will ich mehr?

Von dem <u>Verzeichniß der Correkturen</u> zur Symph. habe ich einen Auszug der bedeutendsten u. störendsten Fehler gemacht und derselbe ist bereits im Druck u. wird früheren u. späteren Käufern des Werks zu gehen. Für einen späteren Neudruck der Part. u. Stimmen werden meine <u>sämmtlichen</u> Correkturen, auch die Kleinigkeiten, auf den Platten gemacht werden.

Nun, mein hochverehrter Herr und Meister, hätte ich noch eine recht herzliche u. dringende persönliche Bitte an Sie auf dem Herzen: Herr *Simrock* wollte Ihnen bei dem Erscheinen Ihres *op.* 100 eine heimliche Freude durch die Herausgabe eines thematischen Catalogs Ihrer Werke bereiten und hat mich mit der Anfertigung desselben betraut. Nun höre ich aber, daß er Ihnen bereits davon gesprochen und daß Sie darauf gescherzt hätten, bis *op.* 100 würden Sie nie kommen. Da Ihnen also nichts mehr zu verschweigen ist, möchte ich Sie recht herzlich bitten, daß Sie mir für den Catalog, um demselben auch einigen musik<u>geschichtlichen</u> Werth zu verleihen, die <u>Entstehungsdaten</u> Ihrer Werke, <u>soweit,</u> aber auch so <u>genau</u> u. <u>speziell</u>, wie Sie dies aus Aufzeichnungen *resp.* aus dem Gedächtniß vermögen, mittheilen möchten. Wenn Sie die Güte hätten, sich der Erfüllung dieser schweren Bitte geneigt zu zeigen, so würde ich Ihnen ein spezielles Verzeichniß Ihrer ~~W[erke]~~ gedruckten Werke zugehen lassen, in welches Sie dann nur die betreffenden Daten einzutragen brauchten. Herrn *S.* würden Sie ja damit ebenfalls zu Dank verpflichten!

Sie sehen, daß die liebenswürdigen und herzlichen, herzgewinnenden Zeilen, mit denen Sie mein Interesse an Ihren Schöpfungen belohnten, sogleich der angeborenen Verderbtheit der menschlichen Natur Ermuthigung zu egoistischen Zwecken geben, zürnen aber wohl deshalb nicht

Ihrem

aufrichtigen Bewunderer

Robert Keller.

Berlin W., Steglitzer Str. 72.

⊷

Berlin, 12 October 1884

Dear Herr Doctor,

I have recently received two kind letters from you. I would have answered immediately, but I had to talk to Herr Simrock first. Now first about the arrangement: With profound gratitude I recognize the great kindness with which you honor me by approaching me directly and first about the matter in question, although you know quite well that I can undertake nothing without Herr Simrock. That your "Third" proves quite intractable to a four-hand adaptation for *one* piano you yourself have shown, in a way, by arranging it for *two* pianos; that I have carried out the task of satisfying the pressing demand of the "four-handers" for *one* piano, to the best of my knowledge and ability and in faithfulness to the original, I know, and you yourself also do me justice by saying that you treat your piece more freely than I or anyone else may and can; that the passages that pleased you the least in my arrangement are those that indeed caused me the most trouble and yet still satisfied me the least, for this you will also take my word;—I know the existing weaknesses of my arrangement full well and would not want to claim that I would have done much better with my hands less tied;—therefore how could I object, if you are willing to take the trouble of rewriting my arrangement? I can only *welcome* the fact that you are willing to make your beautiful work available to a wider public in a piano arrangement that is in accordance with your intentions! I have told all of this to Herr Simrock as well, and have given him your letter to read, and he says that above all he wants to see you completely satisfied and that the not inconsiderable cost caused by a partial or even complete reengraving will not prevent him from fulfilling your wishes. With this the matter would be settled, and it remains only to append the request that you be so kind as to contribute the equivalent of the publisher's pecuniary sacrifice by attending to the transcription as soon *as possible,* since the arrangement has already been in urgent demand from all sides for quite some time and there is hardly any other explanation left for the delay in its publication other than chicanery by the publishing house (which is not particularly known for being very obliging).—I close my idle talk about this matter with the assurance that there can be no question on my part of misunderstanding your inquiry. I worked conscientiously, and you as well as Herr Simrock acknowledge this; what more do I want?

From the *List of Corrections* for the symphony I have prepared an excerpt of the most important and most annoying errors, and this is already in print and will be made available to previous and future buyers of the work. For a later reprinting of the score and parts *all* of my corrections, including the minor ones, will be made in the plates.

And now, my highly esteemed master, I have another truly sincere and urgent personal request on my mind: Herr Simrock planned to surprise you by issuing a thematic catalog of your works to coincide with the appearance of your opus 100, and he entrusted its preparation to me. But now I learn that he has already spoken with you about it and that you jokingly replied you would never get to opus 100. Since the matter is no longer being kept a secret from you, I would like to ask you kindly to inform me of the *dates of composition* of your works, *as far as,* but also as *exactly* and *specifically* as you are able to recall from notes or from memory, in order to lend the catalog a certain music-*historical* value as well. If you would be so kind as to be favorably inclined toward this difficult request, I would forward to you a special list of your printed works on which then you would need only to enter the relevant dates. Herr Simrock will likewise be obliged to you for this!

You see that the kind and sincere, heart-winning lines with which you rewarded my interest in your creations immediately gave encouragement to the innate corruptness of the human nature toward egoistic goals; however, you are probably not angry on this account with

Your

sincere admirer,

Robert Keller

Berlin W., Steglitzerstrasse 72

❖

In his brief response, written on a postcard (his favored means of correspondence during these years), Brahms proffered an apology, should his letter have seemed less than cordial.

→ 24

JOHANNES BRAHMS TO ROBERT KELLER   Mürzzuschlag, 14 October 1884 (Library of Congress)

{Postcard addressed to: Herrn *Robert Keller Berlin. W. Steglitzer Str.* 72.}

Lieber Herr, Haben Sie besten Dank für Ihren frdl. Brief. Ich aber schrieb Ihnen neulich nur lange nicht so herzlich als ich wollte, weil mir die Mißverständniße zu sehr durch den Kopf gingen, denen m. Schreiben bei Ihnen u. Hrn. S. begegnen könnte!

Nächstens weiter
von Ihrem
J. Br.

→

Dear Sir:
     Thank you very much for your kind letter. I, however, did not write to you the other day nearly as cordially as I had wanted, for I was far too preoccupied with the misunderstandings my letter might cause for you and Herr Simrock!

More soon,
from your
J. Br.

→

Brahms attended to his revisions of Keller's arrangement directly, returning it to him (rather than to Simrock) a few days later.

→ 25

JOHANNES BRAHMS TO ROBERT KELLER   Vienna, 18 October 1884 (Library of Congress)

{Postcard addressed to: Herrn *Robert Keller Berlin. W. Steglitzer Str.* 72.}

Heute geht die S[ymphonie] an Sie ab. Sie haben wohl noch ein gedr[ucktes] Ex[emplar] da, falls meines für Satz 2 u. 4 zu undeutlich ist?

Darf ich schließlich noch sagen daß ich die Pedal=Bez: gern striche u. die Instrument=Angabe gern auf das Nöthigste reducirt sähe? Daß ich auch sehr überflüßig geändert habe, werden Sie begreifen u. verzeihen—ich war eben einmal bei [inkblot, underneath perhaps: der] der Arbeit! Ihnen aber nochmals alles Herzlichste!

Ihr

J. Br.

Today the symphony is going back to you. You probably still have a printed copy at hand, in case mine for movements 2 and 4 is too unclear?

May I also add that I would like to delete the pedaling and to see the instrument indications reduced to just the most important ones? That I have also changed things quite unnecessarily you will understand and for-give—I simply got carried away doing this!

But once again, all the best!

Yours,

J. Br.

For several years Simrock continued to issue the Third Symphony from uncorrected plates, with the corrigenda list inserted. As Robert Pascall has noted,[8] in 1889 the British Library purchased such an unrevised copy, and in 1892 Brahms complained that he owned only "a first printing, into which a bifolio containing a catalog of printer's errors is appended" (16 December 1892; 12:90). Sometime during the 1890s, however, the plates for the score were revised, for in 1899, as Pascall reported, Paul Hirsch acquired a corrected edition (British Museum, Hirsch M 806), issued with-out change of publisher's number and containing more of Keller's cor-rections than had appeared on the corrigenda list.

The final extant communication from Brahms to Keller concerning the Third Symphony good-naturedly calls attention to two errors that Keller had overlooked.

◆ 26

JOHANNES BRAHMS TO ROBERT KELLER Vienna, 26 October 1884 (Library of Congress)

{Postcard addressed to: Herrn *Robert Keller Berlin. W. Steglitzerstr: 72.*}

Damit Sie nicht zu eitel werden u. sich für unfehlbar halten, melde ich, daß in der F dur-Partitur S. 11 beim A dur [1, bar 36] ein nöthiger Tenor-schlüßel für das *Fagott* fehlt u. S. 24 [1, bar 101] ein ♭ vor *e* f. d. *Contrabass!*

Ihr herzlich grüßender
J. Br.

◕

So that you do not become too conceited and consider yourself infallible, I announce that in the F major score on p. 11, in A major [1, bar 36], a necessary tenor clef for the bassoon is missing, and on p. 24 [1, bar 101], a ♭ before E for the contrabass!

Kind regards,
J. Br.

The Brahms
Thematisches Verzeichniss,
the Fourth Symphony, and
the Piano Trio in C Minor

In a letter to Brahms of 4 September 1884, Fritz Simrock broached the idea of publishing a catalog of Brahms's works: "At the same time as your Op. 100, I want to publish a *thematic* catalog of your collected works released up until then—including citations of all arrangements, etc.; it has already been in preparation for some time—you don't have any objections? And again for the second hundred, etc.! Therefore: get working at it quickly, so that we don't need to wait as long for the continuation as for the first installment!!" (no. 138). Brahms's reaction to Simrock's plan—as also to Simrock's advice to liquidate the investments in Russian gold that he had made earlier in the year (no. 138)—was unenthusiastic: "I must now . . . cut a new quill and write other letters to other *respectable* people; soon I will reply fully regarding the catalog and Russians. So then—you will make a fool of yourself if you count on a bombardment of Warsaw and three-Kaisers-flying-in-the-air [*Drei=Kaiser=in=die=Luft=fliegen*]—likewise, if you believe that I will write up to Op. 100!" (8 September 1884; 11:70).

But Simrock was not to be deterred, and work on the catalog continued under Robert Keller's supervision. As we learn from Keller's letter to Brahms of 12 October (see item 23 above), the catalog as originally envisioned was to include not only thematic incipits and a listing of arrangements but also dates of composition, which Keller hoped Brahms would provide. No immediate response from Brahms is to be found among the Brahms-Keller or Brahms-Simrock letters, and it is possible that none was given until 16 June 1885, when Brahms wrote Simrock:

> Most hastily, a few words about the catalog plan, which I ask you, however, to share fully with Herr Keller, since I have long owed him communication about this. Thus: I find the whole affair quite nonsensical and unnecessary, but I can really say very little against it, since there are already two catalogs. I would find it more sensible if you

satisfied yourself with publishing a catalog of the "works worthy of recommendation"! That would be such a little, nice, inexpensive advertisement for Senff and Fritzsch [the publishers of the music journals *Signale für die musikalische Welt* and the *Musikalische Wochenblatt*, respectively]! An anthology of poems and poets of my choice would also be nice! Now, however, so that I also have something positive to say: I am completely against the "historical data" that you and Herr Keller have in mind. I consider [this information] not merely unnecessary, but also unseemly. It looks shamefully vain on my part, and that I am not helping with it—and cannot even do it properly—no one will believe.

So by all means leave [this data] out. And the idea that the catalog should appear together with [my] Op. 100 is also repugnant to me. That looks like a jubilee, and you too will come to the conclusion that there is no cause for this. So let it appear earlier, with the next 1 or 2 works, which I will perhaps find in old drawers. For you don't really think that I, a well-situated man, still work? Perhaps you will show this note to [our] friend Hanslick and let him tell you that I am right. (11:98–100)

Simrock followed Brahms's advice to consult the Viennese music critic Eduard Hanslick, who took Simrock's side concerning the inclusion of "historical data." On 20 June 1885 he wrote Brahms: "If by 'historical data' [Simrock] means year numbers (and not also the ladies about whom you were thinking and similar information), then I am of the same mind. I confess that I deeply regret the lack of year numbers in the Schumann and Mendelssohn catalogs and adhere to Simrock's idea for a necessary reform in thematic catalogs, desired by every musician. You should not want to dissuade him from doing this.—Our contemporaries and future generations will thank you for it!" (11:100, n. 1).

Discussion of the thematic catalog disappears from the correspondence until early in 1886, by which time, judging from the publisher's number assigned to the project, the engraving of plates for the catalog had already begun.[1] Thus, when Keller wrote to Brahms to verify the musical texts of three of the incipits, he was already involved in the process of correcting proofs.

•◦ 27

ROBERT KELLER TO JOHANNES BRAHMS   Berlin, 23 January 1886
(Archiv der Gesellschaft der Musikfreunde, Vienna)

Berlin 23. *Januar* 1886.

Hochgeehrter Herr Doctor!

Darf ich Sie vielleicht bitten, mir gefälligst Auskunft zu geben, ob die im Folgenden bezeichneten Noten Druckfehler sind oder nicht? Ich möchte das thematische Verzeichniß gern <u>correct</u> geben.

I) Op. 27. Der 23ᵗᵉ [13th] *Psalm:*

II) Op. 57 Nº 2.

III) Op. 59 Nº8.

Gestern Abend gabs hier einen kleinen Skandal in der Philharmonie. Beim Auftreten *St. Saëns* verlangten die Wagnerianer das Lohengrinvorspiel, riefen „raus!" und unterbrachen eine säuselnde *pp*-Stelle seines Clavierspiels durch lautes Gelächter! Er blieb aber gefasst.

Am 1. *Febr.* soll also auch *Berlin* des Glück haben Ihre vierte Symphonie zu hören! Bei der Correktur der Streicherstimmen habe ich versucht mir ein Bild davon zu construiren, aber es ist sehr mangelhaft geblieben; namentlich charakteristische Züge sind in tiefes Dunkel gehüllt u. können erst auf den Ruf der Bläser ans Licht treten. Hätte man nur wenigstens eine ausgeführte Zeichnung in Form eines 4hdg. oder anderen Arrangements, so würde man schon mit weniger Ungeduld aber mit um so lebhafterer Spannung des farbigen Orchesterbildes harren. Ja, müßte man auch wirklich jeder Vorbereitung entbehren und auf jeden Vorgenuß verzichten, so sollte es Ihren bewundernden Freunden doch vergönnt sein, nach der Aufführung in frischer Erinnerung an die Farbenpracht des Ganzen den feinen Linien der Zeichnung nachspüren und sich der reizenden u. geistvollen Details erfreuen zu können, welche in ihrem Reichthum vollständig zu erfassen bei dem erstmaligen aufregenden Anhören des Originals doch nicht möglich ist. Was bin ich schon gefragt worden in musikal. Kreisen, da man weiß, daß ich die Correctur Ihrer Werke lese und Arrangements derselben verbreche. Niemand will glauben, daß Sie ein so grausamer Mann sind und nichts hergeben. Danken Sie Gott, daß Ihr Verleger ein reicher Mann ist; wäre es ein armer Teufel wie ich, der würde Ihnen die Pistole auf die Brust setzen u. Ihnen so lange ins Gewissen reden, bis Sie zerknirscht ihm das Manuskript an den Kopf würfen und voll Erbarmen ausriefen: „Da! servire den musikhungrigen Schweinen den Braten, und schöpfe Dir das Fett ab, eh' es gerinnt!"

Verzeihen Sie diesen gelinden Wuthausbruch und geben Sie bald freundlichen Bescheid auf obige Anfragen

Ihrem

alten Bewunderer

Robert Keller.

Berlin W. 35. Steglitzer Str. N° 72.

◆◇

Berlin, 23 January 1886

Dear Herr Doctor,

May I perchance ask you kindly to inform me whether the notes marked in the following passages are misprints. I would like to produce the thematic catalog *correctly*.

I) Op. 27. The 23d [13th] Psalm:

II) Op. 57 No. 2

III) Op. 59 No. 8

Last evening there was a minor scandal in the Philharmonic concert. During Saint-Saëns's performance the Wagnerians demanded the Prelude to *Lohengrin*, shouted "get out," and interrupted a whispering pianissimo passage of his piano playing with loud laughter! But he kept his composure!

On February 1st Berlin will also be so fortunate as to hear your Fourth Symphony! While proofreading the string parts, I tried to construct a picture of the work, but it remained rather sketchy; in particular, characteristic features are shrouded in deep darkness and can only be brought to light by the sound of the wind instruments. If one only had at least some kind of a drawing, executed in the form of a four-hand or some other arrangement, then one would await the colorful orchestral picture with less impatience, though with even keener excitement. Indeed, if one really had to do without any preparation and forgo any foretaste of pleasure, then your admiring friends should at least be allowed after the performance to investigate the fine lines of the drawing while the magnificent color of the whole is still fresh in their minds and to delight in the abundance of attractive and ingenious details that are simply impossible to grasp in their entirety during the first exciting hearing of the original. So often have I been asked already in musical circles, since it is known that I proofread your works and perpetrate arrangements of them. No one wants to believe that you are such a cruel man and give away nothing. You should thank God that your publisher is a rich man; if he were a poor devil like me, he would hold his pistol against your breast and appeal to your conscience, until you contritely threw the manuscript at his head and cried out, full of compassion: "There! Serve the roast to the music-hungry pigs, and skim off the fat for yourself, before it congeals!"

Excuse this mildly frenzied outburst and kindly let me know about the questions mentioned above,

> Your
> old admirer,
> *Robert Keller*
> Berlin W. 35, Steglitzerstrasse No. 72

The tone of this letter, with its musical gossip from Berlin and its "mildly frenzied outburst" in anticipation of hearing the first performance of the Fourth Symphony in Berlin (1 February 1886), is remarkably less formal than Keller's earlier letters to Brahms.[2]

After the Fourth Symphony's premiere in Meiningen on 25 October 1885, the string parts had been sent to Simrock for engraving (12:107). Keller's first exposure to the new symphony took place at that time, although he was privy to the string parts only, the preparation of both the two-piano and the four-hand piano arrangements of this symphony being undertaken this time by the composer himself. Brahms replied immediately to Keller's letter.

∞ 28

JOHANNES BRAHMS TO ROBERT KELLER   Vienna, 25 January 1886 (Library of Congress)

{Envelope addressed to: Herrn *Robert Keller Berlin. W. 35* Stieglitzerstr: 72.}

Geehrter u. lieber
   Herr *Keller,*
Das *b* im Psalm ist ein Druckfehler u. soll *g* heißen.
Die beiden andern fragl. Stellen sind wohl leider richtig, könnten aber deutlicher u. besser gesagt sein. Etwa:

op. 57

u. 59.

   Sie sehen wie gut es wäre wenn ein Correktor wie Sie immer zu rechter Zeit da wäre u. auch spräche! Und sie [changed to:] Sie sehen daß man immer zu eilig u. flüchtig herausgiebt!
Da wollen Sie mich noch drängen mit der Sinfonie! Hat S. erst den Cl.=A., kann ich die Partitur nicht mehr lange zurückhalten. Leider nur kann ich nicht hoffen daß das Stück durch das bloße Liegen=bleiben besser werde!
                              Herzlichen Gruß
                              Ihres
                              J. Brahms.

∞

My dear Herr Keller,
   The B♭ in the Psalm [Op. 27] is a misprint and should read G. The other two passages in question are correct, I'm afraid, but could be rendered more clearly and better. Perhaps:

You see how good it would be if a proofreader like you were always there at the right time and also would speak up! And you see that one always publishes too hastily and carelessly!

And you still want to rush me with the symphony! Once Simrock has the piano arrangement, I cannot hold back the score much longer. Unfortunately, I cannot expect the piece to improve by merely lying around, either!

Kind regards,
Yours,
J. Brahms

The variant readings for the songs *Wenn du nur zuweilen lächelst,* Op. 57 No. 2, and *Dein blaues Auge,* Op. 59 No. 8, are unique to this letter and thus heretofore unknown. In both cases, more is lost than gained by the proposed revisions. Essential to *Wenn du nur zuweilen lächelst* is the continuous flow of eighth notes that underlies both vocal melody and right-hand accompaniment. A disruption of this motion, especially so early in the song and with no prompting from the poetry (cf. "in Geduld," where an abating of the flow is suggestive of patient waiting), seems injudicious. The revision in *Dein blaues Auge* presents less of a problem, although it needlessly complicates a straightforward accompaniment and, by anticipating the "dissonant" E♭, robs it of its harmonic sensualism.[3] Neither revised reading was adopted by Keller in the Brahms catalog.

The series of first performances of the Fourth Symphony in cities throughout Germany, Holland, Austria, and England continued through June 1886, at which time the autograph score (Allgemeine Musikgesellschaft, Zurich) and the full set of orchestral parts (now lost) were finally submitted to Simrock for publication. On 25 June, in a letter to Fritz Simrock, Brahms sent Keller instructions: "I ask Herr Keller to let the 3d movement be called *Allegro,* not *Presto;* also, many differences remain between the score and the parts. Thus in the parts there occasionally are superfluous *espress.,* more often – – (bars) instead of ⌢ in the violins, *dim.* instead of ⟩, etc. If Herr Keller is more a violinist than I, he would be doing me a favor if he would recommend here and there for pizzicato chords more *harmonious* or comfortable fingerings!" (11:124). Two days later, in a letter to Simrock, Brahms transmitted to Keller a revision of the contrabassoon in bars 64–65 of the Finale to match the contrabasses and called his attention to missing rests on several pages (11:124).

By mid-August proofs of the full score of the symphony were ready for Brahms's inspection. A few days' advance notice of their arrival was given by Keller, who was then on vacation in the small Swiss town of Weesen.

➺ 29

ROBERT KELLER TO JOHANNES BRAHMS   Weesen am Wallensee, Mariahalden, 7 August 1886 (Archiv der Gesellschaft der Musikfreunde, Vienna)

{Postcard addressed to: Herrn *Dr. Johannes Brahms* z[ur] Z[eit] [at the present time] in *Thun* beim Kaufmann [c/o the merchant] *Spring;* return address stamped on front: *E. Ryffel-Streiff Hôtel & Pension Mariahalden Weesen Wallensee*}

Weesen am Wallensee, Mariahalden.
7 August 86.

Hochgeehrter Herr Doctor!

In den ersten Tagen nächster Woche erhalten Sie von mir die 1 Corr. Ihres op. 98 zur gef[älligen] Revision und ich wollte hierdurch nur anfragen, ob es nöthig ist, Ihnen das Manuscript mitzusenden oder nicht? Der Druck stimmt nach meiner Correktur genau mit dem Manuscript, und deshalb sehe ich eigentlich die Uebersendung des letzteren für unnütz an, da Sie daraus nichts weiter ersehen könnten. Ein so kostbares Document möchte ich nicht gerne ohne zwingende Ursache hin u. hersenden. Vielleicht haben Sie die Güte mir eine Zeile auf diese Anfrage nach hier zu schreiben. Die Correctur hat mir riesige Freude gemacht; wie verstehen Sie zu arbeiten!! Mit hochachtungsvollstem Gruß

Ihr
ganz ergebener
Robert Keller.

➻

Weesen am Wallensee, Mariahalden
7 August 1886

Dear Herr Doctor,

Early next week you will receive from me the first galleys of your [Fourth Symphony,] Op. 98, for correction at your convenience, and I just wanted to ask now whether or not it is necessary to send the manuscript along with them. After my corrections the print will agree exactly with the manuscript, and therefore I consider it unnecessary to return the latter, since you could derive nothing further from it. I do not like sending such a precious document back and forth unless it is absolutely necessary. Perhaps you will be so good as to send me a line or two, at this address, concerning this matter. I enjoyed doing the proofreading very much; you really know your craft!! With most respectful greetings,

Yours sincerely,
Robert Keller

◄●

Apparently Brahms never had an opportunity to proofread the score of the symphony in comparison with the autograph engraver's model.

Keller's next letter to Brahms mentions the proofs, but its main purpose was to inform the composer, who was spending his vacation in Thun, of the delights of Weesen and to encourage him to visit.

➤ 30

ROBERT KELLER TO JOHANNES BRAHMS Weesen am Wallensee, Mariahalden, 10 August 1886 (Archiv der Gesellschaft der Musikfreunde, Vienna)

{Postcard addressed to: Herrn *Dr. Johannes Brahms* z[ur] Z[eit] [at the present time] in *Thun* beim Kaufmann [c/o the merchant] *Spring;* return address stamped on front: *E. Ryffel-Streiff Hôtel & Pension Mariahalden Weesen Wallensee*}

Weesen 10. 8. 86.

Hochgeehrter Herr *Doctor*!

Die Partitur ist wohl nun in Ihren Händen. Sollten Sie hier u. da noch feine u. grobe Fehler finden, so bitte ich zu bedenken daß dies die <u>erste</u> Corr. ist.

Schönsten Dank für Ihre freundl[iche] Karte. Was den Spaziergang zwischen Thun und Weesen betrifft, so würden sich meine <u>Beine</u> dafür wohl ausreichend kräftig erweisen; ich glaube jedoch daß Ihr <u>Beutel</u> mehr Leistungsfähigkeit dafür haben würde als der meinige, u. da das doch der eigentliche *nervus rerum* ist, so wäre es gar nicht so übel, wenn Sie die Corr.

eigenhändig nach *Weesen* zurücktragen und in einer ganz besonders reiz-
vollen Gegend, wo auch eine recht gute Traube wächst, einige Tage mit
uns zu kleinen oder großen Excursionen verwenden wollten. Vielleicht
wäre Hr. *Simrock* mit von der Partie. Ich bin hier mit *Oscar Raif* von der
Hochschule in Berlin u. dem Abgeordneten *Dr.* Hammacher nebst einer
ganzen Gallerie hübscher Damen, obenan unsere anmuthige Wirthin.
Sehr familiäres Leben; Wohnung u. Verpflegung fast so schön wie die Gegend. Ueberlegen Sie sich doch die Sache und steigen Sie einmal liebens-
würdig zu den harmlosen musikalischen Proletariern herab. Wir wollen
Sie dann auch ganz als Unsersgleichen behandeln u. Sie Ihre Ueberlegen-
heit gar nicht fühlen lassen!

Hochachtungsvoll grüßt
Ihr
R. Keller.
Weesen, Mariahalden.

•❖

Weesen, 10 August 1886

Dear Herr Doctor,

By now the score is probably in your hands. Should you still discover
minor or major errors here and there, please remember that these are the
first galleys.

Thank you very much for your friendly card. As far as the walk from
Thun to Weesen is concerned, my *legs* might well prove strong enough;
but I believe that your *purse* might have more capacity for it than mine,
and since that is really the *nervus rerum,* it would not be such a bad idea if
you were to return the galleys to Weesen in person and spend a few days
of shorter or longer excursions with us in an especially charming area,
where also grows a rather good grape. Perhaps Herr Simrock would also
come along. I am here with Oscar Raif of the Hochschule in Berlin and
Deputy Dr. Hammacher as well as a bevy of lovely ladies, above all our
charming landlady. Very relaxed style of life; accommodations and food
almost as nice as the surroundings. Think about it and amiably descend
to the inoffensive musical proletarians. We will treat you entirely like one
of us and will not let you feel your superiority at all!

Sincere greetings,
Yours,
Robert Keller
Weesen, Mariahalden

◀•

There is no record of Brahms having accepted Keller's invitation that year, despite the attractions of wine, women, and scenic beauty. Brahms probably returned the corrected proofs to Simrock in September; the full score of the Fourth Symphony was released in October 1886.

With only two more opuses remaining before the publication of his Op. 100, Brahms raised the question of Simrock's proposed Brahms catalog in a letter of 23 January 1887: "In case you still have your whim about the Brahms Catalog, will you in any case let me see a sample before you send it to press or publish it? Only a sheet. Now fairly slowly with [Op.] 99–101" (11:140). At this point Simrock apparently had already engraved much of the volume, leaving Brahms to wonder in his next letter just how much could still be changed to suit his tastes:

> I had hoped to see the catalog before it was engraved! Now I can of course only praise beyond bounds everything possible, which goes without saying; possible misgivings, though, probably come too late, as the whole thing is no doubt finished? It is no longer useful to explain why I am *very much* against the inclusion of year numbers and against the engraving of the individual variations. These would be highly superfluous in any catalogue and quite uselessly swell it to quite an enormous size, and this is unnecessary here and not pretty. But, as I said, there is much to praise, and it is nevertheless quite good if I too examine the proofs for any possible mistakes.
>
> The honorarium you may wish to reduce substantially; it's a clearance sale item. But it's none of my business how you ruin yourself. (31 January 1887; 11:141)

Criticism of specific aspects of the project followed in four letters to Simrock written during February 1887 (Simrock's side of the correspondence no longer exists):

> Do you not also still want to consider whether it would be better to delete the indication of single page numbers "(Pag. 3–8)," etc.? It is entirely superfluous and, with the waltzes, *Liebeslieder*, rather strange? In such things, clarity is an essential matter, and all that is unnecessary is better left out. The English text is included in the songs owing to business reasons? Otherwise, there is much to be praised about the clarity and everything else; but one should think twice before introducing innovations. (6 February 1887; 11:142)

> If my misgivings concerning the variations are clear to you, and if you agree [with them] even to some degree, then I urgently request

Plates

Plate 1 (above). Original and *ossia* readings for the Violin Concerto in D Major, Op. 77, IV, bars 21–26, as entered on the inside of the back wrapper (p. [57]) of the manuscript of the violin-piano arrangement. Mus.Hs.19.658 from the Musiksammlung of the Öesterreichischen Nationalbibliothek. Reproduced by permission of the Oesterreichische Nationalbibliothek, Vienna.

Plate 2 (right). First page of Robert Keller's *Brahms' Dritte Symphonie. Correkturen u. Notizen* (mid-July 1884). Reproduced by permission of the Library of Congress, Washington DC, from the Gertrude Clark Whittall Collection.

Brahms' dritte Symphonie.
Correkturen u. Notizen.

I. Partitur:

p. 5: Basspos. Takt 3. ♩ ♩ (statt ♩ ♩ vor) Stimme richtig.
Viol. 1. Takt 3 und 5 ist in der Stimme über der letzten Achtel
... im Punkt. ...
... Violoncell. In der Stimme ...
ein ...

— Contrabass ⎫ Takt 3: ♩♩♩ (♩ statt) Pag. 6
Contrafagott ⎭

p. 6: F-Hörner zweit Takt 4 ändert als pag. 29. ...
Bratsche Takt 5 fehlt > über der ... halben Note (>)

p. 7: Clar. letzter Takt Punkt fehlt über den ¼ ♩)
Tromp. Takt 1. " " " erst ...
Violine II. In der Stimmen fehlt Takt 1 und 2 so:

Noch soll gelten?

p. 8: Contrafagott Takt 3 in der Stimme ... über den 4 ...
Viol. I u II. In der Stimme ...

p. 9: Takt 4 fehlt p zu Flöte II.
Bratschenstimme ...

p. 10: C-Horn II Takt 3 fehlt Taktpause.
Viol. I vorletzter Takt — zu kurz, ...
" II " " " "
Bratsche " " " "
Viol. II, Br. und Vcell Takt 3. 4 fehlt der Bogen wie bei Viol. I,
in der Stimme steht er jedoch.

Vcell. Takt 3 fehlt arco. ...
Vcell. u. CBass fehlt Takt 2 der Punkt hinter der ½ ...
Viol. I u. II ist in der Stimme ...

p. 13: Viol. I. II. in der Stimme Takt 1: p marc.
Viol. II und Vcell: Takt 3 in der Stimme
Vcell: 1te Viertel ... noch nicht getheilt!

p. 14. 15.) ...
Hat ...

p. 14. in Clarinetten System müsste vorn in B. stehen.
Vcell Takt 3: ♯♯

Correcturen
zu
Brahms, Dritte Symphonie.

Da die Umstände seinerzeit eine sehr eilige Herausgabe der Partitur und Stimmen nöthig machten, so sind leider eine Menge Fehler und Ungenauigkeiten stehen geblieben, deren wichtigste und störendste hier mitgetheilt werden. Die Herren Orchesterdirigenten werden ersucht, Partitur und Stimmen gefälligst nach diesem Verzeichniss revidiren zu lassen.

Berlin, September 1884.

N. SIMROCK.

Partitur.
Erster Satz.

Seite 5. Takt 3: Bassposaune muss den ganzen Takt f halten: ♩. ♩.
— 11. Takt 6: Fagott I ist der Tenorschlüssel vorzuzeichnen.
—— 15. letzter Takt: Violine II das letzte Viertel Doppelgriff:

—— Takt 3: Contrabass erstes Viertel d statt h.
—— 18. vorletzter Takt: Violine II letztes Viertel e statt fis.
—— 19. letzter Takt: Flöte II 2tes Viertel dis statt h.
—— Takt 1: Bei allen 4 Hörnern muss das 3te u. 4te Viertel abgestossen (nicht gebunden) sein.

—— letzter Takt: Bratsche 5tes Viertel:

gis   h

—— 22. letzter Takt: Bei Bratsche und Violoncello fehlt das ♮ vor dem ersten g.
—— 25. vorletzter Takt: Bratsche: Die 3te Viertelnote nicht mehr ges sondern f.
—— 29. letzter Takt: ___ fehlt bei Hoboen, Fagotten u. C-Hörnern.
—— Takt 2 müssen die F-Hörner so wie an der entsprechenden Stelle auf Seite 6 heissen:

—— Takt 4: Violine II eine 8ve tiefer, so:

—— 30. Takt 1: Violine I: ♭ vor a fehlt.
—— 32. Takt 3 u. 4: Violoncell falsch, muss bleiben wie Takt 1 u. 2.
—— 40. Takt 1: Violine II: ♯ statt ♮g.
—— 42. Takt 4: Bei allen spielenden Stimmen gleichmässig: f ___
—— letzter Takt: Das *dim.* im Streichquintett an den Anfang des Taktes.

Andante.

Seite 45. II. vorletzter Takt: Violoncell I: e statt c.
—— 49 II. letzter Takt: Violine II: 6tes Achtel fis statt h:

Poco Allegretto.

Seite 56 I. Takt 1: Violine II: Achtelpause hinter ♪ fort.
—— 57 II. Takt 4 zu 5: Violoncello fehlt der Bogen von
—— 58 I. vorletzter Takt: Violine I: gis statt fis.
—— 58 II. letzter Takt: Violine I: Das zweite 16tel c statt a.
—— 59 II. Takt 5 u. 6: Hörner müssen es halten, nicht auf c gehen; Beim Violoncell fehlt arco zum Begin des as dur.
—— 63 II. Takt 1: Zur Bratsche fehlt arco.

—— Takt 5: Violine muss heissen:
—— 64 II. Takt 1: Violoncell: arco fehlt.
—— 65 II. Takt 5: C.Bass: arco fehlt.

Finale.

Seite 69. Takt 2: Bratsche: arco fehlt.
—— Takt 7: Horn I: ♭ vor e.
—— 72. Takt 1: Violoncell: Das 1te Viertel g tief (leere Saite).
—— 73. Takt 2: Violoncell: pizz. fehlt.

Seite 76. Takt 3: Contrabass und Contrafagott müssen diesen Takt pausiren!!
—— 77. Takt 6: Clarinette II: ♯ statt ♮ vor c.
—— 86. Takt 3: Hoboe II: ♮ vor das erste d.
—— Violoncello: ♮ statt ♯ vor e.
—— 87. Takt 3: Bratsche: ♮ statt ♯ vor e (letztes Achtel).
—— 88. letzter Takt: Horn I: ⌢ fort, Punkt über das Viertel.
—— Takt 1: Bratsche: ♯ vor c.
—— 90. Takt 2-5: Fagotte, Cfag., Vcell. u. C.Bass Punkt u. marc. Zeichen unter jedes Achtel ♪

—— letzte Takte: stacc. Punkte beim Contrafagott fehlen.
—— 94. Takt 1 u. 2: Flöten doppelt gestrichen.
—— 97. Takt 2: Horn I. ♮ vor f.
—— letzter Takt: Violine II: letztes Achtel f statt des.
—— 98. Takt 4: Contrafagott ♮ vor e.
—— 103. Takt 2: Violoncell u. C.Bass: *dim.* statt *p*; im 3ten Takte *p express.* und arco.
—— 106. letzter Takt: *cresc.* bei allen Streichinstrumenten.
—— 107. letzter Takt: *p* fehlt bei Violinen und Bratsche.
—— 108. Takt 3: *p* zu den Trompeten.
—— 109. Takt 4: *dim.* zur Bratsche.
—— letzter Takt: *pp* zum Contrafagott.

In den Stimmen.
Violine I.

Seite 2. Zeile 7: Bogen von ♩ ♩ fort.
—— 3. —— 3. von unten: Takt 1 u. 2 falsch, muss so heissen:

ben marc.

—— 4. —— 1. letzter Takt: ⌣ unter den Punkten fort.
—— 6. Takt 2: (c fehlt in der Mitte.)
—— Takt 5 u. 7 muss der 2te Bogen fort.
—— 7. Takt 4 fehlt *cresc.*
—— letzte Zeile, letzter Takt *mp express.* (statt *p*)
—— 5. Zeile 5. Takt 3: *p* fort.
—— 6. —— 4 von unten, letzter Takt; das vorletzte Achtel cis statt e.
—— 7. letzte Zeile: Stichnoten der Clarinette: h ♩ für das zweite c ♩; beim Eintritt der Viol., das zweite ⟨⟩ fort; 4 Takte vor dem Schluss fehlt *poco rit.*
—— 8. vorletzte Zeile: *p express.* statt *pp cresc.*
—— letzte Zeile: *p* statt *pp.*
—— 9. Zeile 4 von unten, Takt 1: Das Achtel muss c heissen statt h.
—— 11. —— 4 von unten: *p* statt *mp.*
—— 12. —— 4. Takt 1: *più f sempre.*

Plate 3 (above, right, and on the following page). N. Simrock's *Correcturen zu Brahms, Dritte Symphonie* (September 1884). Bound with first edition, second issue of the Third Symphony, M3.3 B8, op. 90. Reproduced by permission of the Library of Congress, Washington DC, from the collections of the Music Division.

Seite 14. Zeile 1 Takt 1: *mf* statt *f*.
_____ 5 von unten: Takt 1: ⸺ *pp*. Im letzten Takt ⸻ *cresc.* und
im folgenden Takt ⸻
_____ 3 von unten: Takt 1: *p* zu ⸻

Violine II.

Seite 2. Zeile 3 Takt 2 u. 3 muss es heissen:
_____ 5 letzter Takt: *p* statt *pp*.
_____ 7 Takt 2 u. 3: Bogen zwischen ⸻ u. ⸻ fort.
___ 3. ___ 2 Takt 1: *mf* statt *p*; Takt 2: *p* fort; Takt 3: *sf* zum 3ten
Viertel; Takt 4: *f* zur Achteltriole.
_____ letzte Zeile: *poco rit.* einen Takt früher und *p dim.* statt *poco dim.*
___ 4. ___ 1 *rit.* (nicht *poco rit.*) muss erst beim letzten Takt stehen.
_____ 2 Takt 2: *f* zu ⸻
_____ 4 Takt 1: *cresc.*
_____ 5 Takt 1: statt
_____ 4 von unten: *mp* statt *p*.
___ 5. ___ 1 Takt 1: *f* zur Achteltriole. Takt 2: *sf* zum letzten Viertel.
___ 6. ___ 6 Takt 2. Bogen fort. Takt 4: ♮ vor ⸻ h.
_____ 4 von unten Takt 1: *poco f* statt *fp* und vorletztes Achtel cis st. e.
___ 7. ___ 1: *p* statt *mp*, im folgenden Takt *dim.* zum 4ten Viertel.
_____ 3: Takt 2: h statt a im letzten Viertel.
_____ letzte Zeile statt 2 Takte Pause muss es heissen:
und 4 Takte vor dem Schluss fehlt *poco rit.*
___ 8. vorletzte Zeile die letzten 6 Achtel gebunden.
___ 10. Zeile 5: nur *pp* statt *ppp*.
___ 11. ___ 4. Takt 4: und Takt 5 nur
___ 12. ___ 4 letzter Takt: *più f sempre*.
_____ 3 von unten, letzter Takt:♭ vor d.
___ 13. letzte Zeile Takt 4: *mf* statt *f*.
___ 14. erster Takt *col sordino*.
_____ Zeile 4 von unten: letzter Takt: *cresc.*
_____ 3 von unten: letzter Takt: *p*.

Bratsche.

Seite 2. Zeile 3 von unten Takt 4: *mp espress.*
___ 3. beim Buchstaben F: *p* fort.
_____ letzte Zeile: *poco rit.* einen Takt früher.
___ 4. Zeile 1 *rit.* einen Takt später (zum letzten Takt).
_____ 2 Takt 2: *f* zum ersten Viertel.
_____ 4 von unten: *cresc.* fort. Im letzten Takt: *mp espress.* statt *p*.
___ 5. ___ 1 letzter Takt: *cresc.* und zum letzten Viertel *f*.
_____ 2 Takt 2: *f* statt *ff*.
___ 6. Andante statt Andante con moto.
_____ Bei D: *mf* statt *mp*.
___ 9. Bei G fehlt arco.
___ 10. Zeile 2-4 muss genau mit der Partitur übereinstimmen!
___ 12. ___ 5 Takt 1: *più f sempre*.
___ 13. ___ 3 Takt 4: *p* ⸺ .
_____ 4 Takt 1: ♮ vor a.
___ 14. ___ 1 Takt 3:♯ vor e; das letzte 1/16 muss b heissen statt f
_____ 5 von unten: *cresc.* und in diesem und dem folgenden
Takte ⸺ statt ⸻ .
_____ letzte Zeile nach dem Takt Pause fehlt *dim.*

Violoncell.

Seite 2. Zeile 1: Die vier *sf* fort.
_____ 4. von unten Takt 1: *p*.
_____ letzte Zeile Takt 2: ⸺ fort; im folgenden Takt: *mp espress.* st. *p*.
___ 3. Zeile 7 Takt 1 u. 3: Das punktirte Viertel mit dem ersten Achtel gebunden.
_____ Beim Buchstaben F das *p* fort.
_____ letzte Zeile: Punkte unter alle Viertelnoten.
___ 4. Zeile 4 u. 5: Alle *sf* fort.
_____ 3. von unten Takt 3: *p* zum 2ten Viertel.
_____ 2. von unten ⸺ fort: Takt 2: *mf espress.*
___ 5. ___ 2. Takt 3: *f* zum letzten Viertel; im vorl. T. nur *f* (statt *ff mf*)
und im letzten Takt das *mf* fort.
_____ 6. Takt 2: *cresc.*
_____ letzte Zeile: *p dim.* statt *dim.*
___ 6. Zeile 5: ⸺ ⸻ fort.
_____ 8: *pp* fort.
_____ letzte Zeile: *mf cresc.* und das ⸺ *f* fort.

Contrabass.

Seite 3 im Anfang: *fsf* statt einfach *sf*.
_____ Zeile 3 letzter Takt: *p* statt *pp*.
_____ 5 von unten Takt 4: *mf*; Takt 6: *sf* zum 3ten Viertel; Takt 7: *p*
fort, aber *f* zum letzten Viertel.
_____ Bei E: *f* statt *mf*; bei F: das *p* fort.
___ 4. Zeile 3: *poco rit.* einen Takt früher.
_____ 5: *rit.* (nicht *poco rit.*) einen Takt später; in demselben Takt 2
unten *cresc.* und bei Tempo 1: *f*.
_____ vorletzte Zeile Takt 4: *f* zum letzten Viertel; Takt 5: ⸺ *sf* und
Takt 6: *f* statt *ff*.
_____ letzte Zeile Takt 3: *p* fort.
___ 5. Zeile 3 von unten Takt 3.4: ⸺ fort.
___ 6. ___ 6: ⸺ ⸻ fort.
_____ letzte Zeile Takt 1: ⸺ Takt 2: ⸺ Takt 3: ⸺ fort.
Takt 4: ⸺
___ 7. Zeile 1: ⸺ einen Takt früher.
___ 8. ___ 2 Takt 2: *dim.* zum letzten Achtel.
___ 9. letzte Zeile: Die beiden letzten ⸺ fort.
___ 10. Zeile 2 vorletzter Takt: *più f sempre*.
_____ 4 u. 5 unter jedes einzelne Achtel Punkt und > (♪)
___ 11. ___ 5 Takt 3: *mf dim.* statt *f dim.*
_____ 8 vorletzter Takt: *dim.*

Flöte I.

Seite 3. Zeile 8. Takt 1: *f* ⸺
___ 5. ___ 2: *mp* statt *p*.
___ 6. letzte Zeile Takt 1 falsch, muss heissen:

Flöte II.

Seite 1. Zeile 3. Nach den 3 Takten Pause fehlt *p*.
___ 3. ___ 5. Takt 1: *f* ⸺
___ 4. ___ 2. Nach den 4 Takten Pause fehlt *dolce*.

Hoboe I.

Seite 2. Zeile 7. Takt 2 : ⸺
___ 3. ___ 6. letzter Takt: *f* ⸺

Hoboe II.

Seite 2. Zeile 3. Takt 1: ⸺ und letzte Zeile Takt 1: *f* ⸺

Clarinette I.

Seite 2. Zeile 1. Takt 1: ♭ vor das letzte Viertel g ! Takt 4: ♭ vor e !
___ 8. Takt 2: ♭ vor d !
___ 3. ___ 6. vorletzter Takt: *f* ⸺
___ 6. vorletzte Zeile Takt 5: halbe Note ⸺ a statt ⸺ h !

Clarinette II.

Seite 3. Zeile 5 vorletzter Takt: *f* ⸺

Fagott I.

Seite 2. Zeile 4 von unten Takt 2: ⸺ und Buchstabe I fehlt auf dem 2ten

Taktstriche

_____ 3 v. u. T. 5: *più p* u. im letzt. T: *p s.v.*
___ 3. ___ 7 Takt 4: *f* ⸺

Flöte I.

Seite 4. Zeile 1. Takt 4 : ⟍ über die Triole .
————— letzte Zeile nach der Taktpause : *più p* .
——— 5. bei G : *dolce* ; 2 Takte vorher ⟍ .
——— Zeile 4 von unten vorletzter Takt : ♮ vor das letzte Achtel h !
——— 7. ——— 3 von unten Takt 1–4 : (♪) unter jedes einzelne Achtel Punkt u. >

Fagott II.

Seite 1. vorletzte Zeile Takt 4 : ♯ vor d 𝄽 !
——— 2. Zeile 6. Takt 1 : ⟍ .
——— 3. ——— 5. letzter Takt : *f* ⟍ .
——— 5. ——— 7. Takt 3 : ♭ vor ♭ d !
——— letzte Zeile Takt 4 : ♭ vor e !
——— 6. Zeile 4 von unten Takt 6 : ♮ vor e !
——— 7. ——— 7 Takt 5 : ♮ vor a !
——— Buchstabe K Takt 3–6 : Unter jedes Achtel Punkt und > (𝄽)
——— vorletzte Zeile, vorletzter Takt : *ff* statt *f* .

Contrafagott.

Seite 1 : Im Anfang : *sf sf* ; Zeile 2 : Das dritte *sf* fort .
——— Buchstabe G Takt 2 : ♭♪. ♪. die beiden des gebunden !
——————— M Takt 2 : ⟍ letzter Takt : *p* < > .
——— 2. Zeile 6. Takt 3 ist zu pausiren !!
——— 3. Zur letzten Note auf der Seite *pp* .

Horn I in C.

Seite 1. Zeile 5 letzter Takt : Punkte über das 3te u. 4te Viertel statt Bogen .
——— Einen Takt vor Buchstabe I : ⟍ .
——— 2. Zeile 4. Takt 1 : *f* ⟍ .
——————— 3 von unten vorletzter Takt : *f* statt *mf* .
——— 3. ——— 3. Takt 2 : Punkt hinter die halbe Note as .
——— 6. Takt 1 : es 𝄽 statt c !!
——— 5. ——— 6. Takt 2 : ♮ vor das erste f !

Horn II in C.

Seite 1. Zeile 2 : Nach den 2 Takten Pause : *f* .
——— 6. Takt 1 : Punkte über das 3te u. 4te Viertel statt Bogen .
——————— 3. von unten letzter Takt : ⟍ .
——— 2. ——— 2. von unten : *f* statt des 2ten *mf* .
——— 3. ——— 6. Takt 2 : 𝄽 es statt c ; das es vor dem Buchst. D 1/8 st. 1/4 !
——— Einen Takt vor Buchstabe I : *p* statt *pp* .
——— 5. Zeile 6 vorletzter Takt : ♮ statt ♭ vor e !!

Horn III in F.

Seite 1. Zeile 1. Takt 2 : ♮ fort ; es bleibt den ganzen Takt !
——————— 4. Takt 1 : 𝄽 statt 𝄽
——————— 7. Takt 4 : Punkte über das 3te u. 4te Viertel statt Bogen .
——————— 3 von unten Takt 10 muss heissen : 𝄽
——— 2. ——— 3 von unten . Der Bogen von 𝄽 durch den vorl. Taktstrich fort .
——— 3. ——— 5. Takt 14 muss heissen : 𝄽 (es statt ges) .
——————— 8. Die Bogen über den Vierteltriolen fort ; Punkt über das Viertel g .

Horn IV in F.

Seite 1. Zeile 7. Takt 1 : Punkte über das 3te u. 4te Viertel statt Bogen .
——— vorletzte Zeile Takt 3 von hinten : 𝄽 1/4 Pause statt Punkt hinter
                                             die halbe Note e .
——— 2. Zeile 4 von unten Takt 2 : *pp* < .
——————— 3 von unten vorletzter Takt : 𝄽 1/2 g gebunden an d. Viertel .
——————— 2 von unten . Der Bogen von 𝄽 fort .
——— 3. ——— 4 von unten : ⌒ über der Triole ♩ ♩ bei *ff* fort ; Punkt un-
                                             ter das Viertel .

Tenor-Posaune.

Seite 1. Buchstabe L : ♮ vor e !

Bass-Posaune.

Seite 1 vorletzte Zeile : ⟍ |*dolce*| einen Takt später !
——— 2. Buchstabe F : *sf* statt *f* .
——————— Zeile 6. Takt 4 : 𝄽 1/4 statt 1/2 Note !
——————— 4. von unten : *sf* statt *f* und ⟍ fort .

Plate 4 (above). Last and first pages from Brahms's letter to Keller, circa 12 February 1887, written on Hans von Bülow's stationery (item 31). Reproduced by permission of the Library of Congress, Washington DC, from the Gertrude Clark Whittall Collection.

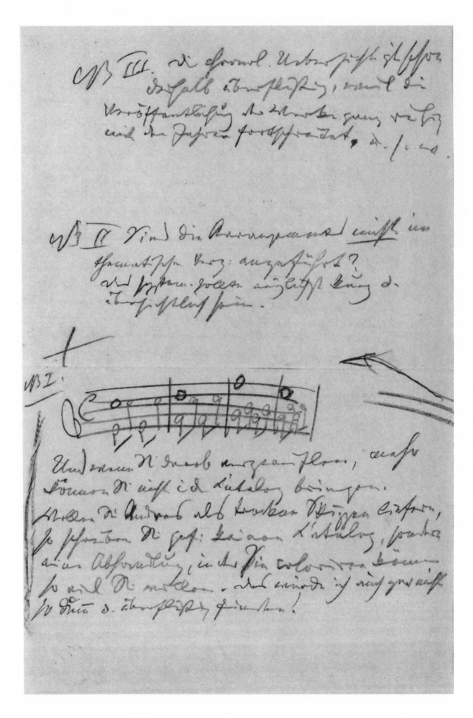

Plate 5 (above and right). First page of Robert Keller's draft for a foreword to the Brahms *Thematisches Verzeichniss,* with Brahms's annotations on facing page, March 1887 (item 33). Reproduced by permission of the Library of Congress, Washington DC, from the Gertrude Clark Whittall Collection.

Vorwort.

Die Herausgabe dieses Kataloges soll zunächst einem praktischen Bedürfnisse helfend entgegenkommen. Bei der stets wachsenden Zahl der erschienenen Werke von Johannes Brahms wird ein vollständig Auskunft gebendes Nachschlagebuch schon längst vermisst.

Im Allgemeinen sind für Zweck und Anordnung des Kataloges vorhandene ähnliche Arbeiten, so weit sie sich benützt machen, und namentlich der Beethoven-Katalog von Nottebohm maßgebend gewesen. Die einigen Neuerungen werden sich zunächst selbst rechtfertigen. Sie bestehen in Folgendem:

Im Thematische Theil ist bei den einzelnen Liedern der erforderliche Stimmenumfang angegeben und ergiebt sich durch Aufführung der Tonart der benützten Ausgabe. Die Beifügung des englischen Textes geboten Zweckmäßigkeitsgründe. — Die Themen sind nicht in trockenen Skizzen, sondern in vollem Colorit hingestellt worden, wozu oft mehr als zwei Liniensysteme erforderlich waren. — Für das systematische Verzeichniß sind auch die Bearbeitungen aufgenommen; es sollte gezeigt werden, wie viele und welche der Werke von gewissen Instrumenten und Instrumentengruppen ausgeführt werden können. — Die chronologische Übersicht mußte sich auf das Erscheinen der Werke in der Öffentlichkeit beschränken; ein sicherer Einblick in die Werkstätte und auf im vollem Schaffen stehenden Deutschland erscheinen nicht statthaft. — Die alphabetischen Register sind begünnerer Nachschlagen wegen auf zwei beschränkt: das eine enthält zugehörend Unterschriften und Textanfänge der Gesangswerke, das andere faßt mit der alphabetischen Aufzählung der Werke, die Vorlagen u. s. w. die Widmungen, die Textdichter, Unterhalber und Bearbeiter (durch übersichtliche Zeichen deutlich unterschieden) zusammen und erspart einzel-Verzeichniße derselben.

NS I
NS II
NS III

Op. 68.
(Erste) Symphonie *(C moll)*
für grosses Orchester.
N. Simrock in Berlin. 1877.

Verlags-No 7957. Partitur [Pag. 8—100] Preis 80 M. netto.

Orchesterstimmen (2 Fl., 2 Ob., 2 Cl., 2 Fag., Contrafag., 4 Hörner, 2 Tromp.,
8 Posaunen, Pauken und Streichorchester) Preis 86 M.
Einzeln: Viol.I.,II., Bratsche Pr. à 8 M.Vcll. Pr. 2 M. 50 Pr. Contrabass Preis 2 M.
Für Pianoforte zu 4 Händen vom Componisten.1878.[Pag. 2—67] Pr. 12 M.
Für zwei Pianoforte zu 8 Händen von ROBERT KELLER.1878. Pr. 15 M.
Für Pianoforte zu 2 Händen von ROBERT KELLER. 1880. Pr. 8 M.

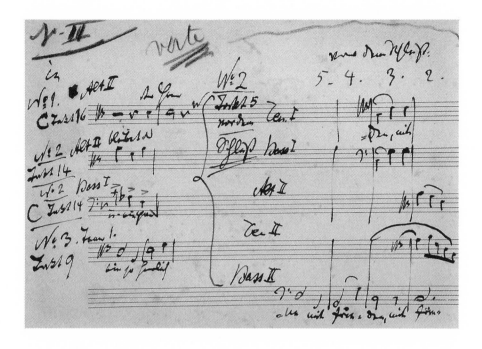

Plate 6 (left). Page for the First Symphony in the Brahms *Thematisches Verzeichniss* (Berlin: N. Simrock, 1887).

Plate 7 (above). Corrections for the *Fest- und Gedenksprüche,* Op. 109, sent by Brahms to Keller, circa 13 June 1889 (item 48). Reproduced by permission of the Library of Congress, Washington DC, from the Gertrude Clark Whittall Collection.

that you not delay the alteration, [that you] not issue the catalog without it! With the Paganini Variations, for example, it must surely be laughable. (8 February 1887; 11:142–43)

English text has nothing to do with German songs. Why don't you say that it is important for your catalog and the market in England? Then I have nothing to say against it. But only not straight out, always around the corner! (24 February 1887; 11:143)

If you therefore had nothing else to consider, I do not comprehend that you still speak a word *in favor of* the English text. Save, perhaps, that it's how things now stand and it is difficult to remove. However, if this would still be possible together with the other quite extensive changes, then I ask you to consider the matter once again. The German song that I compose has absolutely nothing to do with the English translation; these are only belatedly pasted in by the publisher for commercial reasons—there's no need to say anything further. Will you now, as a consequence, also want *to publish alphabetically* in the appendix the English titles and the English incipits!?!?!?!?

That is completely fitting!!

I ask, however, that you always bear in mind that I do not get worked up [about this] personally! I'm sorry for the pretty book if, after this and that, it isn't at least done perfectly. Do me a favor and put the Beethoven or Schubert catalog on your desk, so that you will have a model to look at!

Forgive the eternal wrangling, but it really is well meant and entirely friendly. (27 February 1887; 11:144)

The two thematic catalogs that Brahms recommended as models were prepared by his friend and colleague Gustav Nottebohm and published by Breitkopf & Härtel, the Beethoven catalog in 1865, the Schubert catalog in 1874.[4]

A series of communications between Brahms and Keller, dating from February–April 1887, treats the issues that Brahms raised in his letters to Simrock as well as other problems. Brahms's first letter to Keller was penned in response to a letter from Keller no longer extant.

➳ 31

JOHANNES BRAHMS TO ROBERT KELLER Vienna, circa 12 February 1887 (Library of Congress)

{Note: In the left margin a line in blue crayon runs the length of the fifth paragraph.}

Lieber u. geehrter Herr K.

Es ist zunächst ganz selbstverständlich daß der Kostenpunkt unserer Sache Sie gar nichts angeht.

Ich weiß nicht ob Hr. S. Ihnen sonst mitgetheilt hat, daß ich immer gegen die Herausgabe eines Catalogs m. Sachen war u. sie (oder ihn) überflüßig finde.

Soll er nun einmal erscheinen so sehe ich ihn zunächst nicht als *J. Br.* an, sondern interessire mich für solche Arbeit an sich u. würde viel leidenschaftlicher mitreden wenn sie *Beethoven* oder wen anginge. [Illegible, corrected]

Persönlich dagegen werde ich berührt von Neuerungen wie die *Var:* Anfänge u. — was Ihr Brief ahnen läßt, wenn mehr als 2 Systeme angewandt würden.

Abgesehen von dem, was sonst dagegen spricht, sieht dies nämlich ungemein anspruchsvoll u. eitel aus; die Meinung aber, daß ich mir selbst dies Denkmal setze, werden Sie Niemanden ausreden können. Deshalb, ich fühle es immer mehr, muß ich durchaus wünschen das [*sic*] hier u. in Allem auf das sonst Uebliche (Bescheidene) zurückgegangen werde.

Da dies nun mich selbst angeht u. ich schließlich Spaß an der Sache haben werde, so würde ich sehr gern die Kosten tragen oder mittragen. Sagen Sie mir doch [added:] um [then:] was so beil. es sich handelt.

So weit auch für Hrn. S. u. bitte ihn lesen zu laßen.

Nun entschuldigen Sie wenn ich auch ~~sonst~~ außerdem Ihnen nicht Recht geben kann. Durch die ersten 2 Takte einer *Var:* zeigen Sie keine Spur der *Variationen*=Kunst, dagegen müßen 2 Seiten mit 20–50 solchen Anfängen sonderbar monoton u. unbedeutend aussehen. Auf dem Bogen des Cat. den ich sah, kamen doch nicht mehr wie 2 Systeme vor? Sollten Sie wirklich davon abgehen, würde mir dies allerdings auch höchst unsympathisch sein, es müßte aber auch mehr [added:] als [then:] nöthig dastehn. Desto weniger Worte u. Noten im C. desto besser, meine ich. Es soll nichts Nöthiges fehlen u. nichts Ueberflüßiges dastehen.

Der englische Text hat mit unsern deutschen Liedern absolut nichts zu thun — er müßte denn für den Absatz in E[ngland] nöthig sein. (Sie könnten ebenso dem lateinischen eine deutsche Uebers[etzung] beifügen.)

Die Seitenzahlen einzeln anzuführen finde ich überflüßig, weil die Verhältniße beiläufig immer dieselben sind.

— Ich behaupte aber nicht, immer im Recht zu sein! Ich habe m. Meinung, wie Sie u. Hr. S. die Ihre!

Nur bitte ich nicht den Schumann=Catalog als Muster zu nennen. Nehmen Sie den Beethoven=Cat. zur Hand u. bedenken dann bei jeder Neuerung, die Ihnen einfällt, ob sie dieses Buch auch verbessern würde oder die Uebersichtlichkeit beeinträchtigen u. s. w.

Herzlichen Gruß dazu u. entschuldigen Sie flüchtiges Schreiben u. alles Mögliche u. laßen ein Wort hören

Ihr ergebener
J. Brahms

◆

My dear Herr K.,

First of all, quite obviously, the financial aspect of our project is absolutely no concern of yours.

I don't know whether Herr Simrock has also told you that I was always against the publication of a catalog of my things and consider them (or it) superfluous.

Yet if it is to appear, I do not look at it primarily as J. Br., but rather I am interested in this kind of work for its own sake and would participate more enthusiastically if it involved Beethoven or whomever.

Personally, though, I am bothered by innovations like the incipits of the variations and—as your letter forebodes, if more than 2 staves were used.

Aside from whatever else speaks against it, this of course looks extremely pretentious and vain; but you will never be able to dissuade anyone from the notion that I erected this monument to myself. Therefore, as I feel it more and more, I must insist here and everywhere else on going back to the conventional (the modest).

Since this involves me personally and I will eventually get some fun out of it, I would very much like to bear the costs or to share them. Do tell me how much, approximately, it will be.

Up to here intended also for Herr Simrock, and please let him read it.

Now please forgive me if I also cannot agree with you either. By showing the first two bars of a variation you do not convey the slightest hint of the art of writing variations; on the other hand, 2 pages with 20–50 such incipits must look strangely monotonous and insignificant. On the leaves of the catalog that I saw there were no more than 2 staves, were there? Should you actually deviate from that, I would certainly find it highly distasteful, and more than is necessary would be there. The fewer words and notes in the catalog the better, I think. Nothing important ought to be left out and nothing superfluous put in.

The English text has absolutely nothing to do with our German songs—unless it is necessary for sales in England. (You might just as well add a German translation to the Latin texts.)

The citing of page numbers separately I find superfluous, because the proportions are always roughly the same.

—I do not claim, though, always to be right! I have my opinion, as you and Herr Simrock have yours!

But please do not cite the Schumann catalog as a model. Take the Beethoven catalog in hand and, with each innovation that occurs to you, consider whether it would also improve that book or would detract from its clarity, etc.

With kind regards, and please excuse my hasty writing and this and that and let me hear from you,

Yours sincerely,

J. Brahms

❦

Brahms's tactfulness in his dealings with Keller is evidenced in the two-part organization of this letter. Since it was clear that publication of a thematic catalog of his works could not be prevented, Brahms became determined to exert some control over how it would look, in order to minimize its pretentiousness. (By writing this letter on stationery bearing a lithographically reproduced photograph of "Dr. Hans v. Bülow" and using the filched paper upside down, Brahms offered further commentary on the vanity of the illustrious; see plate 4.) Nottebohm's Beethoven catalog, rather than Alfred Dörffel's Schumann catalog (Breitkopf & Härtel, 1860), was to be taken as a model; only original texts were to appear in the incipits of vocal works; no more than two staves were to be used; only incipits for themes were to be included for sets of variations; the numbers of pages in editions were to be omitted; and the fewer words, the better.

As we shall see, Brahms did not succeed on all counts. One aspect of this venture, however, he could control: to prevent publication of the thematic catalog from occurring on the occasion of his Op. 100, he submitted three rather than two works for release in the spring of 1887—the F Major

Violoncello Sonata, Op. 99; the A Major Violin Sonata, Op. 100; and the C Minor Piano Trio, Op. 101. Brahms's next communication with Keller dealt with a notational revision in the C Minor Trio suggested by Keller.

◆◆ 32

JOHANNES BRAHMS TO ROBERT KELLER   Vienna, 1 March 1887 (Library of Congress)

{Postcard addressed to: Herrn *Robert Keller Berlin. W. Steglitzerstr: 72.*}

{Note: In the left margin a line in blue crayon runs the length of the message.}

Wegen der *Duolen* im Finale des Trio [Op. 101, bars 11–12, etc.] bin ich Ihrer Meinung u. schrieb nur anders, weil ich meinte, es sei so lesbarer. Die betr. Aenderung mache ich nicht — weil Sie diese für den Stecher wieder lesbarer machen können!

Ihr

J. Br.

◆◆

Concerning the duplets in the Finale of the Trio [Op. 101, bars 11–12, etc.], I agree with you, and I only notated it differently because I thought it would be easier to read. I will not make the change in question—because you can again make this easier for the engraver to read!

Yours,

J. Br.

◆◆

As can be seen in the copyist's manuscript that served as the engraver's model for the Trio (Brahms Archiv, Staats- und Universitätsbibliothek, Hamburg), Brahms originally notated the duplets in bars 11–12 and elsewhere in the Finale as quarter notes. On Keller's suggestion, they were changed to eighth notes.

In March 1887 Robert Keller sent Brahms a draft of his foreword for the thematic catalog (see plate 5). Judging from the postscript in Brahms's reply, this document was accompanied by proofs for some or all of the catalog itself. Using both blue crayon and lead pencil, Brahms registered a number of stern objections directly on Keller's draft, crossing out certain words that he found offensive and underlining other passages that he cross-referenced to comments that he wrote on the empty pages facing Keller's text as well as in space available at the end of the text. Brahms keyed his three comments for page I with NB designations and roman numerals in the left margin and connected the first of these comments to the text with a pair of lines in blue crayon; his two comments for page II he linked to the text with pairs of lines written in pencil. Closing remarks and a postscript complete Brahms's annotations.

➡ 33

Robert Keller's Draft of a Foreword to the Simrock *Brahms Thematisches Verzeichniss*, Berlin, March 1887, with Comments by Johannes Brahms, Vienna, 16 March 1887 (Library of Congress)

{Envelope addressed to: Herrn *Robert Keller. Berlin. W.* Steglitzerstr: 72}

I

Vorwort.

Die Herausgabe dieses Catalogs soll zunächst einem praktischen Bedürfnisse helfend entgegenkommen. Bei der hoch [last word underlined in blue and crossed out in pencil by Brahms] angewachsenen Zahl der erschienenen Werke von Johannes Brahms wird ein allseitig Auskunft gebendes <u>Nachschlagebuch</u> schon längst vermisst.

Im Allgemeinen sind für <u>Inhalt</u> und <u>Anordnung</u> des Catalogs vorhandene ähnliche Arbeiten, so weit sie sich bewährt haben, und namentlich der Beethoven=Catalog von Nottebohm maßgebend gewesen. Die wenigen Neuerungen werden sich zumeist selbst rechtfertigen. Sie bestehen in Folgendem:

Im <u>thematischen Theil</u> ist bei den einzelnen Liedern der erforderliche <u>Stimmumfang</u> angegeben und ergänzt sich durch Anführung der Tonarten der transponirten Ausgaben. Die Beifügung des <u>englischen Textes</u> geboten Zweckmäßigkeitsgründe. — Die <u>Themen</u> sind nicht in trockenen Skizzen [last two words underlined in blue by Brahms], sondern in vollem Colorit [last two words underlined in blue by Brahms; comment for this passage under NB I] hingestellt worden, wozu oft mehr als zwei Liniensÿsteme erforderlich waren. — ~~Im sÿstematischen~~ In das sÿstematische <u>Verzeichniß</u> [last word underlined in blue by Brahms] sind auch <u>die Bearbei-</u>

tungen [last word underlined in blue by Brahms; comment under NB II] aufgenommen; es sollte gezeigt werden, wie viele und welche der Werke von gewissen Instrumenten und Instrumentengruppen ausgeführt werden können. — Die chronologische Uebersicht musste sich auf das Erscheinen der Werke in der Oeffentlichkeit beschränken; indiscrete Einblicke in die Werkstätte eines noch in vollem Schaffen stehenden Künstlers erschienen nicht statthaft. [Last sentence marked by Brahms with a blue line in the margin; comment under NB III.] — Die alphabetischen Register sind bequemeren Nachschlagens wegen auf zwei beschränkt: das eine enthält ungetrennt Ueberschriften und Textanfänge der Gesangswerke [this line marked by Brahms with a blue line in the margin], das andere fasst mit der alphabetischen Aufzählung der Werke, der Verleger u.s.w. die Widmungen, die Textdichter, und Uebersetzer und Bearbeiter (durch übersichtliche Zeichen ordentlich [changed to:] deutlich unterschieden) zusammen und erspart Einzel=Verzeichnisse derselben.

II

Bildnisse und Photographien blieben unberücksichtigt.

Der Literatur über Brahms werde an dieser Stelle in Kürze gedacht. Sie ist noch nicht umfangreich und besteht außer:

Deiters, Herm., Johannes Brahms. (Samml. musikal. Vorträge. Herausgegeben von Paul Graf Waldersee № 23. 24) 8º 56 S. Leipzig, Breitkopf & Härtel. Pr. 2,M.

Köhler, Louis. Johannes Brahms und seine Stellung in der Musikgeschichte. 8º Hannover, Simon. Pr. +M. 20 Pf.

La Mara, Johannes Brahms. (In: „Musikalische Studienköpfe" Band III.
 Pr. broch. 3 M. n., geb. 4 M. n.) Leipzig, Schmidt & Günther.

nur aus in Journalen zerstreuten Artikeln von vorübergehendem Werth. [Brahms crossed out the paragraphs on pictures and the literature in pencil and marked them with a blue line in the margin; his respective comment is given below as comment 1.]

So glaubt der Herausgeber auf alle dringenden Anfragen Bescheid gegeben zu haben und giebt sich schließlich der Hoffnung hin, daß seine Arbeit einen getreuen Abriß des bisherigen Schaffens unseres — jetzt wohl unbestritten [last three words underlined in blue by Brahms] — größten lebenden Tonmeisters [last word underlined in blue by Brahms; his respective comment is given below as comment 2] geben und als eine brauchbare Vorstudie zu späteren umfassenden Werken über denselben verwendbar sein mögen!

Berlin, im *März* 1887.

R. K.

[Facing p. I:]

NB I.

Und wenn Sie darob verzweiflen, mehr können Sie nicht in den Catalog bringen. Wollen Sie Andres als trockene Skizzen liefern, so schreiben Sie gef[älligst] keinen Catalog, sondern eine Abhandlung, in der Sie coloriren können so viel Sie wollen. Das würde ich auch gar nicht so dumm u. überflüßig finden!

[NB I is marked by Brahms with a blue line in the margin]

NB II   Sind die Arrangements <u>nicht</u> im thematischen Verz: angeführt? Das system. sollte möglichst kurz u. übersichtlich sein.

NB III   Die chronol. Uebersicht ist schon deshalb überflüßig, weil die Veröffentlichung der Werke ganz ruhig mit den Jahren fortschreitet, u. s. w.

[Comment 1, facing p. II:]

Ist unter den Umständen wirklich jedes Wort, jede Erwiderung überflüßig.

[Comment 2, facing p. II:]

mit der Firma *Simrock* auf dem Titel — sehr schmeichelhaft! Wollen wir nicht abwarten daß es Andre sagen?

[Closing remarks on bottom half of p. II:]

Herzl. Gruß dazu u. wo möglich sein Sie nicht bös aber ich kann nicht noch einmal von Vorne anfangen.

Schreiben Sie obenerwähnte Abhandlung ich will Ihnen sogar helfen, ernstlich helfen dabei u. schließlich danken.

[Facing p. II:]

(P. S. Der Catalog, (leider oben so respektlos behandelt!) geht Heute
(an Hrn. S. zurück.

❧

I

Foreword

The publication of this catalog is intended primarily to help fulfill a practical need. In view of the considerably [last word underlined in blue crayon and crossed out in pencil by Brahms] increasing number of published works by Johannes Brahms, a *reference book* giving comprehensive information seems long overdue.

In general this catalog has taken as its models for *content* and *structure* similar catalogs that have already proved their worth, especially the Beethoven Catalog by Nottebohm. The few innovations are for the most part self-explanatory. They consist of the following:

In the *thematic portion* the requisite *vocal range* is given for each song and supplemented with an indication of the song's key in the transposed edition. Practical considerations dictated the addition of the *English texts.*— The *themes* are not rendered as dry sketches [last two words underlined in blue crayon by Brahms], but in full color [last two words underlined in blue crayon by Brahms; comment for this passage under NB I], which frequently required more than two staves.—In the *systematic catalog* [last word underlined in blue crayon by Brahms] *the arrangements* [last word underlined in blue crayon by Brahms; comment under NB II] are also included; this is to show how many and which of the works can be performed by certain instruments and groups of instruments.—The *chronological survey* had to be limited to the dates the works were published; indiscreet glimpses into the workshop of an artist still at the height of his creative powers did not seem permissible. [Last sentence marked by Brahms with a blue line in the margin; comment under NB III.]—For more convenient reference, the *alphabetical registers* were limited to two: *one* containing both the *titles* and the *text incipits* of the vocal works [this line of text marked by Brahms with a blue line in the margin], the *other* presenting all in one list, in alphabetical order, the *works*, the *publishers,* as well as the *dedicatees*, the *poets of the texts, translators,* and *arrangers* (each clearly differentiated by distinct symbols), which saves having to publish separate registers.

II

Portraits and *photographs* remained unconsidered.

At this point a brief mention of the *literature* on Brahms seems appropriate. As yet it is not very extensive and consists only of:

Deiters, Herm., Johannes Brahms. (Sammlung musikalischer Vorträge. Edited by Paul Graf Waldersee. No. 23, 24) Octavo, 56 pp. Leipzig, Breitkopf & Härtel. Price: 2 Marks.

Köhler, Louis. Johannes Brahms und seine Stellung in der Musikgeschichte. Octavo. Hannover, Simon. Price: 1 Mark, 20 Pfennig.

La Mara, Johannes Brahms. (In: Musikalische Studienköpfe, vol. 3. Price: paper, 3 Marks; hardcover, 4 Marks) Leipzig: Schmidt & Günther.

as well as articles of transitory value published in various journals. [Brahms crossed out the paragraphs on pictures and the literature in pencil and marked them with a blue line in the margin; his respective comment is given below as comment 1.]

Thus the editor trusts to have given information on all urgent questions and in the end hopes that his work gives a faithful summary of the heretofore published oeuvre of our—now probably undisputed [last three words underlined in blue crayon by Brahms]—greatest living composer [last word underlined in blue crayon by Brahms; his respective comment is given below as comment 2] and that it may serve as a useful *preparatory tool* for future comprehensive works on his oeuvre!

Berlin, March 1887.

R. K.

[Facing p. 1:]

NB I.

And even if you despair on that account, you cannot squeeze more into the catalog. If you wish to supply anything other than dry sketches, then please do not write a catalog, but rather an essay in which you can color as much as you wish. That I would not at all consider so stupid and superfluous!

[NB I is marked by Brahms with a blue line in the margin]

NB II Are the arrangements *not* mentioned in the thematic catalog? The systematic section should be as brief and as easy to take in at a glance as possible.

NB III The chronological survey is superfluous for the very reason that the publication of my works continues altogether evenly over the years, etc.

[Comment 1, facing p. II:]
Under these circumstances, every word, every reply is in fact superfluous.

[Comment 2, facing p. 11:]
With the Simrock firm on the title page—very flattering! Do we not want to wait and see whether others say it?

[Closing remarks on bottom half of p. 11:]
I include kind regards, and if possible do not be angry, but I cannot start all over again.

Do write the essay mentioned above; I even want to help you, seriously help you with it and be grateful to you in the end.

[Facing p. 11:]
(P.S. The catalog (treated so disrespectfully above, I'm afraid) goes back
(to Herr Simrock today.

❧

Keller's distinction between themes rendered as "dry sketches" and those "in full color" especially aroused Brahms's ire, and he countered with the theme of the Finale of Mozart's *Jupiter* Symphony (No. 41 in C major, K. 551) written on just *one* staff (an unfair example, since the opening of this theme consists only of melody and tremolo). The essay that Brahms volunteered to help Keller write never came to fruition.

Brahms returned the materials for the thematic catalog to Simrock on 16 March 1887, with a brief note congratulating Simrock on the birth of a grandchild and apologizing that he had to enclose "such a vexatious packet." "The catalog is becoming ever more dreadful for me" (11:145).

In his next letter to Keller, written in response to an acknowledgment of receipt of the revised draft, Brahms commented further on the elaborate "systematic" section envisioned by Keller, referring him to a simpler index in the *Verzeichniss der in Druck erschienenen Compositionen von Johannes Brahms* issued by P. Pabst of Leipzig.

➤ 34

JOHANNES BRAHMS TO ROBERT KELLER   Vienna, 24 March 1887
(Library of Congress)

{Envelope addressed to: Herrn Robert Keller. <u>Berlin. W.</u> 72 Steglitzerstr:}

Lieber Hr. K.
Ich scheue mich immer so energisch in praktischen Dingen mitzureden. An Ihrer Stelle aber ließe ich den „schlichthaarigen Jünglingen" zu Ge-

fallen die häßliche Beule nicht. Für diese genügt jeder Zettel, der irgend
wo beigelegt wird.

Ich nehme eben das bei Papst [*sic*] ersch. Verz: m. Sachen in die Hand u.
sehe zu m. Vergnügen das systematische Verz: viel einfacher als bei Ihnen
u. durchaus klar, übersichtlich u. genügend. Zu besonderer Wollust ist für
die Chaconne von Bach u. die linke Hand [Anh. 1a, No. 1/v] kein
Extra=Cabinet eingerichtet!!

Dagegen — eine Weitläufigkeit, oder eine Theilung dort behagt mir wohl
u. ich finde sie auch im Schubert= o. Schumann=Catalog.

Die Texte sind in 2 Abtheil. aufgestellt. Erst die Titel, dann die
Text=Anfänge. Aber — ich bitte nur immer wieder, nicht unnütz auf-
bauschen, so einfach u. kurz wie möglich.

Sie verwöhnen mich übrigens sehr, wenn Sie meine Rücksendungen
freundlich finden!

Mit bestem Gruß

Ihr

J. Brahms

Dear Herr K.,

I always shrink from interfering so energetically in practical things.

If I were you, however, to please the "straight-haired youths" I would
not leave the hideous lump. For them any slip of paper added anywhere
will suffice.

I just picked up the catalog of my things published by Papst [*sic*] and
to my pleasure discovered that the systematic catalog is much simpler than
yours and absolutely clear, easy to take in at a glance, and sufficient. To
my special delight there is no separate section provided for the Chaconne
by Bach and the left hand [Anh. 1a, No. 1/v]!!

On the other hand—a spaciousness, or a subdivision there appeals to
me, and I find it also in the Schubert and Schumann Catalogs.

The texts are set up in two sections. First the titles, then the text incipits.
But—again I ask you not to inflate things unnecessarily, to keep things as
simple and brief as possible.

By the way, you indulge me too much when you consider my responses
kind!

With best regards,

Yours,

J. Brahms

Extensive revisions of the thematic catalog must have been undertaken in early April, for the final publication varies greatly from the version on which Brahms had commented in February and that Keller had described in the draft of his foreword (see plate 6). Although the numbers of pages in the published editions were retained and English translations given for the vocal works, Brahms's sets of keyboard variations were represented only by incipits for their themes. All the chamber and orchestral works were reduced to two staves, and vocal works were kept to three or four staves. Keller's "chronological survey" was eliminated from the "systematic catalog" at the end of the volume, dates of publication being provided as part of the entries in the main catalog. The alphabetical register for titles and text incipits of vocal works was kept, but the mixed alphabetical register of works, publishers, dedicatees, poets, translators, and arrangers was replaced by a "systematic catalog" of works according to performance medium, a separate "overview" of arrangements by Brahms and others (also according to medium), and an alphabetical index of names and works. Furthermore, Keller's entire foreword was eliminated, the final organization of the volume no doubt being deemed clear enough to make further explanation unnecessary.

In his last letter to Keller concerning the project Brahms's mood had improved. With most of his points won, he registered his approval of the catalog, giving Keller full credit and sincerely praising him for his "fine work."

⇒ 35

JOHANNES BRAHMS TO ROBERT KELLER   Vienna, 14 April 1887
(Library of Congress)

{Envelope addressed to: Herrn *Robert Keller. Berlin. W.* 72, Steglitzerstraße.}

Lieber u. geehrter Herr,

Der Catalog fängt an mir bedeutend zu gefallen u. jedenfalls sein Sie überzeugt daß ich keine seiner hohen Vortrefflichkeiten übersehe, die laut ihren Meister loben — nämlich Sie! Ich komme also das letzte Mal u. bitte nur um wenige — Striche. Vor allem noch für einige historischmerkwürdige Notizen — man muß künftigen Forschern was übrig laßen! S. 11 Serenade [Op. 16], S. 31 Trio [Op. 40], S. 41 „Sonntag" [Op. 47 No. 3] u. S. 98 „Lied" wo ich einfach den 2/4 Takt hinzusetzen bitte.

Den kleinen Druckfehler im Psalm [Op. 27] S. 18 würde ich stillschweigend verbessern—dagegen hätten Sie wohl den sehr bösen im Walzer [Op. 39] S. 30 bemerken können! Er steht im Original, ist aber im 2 händ. Arr: verbessert——Sie sehen, ich steige Ihren kritischen Forschungen in die tiefsten Tiefen nach!

Möchten Sie nicht S. 63 den Tenor [*All' meine Herzgedanken*, Op. 62 No. 5] so schreiben: ? u. die Bratsche S. 93 [*Geistliches Wiegenlied*, Op. 91 No. 2] im Baßschl.? Daß im Catalog 50 mal „in Musik gesetzt" u. 50 mal „componirt für" vorkommt, läßt sich nicht mehr ändern?

Die Arrang: S. 131, 2, für sich, gefällt mir ganz außerordentlich u. sind Sie mit der Anordnung zufrieden oder über Alles u. alle mein Einreden überhaupt höchst verdrießlich?!?

Wenn Sie nun einmal die Freude haben, von den Werken eines Bessern einen Catalog zu machen, sollten Sie sich doch zum Prinzip nehmen, als thematische Angabe nur das Nöthigste, das Wesentliche zu bringen, eine Art Cl.=Auszug, der die Melodie u. eine Andeutung, eine möglichst übersichtliche u. leicht verständliche Andeutung des Uebrigen enthält.

Es kann doch nicht Jeder die betr. Sache so auswendig wißen wie wir Beide meine Sachen u. das gehört dazu um z. B. in den Sinfonien, Triumpf= u. Schicksalslied [Opp. 55, 54] zu finden was man sucht, zu verstehen was da steht.

Ich möchte wohl das thematische Verzeichniß der 120 Cantaten von Bach, von Ihnen bearbeitet — sehen — aber nicht besitzen u. benutzen!

Nun haben Sie aber schönsten Dank für die große — vor Allem die große Geduld die Sie für die Arbeit u. gar für mich hatten!
Wenn Ihnen nur nicht alle Freude an Ihrer schönen Arbeit durch mein Hineinreden genommen ist!

Von Herzen grüßend
Ihr ergebener
J. Brahms.

My dear Sir,

The catalog is beginning to please me considerably, and in any case you may rest assured that I am overlooking none of its fine qualities, which loudly extol their master—namely you! Thus I am here for the last time and merely to ask for a few—cuts.

Above all, with respect to some peculiar historical notes—one ought to leave something to future researchers. P. 11, Serenade [Op. 16], p. 31,

Trio [Op. 40], p. 41 *Sonntag* [Op. 47 No. 3], and p. 98 *Lied,* where I ask that you simply add the 2/4 time signature.

The minor misprint in the Psalm [Op. 27], p. 18, I would correct tacitly—but you ought to have noticed the very bad one in the Waltzes [Op. 39], p. 30! It is in the original, but was corrected in the two-hand arrangement——you see, I follow your critical research with the most profound profundity!

Don't you want to notate the tenor on p. 63 [*All' meine Herzgedanken,*

Op. 62 No. 5] like this: ? and the viola

on p. 93 [*Geistliches Wiegenlied,* Op. 91 No. 2] in the bass clef? I suppose it is too late to do anything about the *"in Musik gesetzt"* and *"componirt für,"* each of which occurs about fifty times in the catalog?

I am extremely pleased that the arrangements appear separately on pp. 131–32; and are you satisfied with the layout now or extremely irritated about everything, and particularly about all my interfering?!?

If you ever have the pleasure of compiling a catalog of a better composer, you should make a point of giving only the bare minimum, the essential, as the thematic incipit, a kind of piano reduction containing the melody and an indication, as clearly arranged and easily understandable as possible, of everything else.

Not everyone can be expected to know each piece as well as we both know my things, but one would have to in the case of, for example, the symphonies, the *Triumphlied* [Op. 55], and the *Schicksalslied* [Op. 54] in order to find what one is looking for, to understand what is given there.

I would certainly like to see a thematic catalog of the 120 cantatas *by Bach* compiled by you—see—but not own and use it!

But now may I thank you for the extraordinary—above all the extraordinary patience you had with the work and especially with me!

If all the joy in your fine work has not been taken away from you by my meddling!

> With heartfelt regards,
> Yours sincerely,
> *J. Brahms*

❦

Again Brahms used an inverted sheet of Hans von Bülow's photograph stationery (see item 31). The "peculiar historical notes" that were to provide grist for the mills of future scholars seem for the most part to have involved issues of compositional history raised by Keller's annotations: in dating the early A Major Serenade, Op. 16, Keller had cited a "new edition, revised by the author" and released by Simrock in 1875, noting that the first edition had appeared in 1860; and the E♭ Major Horn Trio, Op. 40, whose date of publication Keller gave as "1868," was actually released two years earlier. The issue Brahms took with *Sonntag,* Op. 47 No. 3, may have involved the distinction that users of the catalog could be expected to discern between the two solo piano arrangements of this song cited on page 41, one by Theodor Kirchner "for pianoforte in free transcription," the other by Gustav Lange "freely arranged for pianoforte." The identity of the unspecified *Lied* on page 98 is unclear; the first three songs in the *Sieben Lieder,* Op. 95, appear on that page. Perhaps the "historical problem" was the relation of the solo setting of *Das Mädchen,* Op. 95 No. 1, to its choral counterpart, Op. 93a No. 2, a connection cited by Keller in a note below the incipit; the missing "$\frac{2}{4}$ time signature" may have been a common-time signature missing after the $\frac{3}{4}$ in this mixed-meter song. The misprints that Brahms called to Keller's attention were all corrected before the catalog was issued.

The Double Concerto

The correspondence between Brahms and Keller concerning the Concerto in A Minor for Violin and Violoncello, Op. 102, consists of only two items—Keller's handwritten copy of a postcard from Brahms (the original is now lost) and the draft that he made of his response to this postcard (the actual letter is now lost). Composed during the summer of 1887, the concerto received its premiere in Cologne on 18 October, with Joseph Joachim and Robert Hausmann as soloists and Brahms conducting. Additional performances followed in Germany, Switzerland, and England. Brahms sent his piano reduction to Simrock in February 1888; it was published in May, the solo parts and full score in June. Brahms's postcard to Keller concerns the last-minute reinstatement of a reading for the solo violin.

⇥ 36

JOHANNES BRAHMS TO ROBERT KELLER   Vienna, 22 April 1888
(Library of Congress)

Postkarte v. *Joh.* Brahms.

Postst[empel] *Wieden in Wien*
22/4 4. N. (88?)
~~nein~~ [by an unknown hand]

(Correspondenz-Karte.)
(An)
Herrn *Robert Keller.*
       (in) *Berlin. W.*
       Steglitzerstrasse 72.
   (Oder Friedrichstraße 171 bei *N. Simrock.*)

Geehrtester, Im ersten Satz des Concerts [Op. 102] habe ich in der Solo-Geige die beiden letzten Takte vor **G.** [bars 191–92] geändert. Wollen Sie so gut sein diese Aenderung wieder zu streichen; es gilt das alte einfache,

das, was da stand. In Partitur u. Cl. A. Hoffentlich ist die Correktur noch
bei Ihnen, sonst schreiben Sie vielleicht fr[eun]dlichst ein Wort an Röder
— es würde sonst unnütz corrigirt. Die beiden Takte vor **G.** bleiben in der
Geige einfach wie sie sind.

Mit bestem Gruß
Ihr
J Brahms.

ˣMöchten Sie wohl ein Wort
sagen daß <u>dies</u> angekommen ist?!
Herzl. Dank.

[Note added by Keller:]

ˣ(mit Bleistift!)

◆

Postcard from Joh. Brahms

Postmark: Wieden in Wien
22/4 4. N. (88?)
n̶o̶ [by an unknown hand]

(Correspondence card)
(To)
Herr Robert Keller
   (in) Berlin, W.
  Steglitzerstrasse 72
(or Friedrichstraße 171 c/o N. Simrock)

Dear Sir,

In the first movement of the [Double] Concerto [Op. 102] I changed
the last two bars before letter **G** [bars 191–92] in the solo violin. Will you
kindly cross out this change; the old, simple reading stays, the one that
was there before. In the score and the piano reduction. I hope that you
still have the proofs; if not, would you perhaps kindly write a note to
Röder—otherwise there would be unnecessary correcting. The two bars
before letter **G** in the violin remain simply as they are.

With best regards,
Yours,
J. Brahms.

ˣ Would you kindly acknowledge
receipt of *this note*?!
Thank you.

[Note added by Keller:]
ˣ (in pencil)

❧

Since the proofs for this work are no longer extant and the engraver's model for the full score (a copy prepared by William Kupfer; private collection, Germany) is free of correction at this point (except for the alteration of the last note of bar 192 from a single pitch, A, to a dyad, C′–E♭′), one cannot say with certainty what the reading was that Brahms rejected. However, immediately before Brahms wrote Keller, Joachim had written Brahms about this passage, urging him to use the simpler reading (which in Joachim's musical example included the C′–E♭′ dyad), because playing through the work he had "once more attempted to bring in the double stops, without success" (20 April 1888; 6:246). Perhaps Brahms had thought to have the solo violin play in the exposition the same sort of double stops demanded in the recapitulation, bars 361–62:

Keller's friendly reply to Brahms was penned the very next day. (Only a draft for this letter survives; in the German text that follows, all abbreviations used by Keller have been realized without editorial brackets, for the sake of clarity.)

➥ 37

Robert Keller to Johannes Brahms   Berlin, 23 April 1888
(Library of Congress)

(An Brahms.)

Berlin 23. 4. 8̶7̶ [corrected in purple ink to:] 1888

Hochgeehrter Herr Doctor!
    Ihre Karte habe ich erhalten und es war noch Zeit die unnöthige Correktur abzuwenden.
    Vor kurzem habe ich Ihre Lieder (die ernstesten!) von einem jungen Mädchen, Fräulein Köckert aus Genf, so singen hören, wie nie vorher. Das

ist eine geborene Brahms-Sängerin. Es rieselt einem kalt über, wenn sie singt: „Der Tod, das ist die kühle Nacht" [Op. 96 No. 1] oder „Ach, wende diesen Blick" [Op. 57 No. 4]. Das müßten Sie hören! Vielleicht läßt es sich veranstalten, wenn Sie im Sommer wieder in die Schweiz kommen. Öffentlich ist sie noch nicht aufgetreten.

Ihr Concert [Op. 102] wächst mit der nähern Bekanntschaft immer tiefer ins Herz, beim ersten hören schien mir der letzte Satz nicht brahmsig genug.

Hochachtungsvollsten Gruß Ihres Robert Keller.

Meine Wohnung ist jetzt wieder Steglitzer Straße 1.

•◆

(*To Brahms.*)

Berlin, 23 April 1887 [corrected
in purple ink to:] 1888

Dear Herr Doctor!

I received your card and it was just in time to prevent the unnecessary correction.

Recently I heard your songs (the most serious ones!) sung by a young lady, Fräulein Köckert from Geneva, as I never heard them before. She is a born Brahms singer. A shudder runs up and down your spine when she sings *Der Tod, das ist die kühle Nacht* [Op. 96 No. 1] or *Ach, wende diesen Blick* [Op. 57 No. 4]. You must hear her! Perhaps it can be arranged when you come to Switzerland again in the summer. She has not performed in public yet.

The better I get to know your [Double] Concerto [Op. 102] the more precious it becomes to me; when I first heard it, the last movement did not seem Brahmsian enough to me.

Most respectful regards, Yours, Robert Keller

From now on my address is once again Steglitzer Straße 1.

◆•

At the top of the sheet containing this draft Keller made a brief list of editorial comments relating to the piano reduction of the Double Concerto; the page and staff references are to the first edition.

•◆

S. 6 [I, ca. bars 72–86]. Das Mskrpt gibt keine Veranlassung kleine Noten zu stechen

S. 20. unten [I, ca. bars 313–17, possibly bar 315, violin and violoncello]: Das Mskpt ist richtig, Abkürzung falsch vom Stecher verstanden.

S. 28 [II, ca. bars 3, 5, 7, etc., piano]. Die tiefe 8 wird immer dazuge-stochen.

S. 32. 33 [II, ca. bars 79–95, 97–99, violin and violoncello] ebenso.

S. 39 Syst. 2 [III, ca. bars 135–41]: Manuscript richtig, jedoch <u>nicht ganz unzweifelhaft.</u>

p. 6 [I, ca. bars 72–86]. According to the manuscript there is no reason for small notes.

p. 20, bottom of page [I, ca. bars 313–17, possibly bar 315, violin and violoncello]: The manuscript is correct; abbreviation misunderstood by the engraver.

p. 28 [II, ca. bars 3, 5, 7, etc., piano]. The lower octave always has to be engraved as well.

pp. 32, 33 [II, ca. bars 79–95, 97–99, violin and violoncello] Likewise.

p. 39, staff 2 [III, ca. bars 135–41]: Manuscript correct, yet *not quite without doubt.*

With the engraver's model for the piano reduction no longer extant, it is difficult to pinpoint all the problems that Keller perceived in the proofs of the first edition. The "lower octave" that was to be engraved on pages 28, 32, and 33 refers, no doubt, to the lower notes of the piano in the doubled melody at the beginning of the second movement and in the solo strings for the reprise. Indeed, when preparing a copy of the second move-ment as a Christmas present from the composer to Laura von Beckerath in 1887 (Andreas von Beckerath, Icking near Munich), Brahms's copyist William Kupfer indicated the lower notes in these passages as 8 _ _ _ _, most likely reproducing the abbreviations in Brahms's autograph of the reduction; in his autograph of the full score (Gesellschaft der Musik-freunde, Vienna) he designated the lower notes in all these passages as *in 8*. Similarly, the confusion on page 20 of the first movement of the reduc-tion may have stemmed from Brahms's use of the abbreviation ✗ in his autograph score to indicate the repetition of the violin and violoncello within bar 315. The passage in the Finale that Keller considered "not quite without doubt" in the manuscript of the reduction may have been bars 137–38, with their dotted rhythm against triplets.

The reference to Fräulein Köckert, a young amateur singer from Geneva, is the first of several to appear in the Brahms-Keller correspondence over the next months.

The *Gesänge,* Op. 104,
the *Lieder,* Opp. 105–7, and
a Holiday in Weesen

In October 1888 N. Simrock published five new opuses of vocal works by Brahms: eleven *Zigeunerlieder* for vocal quartet and piano, Op. 103; five *Gesänge* for mixed choir, Op. 104; and three collections of solo *Lieder,* Opp. 105–7, five songs in each. The *Zigeunerlieder* were a product of the preceding winter. Several of the choral and solo songs, on the other hand, date from the summer of 1886: on the "August" page of his pocket calendar book for 1886 (Stadt- und Landesbibliothek, Vienna) Brahms cited as having been completed during his vacation in Thun, Switzerland, two of the choral pieces (Op. 104 Nos. 3 and 5) and five of the songs (Op. 105 Nos. 1, 2, and 5 and Op. 107 Nos. 1 and 3); three other solo songs had been heard in performance during the winters of 1885 and 1887 (Op. 106 Nos. 2 and 5, and Op. 107 No. 4, respectively). The dates of composition for the remaining choral and solo songs (Op. 104 Nos. 1, 2, and 4; Op. 105 Nos. 3 and 4; Op. 106 Nos. 1–5; and, Op. 107 Nos. 2 and 5) are unknown.[1] Some of these works may stem from the spring and summer of 1886, during the months just before Brahms assembled these collections, but the possibility remains that others were drawn from his portfolio of earlier works. A group of seven postcards and letters between Brahms and Keller supplements a series of communications between Brahms and Simrock in detailing the steps that led to the publication of these songs.

Brahms turned his *Zigeunerlieder* over to Fritz Simrock early in May 1888, when the publisher visited him in Vienna; by mid-June they had been engraved and the proofs sent to Brahms for his scrutiny (5 May 1888, Schumann, 2:343; 16 July 1888, *Brahms Briefwechsel,* 11:190–91). When writing Simrock at the end of May, Brahms had hinted that solo songs might soon be forthcoming: "The solo-voice [version of the *Zigeunerlieder*] you can have, and still others as well" (31 May 1888; 11:184). The first letter from Brahms to Keller reveals that the composer soon delivered on his promise.

◆ 38

Johannes Brahms to Robert Keller   Thun, 29 June 1888
(Library of Congress)

{Postcard addressed to: Herrn *Robert Keller.* (Nöthigenfalls [If necessary]
N. Simrock. Friedrichstr: 171. Berlin. W. Steglitzerstrasse 1. (?)}

Lieber geehrter Herr. Es wäre mir eine sehr angenehme Nachricht, wenn
Sie mir melden könnten daß m. neuen Lieder [Opp. 105–106] noch nicht
beim Stecher sind?! Ich hätte gern Einiges überlegt u. zugelegt.

Sie gehen wohl wieder an Ihren Schweizer See? Ihre vortreffliche Sän-
gerin auch? u. ist unter den neuen Liedern eins oder das andere gut genug
für Sie [*sic*]?

Herzlich grüßend
Ihr ergebener
J. Brahms

Thun.

◆

Dear Sir:

It would be welcome news to me if you could tell me that my new songs
[Opp. 105–6] are *not yet* at the engraver?! I would like to think some more
about them and perhaps add to them.

You will be going to your Swiss lake again, I assume? Your excellent
singer too? and is one or the other of my new songs good enough for her?

Kind regards,
Yours sincerely,
J. Brahms

Thun

◆

In the course of preparing his edition of Brahms's songs for the *Johannes
Brahms Sämtliche Werke,* Eusebius Mandyczewski discovered in the possession of N. Simrock a group of five autographs for the songs Opp. 105–7
that he described as paginated continuously and arranged in the following
order:

> *Klage* (Op. 105 No. 3; Lower Rheinish folk song);
> *Auf dem Kirchhofe* (Op. 105 No. 4; Detlev von Liliencron);
> *Es hing der Reif* (Op. 106 No. 3; Klaus Groth);
> *Meine Lieder* (Op. 106 No. 4; Adolf Frey);
> *Mädchenlied* (Op. 107 No. 5; Paul Heyse).

Mandyczewski concluded that Brahms had originally thought to publish a single volume containing only these songs. This hypothesis receives little support from the extant physical evidence, however, for neither the one surviving bifolio from this group—for *Klage* and *Auf dem Kirchhofe* (Stadt- und Landesbibliothek, Vienna)—nor a facsimile of the first page of the *Mädchenlied* (published in *Liepmannssohn-Versteigerungs-Katalog* 59, which offered this song together with *Es hing der Reif* and *Meine Lieder* for sale as a group) shows signs of pagination.[2] Only the structure of the manuscripts containing these five songs—apparently a single bifolio plus a gathering or pairing of two other bifolios—speaks for viewing the songs as having originally formed a single opus.[3]

Yet certain cyclic features, not unlike the unifying elements that prompted Brahms to view his opuses of songs as "bouquets" carefully assembled rather than as random collections, can be discerned within this group of songs.[4] Their texts focus on betrayed love and death as one's only solace, and the first three songs are linked by images of winter, freezing, and frost. The group opens and closes with folklike strophic songs of *Liebesleid:* the first song is strictly strophic, while the final song is strophic for two stanzas, its third stanza set as a variation of the first two and its final stanza functioning as a coda—to the song and, given its length and broadened pace, to the "cycle" as a whole (a role that it also plays as the final song of Op. 107). Between these two "folk songs" are three through-composed "art songs."

The progression of keys for the five songs also contributes to the cyclic nature of the group. The first two songs posit a tonic-to-dominant polarity on F, the keys of the second through fourth songs are related by minor thirds, and the fourth and fifth songs resolve minor dominant to minor tonic, but on B, a tritone away from the opening plateau, thereby reflecting tonally the ambivalence of the last line of the final song, "Ich weiß es nicht!":

Op. 105/3	105/4	106/3	106/4	107/5
F (d) F	c/C	a	f♯	b, with picardy third
I	v/v	iii		
		vii	v	i

For lack of any documentary evidence to the contrary, these five songs have been attributed to the year of their publication. It is possible that they were conceived as a cycle and composed not long before being submitted to Simrock.

The expansion of this group of five songs into three collections totaling fifteen Lieder apparently took place in several stages, as Brahms reviewed his portfolio of earlier songs. By 18 July, in a letter to Fritz Simrock, Brahms was speaking of two opuses of songs, designating "the low songs" as Op. 105, "the high [songs]" as Op. 106 (11:192). The next day he informed his publisher of his intention to submit "an additional volume" and asked that Op. 106 not be given to the engraver yet, for these songs were to be ordered differently (11:193). At the end of the month the order of Opp. 106 and 107 had still not been finalized; on 31 July Brahms suggested to Simrock that it would be nice if they determined the order together when Simrock visited him at Thun in mid-August. One of the songs that changed collections was *Salamander*, eventually published as Op. 107 No. 2 but designated as Op. 106 No. 3 on the first page of the autograph engraver's model (private collection, Bern).

From Brahms's letter to Simrock of 18 July we learn that the order of Op. 105 also underwent alterations: Brahms informed his publisher that he was sending him a song to serve as No. 3 and that *Verrat* would then become No. 5. If we accept Mandyczewski's hypothesis about the original collection of five songs, the new third song for Op. 105 must have been either *Wie Melodien sieht es mir* or *Immer leiser wird mein Schlummer* (both of which had been in Brahms's portfolio since the summer of 1886). From Brahms's next letter to Keller we learn that at least one of the songs already sent to the publisher had undergone alterations significant enough for Brahms to request the return of the autograph.

➡ 39

JOHANNES BRAHMS TO ROBERT KELLER Thun, 4 July 1888 (Library of Congress)

{Envelope addressed to: Herrn *Robert Keller. Berlin. W. Steglitzerstrasse* 1.}

Geehrtester Herr,

Besten Dank für Ihre freundl. Zeilen u. da ich nun einmal statt der Firma Sie incommodirt habe, so thue ich es weiter! Es handelt sich nicht um die ungrischen sondern um spätere Lieder. Da diese also noch gar nicht in Ihre fleißigen Hände gekommen sind, so kann ich wohl annehmen daß sie auch noch nicht beim Stecher sind. Jedenfalls hätte ich gern das inl[iegend] bezeichnete vor dem Stich zurück — um sogleich eine andre Lesart zurück zu schicken. Möchten Sie dies gelegentlich im Geschäft veranlaßen?

Ihr liebes *Weesen* ist mir leider so entlegen u. in jener Zeit ist es gar so unangenehm in der Schweiz zu reisen. Ich käme gar gern u. freute mich auch bei der Gelegenheit Ihr liebes Wesen (jetzt meine ich ein andres) zu hören.

Herzl. Gruß

Ihres ergebenen

J. Brahms.

◆◆

Dear Sir:

Many thanks for your kind note, and, since I have begun to bother you instead of the firm, I will continue to do so! I was not talking about the Hungarian songs [Op. 103], but later ones. Since they have not even gone through your diligent hands yet, I can assume that they have not yet gone to the engraver either. In any case, *before* engraving takes place I would like to have back the one indicated on the enclosure—in order to send back a different reading immediately. Would you arrange for this with the firm, at your convenience?

Your dear Weesen is unfortunately very much out of the way for me, and at that time of year traveling in Switzerland is so unpleasant. I would really like to come, and on that occasion would enjoy listening to your dear Wesen (now I mean a different one).

Kind regards,

Yours sincerely,

J. Brahms

◆◆

Since virtually all the manuscript sources for these late songs are missing, it is impossible to determine which song Brahms wanted to revise. The few surviving manuscripts show no signs of significant recomposition, nor do the few descriptions we have of lost manuscripts speak of major variants or alterations.

In his letter of 29 June, Brahms had inquired of Keller whether he would be spending his vacation on "your Swiss lake" and in the company of his favorite singer, Fräulein Köckert. Keller responded with an invitation for Brahms to visit him, an idea that Brahms welcomed, allowing him, as it did, to enjoy both *Weesen* and *Wesen*. Brahms made the trip from his summer residence on the Thunersee to Keller's on the Wallensee early in August.

⇥ 40

Johannes Brahms to Robert Keller   Thun, 1 August 1888
(Library of Congress)

{Postcard addressed to: Herrn *Robert Keller Hotel Mariahalden Weesen. am
Wallensee.*}

Geehrtester u. lieber Hr. K.

Falls nichts Besondres dazwischen kommt, denke ich Sonntag mit der
Brünigbahn zu fahren u. Abends bei Ihnen zu sein. Ein Zimmerchen finde
ich wohl in Ihrer Marien=Stiftung? Und recht viel schöne Schubert'sche
Lieder haben Sie auf dem Programm für

Ihren herzl. grüßenden
J. Brahms

⇥

My dear Herr K.,

If nothing unexpected comes up, I plan to take the Brünig train on
Sunday and to be with you by evening. I will probably be able to get a little
room in your Marien-Stiftung? And you will have lots of nice Schubert
songs on the agenda for

Your, with kind regards,
J. Brahms

◆●

On the same day Brahms wrote Simrock of his plans to visit Keller: "I am
thinking of traveling to Weesen on Sunday and to return probably on
Wednesday" (11:195). Brahms's modest needs in accommodations are reflected in his observation that a little rented room in the local convent
would suit him. The lure of a fine Lieder singer surely proved as powerful
as the promise of camaraderie and beautiful scenery.

Brahms's five *Gesänge* for mixed choir, released as Op. 104 in October
1888, were submitted to Simrock on 18 July:

> Together with the proofs [for the *Zigeunerlieder,* Op. 103] I am
> sending you a volume of *Gesänge für gemischten Chor* and want to call
> them Op. 104. . . . Unfortunately, I cannot send parts . . . after much
> correcting they are unusable as engraver's models. The song by

[Klaus] Groth therein [*Im Herbst,* Op. 104 No. 5] may *not* be "engraved out" in score and parts—with it one can easily and simply omit the second stanza. The choral pieces are for four, five, and six voices. It seems practical to me if the first and second alto and the first and second bass were put together in the same parts, thus only four parts to be engraved!? (11:192)

Although these five choral songs had already undergone revisions sufficient to render the manuscript parts unusable by the engraver, the process of refinement was not yet at an end. Three days after sending the songs to Simrock, Brahms again wrote his publisher, enclosing a revision for *Im Herbst:* "In the last choral song (Kl. Groth) I ask that the 7th, 8th, and 9th bars before the end be glued over with the little slip of paper!" (11:193). The engraver's model for this piece is not extant, but comparison of an earlier version in A minor/major, dating from the summer of 1886 and preserved in two manuscript copies,[5] with the published version in C minor/major suggests the nature of this revision:

Version of 1886

Version of 1888

(The earlier and final versions differ significantly in other passages as well: Brahms altered details of rhythm, text underlay, and voice leading in bars 6–8 and 11–15 [bars 25–27 and 30–34] and completely recast bars 44–48 and 55–58.)[6]

Brahms's next letter to Keller also speaks of compositional revisions in one of the choral *Gesänge*.

◆ 41

JOHANNES BRAHMS TO ROBERT KELLER   Thun, 7 September 1888
(Library of Congress)

{Postcard addressed to: Herrn *Robert Keller. Pension Mariahalden. Weesen (St. Gallen).*}

Lieber Hr. K. Die Correktur [for Op. 104] geht Heute noch ab, kann also das freundliche liebe *Weesen* noch grüßen. Blieben Sie nur einige Tage länger so würde ich auf der Heimreise aussteigen!
2 schlimmere Correkturen kommen vor, die aber sehr nöthig sind. Geht das auf S. 16 [Op. 104 No. 3, bars 27–28] ohne Neustich? Doch wohl? Vater *Köckert* hat mir (wohl aus Zartheit) nichts von der Verlobung gesagt, so weiß ich nichts als Ihre kurze harte Notiz. Sie Unglücklicher! Nun seien Sie aber schönstens gegrüßt u. denken bei der letzten guten Flasche freundlich

Ihres

J. Br.

◆

Dear Herr K.,

   I am returning the proofs [for Op. 104] today; thus they can still pay their respects to friendly, dear Weesen. If only you were staying a few days longer, I would interrupt my trip home!

   There are two corrections of a more serious nature that are, however, very necessary. Can the one on p. 16 [Op. 104 No. 3, bars 27–28] be done without reengraving [the entire page]? Probably yes? Frl. Köckert's father said nothing to me (probably out of delicacy) about the engagement, so I know nothing except what you said in your short, cruel note. You unlucky fellow! But for now, best regards, and when you empty the last good bottle, kindly remember

Your

J. Br.

◆

The poet of *Letztes Glück*, Op. 104 No. 3, was Brahms's future biographer Max Kalbeck. On 15 August Brahms sent Kalbeck an autograph manuscript of his setting that varies in certain details from the published reading (facsimile in Kalbeck, vol. 4, following p. 144), the most important of which is the alteration about which Brahms wrote Keller:

Kalbeck manuscript (August 1888)

Simrock edition (October 1888)

A basic organizational premise in this work is the reassignment of musical material to different voices in different phrases, for instance, the sequences of descending thirds that occur first in parallel thirds in the altos (bars 1–4) and basses (bars 10–13), then in contrary motion in the soprano 1 and bass 2 (bars 19–21) and soprano 2 and bass 2 (bars 31–33), and again in parallel thirds in the altos (bars 41–43). The insertion of an additional measure at bar 27 creates a similar exchange of materials for the lines "lebt das Herz in Frühlingträume" (bars 23–27, soprano 1 and bass 2 in parallel tenths; bars 27–31, tenor and bass 1 in parallel thirds) and "bei den späten Hagerosen" (bars 35–41, soprano 1 and bass 1 in parallel tenths, in stretto with tenor and bass 2 in contrary motion, the contrapuntal intensification preparing for the recapitulation that begins at bar 41).

The reference to the engagement of Fräulein Köckert is somewhat oblique, but it is unlikely that the sixty-year-old Keller held any particular hopes for himself. Brahms was, of course, not unfamiliar with the attraction of young ladies with fine voices. In the early 1860s he had been especially fond of a young Lieder singer in Vienna, Ottilie Hauer, and "would have made a fool of myself, if, as luck would have it, someone [Dr. Edward

Ebner of Budapest] had not snatched her up at Christmas [1863]."[7] In later years he enjoyed "autumn-spring" fascinations for the contraltos Hermine Spies (who openly admitted her own "Johannes-passion")[8] and Alice Barbi. Both eventually married others. To Keller, Brahms suggests solace in wine; he himself was fortunate to be able to express his feelings through songs.

The next communication informed Keller of Brahms's imminent change of address, at the end of his sojourn in Thun.

➤ 42

JOHANNES BRAHMS TO ROBERT KELLER   Thun, 12 September 1888 (Library of Congress)

{Postcard addressed to: Herrn *Robert Keller Pension Mariahalden Weesen am Wallensee* [this address crossed out and changed in an unknown hand to:] *Berlin* [and to the left, added in green ink:] Steglitzerstr. //}

Falls Sie noch dort sein sollten, sagen Sie mir dies noch mit einem Wort (u: auch wie lange) nach *Zürich* bei Capellm. *Hegar.*
   M. Adreße ist alsdann für Corr: *etc.*

	Wien. IV. *Karlsg.* 4
[Added in pencil:]	Ihr eiliger
Ich fahre Uebermorgen	herzlich erg.
früh von Z. ab.	*J. B.*

➤

In case you should still be there, let me know this with just a word (and also how much longer) in care of Capellmeister Hegar in Zurich.
   After this my address for proofs, etc., will be

	Vienna IV, Karlsgasse 4
[Added in pencil:]	In great haste,
I'm leaving Zurich	Yours sincerely,
the morning of the	J. B.
day after tomorrow.	

➤

The proofs that Brahms was expecting were those for the *Lieder,* Opp. 106 and 107; the day before he had written Fritz Simrock from Thun: "Opp. 106 and 107 will not, I hope, come to this place!" (11:198).

The touching openness of Keller's next letter to Brahms suggests that, with the composer's visit to Weesen early in August, the relationship between the two men entered a new phase. The activities described in this letter would take on a special meaning if they occurred in the wake of a disappointment in love.

➼ 43

ROBERT KELLER TO JOHANNES BRAHMS Berlin, 24 September 1888 (Archiv der Gesellschaft der Musikfreunde, Vienna)

Berlin 24 Sept. 88.

Hochverehrter Herr Doctor!

Jetzt, wo ich bestimmt weiß, daß Sie wieder in Wien sind, zögere ich nicht länger Ihnen meinen Dank zu sagen für die beiden freundlichen Karten, welche uns ein nochmaliges Zusammensein mit Ihnen in Aussicht stellten! Es waren ein Paar heitere Tage [crossed out:] in Aussicht [corrected above:] gekommen, [then:] und ich hatte mit Raif und einer uns befreundeten jungen Frau [added:] (Wittwe) [then:] aus Berlin eine Partie ins Lintthal [Linththal] gemacht; das gute Wetter lockte uns höher und höher, und da sich unsere anmuthige Reisegefährtin tapfer und ausdauernd erwies, gingen wir bis zur Clubhütte am Muttensee (2500 Meter). Es war wegen Neuschnee nicht ganz ohne Gefahr, aber wir gingen sehr vorsichtig zu Werke und kamen glücklich mit ihr hinauf. x) [along left margin:] x) Als ausbedungenen Führerlohn bekam jeder einen Kuß. [then:] Die Hütte lag ganz umgeben von Schnee auf einem vegetationslosen Felsplateau an einem zugefrorenen See, umgeben von der denkbar großartigsten Hochalpenscenerie. Wir wären gern mehr als <u>einen</u> Tag oben geblieben, [added:] (das Kochen u. Wirthschaften zu drei war zu amüsant) [then:] aber aufsteigende Nebel drängten zum Abstieg, der auch wieder ganz glücklich von statten ging. In Weesen fand ich Ihre <u>erste</u> Karte, aber leider war meine Reisezeit zu Ende und die <u>zweite</u> musste mir schon nach Berlin nachgeschickt werden. Die Hoffnung auf den nächsten Sommer, indem [*sic*] Sie uns ja einen längeren Besuch zugesagt haben, muß mich trösten. Wir haben noch sehr vergnügte Tage gehabt und die Gesellschft war derart daß es möglich war das ungünstige Wetter zu verschmerzen. Die Zeit ist blitzschnell vergangen und jetzt heißt es wieder 10 Monate ochsen um 2 Monate eigener Freiherr sein zu können. — Ihre Zigeunerlieder [Op. 103] werden [added:] hier [then:] außer v. Fr. Joachim auch v. Frl. Schmidtlein aufgeführt werden; ich glaube, die werden populär. Man kriegt die Dinger nicht aus dem Sinn, die Babette v. Mariahalden konnte sie sogar auswendig u. sagte sie wolle nach Berlin kommen u. sie im Concert singen. Auch die andern Chor= und Solo=Lieder [Opp. 104–7] müssen Ihren Ruhm mehren. „Es hing der Reif" „Meine Lieder" „Auf dem See" [Op. 106 Nos. 3, 4, and 2, respectively] gehen <u>mir</u> besonders <u>tief</u> zu Herzen, für alles andere habe ich enormes Verständniß, nur für den „Salamander" [Op. 107 No. 2] bin ich zu dumm und streiche den Text aus um mich an den Tönen allein zu erfreuen oder umgekehrt.

Nun, hochverehrter Herr Doctor, schließe ich und mache nur noch von der Erlaubniß Gebrauch, Sie an die Sendung <u>Ihrer Photographie</u> erinnern zu dürfen; bitte schreiben Sie auch Ihren Namen darauf! Wenn Sie für das mitfolgende Bild Ihres treuen Verehrers keinen Platz in Ihrem Album finden, so werfern Sie das Scheusal ruhig in die Wolfsschlucht!

Alle durch Ihre Anwesenheit in Weesen Beglückten senden Ihnen freundlichdankbaren Gruß, den herzlichsten aber

Ihr

treuergebener

Robert Keller.

Berlin W. Steglitzerstr. 1.

•◆

Berlin, 24 Sept. 1888

Dear Herr Doctor,

Now that I know for sure that you are back in Vienna, I will not hesitate any longer to thank you for your two kind postcards that held out the prospect to us of another visit from you! We had a couple of clear days, and I went hiking in the Linthtal with Raif and a young lady [added:] (widow) [then:] from Berlin, a mutual friend of ours; the good weather enticed us to climb higher and higher, and since our attractive companion proved to be courageous and an enduring hiker, we went up to the club cabin at Muttensee (2,500 meters). Because of the new snow, it was a little dangerous, but we proceeded very cautiously and got up there without any mishap.[x)] [along left margin:] [x)] Each of us got a kiss, the reward we had agreed on for being her guides. [then:] The cabin, completely surrounded by snow, was situated on a rocky plateau with no vegetation, near a frozen lake, with the most magnificent high-alpine scenery imaginable. We would have liked to have stayed up there longer than *one* day, [added:] (cooking and keeping house *à trois* was a lot of fun) [then:] but rising fog made our descent urgent; it also went quite well. In Weesen I found your *first* card, but unfortunately my holidays had come to an end and the *second* card had to be forwarded to me in Berlin. The prospect of the longer visit that you have promised us for next summer must serve as my consolation. We still had some very enjoyable days, and the company was such that it was possible to put up with the poor weather. The time went by like a flash, and now it is another 10 months of hard work in order to be able to be one's own boss for 2 months. — Your *Zigeunerlieder* [Op. 103] will be performed [added:] here [then:] by Frau Joachim as well as by Fräulein Schmidtlein; I'm sure they will become popular. It is impossible to get them out of one's mind; Babette in Mariahalden even knew them by heart and said she wanted to come to Berlin and sing them in a concert. The other songs for chorus and solo voice [Opp. 104–7] are also bound to add to your reputation. *Es hing der Reif, Meine Lieder, Auf dem See* [Op. 106 Nos. 3, 4, and 2, respectively] touch *me* quite *deeply;* I appreciate all of the others enormously, except that I am too dumb for the *Salamander* [Op. 107 No. 2] and cover the text in order to enjoy the music by itself or vice versa.

Now, dear Herr Doctor, I must close, but may I avail myself of your permission to remind you to send *your photograph;* please sign it, too! If you find no room in your album for the enclosed photograph of your faithful admirer, then don't hesitate to throw the dreadful thing into the abyss.

All who enjoyed your presence in Weesen send you their kind and grateful regards, the most heartfelt ones, however, from

Your

very devoted,

Robert Keller

Berlin W. Steglitzerstrasse 1

◆•

This letter provides a glimpse of the humdrum life of the music teacher and editor. All the more then was involvement in the production of Brahms's new works a bright point in Keller's existence.

Brahms's *Zigeunerlieder* seem to have made an immediate and lasting impression on all strata of singers, as they still do. Frau Amalie Joachim, wife of the famous violinist, was one of the foremost singers of her day; she sang the alto part in the vocal quartet that premiered the *Zigeunerlieder* in Berlin on 31 October 1888.

The poem by Carl Lemcke set by Brahms in *Salamander* reads as follows:

Es saß ein Salamander	A salamander was sitting
Auf einem kühlen Stein,	on a cool stone,
Da warf ein böses Mädchen	when a wicked girl threw
Ins Feuer ihn hinein.	it into the fire.

{131}

Sie meint, er soll verbrennen,	She thought it would burn up,
Ihm ward erst wohl zu Mut,—	but only then did it feel fine—
Wohl wie mir kühlem Teufel	just as fiery love does
Die heiße Liebe tut.	to a cool devil like me.

The humor of the song *Salamander*, which eluded Keller, has been aptly described by Max Friedlaender:

> Brahms intended the song to be sung "with humor" [*Mit Laune*], and whimsically, with exceeding humor, was the little piece composed, which becomes ever more apparent upon closer acquaintance. It begins almost in the student style, like the melody to a drinking song, yet the accompaniment strews supporting figuration at once running and sustaining, which suggests a true concert piece. In the major section it goes on merrily enough: the parodistic movement in thirds at "verbrennen" is mimicked by the piano, and at the end the salamander seems to rush about completely at ease in the hot glow (bar 7 from the end) and lashing its little tail around with pleasure (bar 3 from the end).—Among [other] details, the comfortable modulation into major with the passage "ihm ward erst wohl zu Mut," as also the reinterpretation of the first stanza's minor ritornello at the end [of the song] (likewise into the major), should be mentioned.[9]

The photograph that Keller sent Brahms is unfortunately no longer part of Brahms's estate (Gesellschaft der Musikfreunde and Historisches Museum der Stadt Wien, Vienna).

Brahms acknowledged Keller's letter with a few lines jotted on a postcard.

➥ 44

JOHANNES BRAHMS TO ROBERT KELLER Vienna, circa 4 October 1888 (Library of Congress)

Herzlichen Dank für Bild u. Brief. Das nächste Mal mache ich die Berg=Parthieen [*sic*] mit — das ist einträglicher als Lieder=begleiten!

Bestens

Ihr

J. B.

➥

Many thanks for picture and letter. Next time I will join you on your mountain excursions—that seems more rewarding than accompanying songs!

Best regards,

Yours,

J. B.

The String Sextet, Op. 18, in Keller's "Piano Sonata" Version

In the autumn of 1888 Robert Keller informed Brahms that he had prepared an arrangement of the String Sextet in B♭ Major, Op. 18, as a *Sonata . . . of Medium Difficulty* (*Sonate . . . in mittelschwerer Spielart*) for solo piano. Knowing that Brahms usually did not wish to be sent arrangements of his works by others before they were published (see the exchange concerning Keller's four-hand arrangement of the Third Symphony above), Keller wrote Brahms asking whether he wished to see this adaptation before it was sent to the engraver. In his letter, which is no longer extant, Keller must have suggested that Brahms disliked all arrangements. The composer's response drew the line on this issue quite clearly.

❧ 45

Johannes Brahms to Robert Keller   Vienna, 17 November 1888 (Library of Congress)

{Envelope addressed to: Herrn *Robert Keller. Berlin. W. Steglitzerstrasse* 1.}

Geehrter u. lieber Herr,
Ich habe gegen keinerlei Arrangements etwas einzuwenden, wenn der Titel deutlich ist u. der Name des betr[effenden] Bearbeiters dabeisteht. Ich meine das ist Geschäftssache u. geht mich nichts an. Von Ihrer Arbeit könnte ich höchstens fürchten, daß sie zu pietätvoll, nicht flott u. frei genug ist!
Wie Sie „mittlere Schwierigkeit" fertig gebracht haben bin ich begierig!
Ich weiß nicht ob ich Sie veranlaßen soll mir die S[onata, modeled on the Sextet, Op. 18] vor dem Stich zu senden.

Halten Sie das, bitte, wie es Ihnen angenehm ist.

Was die Leute aber alles wißen! Sie nun: daß d[ie] ich die Arrangements haße. So in Bausch u. Bogen? Das wäre doch wohl nicht grade gescheit?!

Herzlich grüßend

Ihr

J. Br.

•◆

My dear Sir,

I am not opposed to arrangements of any kind, as long as the title makes this clear and the name of the particular arranger is given. I think that is a business matter and no concern of mine.

The greatest fear I could have about your work is that it is too reverent, not lively and free enough!

I am eager to see how you managed to come up with "medium difficulty"!

I do not know whether I should ask you to send me the Sonata [modeled on the String Sextet, Op. 18] before it is engraved.

You decide, please, what you think is best.

Surprising what people know! Now you: that I hate arrangements. As a whole? That wouldn't be very smart of me, would it?!

Kind regards,

Yours,

J. Br.

◆•

Keller took this letter as permission to forward his "Sonata" to Brahms, who promptly looked it over, marked a few questionable passages, and returned it to Keller, offering on a postcard sent separately his regrets for the cursory review.

•◦ 46

JOHANNES BRAHMS TO ROBERT KELLER Vienna, 22 November 1888 (Library of Congress)

{Postcard addressed to: Herrn *Rob: Keller Berlin. W. Steglitzerstrasse* 1.}

Ihre S[onata, modeled on the Sextet, Op. 18] geht mit diesem zurück u. Sie verzeihen wohl wenn ich nicht grade sehr viel u. geduldig micht damit beschäftigen konnte. Einige ?=Notizen können Sie im Nein=Falle leicht auswischen! Den Hauptfehler hat die S[onata] „mittlerer Schwierigkeit" von ihrem Großvater, die zu arge Länge!

Bestens

Ihr *J. B.*

●○

Your Sonata [modeled on the String Sextet, Op. 18] goes back to you with this letter, and you will forgive me, I am sure, for not having been able to expend very much time and patience on it. You can easily erase the few ? signs if you do not agree with them! The Sonata "of medium difficulty" inherited its main defect from its grandfather—its dreadful length!

Best regards,

Yours, J. B.

◇●

Keller's arrangement was published by N. Simrock in 1889. Unfortunately, Brahms's misgivings about how the project would turn out proved to be well founded. For an adaptation touted as a "sonata for piano," Keller's arrangement fell woefully short of Brahms's standards in pianistic writing.

Unbeknownst to Keller, Brahms himself had prepared a solo piano arrangement of the theme-and-variations movement of the Sextet as a birthday present for Clara Schumann in 1860. Unhindered by the goal of writing a piano piece "of medium difficulty," Brahms created a virtuoso work worthy of its new medium that both he and Clara Schumann performed in concert. (Frau Schumann premiered the arrangement in Frankfurt am Main on 31 October 1865,[1] and Brahms performed it on his concert of 20 February 1869 in the Kleine Redoutensaal in Vienna.[2]) The chordal nature of much of the movement facilitates its transformation for solo piano, lessening the problem of translating musical material created for strings into figuration idiomatic for the piano. The shortcomings of Keller's version lie mainly in his inability to convey the grandeur of the original. Compare, for example, his rendition of the varied repetition of the first phrase of the theme with Brahms's:

{137}

Keller:

Brahms:

The problem is compounded in the varied repetition of the second phrase, where Keller's arrangement follows the shift of the melody into a higher octave but neglects to underlay it with an accompanimental pattern of sufficient breadth and depth to achieve the climactic closure present in the Sextet:

Keller:

Brahms:

The other movements of Keller's "sonata" are even less successful. Little attempt has been made to transform the original string writing into pianistic figuration, and in many passages Keller's too literal transcription has resulted in low-register dyads that on the piano only weakly support the material above them. One can easily imagine which passages Brahms tagged with question marks.

A Friendly Invitation

On 28 February 1889, Brahms left Vienna on a trip to Berlin to join the festivities marking the golden jubilee of Joseph Joachim's career as a performer, which was celebrated at the Hochschule on 1 March.[1] Brahms remained in the capital for a week, conducting two Philharmonic concerts; the Brahms works on the first program, presented on 4 March, were the Academic Festival Overture, Op. 80, and the First Piano Concerto, Op. 15, with Hans von Bülow as soloist; the second concert, on 7 March, included these two works as well as the Tragic Overture, Op. 81, and the Violin Concerto, Op. 77, with Adolf Brodsky as soloist.[2] In the midst of these events, Brahms spent an evening with friends and colleagues, to which he invited Robert Keller.

❧ 47

JOHANNES BRAHMS TO ROBERT KELLER   Berlin, 5 March 1889
(Library of Congress)

{Postcard addressed to: Herrn *Robert Keller Berlin W. Steglitzerstrasse* 1. Note: This postcard is written hastily in pencil.}

G. H. Soviel ich weiß u. sagen kann sind wir den Abend hier im ganz gemüthlichen Asc[anischen] Hof! Vielleicht kommen Sie u. Ihre Freundin auch?

Bestens
Ihr
J. Br.

❧

Dear Sir,

As far as I know and can say, we will be spending the evening in the rather pleasant Ascanischer Hof! Perhaps you and your lady friend will come too?

My best,
Yours,
J. Br.

❧

The Ascanischer Hof, located on the Ascanischer Platz (just outside the Anhaltische Tor and across from the Anhalter Bahnhof), would have been a natural postconcert gathering place, situated as it was in the neighborhood of the old building of the Berlin Philharmonic Orchestra. (The hotel was destroyed during World War II.)

The *Fest- und Gedenksprüche,* Op. 109

During the spring of 1889, while residing in Bad Ischl, Brahms completed his *Fest- und Gedenksprüche* for eight-voice choir, a cappella, Op. 109—three polychoral settings of biblical texts selected and organized by the composer. Work on these compositions may have taken place as early as the winter of 1888.[1] By 26 April 1889 Brahms was able to send a manuscript of the pieces to his good friend Theodor Billroth on the occasion of the surgeon's sixtieth birthday (Billroth, 444).

The impetus for the composition of these pieces "steeped in solemn joy and radiant serenity, . . . the ideal prologue for any ceremony,"[2] may have been the deaths of Kaisers Wilhelm I and Friedrich III and the crowning of Kaiser Wilhelm II, all in 1888. As Brahms wrote Hans von Bülow, the pieces (originally entitled *Deutsche Fest- und Gedenksprüche*) were "meant for national festival and memorial days" and were suitable for "Leipzig Day, Sedan Day, and the Coronation of the Kaiser."[3]

Yet the premiere of Op. 109 took place, not on the occasion of a national event, but in conjunction with a long-overdue honor conferred on its composer. On 23 May 1889 Brahms received a telegram from Carl Petersen, the burgomaster of Hamburg, informing him that he was to be granted the Honorary Freedom of Hamburg.[4] Working behind the scenes to arrange this special privilege had been Hans von Bülow, who had moved from Meiningen to Hamburg in 1886. Bülow's aim was, in some part, to right the wrong done to Brahms in the 1860s when he had been passed over twice for the position of music director of the Philharmonic Orchestra in his native city. In appreciation for this belated honor, Brahms entrusted the first performance of the *Fest- und Gedenksprüche* to the Hamburg Cäcilien-Verein, a choral society of approximately 350 singers. The premiere took place on 9 September during the Hamburg Commercial and Industrial Exhibition. Five days later Brahms was formally presented his diploma of honorary citizenship. When the pieces were published in February 1890, Brahms dedicated them to Burgomaster Petersen.[5]

The autograph manuscript of the *Fest- und Gedenksprüche* (Gesellschaft der Musikfreunde, Vienna) reveals numerous revisions and variants from the published reading. Twice in June 1889, first on the eleventh and again on the thirteenth, Brahms sent lists of revisions to Fritz Simrock (11:222, 223); moreover, after the Hamburg premiere, and in anticipation of a second performance, under Franz Wüllner in Cologne in December, Brahms revised the pieces once more (15:161), sending a set of corrected parts to Simrock on 4 November (12:10). On a single sheet of music paper (Gesellschaft der Musikfreunde, Vienna; A 120), using the space left empty after he had entered a draft for the texts of the three Motets, Op. 110, Brahms tabulated a series of revisions for the *Fest- und Gedenksprüche*. Study of this manuscript (hereafter the "Vienna list") in comparison with the following list of revisions prepared for Keller allows a reconstruction of the stages of revision (see also plate 7).

•• 48

JOHANNES BRAHMS TO ROBERT KELLER   Bad Ischl, circa 13 June 1889 (Library of Congress)

{Note: This letter is written on a piece of music paper cut from the corner of a larger sheet.}

Hrn. <u>Rob. Keller</u> [underlined in blue crayon]
   zu freundlicher Beachtung u. mit herzlichen Grüßen an ihn, s. Z. auch an das u. die lieblichen Wesen, die leider dies Jahr nicht zu sehen kriegt
sein

[added in blue crayon:]   herzl. ergebener
   <u>verte</u>   *J. B.*

[on the reverse side:]

[in blue crayon:]

N. II   verte ⟶

[then in ink:]

in   vor dem Schluß:

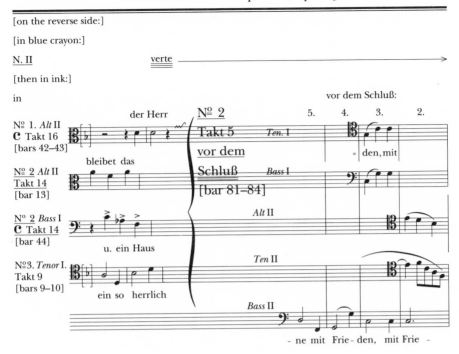

Herr *Rob. Keller* [underlined in blue crayon]

for his kind attention, and with fond greetings to him and in due course also to that and those lovely *Wesen* whom this year, unfortunately, the undersigned will not be able to see.

Yours sincerely,
J. B.

[added in blue crayon:]
verte

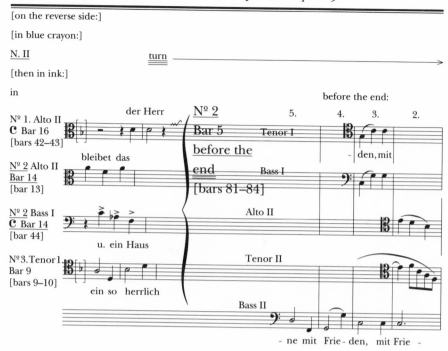

On the Vienna list, the revisions communicated here to Keller appear together, squeezed into the bottom right-hand corner of the recto page and continued onto the verso (hereafter the "second group"). On the recto page, to the left of the second group, is another series of revisions (hereafter, the "first group"),[6] and on the verso page, below the second group, are a series of sketches for additional revisions (hereafter the "third group"), some of which Brahms did not adopt for the published reading.[7] It is likely that the revisions in the first group are the ones that Brahms sent Simrock on 11 June, those in the second group the corrections forwarded on 13 June, and those in the third group the alterations that Brahms considered making after the Hamburg performance.

The Final Correspondence

An exchange of letters between Brahms and Keller, perhaps the final one, took place late in May 1890. Only the envelope is extant for the letter from Brahms that initiated the exchange:

➜ 49

JOHANNES BRAHMS TO ROBERT KELLER   Bad Ischl, 25 May 1890 (Library of Congress)

{Envelope addressed to: Herr *Robert Keller* pr. Adr. *N. Simrock Berlin W.* Friedrichstraße 171; to the left, in an unidentified hand: Brahms}

➜

Keller's reply reveals that Brahms had written kind words concerning his arrangement of the First Symphony for two pianos. As we have seen, Brahms never thought highly of Keller's keyboard transcriptions. With the two-piano versions of the First and Second Symphonies, however, he was pleased, as he informed Fritz Simrock as well (12:23–25; cited in the introduction). At last Keller received from Brahms the approbation he had so long been denied.

Writing during the early phase of a progressive illness to which he would succumb in June 1891, Keller is wistfully retrospective, as he recalls the happy summer days he had spent at Weesen three years before.

➜ 50

ROBERT KELLER TO JOHANNES BRAHMS   Berlin, 30 May 1890 (Archiv der Gesellschaft der Musikfreunde, Vienna)

Berlin 30. May 1890.

Hochgeehrter Herr Doctor!

Sie haben mir eine sehr große Freude gemacht durch Ihre gütige Zuschrift und das darin enthaltene günstige Urtheil über meine Arbeit und ich weiß nicht, wie ich meinem Danke dafür Ausdruck geben soll. Es kommt mancherlei zusammen. Ich bin im Winter gefallen und habe mir die linke Hand verstaucht. Dann stellte sich ein Kopfschmerz ein und ich glaubte, der sei eine Folge des Falles. Mein eigener und Herrn *Simrocks* Arzt versichern jedoch, der Fall könne es nicht bewirkt haben, der Schmerz sei rheumatischer oder nervöser Natur, ein „Ausspannen" werde mich kuriren. So muß ich denn, da ich jetzt noch nicht fort kann, alle möglichen Hülfsmittel anwenden; Cigarren u. Bier soll ich meiden, geistige Thätigkeit auf ein *minimum* beschränken, heftigere Anfälle durch Phenacetin beschwichtigen und viel spaziren gehen. Dadurch ist meine Stimmung sehr gedrückt und Ihr Brief fiel wie ein Lichtstrahl auf mich. Ihre Freundlichkeit war eine wahre Arzenei für meinen armen Kopf, ich hatte mich vor Ihrem Urtheil gefürchtet und nun fiel es so gut aus. Nun bin ich für die 2te Symphonie nicht mehr bange, denn sie ist nach gleichen Grundsätzen gearbeitet, und ich will mit der Abschrift eilen (wenn die Schonzeit vorüber ist, die mir der Arzt verschrieben hat) so viel als möglich.

Daß Ihnen, Herr Doctor, die paar Tage von Weesen noch in freundlicher Erinnerung sind, macht mich ganz stolz und glücklich. Im vorigen Sommer konnte ich nicht hin, aber diesen Sommer wird es durch Ihre beiden Symphonien möglich werden. Ob es aber so schön wird ist zu bezweifeln: Sie und Ihre Lieder, Ihre Begleitung und Frl. Köckerts Gesang, wo sind sie? Sie weilen in Ischl, von wo aus Weesen doch etwas mehr als ein Ausflug ist u. Frl. K. schwingt als Frau v. Hessert den Kochlöffel und wartet ihr kleines Mädchen. Aber die alten Berge stehen noch und der grüne See ist nicht ausgetrocknet.

Ein Paar Wochen Geduld muß ich also wegen der 2ten Symph. noch von Ihnen erbitten, die Sie mir wohl gern gewähren und so empfehle ich mich denn auch ferner Ihrem Wohlwollen als ein begeisterter Apostel Ihres Evangeliums u. mit hochachtungsvollstem Gruße,

Ihr

dankbarer
Robert Keller.
(*Berlin W. Steglitzer Str.* 1.)

Berlin, 30 May 1890

Dear Herr Doctor,

Your kind letter containing your favorable opinion of my work has made me extremely happy, and I do not know how I shall express my gratitude. Much has happened. Last winter I fell and sprained my left hand. After that a headache set in, and I thought it might be a result of the fall. My own and also Herr Simrock's doctor assured me, though, that the fall did not cause it, that the pain is rheumatic and neuralgic in origin, and that "a good rest" will cure me. Thus, since I cannot leave here yet, I have to apply all sorts of remedies; I am to avoid cigars and beer, reduce intellectual activity to a minimum, treat severe attacks with phenacitin, and take many walks. As a result, I am feeling quite depressed, and *your letter* brought a ray of sunshine into my life. Your kindness was a real tonic for my poor head; I had been afraid of your verdict, and now it has turned out so well. Now I don't have to worry about the Second Symphony any longer, since it has been arranged according to the same principles, and I will hurry with the copy as much as possible (once the rest period prescribed by my doctor is over).

It makes me proud and happy that you, Herr Doctor, still have such fond memories of the few days you spent in Weesen. Last summer I could not go there, but this summer your two symphonies will make it possible. I doubt, though, that it will be as nice; you and your songs, your accompanying and Frl. Köckert's singing, where are they? *You* are staying in Ischl, which is more than a day trip away from Weesen, and Frl. Köckert is wielding the ladle as Frau von Hessert and looking after her little girl. But the old mountains are still there and the green lake has not dried up.

For the Second Symphony I will have to ask your patience for a few more weeks, which you will be glad to grant me, I'm sure, and thus I will take my leave of your goodwill, as an enthusiastic apostle of your gospel and with respectful greetings,

Your

grateful,

Robert Keller

(Berlin W., Steglitzer Strasse 1)

◆●

Keller's arrangements of the two symphonies were released in the autumn of 1890. During the winter months he supervised the publication of Brahms's revised version of the B Major Piano Trio, Op. 8, and the G Major String Quintet, Op. 111, which were released in February 1891; he also prepared a four-hand transcription of the Trio that was issued early in the spring. These were to be the final services rendered by Robert Keller to his revered Brahms.

Appendixes

Two Inventories
of the Brahms-Keller
Correspondence

The collection of Brahms-Keller letters in the Library of Congress is accompanied by two inventories, one listing thirty-five items, ranging in date from 28 September 1877 to 25 May 1890, the other listing thirty-one items, from 28 September 1877 to 23 April 1888 (a second page for this inventory is apparently missing). All of the items listed on the two inventories are extant in the collection. Judging from the handwriting, both inventories were prepared by the same, unidentified person, the first as a rough draft, the second as a fair copy.

The inventories attempt to place the Brahms-Keller letters in a chronological sequence, a process begun by Keller himself when he entered on each of the letters from Brahms (and one of the letters from Simrock) a complex cataloging number. (That Keller was responsible for this numbering system is confirmed by his signature after the number on item 6 and by other comments in his hand entered on the letters in conjunction with these numbers.) For items 1–29 Keller's *sigla* consist of an original number and a revised number; starting with item 32, only the revised numbering system was applied (items 30–31 were not in Keller's possession). In the process of revising his numbering system, Keller changed the sequence of the letters, no doubt to reflect his second thoughts about their chronological order.

The initial Keller numbers consisted of a constant four-digit prefix number (*1412*) plus a variable two-digit suffix number (*1412,19, 1412,20,* etc.; see the table below). When Keller renumbered the letters, he crossed out the original two-digit suffix and replaced it with a new suffix consisting of the letter *B* plus a variable one-or two-digit number. Thus, *1412,19* became *1412,B4, 1412,20* became *1412,B3,* etc. Starting with item 32, Keller added his *B* numbers directly to the constant prefix number—thus *1412,B22* etc. (Keller also assigned complex numbers to the remaining letters to him from Simrock and to the drafts of some of his letters to

Brahms, treating them, however, as adjuncts to the Brahms letters and giving them numbers derived from those on the Brahms letters—thus, *ad 1412,38a,* subsequently changed to *ad 1412,B18a.*)

The earliest letter from Brahms to Keller bears the number *1412,19,* suggesting that eighteen additional pieces of correspondence from Brahms preceded the first extant letter. When Keller revised his *sigla* using *B* numbers, however, he began with *B3,* which allows for only two items before the first extant letter. Also missing is a letter bearing the initial number *1412,32;* this item was already absent from the correspondence when Keller assigned the *B* numbers.

Inventory 1, the rough draft, lists only the autograph letters from Brahms to Keller and assigns them two sets of consecutive numbers, one starting with *14,* the other with *1.* This inventory also cites the *B* portion of Keller's renumbered *sigla* and gives for each letter a short description ("Brief ohne Datum," "Brief mit Couvert," "Postkarte," etc.), the size of the paper on which the letter is written ("8°," etc.), the number of pages, and a brief summary of the letter's contents. Omitted from this inventory are the drafts of letters from Keller to Brahms, the letters from Simrock to Keller, and the two sets of corrections for the Third Symphony.

The person who prepared inventory 1 also entered dates, in pencil, on a number of the letters (for information about specific letters, see appendix B). His inventory contains many revisions, and his final ordering of the letters differs from Keller's.

Inventory 2 lists the drafts of letters from Keller to Brahms, the letters from Simrock to Keller, and the two sets of corrections for the Third Symphony, as well as the letters from Brahms to Keller, and assigns to each a new number ("Meine Nr"). The inventory also gives the Keller number (both original and revised), the place and date of the letter, a short description ("Brief," "Brief m. Umschlag," "Postkarte," etc.), the size ("8°," etc.), and the number of pages.

Table. Various Numberings for the Brahms-Keller Correspondence.

Numbers in Present Volume	Writer	Date	Keller Numbers[a]	Numbers on Inventory 1	Numbers on Inventory 2
1	Brahms	28/9/77	1412,20|B3	14/1	1
2	Keller	27/3/78	GdM		
3	Brahms	ca. 4/4/78	1412,19|B4	15/2	2
4	Brahms	5/2/79	1412,21|B5	16/3	3
5	Brahms	ca. 6/7/79	1412,22|B6	17/4	4
6	Brahms	ca. 23/8/79	1412,24|B8	18/5	5
7	Keller	27/8/79	GdM		
7a	Keller	27/8/79	—	—	6
8	Brahms	ca. 10/9/79	1412,23|B7	—[b]	7
9	Brahms	8/80	1412,28|B9	19/6	8
10	Keller	30/8/80	GdM		
11	Brahms	4/9/80	1412,29|B10	20/7	9
12	Brahms	23/4/82	1412,30|B13	21/8	10
13	Brahms	28/4/82	1412,31|B14	22/9	11
14	Brahms	ca. 12/5/82	1412,27|B11	23/10	13[c]
15	Simrock	14/5/82	1412,25 ad B11	—	12
16	Brahms	24/7/82	1412,26|B12	24/11	14
17	Corr. to Sym. 3	early 6/84	—	—[d]	—
18	Brahms	10/6/84	1412,33|B15	25/12	15
19	Keller	mid-7/84	GdM		
App. D	Corr. to Sym. 3	mid-7/84	—	—	—
20	Brahms	11/9/84	1412,34|B16	26/13	16
21	Brahms	ca. 8/10/84	1412,38|B18	27/14	17
22	Simrock	9–10/10/84	ad 1412,38a B18a	—	18
23	Keller	12/10/84	GdM		
23a	Keller	12/10/84	ad 1412,38b	—	19
24	Brahms	14/10/84	1412,35|B17	29/16[e]	20
25	Brahms	18/10/84	1412,36|B19	30/17	21
26	Brahms	26/10/84	1412,37|B20	31/18	22
27	Keller	23/1/86	GdM		
27a	Keller	23/1/86	ad 1412,39	—	23
28	Brahms	25/1/86	1412,39|B21	32/19	24

Numbers in Present Volume	Writer	Date	Keller Numbers[a]	Numbers on Inventory 1	Numbers on Inventory 2
29	Keller	7/8/86	GdM		
30	Keller	10/8/86	GdM		
31	Brahms	ca. 12/2/87	1412,B22	33/20	25
32	Brahms	1/3/87	1412,B23	34/21	26
33	Foreword, Keller	16/3/87	1412,B24	35/22	27
34	Brahms	24/3/87	1412,B25	36/23	28
35	Brahms	14/4/87	1412,B26	37/24	29
36	Brahms	22/4/88	1412,B27	—[f]	30
37	Keller	23/4/88	ad 1412,B27	—	31
38	Brahms	29/6/88	1412,B28	38/25	—
39	Brahms	4/7/88	1412,B29	39/26	—
40	Brahms	1/8/88	1412,B30	40/27	—
41	Brahms	7/9/88	1412,B31	41/28	—
42	Brahms	12/9/88	1412,B32	42/29	—
43	Keller	24/9/88	GdM		
44	Simrock	ca. 4/10/88	ad 2522	43/30	—
45	Brahms	17/11/88	1412,B33	44/31	—
46	Brahms	22/11/88	1412,B34	45/32	—
47	Brahms	5/3/89	1412,B35	46/33	—
48	Brahms	ca. 13/6/89	—	47/34	—
49	Brahms	25/5/90	—	—/35[g]	—
50	Keller	30/5/90	GdM		

a. GdM indicates that the letter in question is held by the Gesellschaft der Musikfreunde.

b. Item 8 was probably not listed on inventory 1 because only a copy of it, in Keller's hand, is found in the correspondence, the original letter having been given away by Keller in 1887.

c. On inventory 2, the Keller number is 1412,25|B11, but on the letter it is 1412,27|B11.

d. On item 17 is the annotation, in pencil and in an unidentified hand, "zu K.12."

e. Owing to revisions in inventory 1, the number 28/15 was left unassigned.

f. Item 36 is probably not listed on inventory 1 because only a copy of it, in Keller's hand, is found in the correspondence.

g. Item 49 is crossed out on inventory 1. This item is only an envelope; the letter is lost, which is no doubt why it has no Keller number and was not listed on inventory 2.

Dating Brahms's Letters
to Robert Keller

Brahms did not write a date on most of his letters and postcards to Robert Keller. Many of the undated letters survive together with their envelopes; these letters, as well as the postcards, can be assigned dates on the basis of their postmarks. Some of the letters without envelopes were labeled by Keller with the date of receipt; the date of posting would have been one or two days earlier. The person who prepared the two inventories that accompany these letters (hereafter *inventory hand;* see appendix A) also entered dates, in pencil, on a few of the letters. Keller's dates and those of the inventory hand can usually be confirmed by comparison with the correspondence between Brahms and Fritz Simrock.

The basis for dating each of the undated items is described below. References to *Hofmann* are to Renate and Kurt Hofmann, *Johannes Brahms Zeittafel zu Leben und Werk.*

Item 1. Inventory hand, in pencil in upper-right-hand corner of first page: *28. 9. 77.* Based on the correspondence from Brahms to Simrock (19:47–48, 49–50), this date is correct. Brahms was in Lichtenthal bei Baden-Baden 17–30 September 1877 (Hofmann, 136).

Item 3. Postmark on envelope: Berlin, 6 April 1878; delivery date of 7 April stamped on back of envelope. Brahms wrote Keller's name on the envelope but provided no street address; apparently enclosed in a letter to Fritz Simrock (10:70–71) that Max Kalbeck dated [Vienna, 3] April 1878; forwarded by Simrock to Keller. (Kalbeck's editorial dates are based on either the postmark or the date of receipt; he did not differentiate between the two but gave both in brackets; see 9:18, Anmerkung.) According to Hofmann, 140, Brahms was in Vienna 3–4 April 1878. At the end of the letter, entered in pencil by inventory hand: *6. 4. 78,* changed to *Wien | 4. 4. 78.*

Item 4. In Keller's hand: (*Wegen Datum s. transp. Lieder!*) | *Febr. 1879*. ([For the date, see the transposed songs] February 1879); enclosed in letter to Simrock (10:104–5) that Kalbeck dated [Vienna, 5 February 1879].

Item 5. Postmark on envelope: Pörtschach, 6 July 1879; delivery date of 9 July. Although Brahms dated the letter *Juni 79,* the correspondence between Brahms and Simrock demonstrates that it could not have been written until early July 1879.

Item 6. In Keller's hand, in the upper-right-hand corner of the first page: *erhalten 25 August 1879.* | *R Keller.* (received on 25 August 1879. R. Keller); probably posted two days earlier, at which time, according to Hofmann, 146, Brahms was in Pörtschach am Wörthersee.

Item 8. In Keller's hand, in the upper-left-hand corner: *Copie.;* a heading, with the last clause framed in pencil: *Brief v. J. Brahms* | *erh. 12 Sept. 1879, 24/12 87 an Sadi* [or *Ladi*] *geschenkt.* (Letter from J. Brahms, received on 12 Sept. 1879, given to Sadi [or Ladi] on 24 December 1887); probably posted two days earlier, at which time, according to Hofmann, 146, Brahms was in Pörtschach am Wörthersee.

Item 11. Postmark on postcard: Ischl, 4 September 1880; delivery date of 6 September.

Item 12. Postmark on postcard: Wieden-Wien, 23 April 1882; delivery date of 24 April.

Item 13. Postmark on postcard: Wieden-Wien, 28 April 1882; delivery date of 29 April.

Item 14. In Keller's hand, in upper-right-hand corner of first page: *Mai oder Juni 1882;* subsequently, *oder Juni* crossed out in pencil; enclosed in packet sent to Simrock (10:207–8) that Kalbeck dated [Vienna, 12 May 1882]; forwarded by Simrock to Keller on 14 May (see item 15).

Item 16. Postmark on postcard: Ischl, 24 July 1882; delivery date of 27 July; in Keller's hand: *erh. in Weesen Ende Juli 82* (received in Weesen, at the end of July 1882); in an unidentified hand, at the end of the message: *beantw[ortet]* | *26/7* (answered on 26 July).

Item 17. Correction sheet returned to Keller with annotations together with letter of 10 June 1884 (item 18).

Item 18. Postmark on envelope: Wieden-Wien, 10 June 1884; delivery date of 11 June.

Item 20. Postmark on envelope: Mürzzuschlag, 11 September 1884; delivery date of 12 September; in Keller's hand, on last page: *Mürzzuschlag d. 11. 9. 1884.*

Item 21. In Keller's hand, in upper-right-hand corner of first page: *erh. 19 Oktober 1884* (received 19 October 1884); enclosed in letter to Simrock (11:73–74) that Kalbeck dated [Mürzzuschlag, 8 October 1884].

Item 22. In Keller's hand, in upper-left-hand corner of first page: *10 Octbr: 1889*, which probably indicates the date of receipt.

Item 24. Postmark on postcard: Mürzzuschlag, 14 October 1884.

Item 25. Postmark on postcard: Wieden-Wien, 18 October 1884; delivery date of 20 October.

Item 26. Postmark on postcard unclear, but probably: Wieden-Wien, 26 October 1884; delivery date of 29 October; in Keller's hand, in upper-right-hand corner of message side: *erh. 29 Oct. 84.* (received on 29 October 1884).

Item 28. Postmark on envelope: Wieden-Wien, 25 January 1886; delivery date of 26 January; in Keller's hand, in upper-right-hand corner of first page: *erhalten 26 Januar | 1886.* (received on 26 January 1886).

Item 31. In Keller's hand, in upper-right-hand corner of first page: *erh. 14 Februar 1887* (received on 14 February 1887); probably posted two days earlier, at which time, according to Hofmann, 198, Brahms was in Vienna.

Item 32. Postmark on postcard: Wieden-Wien, 1 March 1887; delivery date of 2 March; in Keller's hand, in upper-right-hand corner of address side: *erh. 2 März 1887* (received on 2 March 1887).

Item 33. Postmark on envelope: Wieden-Wien, 16 March 1887; delivery date of 17 March.

Item 34. Postmark on envelope: Wieden-Wien, 24 March 1887; delivery date of 25 March; in Keller's hand, in upper-right-hand corner of first page: *erh. 25. 3. 87.* (received 25 March 1887).

Item 35. Postmark on envelope: Wieden-Wien, 14 April 1887; delivery date of 15 April; in Keller's hand, in upper-right-hand corner of first page: *erh. 15 April 1887. (received on 15 April 1887).*

Item 36. Postmark on postcard and delivery date, as transcribed by Keller: *Wieden in Wien | 22/4 4.N. (88?)* and *35 | 23/4 | VI*, respectively. The year must have been unclear on the original postcard, but the contents place the postcard in the year 1888.

Item 38. Postmark on postcard: Thun, 29 June 1888; delivery date of 1 July.

Item 39. Postmark on postcard: Thun, 4 July 1888; delivery date of 6 July.

Item 40. Postmark on postcard: Thun, 1 August 1888; delivery date of 2 August.

Item 41. Postmark on postcard: Thun, 7 September 1888; delivery date of 8 September.

Item 42. Postmark on postcard: Thun, 12 September 1888; forwarded from Weesen am Wallensee to Berlin on 13 September 1888; delivery date in Berlin of 15 September.

Item 44. In Keller's hand, in upper-right-hand corner: *erh. 6. 10. 88.* (received on 6 October 1888); probably posted two days earlier, at which time, according to Hofmann, 206, Brahms was in Vienna.

Item 45. Postmark on envelope: Wieder-Wien, 17 November 1888; delivery date of 19 November; in Keller's hand, in upper-right-hand corner of first page: *erh. 19. 11. 88. | Poststempel Wien 17. 11.* (received on 19 November 1888, postmark Vienna, 17 November).

Item 46. Postmark on postcard: Wieden-Wien, 22 November 1888; delivery date of 23 November.

Item 47. Postmark on postcard: Berlin, 5 March 1889; delivery date of 5 March.

Item 48. In Keller's hand, in upper-right-hand corner of first page: *erh. 18 Juni | 1889.* (received on 18 June 1889); probably posted several days earlier to Simrock, then forwarded to Keller; possibly the correction sheet sent to Simrock on 13 June (see commentary); at that time, according to Hofmann, 208, Brahms was in Bad Ischl.

Item 49. Postmark on envelope: Ischl, 25 May 1890; delivery date of 27 May.

APPENDIX C

Paper Information

Item	Date	Structure	Measurements[a]	Watermarks[b]
1	28/9/77	1 bifolio	21.4 × 27.5	C/L
2	27/3/78	1 bifolio	28.7 × 45.1	None
3	ca. 4/4/78	1 bifolio	15.5 × 19.5	C/L
		Envelope	8.1 × 10.4	None[c]
4	ca. 5/2/79	1 bifolio	14.2 × 22.0	C/L
5	6/7/79	1 bifolio	17.7 × 22.0	C/L
		Envelope	9.2 × 12.0	None
6	ca. 23/8/79	1 bifolio	17.7 × 22.0	C/L
		Envelope	9.2 × 12.0	None
7	27/8/79	Gathering of 2 bifolios	22.5 × 28.7	None
7a	27/8/79	1 sheet	22.1 × 14.0	None
8	ca. 10/9/79	1 sheet	14.0 × 16.6	None
9	8/80	1 bifolio	20.3 × 25.0	C/L
10	30/8/80	1 bifolio	20.1 × 25.4	C/L
11	4/9/80	Postcard	8.3 × 14	None
12	23/4/82	Postcard	8.3 × 14	None
13	28/4/82	Postcard	8.3 × 14	None
14	ca. 12/5/82	1 bifolio	21.5 × 26.9	C/L
15	14/5/82	1 sheet	21.8 × 13.8	None[d]
16	24/7/82	Postcard	8.3 × 14.1	None
17	Corr. sheet for Sym. 3, Op. 90, early June 84	1 sheet, music paper[e]	Irregular edges, ca. 14.5 × 12	None
18	10/6/84	1 bifolio	13.3 × 16.7	C/L
		Envelope	10.5 × 13.4	None
19	Mid-July 84	1 bifolio	22.0 × 29.4	C/L
App. D	Corr. sheets for Sym. 3, Op. 90, mid-July 84	Gathering of 4 bifolios + gathering of 2 bifolios + 1 bifolio	22.0 × 28.4	C/L

Item	Date	Structure	Measurements[a]	Watermarks[b]
20	11/9/84	1 bifolio (now 2 sheets)	17.7 × 22.7	C/L
		Envelope	12.5 × 15.6	None
21	ca. 8/10/84	1 bifolio	18.7 × 22.8	C/L
		Envelope	9.4 × 12.2	None
22	9 or 10/10/84	1 sheet (upper half of larger sheet)	14.3 × 22.0	C/L
23	12/10/84	1 bifolio	22.0 × 28.5	C/L
23a	12/10/84	1 sheet (right half of larger sheet)	22.1 × 14.2	None
24	14/10/84	Postcard	8.3 × 14.0	None
25	18/10/84	Postcard	8.4 × 14.0	None
26	26/10/84	Postcard	8.3 × 14.0	None
27	23/1/86	1 bifolio	22.0 × 28.4	C/L
27a	23/1/86	1 sheet	22.9 × 14.5	None[f]
28	25/1/86	1 bifolio	17.5 × 22.0	C/L
29	7/8/86	Postcard	9.5 × 14.3	C/L
30	10/8/86	Postcard	9.5 × 14.4	C/L
31	ca. 12/2/87	1 bifolio	21.8 × 28.3	C/L[g]
32	1/3/87	Postcard	8.5 × 14.0	None
33	Foreword to 1887 *Brahms Verzeichniss*, 16/3/87	1 bifolio	21.9 × 28.2	C/L
		Envelope	12.5 × 15.5	None
34	24/3/87	1 bifolio	17.0 × 26.0	MARY MILL | IVORY PAPER
		Envelope	9.3 × 14.2	Ditto
35	14/4/87	1 bifolio	21.9 × 28.4	C/L[g]
		Envelope	12.5 × 15.5	
36	22/4/88	1 sheet	Irregular, 12.5 × 11.3	Crown over (i.e., super-imposed A, S, H)
37	23/4/88	1 sheet	16.5 × 10.6	None
38	29/6/88	Postcard	9.3 × 14.2	None
39	4/7/88	1 bifolio	16.4 × 21.5	None[h]

Item	Date	Structure	Measurements[a]	Watermarks[b]
		Envelope	9.5 × 12.0	None
40	1/8/88	Postcard	9.3 × 14.3	None
41	7/9/88	Postcard	9.4 × 14.3	None
42	12/9/88	Postcard	9.4 × 14.3	None
43	24/9/88	1 bifolio	20.7 × 26.1	None[i]
44	ca. 4/10/88	1 sheet	14.1 × 22.2	Graph grid, .45 cm. squares
45	17/11/88	1 bifolio	20.6 × 26.5	ABBAYE MILL ǀ CREAM LAID ǀ (i.e., overlapped O B C)
		Envelope	11.1 × 14.9	None[j]
46	22/11/88	Postcard	8.4 × 14.0	None
47	5/3/89	Postcard	9.1 × 14.0	None
48	ca. 13/6/89	1 sheet, music paper[k]	Irregular, 12.5 × 18.3	None
49	25/5/90	Envelope	8.9 × 15.5	None[l]
50	30/5/90	1 bifolio	22.1 × 28.3	C/L

a. Measurement for *height* × *width* of sheet or of the bifolio laid open in centimeters.

b. The abbreviation *C/L* indicates that no watermark is present, only chain and laid lines.

c. Embossed on reverse, bottom right: THEYER & HARDTMUTH WIEN.

d. Printed letterhead: N. SIMROCK ǀ 171. Friedrichstrasse 171. ǀ BERLIN W.

e. Ten light-tan staves; upper-left-hand corner of a sheet of music paper, with most of left margin torn off. Width of staves (in cm.): .65, .65, .65, .65, .6+, .65, .65, .60, .60, incomplete staff; distance between staves (in cm.): .7, .6, .6, .6, .6−, .6+, .6+, .6, .7; upper margin: 2.6 cm.

f. On reverse side, the bottom portion of a printed advertisement for cigars sold by H. W. Rerhausen, Cigarrenhandlung, Berlin W., Potsdamer Straße 106B, on the corner of Steglitzer Straße (i.e., Keller's local tobacco store).

g. Lithographic photograph of *Dr. Hans v. Bülow* (see plate 4).

h. Paper textured with horizontal lines.

i. Graph paper, blue ink, .5 cm. squares.

j. Green-gray color.

k. Five printed black staves, the upper corner of a larger sheet; widths of staves: all .75 cm.; distances between staves: all 1.1 cm.; upper margin: ca 3.5 cm.

l. Blue-green color.

Correction Sheets for the Third Symphony, Op. 90

Robert Keller's *Corrections and Notes* for the first issue of the Third Symphony, sent to Brahms in mid-July 1884, consists of two sections. *Partitur* is devoted to questions and comments about the full score and its variants from the orchestral parts; *Orchesterstimmen* focuses on problems specifically in the parts. While Keller used a dark brown ink for most of the document, he distinguished his queries in the *Partitur* section about problems in the orchestral parts by entering them in magenta ink. To flag certain entries, Keller employed other writing implements, as he explained in his cover letter to Brahms (item 19): blue crayon, for the words *Hauptfehler!* (or the abbreviation *H Fehler!*), *wichtig!* and *sehr wichtig!* after important queries concerning the score, for question marks before or after entries, and to underline the beginnings of certain entries; and red crayon, for marking *X*s in the margin before important queries about the orchestral parts. Brahms responsed in lead pencil, orange and blue crayons, and purple ink.

In the following transcription Keller's queries are given in the left-hand column, Brahms's answers in the right, with indications of how they relate to Keller's text. The portions of the original document written in magenta and purple ink, in blue, red, and orange crayon, and in lead pencil are designated as such. The rest of the text may be assumed to have been written in dark brown ink, with the following exceptions: all the *X*s in the left margin were written in red crayon in the original document, all the question marks in the left margin and all the page numbers in blue crayon. Each entry has been treated as a separate entity; the end of an entry cancels all special designations of ink, pencil, and crayon colors.

Words underscored in the transcription with solid lines were underlined in dark brown ink in the original document; words underscored with broken lines were underlined in blue crayon. Letters representing musical notes have been changed to capitals in the translation, except where a distinction was made in the original between lower case (to indicate a higher register) and capital letters. Those corrections included on the errata list subsequently published by N. Simrock are designated with an asterisk.

(1

Brahms's dritte *Symphonie.*
Correkturen u. Notizen

1. <u>Partitur:</u>

*   p. 1. [changed to:] <u>5</u>: [then:] <u>*Basspos.*</u> Takt 3.   [Lead pencil, above the

♩. ♩. (statt ♩. ♩ 𝄾 𝄾) <u>Stimme</u> richtig.   second musical

[blue crayon, over the last two words:]   example:] N͡B

Hauptfehler!

[Next two entries in magenta ink:]

—   *Viol.* 1. Takt 3 und 5 ist in der Stimme über   [Lead pencil, "Punkt"

dem letzten Achtel ein Punkt. Dies und   underlined, and in the

manches andre auf Stricharten bezügl. ist   left margin:] weg!

wahrscheinlich von einem Orchester-

spieler in die Stimme hineincorrigirt,

welche als Vorlage f. d. Stich gedient hat.

—   *Violoncell.* In der Stimme steht auf dem 1<u>sten</u>   [Lead pencil, "*sf*"

Viertel jedes Taktes [bars 3ff.] ein *sf*.   underlined, and at the

     end:] weg!

—   *Contrabass* ⎫ Takt 3: *f sf* (*f* fehlt)
       Contrafagott ⎭

X   p. 2. [changed to:] <u>6</u>: [and underlined twice in   [Lead pencil, inserted

red crayon; then:] *F-Hörner* sind Takt 4   after "—":] besser Pag. 6.

[bar 10] anders als pag. 29 [bar 131] —

[blue crayon, over —:]? [then:] Die 1/4

Pause braucht nur einmal in der Mitte des

Systems zu stehen.

Bratsche Takt 5 [bar 11] fehlt > über der   [Lead pencil, at the end

1<u>sten</u> halben Note.   of the entry:] (>)

Brahms's Third Symphony
Corrections and Notes

---

1. Score

* p. 1 [changed to:] 5: [then:] *Bass trombone*, bar 3: [Lead pencil, above the second musical example:] N͟B

♩. ♩ (instead of ♩. ♩ 𝄽 𝄾). The *part* is correct. [blue crayon, over the final two words:] Major error!

[Next two entries in magenta ink:]

— Violin I, bars 3 and 5: There is a dot over the final eighth note in the part. This and many other markings concerning bowing were apparently entered by an orchestra player into the part that served as the model for the engraving. [Lead pencil, "dot" underlined, and in the left margin:] out!

— Violoncello: In the part there is a *sf* over the 1st quarter note of each bar [bars 3ff.] [Lead pencil, "*sf*" underlined, and at the end:] out!

— Contrabass ⎫ Bar 3: *f sf* (*f* is missing.)
  Contrabassoon ⎭

X p. 2 [changed to:] *6*: [and underlined twice in red crayon; then:] *Horns in F,* bar 4 [bar 10], are *different* than on page 29 [bar 131].—[blue crayon, over —:]? [then:] The 1/4 rest only needs to be employed once, in the middle of the staff. [Lead pencil, inserted after "—":] better on page 6.

Viola, bar 5 [bar 11] is missing a > over the 1st half note. [Lead pencil, at the end of the entry:] (>)

p. 3. [changed to:] 7: [then:] <u>*Clar.*</u> letzter Takt
[bar 18] Punkt fehlt über dem 1/4 $\frac{g}{e}$)

<u>*Tromp.*</u> Takt 1 [bar 13]. " " " " [i.e., Punkt
fehlt über dem] ersten Viertel.

X   [Blue crayon:] ? [dark brown ink:]
<u>*Violine*</u> II. In der Stimme heißt Takt 1 und
2 [bars 13 and 14] so:

Was soll gelten? [blue crayon:] Part[itur].

X p. 8. [Magenta ink:] <u>*Contrafagott*</u> Takt 3 [bar 21]
in der Stimme steht *sf* unter dem 4$\underline{^{tel}}$ *a.*
[blue crayon:]   ♫

X   [Magenta ink:] <u>*Viol.*</u> I. II. In den Stimmen
[bars 19ff.] geht der Bogen immer nur bis
ans 6$\underline{^{te}}$ Triolen=Achtel! [blue crayon:]?

p. 9. <u>Takt</u> 4 [bar 27] fehlt *p* zu *Flöte* II.

X   [Magenta ink:] <u>*Bratschen*</u>stimme Beide
Bogen [bars 27, 28] nur bis ans letzte
Achtel. [blue crayon:]?

p. 10. <u>*C-Horn*</u> II Takt 3 [bar 31] fehlt Taktpause.

{
<u>*Viol.*</u> I vorletzter Takt [bar 33]   —◁ zu kurz, vom ersten ♩ ab.

"   II   "   "   "   "   *a.*   "

<u>*Bratsche*</u>   "   "   "   "   *a.*   "
}

<u>*Viol.*</u> II, *Br.* und *Vcell* Takt 3. 4 [bars 31, 32]
fehlt der Bogen wie bei *Viol.* I., in den
Stimmen steht er jedoch.

p. 3   [changed to:] 7: [then:] *Clarinet,* final bar
[bar 18]: Dot is missing over the 1/4 note $\substack{C \\ E}$).

Trumpet, bar 1 [bar 13]: " " " [i.e., Dot
is missing over the] first quarter note.

X   [Blue crayon:] ? [dark brown ink:] *Violin II:*
In the part bars 1 and 2 [bars 13 and 14]

read like this:

Which do you want? [blue crayon:] Score

X p. 8   [Magenta ink:] *Contrabassoon,* bar 3 [bar
21], in the part there is a *sf* below the
quarter note A. [blue crayon:]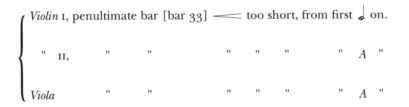

X   [Magenta ink:] *Violin I, II:* In the parts [bars
19ff.] the slurs always extend only to the
6th eighth note of the triplet! [blue
crayon:] ?

p. 9   *Bar 4* [bar 27]: *p* is missing in Flute II.

X   [Magenta ink:] *Viola* part: Both slurs [bars
27, 28] extend only to the final eighth note.
[blue crayon:] ?

p. 10   *Horn in C II,* bar 3 [bar 31]: A whole rest is missing.

⎧   *Violin I,* penultimate bar [bar 33] ──◁ too short, from first ♩ on.
⎨   " II,   "   "   "   "   "   " A "
⎩   *Viola*   "   "   "   "   "   " A "

Violin II, Viola, Violoncello, bar 3, 4 [bars
31, 32]: The slur, as in the Violin I, is
missing, though present in the parts.

Vcell. Takt 3 [bar 31] fehlt <u>*arco.*</u> [blue crayon:] Hauptfehler!

Vcell. u. *CBass* fehlt Takt 2 [bar 30] der Punkt hinter der 1/2 Pause.

X   *Viol.* I. u. II [magenta ink:] ist in den Stimmen  und [bars 33–34] gebunden [blue crayon:] ?   [Blue crayon, ties crossed out and marked:] del

p. 13.[Magenta ink:] *Viol.* I. II. in den Stimmen Takt 1 [bar 44]: *p marc*

[Magenta ink:] *Viol.* II. und *Vcell:* Takt 3 [bar 46] in den Stimmen ⟩⟩⟩   [Blue crayon, ⟩⟩⟩ crossed out and marked:] del

Vcell: 1stes Viertel ▤ noch nicht gestielt:

p. 14. ⎫ [Magenta ink:] *Bratschenstimme* [bars 53–   [Blue crayon, dynamics
15. ⎭ 55]: [Dark brown ink:] hat Schweller: crossed out and marked:] del

 und

[dynamics in both magenta and dark brown ink]

p. 14.im *Clarinetten* System [bar 51] müßte vorn <u>in *B*.</u> stehen.

Vcell Takt 3 [bar 50]:

2)

p. 15.*Hoboe* II [inserted:] Schreibart [then:]   [Blue crayon, at the end besser so [bars 54–55]:   of the entry:] NB [underlining also by (als *p·* u. *p·*)   Brahms?]

Violoncello, bar 3 [bar 31]: *arco* is missing.
[blue crayon:] Major error!

Violoncello and Contrabass, bar 2 [bar 30]:
Dot is missing after the 1/2 rest.

X	Violin I and II [magenta ink:] There are ties in the parts, 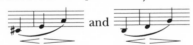 and ⬚. [blue crayon:] ?	[Blue crayon, ties crossed out and marked:] delete

p. 13 [Magenta ink:] Violin I, II, in the parts, bar
   1 [bar 44]: *p marc.*

[Magenta ink:] Violin II and Violoncello,
bar 3 [bar 46]: ═════ in the parts. | [Blue crayon, ═════ crossed out and marked:] delete

Violoncello: 1st quarter note ▤ , i.e., *not
yet divisi*

| p. 14 ⎫ 15 ⎭ | [Magenta ink:] Viola part [bars 53–55]: [Dark brown ink:] has the dynamics:  and ⬚ [dynamics in both magenta and dark brown ink] | [Blue crayon, dynamics crossed out and marked:] delete |

p. 14 Clarinet staff [bar 51] must have *"in B."*

Violoncello, bar 3 [bar 50]: ⬚

2)

p. 15 Oboe II [inserted:] Notation [then:]
   better like this [bars 54–55]:
   ⬚ (*than as* ♩·
   and ♩·) | [Blue crayon, at the end of the entry:] NB [underlining also by Brahms?]

Cl. 1 Takt 3. [bar 56] ♮ 𝄾

Viol. 11 Takt 3. [bar 56] ♮ vor dem 2ᵗᵉⁿ *g* u. *f*

𝄾.

*X   " [i.e., Violin 11] Takt 5 [bar 58] fehlt

d ⸻ im letzten Viertel.

*   *Contrabass*
Takt 2. 3 [bars 55, 56] ⸻
(*p* fehlt, *d* st[att] des 2ᵗᵉⁿ *h*) [blue crayon:]
Hauptfehler!

X	p. 16.[Magenta ink:] *Viol.* 1 letzter Takt [bar 63] in der Stimme ⌒ über alle 9 Noten.	[Blue crayon, at the end of the entry:] falsch!
X	17.[Magenta ink:] " [i.e., Viol. 1] letzte Note [bar 67] ⸻ steht in der Stimme *mf* [blue crayon:]?	[Blue crayon, "*mf*" crossed out and marked:] del.
X	[Magenta ink:] *Viol.* 11 Takt 1 [bar 64]: Stimme 2 Bogen erst 9 dann 6 Achtel [blue crayon:]?	[Blue crayon, "2" changed to:] 1.
	p. 18.Takt 1 [bar 68] fehlt der Punkt über dem letzten Viertel bei allen Holzbläsern.	
	Takt 2 [bar 69] fehlt beim Eintritt der *Tromp.* das *f*.	
*	*Viol.* 11 muß das letzte Viertel im vorletzten Takt [bar 71] ⸻ *e* statt *fis* heißen.	
X	[Magenta ink:] " [i.e., Viol. 11] Stimme wieder 2 Bogen bei den Triolen [bar 69] [blue crayon:]? Hauptfehler!	[Blue crayon, "2" changed to:] 1

Clarinet I, bar 3 [bar 56]: ♮ 𝄾

Violin II, bar 3 [bar 56]: ♮ before the 2d *G*

and *F* 𝄾

*X   " [i.e., Violin II], *bar 5* [bar 58]: *D* ⸻ *is missing* in the final quarter beat.

*   Contrabass, *bar 2, 3* [bar 55, 56] ⸻

(*p* is missing, *D* instead of the 2d *B*) [blue crayon:] Major error!

X p. 16 [Magenta ink:] Violin I, final bar [bar 63]: In the part ⸻ over all 9 notes.   [Blue crayon, at the end of the entry:] wrong!

X   17 [Magenta ink:] " [i.e., Violin I]: Last note [bar 67] ⸻ has *mf* in the part. [blue crayon:] ?   [Blue crayon, "*mf*" crossed out and marked:] delete

X   [Magenta ink:] Violin II, bar 1 [bar 64]: Part has 2 slurs, the first for 9 eighth notes, the second for 6. [blue crayon:] ?   [Blue crayon, "2" changed to:] 1

p. 18 Bar 1 [bar 68]: Dot is missing over the final quarter note for all *woodwinds.*

Bar 2 [bar 69]: The *f* is missing at the entrance of the Trumpet.

*   *Violin II:* The final quarter note in the penultimate bar [bar 71] must read ⸻ *E* instead of *F♯*.

X   [Magenta ink:] " [i.e., Violin II]: The part again has 2 slurs at the triplets [bar 69]. [blue crayon:] Major error!   [Blue crayon, "2" changed to:] 1

Bratsche vorletzter Takt [bar 71] fehlt ♮ vor
♩ [blue crayon:] !! Hauptfehler!

*   p. 19._Flöten_ letzter Takt [bar 76] 2tes Viertel: ♯♩
doppelt _dis_. (II _Fl. h_ ganz falsch!) [blue
crayon:] Hauptfehler!

*X ??   Alle 4 _Hörner_ Takt 1 [bar 71b] soll wohl   [Blue crayon, in the left
das 3te u. 4te Viertel _stacc_., nicht ⌒   margin:] _ja_ [⌒
sein? [magenta ink:] Stimmen sind wie   crossed out, and in the
Partitur. [blue crayon:] ??   right margin:] !!
[underlining of "3te u. 4te
Viertel _stacc_." also by
Brahms?]

*   _Bratsche_ vorletztes Viertel [bar 76]
_g_ st. _h_! [blue crayon:] Hauptfehler!

Vcell. u. _CB_ Takt 4 [bar 74] fehlt der Punkt
über dem 5ten Viertel.

_CB_. [bar 71] _più_ (Accent über u fehlt)

p. 20._Viol_ I. Takt _1 [bar 77]: divisi_ u. deshalb
noch einmal ♯ vor _d_:

X   [Magenta ink:] _Viol_. I., II., _Br_. u. _Vc_. steht
im letzten Takt [bar 81] in den Stimmen
ben marc.

X   [Magenta ink:] _CB_.=Stimme im Anfang   [Blue crayon, "_mf_"
[bar 77] _mf_ st. _f_ [blue crayon:] ?   crossed out]

p. 22._Viol_. I Takt 4 [bar 90]: fehlt
Punkt über dem 2ten Achtel.

Viola, penultimate bar [bar 71]: ♮ is missing before ♪ [blue crayon:] !! Major error!

* p. 19 *Flutes,* final bar [bar 76], second quarter note: ♯♪ Both flutes play *D*♯ (Flute II on *B* is completely wrong!). [blue crayon:] Major error!

*X ?? *All 4 Horns,* bar 1 [bar 71b]: Presumably the *3d and 4th quarter notes* should be *stacc.,* not ⌣? [magenta ink:] Parts are same as score. [blue crayon:] ??

[Blue crayon, in the left margin:] *yes* [⌣ crossed out, and in the right margin:] !! [underlining of "3d and 4th *stacc.*" also by Brahms?]

* *Viola,* penultimate quarter note [bar 76]: ♪ *G* instead of *B*! [blue crayon:] Major error!

Violoncello and Contrabass, bar 4 [bar 74]: Dot is missing over the 5th quarter note.

Contrabass [bar 71]: *più* (the accent over the *u* is missing.)

p. 20 *Violin I,* bar 1 [bar 77]: *divisi* and therefore ♯ again before *D:* ♯♯♪

X [Magenta ink:] Violin I, II, Viola, and Violoncello, final bar [bar 81]: *ben marc.* in the parts.

X [Magenta ink:] *Contrabass* part at the beginning [bar 77]: *mf* instead of *f* [blue crayon:] ?

[Blue crayon, "*mf*" crossed out]

p. 22 *Violin* I, bar 4 [bar 90]: ♪♪ Dot is missing over the 2d eighth note.

X ?   *Br., Vc., CB* Takt 4 [bar 90]: [magenta ink:] steht in den Stimmen *p* zum 1<u>sten</u> *resp.* 2<u>ten</u> Viertel, ist wohl falsch? [blue crayon:] ?

[Blue crayon, "*p*" crossed out]

*   *Br.* und *Vcell* letzter Takt [bar 91] fehlt ♮ vor *g*! [blue crayon:] Hauptfehler!

CB. vorl. Takt [bar 90] fehlt Punkt unter *a*!

p. 23. *Hoboe* I letzter Takt [bar 96] fehlt Punkt hinter 1/2 Pause!

Viol. I. Takt 3 [bar 94]   "   " über ♮*c*!

Vcell. das *dim.* [bar 96] muß schon bei den letzten 2 Vierteln des <u>vorletzten</u> Takts [bar 95] stehen!

p. 24. *Bratssche* letzter Takt [bar 102], ⌣ vom letzten Achtel 𝄾!

*<u>X p. 25.</u>[page number underlined in orange crayon] *Bratsche* Takt 5 [bar 107]:

f statt *ges* !
Hauptfehler!

[Purple ink, added after "Bratsche":] = ?Stimme? [and purple ink, in the right-hand margin, circled in orange and blue crayon:] Soll *f* sein! In der Partitur steht leider *ges*!

(3

p. 26. *Fagott* Takt 4 [bar 112] ♭♭) von *h/h*) 𝄾 (unnütz!)

X?   *Viola, Violoncello, Contrabass*, bar 4 [bar 90]:   [Blue crayon, "*p*"
       [then, in magenta ink:] In the parts there is   crossed out]
       a *p* for the 1st or 2d quarter notes; probably
       wrong? [blue crayon:] ?

*   *Viola and Violoncello*, final bar [bar 91]: ♮ is
       missing before *G*! [blue crayon:]
       Major error!

       Contrabass, penultimate bar [bar 90]:
       Dot is missing under *A*!

p. 23 *Oboe I*, final bar [bar 96]: Dot is missing
       after 1/2 rest!

       Violin I, bar 3 [bar 94]: "   " [i.e., Dot is
       missing] over ♮*C*!

       Violoncello: The *dim.* [bar 96] must begin
       already with the last 2 quarter notes of
       the *penultimate* bar [bar 95]!

p. 24 *Viola*, last bar [bar 102]: ⌣ starting from

       the last eighth note ♪!

*X *p. 25* [page number underlined in orange   [Purple ink, added after
       crayon] *Viola*, bar 5 [bar 107]:   "Viola":] =?part? [and
                                                     purple ink, circled in
   orange and blue
       F instead of *G* ♯!   crayon:] Should be *F*!
       Major error!   In the score it
                                                     unfortunately reads *G*♯!

                                                                          (3

p. 26 *Bassoon*, bar 4 [bar 112]: ♭♭) for ♭*B*/*B*) ♪

       (unnecessary!)

X   [Magenta ink:] *Viol.* I. In der Stimme Takt
           2 [bar 110] **pp** [blue crayon:] ?

[Blue crayon, " **pp** " crossed out]

X p. 27. *Viol.* I. vorletzter Takt [bar 121]. [magenta
           ink:] In der Stimme fehlt das *c* im Accord

[Blue crayon, both "?" crossed out and first "?" replaced with a period]

           [♪ notation] welches doch wohl da sein muß?

           [blue crayon:] ? [magenta ink:] Das hohe
           as müßte ja dann auf der *a* Saite gegriffen
           werden.

   p. 28. *Viol.* I. [magenta ink:] In der Stimme Takt
           2 [bar 124] [♪ notation] und Takt 4 [bar
           126] [♪ notation]

[Blue crayon, both slurs crossed out]

           [Magenta ink:] *Vcell=*Stimme *sf* zum 1sten
           Viertel [bars 124ff.] wie bei *CB.* [blue
           crayon:] s. p. 5!

           Viol. II. Das ♮ muß vor der 1sten halben
           Note *a* [bar 124] schon stehen!

*X p. 29. Bei *Hob., Fag.* u. *C-Hörnen* fehlt das [hairpin]
           im letzten Takt [bar 135].

           Bei *Bratsche* das *sf* im vorletzten Takt [bar
           134] fehlt!

*X ??   *Viol.* II. In der Stimme steht Takt 4 [bar
           133]: [♪ notation] (8 tiefer als Part.)
           [blue crayon:]? [dark brown ink:] und im

[Blue crayon, the first musical example underlined, and after it:]
? besser; [the second musical example and "?" after third musical example crossed out]

           letzten Takt [bar 135] [♪ notation] statt [♪ notation]
           [blue crayon:]? [dark brown ink:]

           Welche Lesart soll gelten [blue crayon:]?

*   p. 30. *Viol.* I. Takt 4 [bar 139] fehlt ♭ vor [♪ notation] [blue
           crayon:] Hauptfehler!

X   [Magenta ink:] Violin I, bar 2 [bar 110]: In the part *pp* [Blue crayon:] ?

[Blue crayon, "*pp*" crossed out]

X p. 27 *Violin I.,* penultimate bar [bar 121]: [magenta ink:] In the part, the *C* is missing from the chord ; presumably it *must be there?* [blue crayon:] ? [magenta ink:] Or else the high *A♭* would have to be played on the A string.

[Blue crayon, both "?" crossed out and first "?" replaced with a period]

p. 28 Violin I: [magenta ink:] In the parts, bar 2 [bar 124] and bar 4 [bar 126]

[Blue crayon, both slurs crossed out]

[Magenta ink:] Violoncello part: *sf* for the 1st quarter note [bars 124ff.], as in the Contrabass [blue crayon:] see p. 5!

Violin II: The ♮ should already occur before the 1st half note *A* [bar 124].

*Xp. 29 *Oboes,* Bassoons, and Horns in C: The ——— is missing in the last bar [bar 135].

Viola: The *sf* is missing in the penultimate bar [bar 134]!

*X ??   Violin II. In the parts bar 4 [bar 133] reads: (octave lower than the score) [blue crayon:] ? [dark brown ink:] and in the last bar [bar 135] instead of [blue crayon:] ? [dark brown ink:] Which reading do you want [blue crayon:] ?

[Blue crayon, the first musical example underlined, and after it:] *? better*; [the second musical example and "?" after the third musical example crossed out]

*   p. 30 *Violin I,* bar 4 [bar 139]: ♭ is missing before [blue crayon:] Major error!

Viol. II Takt 5 [bar 140] ist das ♭ vor dem 2$^{\underline{ten}}$ *g* überflüssig!

X   [Magenta ink:] In der *Vcell.* Stimme geht der Bogen in den beiden letzten Takten [bars 140–41] über die 3 Achtel, ohne das 1/4 anzuschließen.

X p. 31.[Magenta ink:] In der *Vcell.* Stimme geht Takt [bar 146] auf einen Bogen:

    p. 32.*Clar.* [bar 149] in A.

X   [Magenta ink:] *Cl.* I Stimme Takt 1 [bar 149]. $\Longrightarrow$ zu den letzten 3 Vierteln.

    [blue crayon:]   [Blue crayon, the dynamic sign crossed out]

X   [Magenta ink:] *Viol.* I, II u. *Br.* letzter Takt [bar 153], steht in den Stimmen *p marc.*

*   *Violoncell* Takt 3–4 [bars 151–52] ist ganz falsch, muß wie Takt 1. 2 [bars 149–50] heißen! [blue crayon:] Hauptfehler!!

    p. 33.*Fagott* I. Takt 1 [bar 154], 2$^{\underline{tes}}$ Viertel: ♮ fehlt 5$^{\underline{te}}$ Linie

    Viol. II. und *Br.*, vorl. Takt [bar 156]: *mp espress.*

    Vcell. Takt 1 [bar 154]: wegen der Theilung noch einmal ♯ vor *g* (5$^{\underline{tes}}$ Viertel.)

X   [Magenta ink:] *Viol.* I. Stimme Bogen [bars 156 and 157] anders als in der   [Blue crayon, the slurs corrected as indicated here with dotted lines]

Partitur  und:

Violin II, bar 5 [bar 140]: The ♭ before the 2d *G* is unnecessary!

X   [Magenta ink:] In the Violoncello part the slurs in the last two bars [bars 140–41] are only over the 3 eighth notes, without including the 1/4 note.

X p. 31 [Magenta ink:] In the Violoncello part the bar [bar 146] has a single slur:

   p. 32 Clarinet [bar 149]: *in A.*

X   [Magenta ink:] Clarinet I part, bar 1 [bar 149]: ⟹ for the final three quarter notes. [blue crayon:] 𝄿   [Blue crayon, the dynamic sign crossed out]

X   [Magenta ink:] Violins I, II, and Viola, final bar [bar 153]: *p marc.* in the parts.

*   *Violoncello,* bars 3–4 [bars 151–52], are *completely wrong,* they must read like bars 1, 2 [bars 149–50]! [blue crayon:] *Major error*!!

   p. 33 Bassoon I bar 1 [bar 154], 2d quarter note: ♮ is missing on the 5th line.

     Violin II and Viola, penultimate bar [bar 156]: *mp espress.*

     Violoncello, bar 1 [bar 154]: owing to the *divisi,* a ♯ is needed again before *G* (5th quarter note).

X   [Magenta ink:] Violin I part: Slurs [bars 156 and 157] different than in the score: [Blue crayon, the slurs corrected as indicated here with dotted lines]

                and

p. 34.*Clar.* [bar 160] <u>in *B.*</u>

Vcell. Takt 2 [bar 160]: ♮*a*

p. 35.*Fag.* II Takt 1 [bar 164]: *p*

Horn II Takt 4 [bar 167] das 2ᵗᵉ ♭
(unnütz!)

X p. 36.*Viol.* I.
      " II. [magenta ink:] ⎞ Stimmen [ca. bars
169–72] haben andre Bogen als Partitur!

p. 37.fehlt im vorl. T. [bar 177] das ♮ vor dem
Viertel *d* bei allen Holzbläsern!

C-Hörner u. *Tromp.* fehlt beim Eintritt [bar
177] das *f*!

X *Viol.* II [magenta ink:] in der Stimme 2
Bogen im letzten Takt [bar 178]!

X p. 38.*Vcell.* [magenta ink:] Stimme Takt 5 [bar
183]: *ff* Takt 6 [bar 178]: *sf* Takt 7 [bar
185]: *sf*

p. 39.*Flöten* über dem letzten Viertel [bar 194]
fehlt das >!

4)

p. 40.*Flöten* Takt 1 [bar 191] fehlt Punkt über
dem 2ᵗᵉⁿ Viertel

C-Hörner Takt 1 [bar 191]:
doppelt zu streichen, Punkt über ♭ h !

F-Hörner Takt 1 [bar 191]: (♮
fehlt)

p. 34 Clarinet [bar 160]: *in B.*

Violoncello, bar 2 [bar 160]: ♮A

p. 35 *Bassoon* II, bar 1 [bar 164]: ***p***

Horn II, bar 4 [bar 167]: The 2d ♭ 𝄢
(unnecessary!)

X   p. 36 Violin I
        "   II   [magenta ink:] ⎫ Parts [ca. bars 169–72]
                                     ⎭
have slurs different from those in the score!

p. 37 *missing* in the penultimate bar [bar 177]:
The ♮ before the quarter note *D* in all the
wind parts!

Horns in C and Trumpets: ***f*** is missing at
the entrance [bar 177]!

X   Violin II [magenta ink:] In the part, 2 slurs
         in the final bar [bar 178]!

X   p. 38 Violoncello [magenta ink:] part, bar 5 [bar
         183]: ***ff*** bar 6 [bar 184]: *sf* bar 7 [bar
         185]: *sf*

p. 39 *Flutes:* The > is missing over the final
         quarter note ♯𝅘𝅥 [bar 194]!

4)

p. 40 *Flutes,* bar 1 [bar 191]: Dot is missing over
         the 2d quarter note 𝄞♯𝅘𝅥

Horns in C, bar 1 [bar 191]: Double
stemmed 𝄞𝅘𝅥♭𝅘𝅥 ; dot over ♭B 𝄢!

Horns in F, bar 1 [bar 191]: 𝄞𝅘𝅥 (♮ is
missing.)

{185}

X ??   Viol. II: Takt 2 [bar 191] steht in der

Stimme: (Partitur ♮g!)

[blue crayon:]? [dark brown ink:]
Was soll gelten? [blue crayon:]??

[Blue crayon, "*f*"
underlined twice in the
musical example, and
♮ before "*g*" crossed
out, and in the right
margin:] *f*

X   *Viol.* II Takt 3 [bar 193] möchte wohl ein ♭
vor ♩ stehen!

CB. Takt 4 [bar 194] fehlt Punkt über dem
sf = *a*!

X   *Vcell.* [magenta ink:] Stimmen vorl. T. [bar
194] > > bei *più f*

p. 41.*Pauken.* Vorl. T. [bar 199] fehlt: <u>*C muta* in</u>
<u>B.</u>

*X? p. 42.Das ═══ (welches bei *Viol.* I [added:]
Takt 2 [bar 202] [then:] etwas früher
anfangen müßte) fehlt im 2<u>ten</u> u. 4<u>ten</u> Takt
[bars 202 and 204] bei den <u>Holzbläsern</u> in
Partitur u. Stimmen.

[Blue crayon, "etwas
früher anfangen müßte"
crossed out]

?   — <u>Takt 4</u> [bar 204] steht bei Bläsern *f* ,
beim *Horn mf* , beim Quartett in der
Partitur *sf* u. in den Stimmen (*Viol.* I. II u.
Br.) *rf* !

?   Könnte das nicht egalisiert werden und

wie? (*mf* ═══ überall?)

[Blue crayon, "m" of
"*mf*," "s" of "*sf*," and
"r" of "*rf*" crossed out,
and in the right margin:]

f = ["m" of "*mf* ═══ "
crossed out, and below:]
═══ im 4<u>tett</u> [Lead
pencil, below the last
line:] Takt 4 *f* überall
═══ nur im 4<u>tett</u>

[The long entry given above for page 42 is bracketed in the left
margin in red crayon; Brahms's last comment is linked to Keller's
query with a line drawn in lead pencil.]

{186}

X?? Violin II: Bar 2 in the part reads:

    (in the score, ♮ *G* !) [blue crayon:] ? [dark brown ink:] *What do you want?* [blue crayon:] ??

                 [Blue crayon, "*F*" underlined twice in the musical example, and ♮ before "*G*" crossed out, and in the right margin:] *F*

X   *Violin* II, bar 3 [bar 193]: There probably should be a ♭ before ♩ !

     Contrabass, bar 4 [bar 194]: Dot is missing over the *sf* = *A* !

X   Violoncello [magenta ink:] parts, penultimate bar [bar 194] > > at *più f*

  p. 41 Timpani, penultimate bar [bar 199]: "*C muta in B.*" is missing.

* X ? p. 42 The ═══ (which should start somewhat earlier in the violin [added:] in bar 2 [bar 202]) [then:] is missing in the second and fourth bars [bars 202 and 204] for the *woodwinds* in the score and parts.

                 [Blue crayon, "should start somewhat earlier" crossed out]

?   — *Bar 4* [bar 204] the wind instruments have *f* , the Horn *mf* , the strings *sf* in the score and *rf* in the parts (Violin I II, Viola)!

?   Could this not be standardized, and how?

     (*mf* ═══ in all cases?)

                 [Blue crayon, "m" of "*mf* ," "s" of "*sf* ," and "r" of "*rf* " crossed out, and in the right margin:]

                 f = ["m" of "*mf* ═══ " crossed out, and below:] "═══ " in the strings [Lead pencil, below the last line:] Bar 4 *f* in all cases, ═══ only in the strings

[The long entry given above for page 42 is bracketed in the left margin in red crayon; Brahms's last comment is linked to Keller's query with a line drawn in lead pencil.]

Viol. II.
Vcell. u. *CB* ⎫ Takt 3 [bar 203] fehlt *p*

* <u>*Quartett*</u> letzter Takt [bar 206] <u>*dim.*</u> an den
Anfang des Taktes!

p. 43.<u>*Horn*</u> IV [bar 214] beim *pp* p̄· fehlt *pp* !

p. 44.<u>*Contrafagott*</u> [bar 224] *p* <> (*p* fehlt)

<u>*Pauken*</u> [bar 218] *p* <u>*cresc.*</u>

<u>*Bratschen*</u> *p dim.* (Takt 5 [bar 221])

X [Magenta ink:] In den Stimmen v. *Vcell.* u.
CB. steht das *p* schon auf dem letzten
Viertel des 3$^{\underline{ten}}$ Taktes [bar 219]!

<u>*Andante.*</u>

p. 45 [System] II. Takt 1. 2. [bars 8–9] Fag.
[changed to:] <u>*Vcell.*</u> 1 Bogen bis *g.*

*X Fag. [crossed out, then:] vorletzter Takt
[bar 15, Violoncello] *e* st. *c.*
<u>Stimme richtig!</u>

X *Br.* [magenta ink:] Takt vor **A** [bar 14]:
in der Stimme Bogen nicht bis
g [bar 15] heran!

p. 46 1. <u>letzter</u> T. [bar 24] *Viol.* II fehlt *p*

<u>*Vcell.*</u> 1 Takt 4 [bar 20] fehlt Punkt hinter
der 1/2 Note *d* !

Violin II

Violoncello and Contrabass ⎱ Bar 3 [bar 203] *p* is missing.

*   *Strings,* final bar [bar 206]: *dim.* at the
beginning of the bar!

p. 43 Horn IV [bar 214]: *pp* is missing at $_{pp}\overline{\overline{\rho}}\cdot$!

p. 44 *Contrabassoon* [bar 224]: *p* < > (*p* is
missing.)

Timpani [bar 218]: *p cresc.*

Viola: p dim. (bar 5 [bar 221])

X   [Magenta ink:] In the Violoncello and
Contrabass parts the *p* occurs already on
the last quarter note of the 3d bar [bar
219]!

Andante

p. 45 [brace] II Bars 1, 2 [bars 8–9], Bassoon
[changed to:] *Violoncello* I: Slur through to *G*

* X   Bassoon [crossed out, then:] *penultimate bar*
[bar 15, Violoncello] *E* instead of *C:*

Part correct!

X   Viola [magenta ink:] One bar before **A** [bar
14]: In the part, the slur does
not extend to *G* [bar 15]!

p. 46 I *Final* bar [bar 24], Violin II: *p* is missing.

Violoncello I, bar 4 [bar 20]: Dot is missing
after the 1/2 note *D*!

{189}

X p. 46 II. Takt 1. [bar 25] [magenta ink:] in der
Viol. II u. *Br.* Stimme geht der Bogen nur
bis zum Ende des 3$\underline{\text{ten}}$ Viertels, und die 4
letzten 16$\underline{\text{tel}}$ haben einen besonderen
Bogen. In der *Vcell*stimme wie Partitur.

p. 47 I. Takt 1. [bar 29] *Cl.* u. *Fag.*

(2$\underline{\text{tes}}$ ♮ fehlt) *Fag.* vorl. Takt [bar

32] Punkt unter das letzte Viertel.

Viol. I.II. Takt 3. 4. [bars 31–32, but
actually bars 30–31] Bogen nur über die 4
Sechzehntel nicht bis ans Viertel!

(5

p. 47 II. *Contrabass* letzter Takt [bar 44] fehlt
!

p. 48 I. [Magenta ink:] *Viol.* I. Stimme [bars 50–51]
Bogen nur bis *a.*

Viol. II. Takt 2 [bar 46]: !

Violcello Takt 6 [bar 50]: *pp* zum letzten
4$\underline{\text{tel}}$!

p. 49 II. *Fagott* II Takt 2 [bar 68]: ♭ vom 2$\underline{\text{ten}}$!

*   *Violine* II letzter Takt [bar 71]:
                                        fis statt *h*!!
[blue crayon:] Hauptfehler!

Vc. u. *CB*: Takt 2 [bar 68]: das unter

dem letzten Viertel !

X p. 50 I. *Hörner* vorl. T. [bar 75]: *f* statt *mf*!

X p. 46 II *Bar* 1 [bar 25] [magenta ink:] In the
Violin II and Viola parts the slur extends
only to the end of the 3d quarter note, and
the final 4 16th notes have a separate slur.
In the Violoncello part as in the score.

p. 47 I Bar 1 [bar 29]: Clarinet ▨ and

Bassoon ▨ (2d ♮ is missing.)

Bassoon, penultimate bar [bar 32]: Dot
under the final quarter note.

Violin I, II, bars 3, 4 [bars 31–32, but
actually bars 30–31]: Slurs only over the 4
sixteenth notes, not extending to the
quarter note!

(5

p. 47 II Contrabass, final bar [bar 44]: ◁▷
is missing!

p. 48 I [Magenta ink:] Violin I, part [bars 50–51]:

Slur extends only to *A.*

Violin II, bar 2 [bar 46]: ▨!

Violoncello, bar 6 [bar 50]: *pp* on the last
quarter note!

p. 49 II Bassoon II, bar 2 [bar 68]: ♭ for the 2d ▨!

*   *Violin* II, final bar [bar 71]: ▨
f♯ instead of *b*!!
[blue crayon:] Major error!

Violoncello and Contrabass, bar 2 [bar 68]:

The ◁ under the final quarter note ▨!

X p. 50 I *Horns,* penultimate bar [bar 75]: *f* instead
of *mf*!

{191}

Vcell. Takt 1 [bar 72] fehlt ═══ !

CB. vorl. T. [bar 75] fehlt *f* !

p. 52   [changed to:] 50 II. *Clarinette* II letzter Takt [bar 80]: ♮ vor *h*!

p. 51 II. *Posaunen* Takt 1 [bar 85]: ♯♪══ Takt 2 [bar 86]: ♭♪══ !

p. 52 I. *Fagott* II: Takt 3. [bar 91] ⌣ von *c* ab!

p. 53 I. *Vcell* Takt 1 [bar 97]: ♮*g*!

p. 53 II. *Viol.* II Takt 1 [bar 101]: *pp* — Auch über die 2ᵗᵉ Triole eine 3!

Vcell. " [i.e., Takt 1] *pp*

X   *Vcell.* u. *CB*: letzter Takt [bar 105] u. pag. 53 [changed to:] 54 1ˢᵗᵉʳ Takt [bar 106] ◁══ | ══▷ [blue crayon:]? [dark brown ink:] richtig in der Stimme? [blue crayon:]?   [Blue crayon, dynamics and final "?" crossed out]

p. 54 I. *Clar.* Takt 5 [bar 110]: ♮*d*! Takt 6 [bar 111]: ♮*a*!

Fag. Takt 5 [bar 110]: ♮*c*!

X   *Viol.* I [bars 110–111] [magenta ink:] in der Stimme ♪♯♪♪♪ Strichart [blue crayon:]?   [Blue crayon, upper slur crossed out.

p. 54 II. *Hob.* II Takt 1 [bar 112]: ♮*e*! Takt 2 [bar 113]: *f* ⌢ *e*

{192}

Violoncello, bar 1 [bar 72]: ⌐══ is missing!

Contrabass, penultimate bar [bar 75]: *f* is missing!

p. 52 [changed to:] 50 II *Clarinet* II, final bar [bar 80]: ♮ before *B*!

p. 51 II *Trombones,* bar 1 [bar 85]: 𝄞♯♪══ bar 2 [bar 86]: 𝄞♭♪══ !

p. 52 I *Bassoon* II, bar 3 [bar 91]: ⌣ starting with *C*!

p. 53 I *Violoncello,* bar 1 [bar 97]: ♮*G*!

p. 53 II *Violin* II, bar 1 [bar 101]: *pp* — Also a *3* over the 2nd triplet!

Violoncello, " [i.e., bar 1] *pp*

X   *Violoncello* and Contrabass, final bar [bar 105], and page 53 [changed to:] 54, 1st bar [bar 106]: ⌐═ | ═⌐ [blue crayon:] ?   [Blue crayon, dynamics and final "?" crossed out]

[dark brown ink:] correct in the part? [blue crayon:] ?

p. 54 I *Clarinet,* bar 5 [bar 110]: ♮*D*! Bar 6 [bar 111]: ♮*A*!

Bassoon, bar 5 [bar 110]: ♮*C*!

X   Violin I [bars 110–11] [magenta ink:] In the part, bowing like this: 𝄞♯♪♪♪   [Blue crayon, upper slur crossed out]

[blue pencil:] ?

p. 54 II *Oboe* II, bar 1 [bar 112]: ♮*E*! *Bar 2* [bar 113]: *F̑ E*

{193}

Cl. I. Takt 1 [bar 112]: ♯*f*!

p. 55 I. *Fag.* II. Takt 5 [bar 123]: ♮*a*!

Vcell. Takt 2 [bar 120]: ♮ 𝄾!

p. 55 II. *Bassposaune* Takt 2. 3 [bars 128–29]:

p ◁ | ▷ !

X *Viol.* I [deleted:] und II [then:] Takt 4 [bar 130]: [magenta ink:] in den Stimmen ◁°▷! [blue crayon:]? [Blue crayon:] Nein.

X ? *Viol.* II. [magenta ink:] steht in der Stimme [bar 130] Taktpause statt ganze Note *c*! [blue crayon:]? [Blue crayon, under "Taktpause":] falsch [underlining of "Taktpause" and "ganze Note" also possibly by Brahms]

Poco Allegretto.

* pag. 56 I. *Viol.* II [added:] Takt 1 [then:]

Achtelpause am Schluß hinter ♪𝄾! [blue crayon:] Hauptfehler!

p. 57 I. *Clar.* letzter Takt [bar 20] ⌒ nicht über das letzte 8ᵗᵉˡ hinaus!

Viol. II letzter Takt u. 57 II 1ˢᵗᵉʳ Takt [bars 20–21] ◁ ▷ Takt. 2. [bar 22] ! [added in blue crayon before "Viol II":] *Fag.* u.

* p. 57 II. *Vcell.* Takt 5 zu 6 [changed in blue crayon to:] 4 zu 5 [bars 24–25] [dark brown ink:] [Blue crayon, correct slur added to the musical example]

♩⌒♩ (Bogen *g g* fehlt!) [magenta ink:]

X in der Stimme Strichart so:

 [blue crayon:]?

Clarinet I, bar 1 [bar 112]: ♯*F* !

p. 55 I *Bassoon* II, bar 5 [bar 123]: ♮*A* !

Violoncello, bar 2 [bar 120]: ♮𝄽 !

p. 55 II *Bass trombone,* bar 2, 3 [bars 128–29]:

p ＜ | ＞ !

X   Violin I [deleted:] and II [then:] bar 4 [bar   [Blue crayon:] *No*
130]: [magenta ink:] in the parts ＜°＞ !
[blue crayon:] ?

X ?   *Violin II* [magenta ink:] In the part there is a   [Blue crayon, under
one-bar rest instead of a *whole note C* ! [blue   "one-bar rest":] *wrong*
crayon:] ?   [underlining of "one-
     bar rest" and "whole
     note" also possibly by
     Brahms]

Poco Allegretto

*   p. 56 I *Violin II* [added:] bar 1 [then:] Eighth-note

rest at the end, after ♪𝄽 ! [blue crayon:]

Major error!

p. 57 I *Clarinet,* final bar [bar 20]: ⌒ not to
extend beyond final eighth note!

Violin II, final bar and p. 57 II, 1st bar [bars

20–21]: ＜   ＞   ! [added in blue
     Bar 2 [bar 22]
crayon before "Violin II":] Bassoon and

*   p. 57 II *Violoncello,* bars 5 to 6 [changed in blue   [Blue crayon, correct
crayon to:] 4 to 5 [bars 24–25] [dark brown   slur added to the
     musical example]
ink:] ♪♪ (Tie ⌒_{G G} is missing!)

X   [magenta ink:] in the parts, bowing like

this: 𝄃♪♪♪♪𝄂 [blue crayon:] ?

* p. 58 I. *Viol.* I. vorl. Takt [bar 35]:

 [blue crayon:]

gis st. *fis*!!
schwerer Fehler!

Vcell. Takt 6 [bar 34]: 2ᵗᵉˢ ♮ vor *a* 𝄢!

Takt 4 [bar 32]: *dolce* zum *Vcell.,* von der

Bratsche 𝄢!

X   *Vcell.* Takt 3 [bar 31]: [magenta ink:] in   [Blue crayon, correct
                                                                          slur added]

der Stimme Strichart:
[blue crayon:]?

6)

Pag. 58 II.*Fagott* I beim Eintritt [bar 40] *p*!

Horn II vorl. Takt [bar 41]: Pause herunter
an die 2ᵗᵉ Linie!

*   *Viol.* I letzter Takt [bar 42]:
                [blue crayon:] Hauptfehler!   *c* st. *as*

X ?   *Vcell.* u. *CB.* vorletzter Takt [bar 41] *pp*   [Blue crayon, both
               oder nur *p* [blue crayon:]? [magenta ink:]   "*pp*" crossed out, "nur
               *Cello*stimme hat *pp*, *CB* Stimme gar nichts!   *p*" underlined; at the
                                                                        end:] *p*

X p. 59 II. *Fag.* II letzter Takt [bar 57]: *p* ═══

*   *Violcello* [bar 53] über 𝄾 fehlt: <u>arco</u>! [blue
                crayon:] Hauptfehler!

p. 60 II. *Fag.* I: Takt 1 [bar 67]: ♭*f*!

*   *p. 58 I Violin I*, penultimate bar [bar 35]:

[blue crayon:]

G♯ instead of F♯!!

Serious error!

Violoncello, bar 6 [bar 34]: 2d ♮ before *A* ♪!

Bar 4 [bar 32]: Add *dolce* to Violoncello, ♪

from Viola!

X   Violoncello, bar 3 [bar 31]: [magenta ink:]   [Blue crayon, correct

In the part, the bowing: 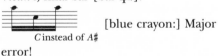   slur added]

[blue crayon:] ?

6)

p. 58 II *Bassoon* 1, at its entrance [bar 40]: *p* !

Horn II, penultimate bar [bar 41]: Move
rest down to the 2nd line!

*   *Violin I*, final bar [bar 42]:

[blue crayon:] Major

C instead of A♯

error!

X ?   *Violoncello* and Contrabass, penultimate bar   [Blue crayon, both "*pp*"
     [bar 41] *pp* or *only p* [blue crayon:] ?   crossed out; "only *p*"
     [magenta ink:] Violoncello part has *pp*,   underlined; at the end:]
     Contrabass part has nothing!   *p*

X p. 59 II *Bassoon* II, final bar [bar 57]: *p* ⸺

*   *Violoncello* [bar 53]: *arco* is missing over ♪ !
     [blue crayon:] Major error!

p. 60 II *Bassoon* I, bar 1 [bar 67]: ♭*F* !

Bratsche letzter Takt [bar 76]: fehlt ═══

CB. [bar 73]

* [Added, to the right of the last five entries, framed in blue crayon, marked with three *X*s in red crayon, and marked again before the musical example with an *X* in red crayon and, in blue crayon:] ??
[the following entry:] <u>Wichtige Frage</u>: Sind die *Hörner* [bars 61–63] richtig, daß sie auf *c* gehen? Sollen sie nicht beide mal *es* 3/8 haben?   ?

[Blue crayon, "<u>Fragen</u>," "??" and "auf *c*" crossed out; after "<u>Wichtige Frage</u>" and also at the end:] ! [above and below the entry:] *es*

X   *Vcell* Takt 6 [bars 72–73]: [magenta ink:] in der Stimme ⌒ nur bis 1/4 *fis*! [blue crayon:]?

[Blue crayon, "bis 1/4 fis" and "?" crossed out]

p. 61 I. II:Die Strichart ⌒⋅ [bars 79ff.] könnte in der Part. überall angegeben sein!

I. *Bratsche* Takt 6 [bar 82]: ♮ vor *g* und ♭ vor *d* überflüssig!

p. 61 II. *Horn* Takt 8 [bar 93] fehlt die Pause, im letzten Takt [bar 98] das *p*

Viol. II Takt 3 [bar 88]: ♭*e*!

[Next group of four entries in magenta ink, with a line in the left margin in red crayon:]

X   Stricharten in den Stimmen anders:

Viol. I Bogen nur bis *es* nicht bis *fis* [bars 96–97]!

Viol. II   "   "   *es* nicht bis *c* [bars 97–98]!

Viola, final bar [bar 76]: ⟩⟩ is missing.

Contrabass [bar 73]:

---

*	[Added, to the right of the last five entries, framed in blue crayon, marked with three Xs in red crayon, and marked again before the musical example with an X in red crayon, and in blue crayon:] ? ? [the following entry:] *Important question:* Are the Horns [bars 61–63] correct, that they are on *C*? Should they not have *E♭*, for three eighths, both times?	[Blue crayon, "*question,*" "? ?" and "on *C*" crossed out; after "*Important question*" and also at the end:] ! [above and below the entry:] *E♭*

 ?

X	*Violoncello,* bar 6 [bars 72–73]: [magenta ink:] In the part, ⌒ extends only to the 1/4 note *F♯*! [blue crayon:] ?	[Blue crayon, "to the 1/4 note *F♯*" and "?" crossed out]

p. 61 I, II The bowing ⌢ [bars 79ff.] could perhaps be indicated in the score throughout!

I *Viola,* bar 6 [bar 82]: ♮ before *G* and ♭ before *D* are unnecessary!

p. 61 II *Horn,* bar 8 [bar 93]: The *rest* is missing; in the final bar [bar 98], the *p* is missing.

Violin II, bar 3 [bar 88]: ♭ before *E* !

[Next group of four entries in magenta ink, with a line in the left margin in red crayon:]

X | Bowing in the parts is different:

Violin I: Slur only until *E♭*, not until *F♯* [bars 96–97]!

Violin II: "   "   *E♭*, not until *C* [bars 97–98]!

Bratsche Takt Bogen [bar 91] schon vom Achtel *as* [bar 90] ab;
(der lange Bogen vom ♮*d* bis ♯*f* fehlte, ist aber bereits gemacht.)

p. 62 I: *Bratsche* [bar 99] fehlt *p* zur 1<u>sten</u> Note!

Vcell. Takt 1 [bar 99]: [magenta ink:] in   [Blue crayon, "*dolce*"
der Stimme *dolce*!   crossed out]

p. 62 II. *Bratsche* [bars 106–8] fehlt

Takt 1.2.   T. 3   !

p. 63 I. *Vcell.* [changed in blue crayon to:] CB.
[bar 118] [then:] *pizz.* !

p. 63 II. *Fagott* Takt 1 [bar 122] fehlt *dolce*!

*   Vcell [changed to:] *Violine* II Takt 5 [bar

126]:   das 3<u>te</u> 16<u>tel</u> *c* fehlt !!

[blue crayon:] Hauptfehler!!

*   *Bratsche* Takt 1 [bar 122]: <u>*arco*</u> fehlt!! [blue
crayon:] Hauptfehler!!

p. 64 I. *Fag.* I. [bar 130] ♮ vor das 1<u>ste</u> *h*! vom 2<u>ten</u> !

Vcell. u. *CB.: Takt 1. [bar 130] più p* (statt
più dolce)!!

p. 64 II. *Clar.* Takt 1 [bar 136]: ⁊ schlecht dafür ⁊ ⁊
in *Clar.* II!

Fag. " [i.e., Takt 1] [bar 136] ebenso ⁊ ⁊ st. ⁊

Viol. I Takt 5 [bar 140]: (statt)
(das 8<u>tel</u> nicht riegeln!)

Viola, slur for the bar [bar 91] already begins with the eighth note A♭ [bar 90]; (the long slur from ♮D to ♯F is missing, but has already been put in.)

Violoncello:

p. 62 i *Viola* [bar 99]: *p* is missing at the 1st note!

Violoncello, bar 1 [bar 99]: [magenta ink:] In the part, *dolce*!

[Blue crayon, "*dolce*" crossed out]

p. 62 ii Viola [bars 106–8]: $\underbrace{}_{\text{Bar 1, 2}} | \underbrace{}_{\text{B. 3}}$ is missing!

p. 63 i Violoncello [changed in blue crayon to:] Contrabass [bar 118] [then:] *pizz.* 𝄼!

p. 63 ii *Bassoon,* bar 1 [bar 122]: *dolce* is missing!

* Violoncello [changed to:] *Violine* ii, bar 5 [bar 126]: the 3d 16th note, *C,* is missing!! [blue crayon:] Major error!!

* *Viola,* bar 1 [bar 122]: *arco* is missing!! [blue crayon:] Major error!!

p. 64 i *Bassoon* i [bar 130]: ♮ before the 1st *B*! before the 2d one, 𝄼!

Violoncello and *Contrabass,* bar 1 [bar 130]: *più p* (instead of *più dolce*)!!

p. 64 ii Clarinet, bar 1 [bar 136]: ♮ is bad; instead put ɣ ɣ in the Clarinet ii!

Bassoon, " [i.e., bar 1] [bar 136]: Likewise, ɣ ɣ instead of ♮

Violin i, bar 5 [bar 140]: (instead of) (not beaming the 8th note!)

{201}

*   *Vcello.* Takt 1 [bar 136]: fehlt <u>*arco!*</u> [blue crayon:] H Fehler!

(7

p. 65 i. *Horn* i Takt 2 [bar 144]: ♭*e!*

        ii. *Fagott* ii Takt 7 [bar 156]: ♭*e!!*

*   *CBass* Takt 5 [bar 154]: <u>*arco*</u> fehlt! [blue crayon:] H Fehler!

Allegro.

     p. 66.   Takt 4. In allen spielenden Stimmen ein ♭ vor die erste Note *h!*

     p. 68.   *CBass* Takt 5 [bar 16]: Bogen nur bis *as,* nicht in den nächsten Takt!

*   p. 69:   *Horn* i Takt 7 [bar 24]: ♭ vor *e!* [blue crayon:] H Fehler!

*   *Bratsche* Takt 2 [bar 19]: <u>*arco*</u> fehlt! [blue crayon:] Hauptfehler!

     p. 70.   Takt 5 [bar 33]. Bei allen beschäftigten Instr. ♭ vor *h!* (wie p. 66)

     p. 71.   Takt 1 zu 2 [bars 38–39] besser in *Fag., Cfag., Vcell* u. *CB* (statt Punkt hinter Taktstrich!)

          Horn i. ii. [bar 40] fehlt *f* beim Eintritt!

          Horn iii. iv. [bar 38] fehlt Punkt über dem 1sten Viertel!

*   Violoncello, bar 1 [bar 136]: *arco* is missing!
[blue crayon:] Major error!

(7

p. 65 I *Horn* I, bar 2 [bar 144]: ♭*E* !

II *Bassoon* II, bar 7 [bar 156]: ♭*E* !!

*   Contrabass, bar 5 [bar 154]: *arco* is missing!
[blue crayon:] Major error!

Allegro

p. 66 *Bar 4.* In *all* playing parts, a ♭ before the first
note *B* !

p. 68 *Contrabass,* bar 5 [bar 16]: Slur only through
A ♭, not into the next bar!

* p. 69 Horn I, bar 7 [bar 24]: ♭ before *E* ! [blue
crayon:] Major error!

*   *Viola,* bar 2 [bar 19]: *arco* is missing! [blue
crayon:] Major error!

p. 70 *Bar* 5 [bar 33]: In all playing instruments,
♭ before *B* ! (as on p. 66)

p. 71 *Bar* 1 to 2 [bars 38–39]: Better
in the Bassoon, Contrabassoon, Violoncello,
and Contrabass (instead of the dot after the
barline!)

Horn I, II [bar 40]: *f* is missing at the
entrance!

Horn III, IV [bar 38]: Dot is missing over the
1st quarter note!

{203}

p. 72.   *Horn* III. IV. Takt 5 [bar 50] fehlt Punkt über *d*!

CBass Takt 1 [bar 46] fehlt Punkt über dem 1$\underline{\underline{\text{sten}}}$ $g\frac{1}{4}$!

*XX?   *Vcell.* Takt 1 [bar 46] [magenta ink:] steht in der Stimme die leere Saite ▬ , das spielt sich wohl besser als das höhere *g* der Partitur. [blue crayon:]??   [Lead pencil, "??" crossed out, and above the musical example:] richtig

*   p. 73.   *Vcell* Takt 2 [bar 56]: fehlt *pizz.*!! [blue crayon:] Hauptfehler! [dark brown ink:] unten fehlt *mf*!

CB [bar 56] muß | das *pizz.* hingegen 𝄐!
kann |

p. 74.   *Fagott* vorletzter Takt [bar 67]: ♮ vor das 1$\underline{\underline{\text{ste}}}$ *f*!

p. 75.   *Horn* 3 [changed to:] III. IV. Takt 2 [bar 70]: Punkt über das 1/4 *c*!

Viol. II.   "   [bar 70]   "   "   "   1/4 ♩
!

*X?p. 76.   *CBass.* [added in blue crayon:] u. *Cfg.* [then:] Takt 3 [bar 80] ist [magenta ink:] in der Stimme Taktpause und das ist nicht richtig? [blue crayon:]???   [Lead pencil, all "?" crossed out; at the beginning:] NB [after "richtig":]! ["nicht" crossed out; "Taktpause" underlined four times]

*   p. 77.   *Clar.* II Takt 6 [bar 90] ▬ (♯ st. ♮ vor *c*) [blue crayon:] Hauptfehler!

p. 72 *Horn* III, IV, bar 5 [bar 50]: Dot is missing
over *D* !

Contrabass, bar 1 [bar 46]: Dot is missing
over the 1st 1/4 note, *G* !

* XX ? *Violoncello*, bar 1 [bar 46] [magenta ink:]   [Lead pencil, "??"
The part has the open string ▬▬ , which   crossed out, and above
is probably easier to play than the higher *G*   the musical example:]
in the score. [blue crayon:] ??   correct

* p. 73 *Violoncello*, bar 2 [bar 56]: *pizz.* is missing!!
[blue crayon:] Major error! [dark brown
ink:] *below, mf* is missing!

Contrabass [bar 56], on the other hand, *pizz.*
must be | ♪ !
can be

p. 74 *Bassoon*, penultimate bar [bar 67]: ♮ before
the 1st *F* !

p. 75 *Horn 3* [changed to:] *III, IV*, bar 2 [bar 70]: Dot over the 1/4 note *C*

Violin II,   "   [bar 70] "   "   " 1/4 note ♪ !

* X ? p. 76 *Contrabass* [added in blue crayon:] and   [Lead pencil, all "?"
Contrabassoon [then:] bar 3 [bar 80]   crossed out; at the
there is [magenta ink:] in the parts a full-   beginning:] NB [after
bar rest and that is not correct? [blue   "correct":] ! ["not"
crayon:] ???   crossed out; "full-bar
     rest" underlined four
     times]

* p. 77 *Clarinet* II, bar 6 [bar 90]: ▬▬ (♯ instead
of ♮ before *C*) [blue crayon:] Major error!

XX? Takt 5. 6. [bars 89–90] ist in der
Bearbeitung für 2 Claviere abweichend in
der Harmonie so:

[blue crayon, entry enclosed in parentheses, and at the end:]?

[Lead pencil, after the musical example:]
nun — kein Unglück!

p. 78. *C-Hörner* Takt 5 [bar 97]: ♮ vor *d*!

Bratschen Takt 1 [bar 93]: Punkte über 4
ersten Achtel!

p. 79. *Fag.* [bar 99] > über dem 1sten 4^{tel} der
Egalität wegen ⅄!

Vcell. Takt 6 [bar 104]: Punkt unter das 1ste
Viertel *as*!

Die *pizz.* Punkte [bar 104] sämmtlich
⅄!!

p. 80. Takt 5 [bar 111] *Fl.* und *Fag.*: ♭ vor *h*! *Clar.*
♮ vor *c*!

X *Viol.* I Takt 7 [bar 113] [magenta ink:] steht in der Stimme *mp* ⎱ beide überflüssig!
X *Viol.* II Takt 7 [bar 113] [magenta ink:] "   "   "   *p* ⎰
[blue crayon, after *mp* and *p*, and at the end:]?

[Lead pencil, "?" at the end crossed out]

p. 81. vorletzter Takt [bar 123]: *Hob.* ♭ vor *h*! *Fag.*
♭ vor *h*!

p. 82. *Vcell.* drittletzter Takt [bar 131] *dim.* wie
im *CB*! (>⅄)

XX ? Bar 5, 6 [bars 89–90]: The harmony is different in the arrangement for two pianos, like this:

[blue crayon, entry enclosed in parentheses, and at the end:] ?

[Lead pencil, after the musical example:] well— no catastrophe!

p. 78 *Horns in C,* bar 5 [bar 97]: ♮ before *D* !

Violas, bar 1 [bar 93]: Dots over the first 4 eighth notes!

p. 79 Bassoon [bar 99]: For the sake of uniformity, > over the 1st quarter note !

Violoncello, bar 6 [bar 104]: Dot under the 1st quarter note, *A*♭ !

all *the pizz. dots!!*

p. 80 Bar 5 [bar 111], *Flute* and *Bassoon:* ♭ before *B* ! *Clarinet,* ♮ before *C* !

X Violin I, bar 7 [bar 113]: [magenta ink:] in the parts, *mp* ⎫
X Violin II, bar 7 [bar 113]: [magenta ink:] " "   " *p* ⎬ both unnecessary!
[blue crayon, after *mp* and *p* , and at the end:] ?

[Lead pencil, "?" at the end crossed out]

p. 81 *Penultimate* bar [bar 123]: *Oboe,* ♭ before *B* ! *Bassoon,* ♭ before *B* !

p. 82 *Violoncello,* third bar from the end [bar 131]: *dim.,* as in the Contrabass! (>,)

| X | [Magenta ink:] In der *Violine* I Stimme [bar 128] steht ════════ *p* und [bar 130] bei ♩ *pp*! [blue crayon:]? | [Lead pencil:] del. |

8)

| X? p. 83. | Takt 7 und 8 [bar 140, 141] *Vcell* und *CB*: [magenta ink:] in den Stimmen steht ════ ════[blue crayon:]? | [Lead pencil, the dynamics crossed out, and above:] del. |

Takt. 7.   8.

* p. 86. *Hoboe* II Takt 3 [bar 157]: fehlt ♮ vor *d*! [blue crayon:] Hauptfehler!

Viol. II und *Br* Takt 1 [bar 155]: die Streichung zu 3 ⊓⊓ ⊓⊓ wäre für das 3te u. 4te Viertel der Schönheit halber vorziehen!

Viol. II Takt 1 [bar 155]: das ◁════ darf erst beim letzten Viertel beginnen!

* *Violoncello* Takt 3 [bar 157] (♮ statt ♯)!! [blue crayon:] Hauptfehler!

p. 87. *Clar.* I Takt 1 [bar 160]: ♮ 𝄽 (unnütz!)

* *Bratsche* Takt 3 [bar 162]: letztes Achtel ♮ st. ♯!! [blue crayon:] Hauptfehler!

* p. 88. *F=Hörner* letzter Takt [bar 167]: ⌒𝄽, aber Punkt über das Viertel!

Trompeten [bar 167: *ff* statt *f*! [Lead pencil:] *ff*!

Viol. I. Im letzten Takt [bar 167] die Noten zu 3 gestrichen wie vorher!

X [Magenta ink:] The Violin I part [bar 128] [Lead pencil:] delete
has ══════ *p* and at ♩ [bar 130], *pp* ! [blue
crayon:] ?

8)

X? p. 83 Bar 7 and 8 [bars 140, 141], Violoncello [Lead pencil, the
and Contrabass: [magenta ink:] The parts dynamics crossed out,
have ══ ══ [blue crayon:] ? and above:] delete
     Bar 7   8

* p. 86 *Oboe* II, bar 3 [bar 157]: ♮ before *D* is
missing! [blue crayon:] Major error!

Violin II and *Viola*, bar 1 [bar 155]: For
aesthetic reasons, beaming the 3d and 4th
quarters in 3s ⊓⊓ ⊓⊓ would be
preferable!

Violin II, bar 1 [bar 155]: The ══◁ may
begin only with the last quarter!

*   *Violoncello*, bar 3 [bar 157]: ♯♮ (♮ instead
                   ♮*E*
of ♯)!! [blue crayon:] Major error!

p. 87 *Clarinet* I, bar 1 [bar 160]: ♮♪
(unnecessary!)

*   *Viola*, bar 3 [bar 162]: Final eighth note ♮
instead of ♯!! [blue crayon:] Major error!

* p. 88 *Horns in F*, final bar [bar 167]: ⌐♪, but
dot over the quarter note!

Trumpets [bar 167]: *ff* instead of *f*! [Lead pencil:] *ff*!

Violin I. In the final bar [bar 167], the notes
beamed in 3s, as before!

{209}

p. 89. In *Viol.* I u. II Streichung schöner und egaler! In beiden Stimmen gleich Takt 1.

2. [bars 168, 169] |⎵⎵⎵⎵| ⎵⎵ ⎵⎵!
                      6   3   3

Takt 3 u. 4 [bars 170, 171] *Viol.* I = *Viol.* II, alles zu 3!

Fagott II Takt 1 [bar 168] ♩ (♭ nöthig!)

X p. 90. *Hoboe* Takt 1 [bar 173] soll wohl ♩ *f*

[Lead pencil, after the first example:] *des* richtig! [both "??" crossed out; "auch ♭♩ des" underlined twice]

heißen? In der Stimme steht auch ♭♩ *des*!

[blue crayon, under the beginning of the entry and at the end:]??

* *Fagott, Cfag., Vc.* u. *CB* Takt 2–5 [bars 174–77] bei jedem einzelnen Achtel Punkt u. > (>)!

* *Cfagott* 3 letzte Takte [bars 178–80] Punkte über jedes Achtel!

Viol. II Takt 5 [bar 177]: ♭ vor *d*!

Vcell Takt 1 [bar 173]: Punkt über das letzte Achtel!

p. 91. *Fl.* u. *Hob.* Takt 2 [bar 182]: ♭ vor *d*!

Contrafagott Takt 1 [bar 181]: *sf sf* wie bei *CB* u. *Vc*!

Horn IV vorl. T. [bar 187]: 2<ᵗᵉˢ> ♭ vor *e* (1<ˢᵗᵉ> Linie) ♪!

Trompeten [bars 186–88]: *f* ——— *ff* !

p. 89 In *Violin* I and II, the beaming more
beautiful and regular! Bars 1 and 2 [bars
168, 169] the same in both parts

! Bars 3 and 4 [bars

170, 171], Violin I = Violin II, all in 3s!

Bassoon II, bar 1 [bar 168]:
(♭ necessary!)

X p. 90 *Oboe,* bar 1 [bar 173], should probably read

F? In the parts there is also *D*♭!
[blue crayon, under the beginning of the
entry, and at the end:] ??

[Lead pencil, after the
first example:] *D*♭ is
correct! [both "??"
crossed out; "also
D♭" underlined twice]

* *Bassoon, Contrabassoon, Violoncello,* and
Contrabass, bars 2–5 [bar 174–77]: Dot and >
(⸰) for each of the eighth notes!

* *Contrabassoon,* final three bars [bars 178–
80]: *Dots* over each eighth note!

Violin II, bar 5 [bar 177]: ♭ before *D* !

Violoncello, bar 1 [bar 173]: Dot over the
final eighth note!

p. 91 *Flute* and Oboe, bar 2 [bar 182]: ♭ before
D !

Contrabassoon, bar 1 [bar 181]: *sf sf*, as in the
Contrabass and Violoncello!

Horn IV, penultimate bar [bar 187]: 2d ♭
before *E* (1st line) !

Trumpets [bars 186–88]: *f* ———— *ff*!

{211}

p. 92.   *Viol.* I Takt 6 [bar 194]: Punkt über dem

zweiten ♪!

Vcell Takt 6 u. 7 [bars 194–95] fehlt die
Triolen_3 über der 1/4 Pause!

CB Takt 6 [bar 194] fehlt *p*!

X   p. 93.   *Horn* I. u. III Takt 2. 3 [bars 198–99]   [Lead pencil, the
fehlen die Schweller ＜ ＞ ＜ ＞   dynamics crossed out;
[in red crayon:] absichtlich?   at the end:] ja

*   p. 94.   *Fl.* Takt 1. 2. [bars 204–5] doppelt
gestrichen!! [blue crayon:] H Fehler!

Hob. Takt 5 [bar 208]: ♮*c*!

Clar. | Takt 4 [bar 207]: ♮*e*! [blue crayon:]
| Hauptfehler!
| Takt 6 [bar 209]: ♮*d*!
| im vorletzten Takt [bar 211]: steht
| die 1/2 Note *d* schlecht auf der 4$^{\underline{\text{ten}}}$
| Linie!

Fag. u. *C-Horn* letzter Takt [bar 212] fehlt
Punkt über dem Viertel!

Bratsche Takt 1 [bar 204]: fehlt *p*!

(9

p. 95.   *Viol.* I Takt 5 und 7 [bars 217, 219] fehlt
der Punkt über ⸭!

p. 96.   *Pauken* [bar 223]: *sf* statt *sff*!

Br., Vc. u. *CB* [bar 223] hingegen: *sff* st.
sf!

p. 92 *Violin* I, bar 6 [bar 194]: Dot over the

second ════ 𝄾!

Violoncello, bars 6 and 7 [bars 194–95]: The
3 for the triplet is missing over the 1/4 rest!

Contrabass, bar 6 [bar 194]: *p̱* is missing!

X p. 93 *Horn* I and III, bars 2, 3 [bars 198–99]: The   [Lead pencil, the
dynamic indications ⊂ ⊃ ⊂ ⊃ are   dynamics crossed out; at
missing. [in red crayon:] intentionally?   the end:] yes

* p. 94 *Flute,* bars 1, 2 [bars 204–5]: Double stem!!
[blue crayon:] Major error!

Oboe, bar 5 [bar 208]:♮*C* !

Clarinet | bar 4 [bar 207]: ♮*E* ! [blue crayon:]
| Major error!
| bar 6 [bar 209]: ♮*D* !
| in the penultimate bar [bar 211]:
| The 1/2 note *D* is poorly placed
| on the 4th line!

Bassoon and Horn in C, final bar [bar 212]:
Dot is missing over the quarter note!

Viola, bar 1 [bar 204]: *p* is missing!

(9

p. 95 *Violin* I, bars 5 and 7 [bars 217, 219]: The
dot over ≣ is missing!

p. 96 *Timpani* [bar 223]: *sf* instead of *sff* !

Viola, Violoncello, and Contrabass, on the
other hand [bar 223]: *sff* instead of *sf* !

*   p. 97.   *C-Hörner* Takt 2 [bar 229]: ♮ vor *f*!

Viol. I. II u. *Br.* letzter Takt [bar 235]:
Punkt über den ersten 4 Achteln! in der
Bratsche außerdem > über dem 2ᵗᵉⁿ u. 4ᵗᵉⁿ
Achtel!

Bratsche Takt 2. 3 [bars 229, 230] fehlt
Punkt über dem Viertel!

*   *Viol.* II. letzte Note [bar 235] *f* statt *des*

[blue crayon:]

Hauptfehler!

*   p. 98.   *Contrafagott* Takt 4 [bar 239]: ♮*e*!! [blue
crayon:] Hauptfehler!

      p. 99.   *Fagott* Takt 1 [bar 243]: ♭*h*!

Viol. I. Takt 2 [bar 244]: Punkt über ♪

Br. letzter Takt [bar 251]: *arco* [blue
crayon:] Hauptfehler!

      p. 100.   *Viol.* I. Takt 4 [bar 255]: fehlt *p*!

Br. Takt 1 [bar 252]: fehlt <u>*arco*</u>! [blue
crayon:] Hauptfehler!

Vcell. Takt 6 [bar 257]: (♮ fehlt)!

XX?   *Vcell.* Takt 2 [bar 253]: [underlined in   [Lead pencil, "??"
           magenta ink, and entry completed in   and "*col sordino*"
           magenta ink:] in der Stimme steht   crossed out]
           <u>*col sordino*</u>! [blue crayon:]??

X p. 101.   *Viol.* I [bar 261] [magenta ink:] in der   [Lead pencil, the
           Stimme *pp* ⎯⎯ *legg.*! [blue crayon:]??   dynamics crossed out]

*   p. 97   *Horn in C,* bar 2 [bar 229]: ♮ before *F* !

Violin I, II, and Viola, final bar [bar 235]:
Dot over the first 4 eighth notes! In the
Viola, in addition, > over the 2d and 4th
eighth notes!

Viola, bar 2, 3 [bars 229, 230]: Dot is
missing over the quarter note!

*   *Violin* II, final note [bar 235]: *F* instead of

D♭ [blue crayon:] Major

error!

*   p. 98   *Contrabassoon,* bar 4 [bar 239]: ♮ *E* !! [blue
crayon:] Major error!

     p. 99   *Bassoon,* bar 1 [bar 243]: ♭ *B* !

Violin 1, bar 2 [bar 244]: Dot over

Viola, final bar [bar 251]: *arco* [blue
crayon:] Major error!

     p. 100 *Violin* I, bar 4 [bar 255]: *p* is missing!

Viola, bar 1 [bar 252]: *arco* is missing! [blue
crayon:] Major error!

Violoncello, bar 6 [bar 257]: (♮ is
missing)!

XX ?   *Violoncello, bar* 2 [bar 253]: [underlined in   [Lead pencil, "??" and
magenta ink, and entry completed in   "*col sordino*" crossed
magenta ink:] In the part, *col sordino!* [blue   out]
crayon:] ??

X p. 101Violin I [bar 261] [magenta ink:]   [Lead pencil, the
in the part! [blue crayon:] ??   dynamics crossed out]

XX?   Takt 3 [bar 263] steht im 2 cl.
Arrangement als letztes Viertel

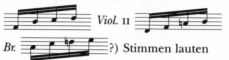 (b moll) in der Part. d.

Sept acc. ♭ biebringen, es könnte ein
Copistenfehler vorliegen (*Viol.* I

Viol. II

Br. ?) Stimmen lauten

aber wie die Partitur! [blue crayon:]?
[entire entry framed in blue crayon]

[Lead pencil, the
entire entry
bracketed, and in the
left margin:] Partitur
richtig. ["?" at the
beginning crossed
out]

p. 103.   *C-Hörner* Takt 3 [bar 271]: *p*!

Vcell. Takt 3 [bar 271] *p espress.*!

*   *Vcell.* und *CB* Takt 2 [bar 270]: *dim.* st. *p*!

*   "   " Takt 3 [bar 271]: fehlt *arco*!
[blue crayon:] Hauptfehler!

p. 105.   *Posaune* III [bar 285] steht die halbe Note *f*
zu weit vor!

p. 106.   *Viol.* I Takt 1. [bar 286] ♮ vor *f* auf dem
1sten Zwischenraum!

*X ??   In allen 5 Streicherstimmen *cresc.* im
letzten Takt [bar 291], unbeschadet
des ⏤! [blue crayon:]?

[Lead pencil, the last
"?" crossed out, and
at the end:] kann
stehen bleiben.

*   p. 107.   letzter Takt [bar 296] fehlt *p* in *Viol.* I, II u.
Br.!

*   p. 108.   *Trompeten* Takt 3 [bar 299] fehlt *p*!

*   p. 109.   *Contrafagott* letzter Takt [bar 309]: fehlt *pp*!

XX ?   In bar 3 [bar 263] of the 2-piano
arrangement the last quarter beat reads

♪♪ (B♭ minor); in the score,

the seventh chord has a ♭; it may be a

copyist's error (Violin I ♪♪ ,

Violin II ♪♪ , Viola

♪♪ ?) The parts, however, are

the same as the score! [blue crayon:] ?
[entire entry framed in blue crayon]

[Lead pencil, the entire
entry bracketed, and in
the left margin:] Score
correct ["?" at the
beginning crossed out]

p. 103 *Horns in C,* bar 3 [bar 271]: *p*!

Violoncello, bar 3 [bar 271]: *p espress.*!

*   *Violoncello* and *Contrabass,* bar 2 [bar 270]:
dim. instead of *p*!

*   "   "   [i.e., Violoncello and
Contrabass], bar 3 [bar 271]: *arco* is
missing! [blue crayon:] Major error!

p. 105 *Trombone* III [bar 285]: The half note *F* is
too far to the right!

p. 106 *Violin* I, bar 1 [bar 286]: ♮ before *F* in the
first space [of the staff]!

* X ??   In all 5 string parts, *cresc.* in the last bar
[bar 291], despite the ⏤!
[blue crayon:] ?

[Lead pencil, the last
"?" crossed out, and at
the end:] can stay

* p. 107 *Last* bar [bar 296]: *p* is missing in Violin I,
II, and Viola!

* p. 108 *Trumpets,* bar 3 [bar 299]: *p* is missing!

* p. 109 *Contrabassoon,* last bar [bar 309]: *pp* is
missing!

*   *Bratsche* Takt 4 [bar 305]: fehlt *dim.*!

[Blue crayon, set off by a blue-crayon line:]
Ende der Partitur, folgen Stimmen.

*   *Viola,* bar 4 [bar 305]: *dim.* is missing!

[Blue crayon, set off by a blue-crayon line:]
End of the score; parts follow.

10)

Orchesterstimmen.

Violine I.

p. 2.   Z.   6. T. 1 [1, bar 27]: fehlt Punkt unter 1/4 *as*.

——   7. T. 3 [bar 41]: das *pp* schon zum letzten Viertel des Taktes 2 [bar 40].

X ——   8. T. 2 [bar 44]: *marc.* steht nicht in der Partitur.

X ——   9. T. 2 [bar 47]: *mp espressivo!* ⟩— unter ⌐ ⌐ !
          Der 3ᵗᵉ Bogen reicht in der Part. bis zum 1/4 *f* des folgenden Taktes.

          Unten: 24 Orchesterstimmen (24 fehlt)!

p. 3.   Z.   4. T. 1 [bar 63]: ≀ ≀ statt 1/2 P.

X ⌐   T. 2 [bar 64]: Hier ist <u>ein</u> Bogen über alle Triolen gleich der Partitur; auf der folgenden Zeile [bar 69] <u>gar keiner</u>; Seite 5 das 1ᵗᵉ mal [bar 173] <u>2</u> Bogen (9 und 6 Achtel); und das 2ᵗᵉ mal [bar 178] wieder nur <u>ein</u> Bogen! In *Violine* II sind alle 4 mal <u>zwei</u> Bogen! In d. *Bratsche* beidemal <u>ein</u> Bogen! In der Partitur immer <u>ein</u> Bogen! [line along left margin in red crayon]

X —— ——   T. 3 [bar 65]: *mp*, in der Part. *mf*!

X ——   Z.   5. T. 2 [bar 67]: *mf* steht nicht in der P.!

——   Z.   6. T. 3 [bar 71b]: fehlt ♮ vor 𝄞!

——   Z.   7. T. 2 [bar 74]: fehlt > über #𝄞!

          ——   T. 3 [bar 76]: fehlt Punkt über #𝄞!

*   ——   Z.   9. sind die 2 ersten Takte [bars 81–82] <u>falsch</u>, die Pause muß immer <u>hinter</u> dem Achtel stehen, also:

[blue crayon:] Hauptfehler!

*   p. 4.   Zeile 1. letzter T [bar 98]: ⌣ zuletzt 𝄾 nur Punkte: [notation]

—   2. T. 2 [bar 100]: *f* ⟩—

X   —   4. T. 2 [bar 110]: *pp* steht nicht in d. Part.

—   5. T. 4 [bar 118]: *poco* 𝄾! *cresc.* <u>oben</u> 𝄾, dafür *cresc.* <u>unten</u> Anfang d. Takts!

*   X   —   6. Takt 2 [bar 121]: [notation] mittle [!] Note *c* fehlt!

*   Takt 5 [bar 124]: ⌢. nicht in d. P.!

*   7 [bar 126]: ⌢ nicht in d. P.!

10)

Orchestral Parts

Violin I

p. 2,   st. 6, b. 1 [1, bar 27]: Dot is missing under 1/4 note A♭.

——   7, b. 3 [bar 41]: The *pp* already for the final quarter note of bar 2 [bar 40].

X ——   8, b. 2 [bar 44]: *marc.* is not in the score.

X ——   9, b. 2 [bar 47]: *mp espressivo* ! ⟩ under ⌒ ! In the score, the 3d slur extends to the 1/4 F of the following bar.

At the bottom: 24 Orchestral Parts (24 missing)!

p. 3,   st. 4, b. 1 [bar 63]: 𝄾 𝄾 instead of 1/2 rest.

X   b. 2 [bar 64]: Here, as in the score, there is *one* slur over all the triplets; on the following staff [bar 69] there is *none;* page 5, the first time [bar 173], 2 slurs (9 and 6 eighths); and the 2d time [bar 178] again only *one* slur! In Violin II all 4 times there are *two* slurs! In the Viola both times *one* slur! In the score always *one* slur! [line along left margin in red crayon]

X ——   b. 3 [bar 65]: *mp*, in the score *mf*!

X ——   st. 5, b. 2 [bar 67]: *mf* is not in the score!

——   st. 6, b. 3 [bar 71b]: ♮ is missing before 𝄞!

——   st. 7, b. 2 [bar 74]: > is missing over ♯♮!

——   b. 3 [bar 76]: Dot is missing over ♯♮!

*   ——   st. 9: The first 2 bars [bars 81–82] are *wrong;* the rest must always follow the eighth note, thus:

[blue crayon:] Major error!

*   p. 4, staff 1, final bar [bar 98]: ⌄ at the end ♪ ; only dots:

——   2, b. 2 [bar 100]: *f* ⟩

X   —— 4, b. 2 [bar 110]: *pp* is not in the score.

—— 5, b. 4 [bar 118]: *poco* ♪! *cresc. above* ♪ ; instead put *cresc. below* the beginning of the bar!

*X   —— 6, bar 2 [bar 121]: middle note *C is missing* !

*   bar 5 [bar 124]: ⌐ not in the score!

*   7 [bar 126]: ⌐ not in the score!

X   — 7. Takt 2. 3 [bars 128, 129]: Der dritte (oberste) Bogen steht nicht in d. P.!

*   — 4 [bar 130]: <u>*cresc.*</u> im Anfang d. Taktes fehlt!

—11. letzter T [bar 150]: *pp* statt *p dol.*

*   —13. l. T [bar 156]: *mp espress.* (st. *p*)!

X   Ueber den letzten 4 Noten steht in der P. nur

ein Bogen ♩ ♪♪♪ !

X p. 5.   Z. 1. T. 1 [bar 157]: Bogen anders in der Part: ♭♩ ♪♯♩ ♫♪

—— T. 3 [bar 159]: *p* zum letzten Viertel fehlt!

Z. 3. T. 1 [bar 167]: Bogen falsch! ♯♪♪ ♪♪♪♪   3 u. 5 (statt 2 und 6) gebunden!

X   Z. 4. T. 2 [bar 172]: Der obere Bogen steht nicht i. d. P.!

X   —— T. 3 [bar 173]: Part. nur ein Bogen!

*   Z. 5. T. 3 [bar 176]: *p* 𝄢!

Z. 10. T. 4 [bar 199]: *ff* fehlt!

X   Z. 11. T. 3 [bar 203]: *rf* ? siehe: <u>Notiz zu Partitur p. 42!</u> [blue crayon:]?

T. 5 [bar 205]: *dim.* in den Anfang des Taktes.

Z. 12. T. 2 [bar 210]: *pp* zum ersten *f*! so: ♩. ♩ *pp*

Z. 13. T. 1 [bar 219]: Punkt fehlt über ♩̇ !

(11

Violine I.

p. 6.   Z. 3. l. T [II, bar 32]: Punkt unter d. letzten 1/4 ♩ fehlt!

X —— Z. 6. T. 4. 5 [bar 50, 51]: Bogen geht i. d. P. bis zum 1/4 *d*!

♪♩ | ♪♪♪ ♪

* —— Z. 8. T. 3 [bar 64]: vorletzte Note falsch! ♩ ♩ (statt ♩ ♩)

—— Z. 9. T. 2 [bar 66]: < > fehlt!

—— Z. 10. T. 2 [bar 69]: < bis zum 6ᵗᵉⁿ Achtel!

—— Z. 11. Takt 1 [bar 70]: *fis fis* über alle 6 Achtel!

p. 7.   Z. 3. T. 3 [bar 82]: <u>*dim.*</u> fehlt!

X —— Z. 10. F T. 3. 4 [bar 108, 109]: der obere Bogen fehlt i. d. Part!

X — 7, bar 2, 3 [bar 128, 129]: The third (uppermost) slur is not in the score!

* —— 4 [bar 130]: *cresc.* is missing at the beginning of the bar!

— 11, final bar [bar 150]: *pp* instead of *p dol.*

* — 13, final bar [bar 156]: *mp espress.* (instead of *p*)!

X Over the final four notes there is only *one* slur ♩ in the score!

X p. 5, st. 1, b. 1 [bar 157]: Slur different in the score:

—— b. 3 [bar 159]: *p* is missing for the final quarter note!

st. 3, b. 1 [bar 167]: Slur wrong! *3 and 5* notes connected (instead of 2 and 6)!

X st. 4, b. 2 [bar 172]: The upper slur is not in the score!

X —— b. 3 [bar 173]: In the score only *one* slur!

* st. 5, b. 3 [bar 176]: *p* !

st. 10, b. 4 [bar 199]: *ff* is missing!

X st. 11, b. 3 [bar 203]: *rf* ? see: *annotation in score, p. 42* ! [blue crayon:] ?

b. 5 [bar 205]: *dim.* at the beginning of the bar.

st. 12, b. 2 [bar 210]: *pp* for the first note *F*! Like this:

st. 13, b. 1 [bar 219]: Dot is missing over *F* !

(11

Violin I

p. 6, st. 3, final bar [II, bar 32]: *Dot* is missing under the final 1/4 note!

X —— st. 6, b. 4, 5 [bar 50, 51]: Slur extends to the 1/4 note *D* in the score!

* —— st. 8, b. 3 [bar 64]: Next to last note *wrong!* (instead of)

—— st. 9, b. 2 [bar 66]: ⎯⎯⎯ is *missing*!

—— st. 10, b. 2 [bar 69]: ⎯⎯ up to the *6th* eighth note!

—— st. 11, bar 1 [bar 70]: F♯ F♯ over *all* 6 8th notes!

p. 7, st. 3, b. 3 [bar 82]: *dim.* is missing!

X —— st. 10, **F**, b. 3, 4 [bar 108, 109]: The upper slur is missing in the score!

—— T. 5 [bar 110]: ⌒ über das 3<u>te</u> u. 4<u>te</u> 8<u>tel</u> fehlt!

* —— Z. 12. [bar 127] Von den Stichnoten ist die letzte falsch! muß ♩ heißen! (st. ♩) _c ^h

* —— —— Zur ganzen Note *p* <≖> [bar 128] fehlt das *p*!

* —— —— Im viertletzten Takte [bar 131] |− ⌐⌐ fehlt: *poco rit.*

p. 8. Z. 6. T. 1 [III, bar 34]: ♮ vor die 1<u>ste</u> Note *h*, von der 3<u>ten</u> ♪!

—— —— T. 5 [bar 38]: ♫ fehlt das ⌐⌐!

—— Z. 9. l. T [bar 61]: ♪ │ (das *p dol.* muß noch ganz hier
stehen u. das ⟩ anfangen!
p dol. │ Auf d. folgenden Zeile kommt
dann unter die 2 ersten
Sechzehntel

⟩, u. das *dol.* ♪!)

—— Z. 10. T. 2 [bar 63]: Das ⟩ muß unter ♪⌐ schon beginnen!

* —— —— — [bar 69]: Statt *pp cresc.* muß es heißen: *pp espress.*!

X —— — Die 2 letzten Bogen <u>berühren</u> sich i. d. P. auf ♮*h* [bar 71]!

* —— Z. 11. E [bar 77]: *p* statt *pp*! — Unter *dolce* muß ⟩ (3
Sechzehntel lang)

—— l. T [bar 80] ⟩ unter der letzten Note ♪⌐ muß <u>offen</u> sein:
⟩

X p. 9. Z. 2 [bar 97]: Der Bogen geht i. d. P. bis ♯*f*!

—— Z. 3 [bar 99]: Unter der ersten Triole [bar 99] fehlt die 3!

—— Z. 4. [bar 107] < bis *d*!

* —— Z. 8. [bar 128] falsche Note: Takt 1: [notation] [blue crayon:]
Hauptfehler! *c* st. *h*!

—— Z. 9. T. 3 [bar 140]: [notation] statt [notation] ♭!

—— Z. 10. l. T [bar 155]: <> auch unten!

p. 10. Z. 1. l. T [IV, bar 4]: ♭♩! (♭ fehlt)

—— Z. 2: *dim.* muß schon unter das letzte Achtel des 2<u>ten</u> Takts [bar 6];
also *dim.* Takt 4 [bar 8] ♪!

—— Z. 4: Ueber dem *sf*=Achtel [bar 29] fehlt ein Punkt!

p. 11. H [bar 134–36] Die ersten drei ⟩ müssen immer bis zur letzten
Note reichen!

p. 12. Z. 2. Takt 1. 2 [bar 150, 151] [notation] | [notation] (< > fehlt)!
ben marc.

* Z. 4. T. 1 [bar 158]: *più f sempre* fehlt!

—— b. 5 [bar 110]: ⌢ is missing over the 3d and 4th eighth notes!

* —— st. 12 [bar 127]: The last of the cue notes is *wrong*! Should read ♩! (instead of ♪)

* —— —— *p* is missing for the whole note *p* ⟨⟩ [bar 128]!

* —— —— In the fourth bar from the end [bar 131] |‑ ♪⌐ *is missing: poco rit.*

p. 8, st. 6, b. 1 [III, bar 34]: ♮ before the 1st note B, 𝄽 from the 3d note!

—— —— b. 5 [bar 38]: ♫ | is missing the ⟨——⟩!

—— st. 9, final bar [bar 61]: (the *p dol.* must go here and

p dol.

the ⟩ begin here! On the following staff, ⟩ then goes under the first 2 sixteenth notes, and the *dol.* 𝄽!)

—— st. 10, b. 2 [bar 63]: The ⟩ must begin already under ♪ |!

* —— —— — [bar 69]: Instead of *pp cresc.* it must read: *pp espress.*!

X —— — The final 2 slurs *touch* in the score at ♮B [bar 71]!

—— st. 11, **E** [bar 77]: *p* instead of *pp*! — ⟩ should be under *dolce* (3 sixteenths long)

—— final bar [bar 80]: ⟩ under the final note ♪ should be *open:* ⟩

X p. 9, st. 2 [bar 97]: The slur extends to #F in the score!

—— st. 3 [bar 99]: Under the first triplet the *3* is missing!

—— st. 4 [bar 107]: ⟨ up to *D* !

* —— st. 8 [bar 128]: *Wrong note:* bar 1 [bar 128]: ♮ ♪ *C* instead of *B♮*!

[blue crayon:] Major error!

—— st. 9, b. 3 [bar 140]: ♫ instead of ♫ ♭!

—— st. 10, final bar [bar 155]: ⟨⟩ below as well!

p. 10, st. 1, final bar [IV, bar 4]: ♭♪! (♭ is missing)

—— st. 2: *dim.* must already be under the final eighth note of the 2d bar [bar 6]; therefore *dim.* in bar 4 [bar 8] 𝄽!

—— st. 4: Over the *sf*-eighth note [bar 29] a dot is missing!

p. 11, **H** [bars 134–36]: The first three ⟩ must always extend to the final note!

p. 12, st. 2, bar 1, 2 [bars 150, 151]: ♫♫ | ♫♫ (⟨ ⟩ is missing)!

ben marc.

* st. 4, bar 1 [bar 158]: *più f sempre* is missing!

Z. 10. T. 3 und 4 [bars 181, 182]: fehlt je ein Punkt (über $\dot{\overline{b}}$ und $\dot{\overline{b}}$)!

Z. 11. die drei letzten Takte [bars 188–90]: ⌣ | ⌣ | ∴ muß auch <u>unten</u> stehen! Die <u>Punkte</u> fehlen auch <u>oben</u>!

12)

Violine I.

p. 13. Zeile 2 Takt 3. 4 [bars 198, 199]: $c \overset{3}{\underset{c}{\downarrow}}$ Beide mal ⌢ 𝄾!

—— letzte Zeile: Takt 3. 4 [bars 244, 245]: Punkt über das einzelne Achtel

$\underset{e}{\overset{e}{\flat}}$ und ♮♪!

*   p. 14. Z. 1. T. l [bar 249]: *mf* statt *f*!

—— Z. 2. T. 2. 3 [bars 261, 262]: ⟹ die ersten 3 mal über ▭!

X   —— T. 4 [bar 263]: (vgl. Notiz zur Part. p. 101) [blue crayon:]?

—— Z. 8. Das ⟸ muß schon Takt 2 [bar 285] bei $\underset{c}{\downarrow}$ anfangen!

—— T. 3 [bar 286]: ♮ vor das tiefe *f* (7tes 16^{tel}!)

* —— Z. 9. T. 1 [bar 288]: *pp* zu $\underset{a}{♪}$!

* —— T. 4 [bar 291]: <u>*cresc.*</u> über die halbe Pause: ⌢ und ⟹ fehlt!

also:

Zeile 10 Takt 1 [bar 292] ebenso.

—— Z. 10. Takt 3 [bar 294]:

Bogen fehlen!

Violine II.

*X⎞
X⎠ p. 2. Z. 3. T. 1. 2. [I, bars 13, 14] in der Part. <u>ganz anders</u>!! [blue crayon:]?? [brown ink:] (s. Part. p. 7.)

—— T. 4. [bar 16] fehlt ⌣ von $\underset{.}{\downarrow}$ zu ♪ !

st. 10, b. 3 and 4 [bars 181, 182]: One dot in each bar is missing (over 🎵 and 🎵)!

st. 11, the final three bars [bars 188–90]: ‿‿| ‿‿| ∴ must also appear *under* the notes! The *dots* are also missing *above*!

12)

Violin I

p. 13, staff 2, bar 3, 4 [bars 198, 199]: $c\ \overset{3}{\underset{}{}}\ c$, both times ⌒𝄾!

—— final staff: bar 3, 4 [bars 244, 245]: Dot over the single eighth notes $\overset{E}{\underset{E}{\flat}}$ and $\overset{E}{\natural\flat}$!

* p. 14, st. 1, b. 1 [bar 249]: *mf* instead of *f*!

—— st. 2, b. 2, 3 [bars 261, 262]: ⸺ the first 3 times over ▬▬!

X —— b. 4 [bar 263]: (cf. the note in the score, p. 101) [blue crayon:] ?

—— st. 8. The ⸺ must begin already in bar 2 [bar 285] with ♩!

—— b. 3 [bar 286]: ♮ before the low *F* (7th 16th note!) $\underset{C}{}$

* —— st. 9, b. 1 [bar 288]: *pp* at $\underset{A}{\eighth}$!

* —— b. 4 [bar 291]: *cresc.* over the half rest: ⌒ and ⸺ are missing!

cresc.

thus:

staff 10, bar 1 [bar 292] likewise.

—— st. 10, b. 3 [bar 294]:

Slurs are missing!

Violin II.

*X⎞ p. 2, st. 3, b. 1, 2 [I, bars 13, 14]: *Completely different* in the score!! [blue
X⎠   crayon:] ?? [brown ink:] *(see score, p. 7)*

—— b. 4 [bar 16]: ‿ is missing from ♩. to ♪ !

—— Z. 5. T. 2 [bar 23]: Punkt über das 1ᵗᵉ Viertel f_{as})!

* —— l. T [bar 26]: *p* st. *pp*!

—— Z. 9. T. 1 [bar 46]: ⟶ 𝄼!

—— T. 2 [bar 47]: *mp* st. *p*! *espress.* unter *arco* in die 4ᵗᵉ Linie!

—— Z. 11. T. 1 [bar 56]: Das 3ᵗᵉ u. 4ᵗᵉ ♮ überflüssig! 𝄼! In den 2 letzten Takten [bars 59, 60] statt der 1/2 P. zwei Viertelpausen!! Ebenso in den 3 folgenden Takte[!] [bars 61–63] auf pag. 3!!

X p. 3. Z. 1. T. 4 [bar 64]: in der Part. nur <u>ein</u> Bogen! — *sf* statt *f* (letztes 1/4)!

* —— Z. 2. T. 1 [bar 65]: *mf* st. *p*!

* —— T. 2 [bar 66]: *p* 𝄼! Punkte über ♮*c* ♯*f*!

* —— T. 3 [bar 67]: *sf* fehlt unter ⬥

* —— T. 4 [bar 68]: *f* fehlt über ♮♩ !

—— T. 5 [bar 69]: in der P. nur <u>ein</u> Bogen!

—— Z. 3. T. 3 [bar 71b]: ♮ (♮ fehlt)! letztes Viertel fehlt $\overset{>}{piùf}$! so:

più f

—— Z. 4. l. T [bar 77]: ♩ ♩ ♩ (erstes ⟹ weiter vor!)

—— Z. 5. 6. und 7 [bars 78–86]: Alle ⟹ müßen bis zur 3ᵗᵉⁿ Note reichen!

—— Z. 7. Takt 1 [bar 86]: unter dem ersten | ⟹ muß | *cresc.* stehen!

—— Z. 10. Takt 2 [bar 100]: *f* ⟹ !

—— Z. 11. T. 1 [bar 104]: ♭♩ (♭ fehlt!)

* —— Z. 12. *poco rit.* — — — — — muß schon 1 Takt früher (T. 2 [bar 108]) stehen!

* statt <u>*poco dim.*</u> muß es heißen: *p dim.*

(13

Violine II.

* p. 4. Z. 1. T. 4 [bar 117]: <u>*poco rit.*</u> 𝄼, erst im 5ᵗᵉⁿ Takt [bar 118] <u>*rit.*</u> – – (ohne *poco*)!

—— st. 5, b. 2 [bar 23]: Dot over the 1st quarter note $^F_{A\flat}$)!

* —— final bar [bar 26]: *p* instead of *pp*!

—— st. 9, b. 1 [bar 46]: ⸻♪!

—— b. 2 [bar 47]: *mp* instead of *p* ! *espress.* under *arco* on the 4th
line [of the staff]!

—— st. 11, b. 1 [bar 56]: The 3d and 4th ♮ are unnecessary! ♪!
In the final 2 bars [bars 59, 60], two quarter rests instead of
the 1/2 rest!! Likewise in the 3 following bars [bars 61–63]
on page 3!!

X p. 3, st. 1, b. 4 [bar 64]: Only *one* slur in the score! — *sf* instead of *f*
(final 1/4 note)!

* —— st. 2, b. 1 [bar 65]: *mf* instead of *p*!

* —— b. 2 [bar 66]: *p* ♪! Dot over ♮*C* ♮*F* !

* —— b. 3 [bar 67]: *sf* is missing under (musical notation)
sf

* —— b. 4 [bar 68]: *f* is missing over (musical notation) !

—— b. 5 [bar 69]: Only *one* slur in the score!

—— st. 3, b. 3 [bar 71b]: (musical notation) (♮ is missing)! Last quarter note *più f* is

missing! thus: (musical notation)
più f

—— st. 4, final bar [bar 77]: (musical notation) (first ⸺ further forward!)

—— st. 5, 6, and 7 [bars 78–86]: All ⸺ must extend to the 3d note!

—— st. 7, bar 1 [bar 86]: Under the first ⎟ ⸺
must be ⎟ *cresc.* !

—— st. 10, bar 2 [bar 100]: *f*⸺!

—— st. 11, b. 1 [bar 104]: (musical notation) (♭ is missing!)

* —— st. 12: *Poco rit.* – – – – – – – must already begin 1 bar earlier (b. 2
[bar 108])!

* Instead of *poco dim.* it must read: *p dim.*

(13

Violin II

* p. 4, st. 1, b. 4 [bar 117]: *poco rit.* ♪ *rit.* – – (without *poco*) not until the
5th bar [bar 118]!

* —— Z. 2. T. 2 [bar 120]: *f* zu ♩ (das 2te *f* bleibt trotzdem!)

* —— Z. 4. T. 1 [bar 130]: *cresc.* fehlt!

X —— T. 4 [bar 133]: in der Part. 8 höher [♪♪] [blue crayon:]?

*X —— Z. 5. T. 1 [bar 135]: in der Part. ♪♪ *g̱ a* st. ♭*a* [blue crayon:]?

—— Z. 6. T. 1 [bar 139]: *p* fehlt!

—— Z. 7. T. 5 [bar 147]: Das ═══ länger bis ♩ !

—— Z. 9. T. 2 [bar 156]: *arco* oben

espressivo darunter } über das 1ste Viertel!

—— Z. 10. T. 1 [bar 159]: *p* zu ♩ fehlt!

—— Z. 12. T. 3. 4. und Takt 1 der folgenden Seite [bars 170–72] statt der 1/2 Pause zwei Viertelpausen!

* p. 5. Z. 1. T. 1 [bar 172]: *f* zu ♪ !

* —— T. 2 [bar 173]: ♮ vor *f* 5te Linie [♪♪]; *sf* unter ♪ fehlt!

—— Z. 2. T. 1 [bar 176]: *sf* fehlt zu [♪]
sf

—— T. 3 [bar 177]: in d. P. nur <u>ein</u> Bogen!

X —— Z. 6. Takt 1 [bar 192]: in der Part. [♪♪♪] wohl richtig! [blue crayon:]? *g* statt ♮*f*; Stimme ist

—— T. 2 [bar 193]: fehlt ♭ vor ♩ !

—— Z. 7. T. 3 [bar 198]: > über die beiden halben Noten *f:* [♩ ♩] !

—— Z. 8. 9. T. 2 [bar 202]: Punkt fehlt über ♭♪ !

X —— T. 4 [bar 204]: *rf*? (s. Part. p. 42!)

—— Z. 10. T. 1 [bar 205]: < > ♪

—— Z. 11. l. T [bar 218]: 1/2 Pause fehlt vor dem Punkt!

—— Z. 12. T. 3 [bar 221]: *dim.* fehlt!

X p. 6. Z. 1. letzter Takt [II, bar 25]: in der P. geht <u>ein</u> Bogen über alle Sechzehntel!

* —— Z. 6. T. 2 [bar 44]: ⌣♪ !

* —— T. 4 [bar 46]: ♮ vor ♩ fehlt!

—— Z. 7. [bar 49] *pp semplice*!

* —— Z. 9. T. 1 [bar 64]: vorletztes Achtel falsch! [♪♪] [blue crayon:] Hauptfehler!
c statt *e*!

* p. 7. Z. 1. l. T [bar 80]: Punkt unter dem ersten 1/16 fehlt! — *p* statt *pp*!

* —— Z. 2. T. 1 [bar 81]: *dim.* über die 16^{tel}!

* —— st. 2, b. 2 [bar 120]: *f* at ♩ (the 2d *f* remains, nevertheless!)

* —— st. 4, b. 1 [bar 130]: *cresc.* is missing!

  X —— b. 4 [bar 133]: An octave higher in the score ♪♪ [blue crayon:] ?

*X —— st. 5, b. 1 [bar 135]: In the score ♪♪ *G A* instead of ♭*A* [blue crayon:] ?

  —— st. 6, b. 1 [bar 139]: *p* is missing!

  —— st. 7, b. 5 [bar 147]: The ⟩ longer, up to ♩!

  —— st. 9, b. 2 [bar 156]: *arco* above

                     espressivo below } over 1st quarter note!

  —— st. 10, b. 1 [bar 159]: *p* is missing at ♩!

  —— st. 12, b. 3, 4, and bar 1 of the following page [bars 170–72], two quarter rests instead of 1/2 rest!

* p. 5, st. 1, b. 1 [bar 172]: *f* at ♩ !

* —— b. 2 [bar 173]: ♮ before *F* 5th line ♪♪ ; *sf* is missing under ♪ !

  —— st. 2, b. 1 [bar 176]: *sf* is missing at ♪

                                                                      sf

  —— b. 3 [bar 177]: In the score, only *one* slur!

  X —— st. 6, bar 1 [bar 192]: In the score, ♪♪ *G* instead of ♮*F*; the part is probably correct! [blue crayon:] ?

  —— b. 2 [bar 193]: ♭ is missing before ♩!

  —— st. 7, b. 3 [bar 198]: > over the two half notes *F*: ♩̇ ♩̇ !

  —— st. 8, 9, b. 2 [bar 202]: Dots are missing over ♭♪ !

  X —— b. 4 [bar 204]: *rf* ? (*see score, p. 42!*)

  —— st. 10, b. 1 [bar 205]: < > ♪

  —— st. 11, final bar [bar 218]: 1/2 rest is missing before the dot!

  —— st. 12, b. 3 [bar 221]: *dim.* is missing!

  X p. 6, st. 1, final bar [11, bar 25]: In the score there is *one* slur over all the sixteenth notes!

* —— st. 6, b. 2 [bar 44]: ⌣♪ !

* —— b. 4 [bar 46]: ♮ is missing before ♩ !

  —— st. 7 [bar 49]: *pp semplice!*

* —— st. 9, b. 1 [bar 64]: Penultimate eighth note *wrong!* ♪♪ [blue crayon:] Major error!   *C* instead of *E* !

* p. 7, st. 1, final bar [bar 80]: Dot is missing under the first 1/16 note! — *p* instead of *pp*!

* —— st. 2, b. 1 [bar 81]: *dim.* over the 16th notes!

* —— Z. 4. T. 2 [bar 87]: falsche Note! ♪♪♪♪ [blue crayon]:
Hauptfehler! *h* statt *a* !

—— Z. 8. T. 2 [bar 102]: Das 2$^{\underline{te}}$ ♭ 𝄿!

*X —— letzte Zeile: statt 2 Takte Pause [bars 129–30] in der Partitur:

1
𝄽 𝅝 [blue crayon:]?
< >

* Im vierten Takt vor dem Schluß [bar 131] fehlt: *poco rit.*!

p. 8. Z. 2. [III] muß das >—— in den 4$^{\underline{ten}}$ Takt [bar 10]!

—— Z. 6. T. 5 [bar 33]: ⌒ vor bis zum letzten Achtel

♪♪♪♪

—— Z. 9. T. 4 [bar 52]: Punkt unter ♮♪ fehlt!

* —— Z. 10: Die beiden letzten Takte [bars 87–88] fehlt Bogen

♭♪♪♯ ♪ ♪♯♪♮

14)

Violine II.

X p. 9. Z. 1: In der Part. reicht der Bogen bis zum letzten ⌒ [bar 98]!

—— Z. 3: muß das <—— beim 2$^{\underline{ten}}$ Achtel von T. 2 [bar 106] beginnen
und bei dem 1/8 ♪ *d* des 3$^{\underline{ten}}$ Takts [bar 107] schließen!

—— Z. 5 [bars 118–119]: <—— nur bis ♩!

—— Z. 6. 1. T [bar 127]: ♪♪♮ Bogen von *e* zu *a* fehlt!

—— Z. 7. 1. T [bar 133]: ⌒ nur bis *d*!

p. 10. Z. 1. T. 4 [IV, bar 4]: fehlt ♭ vor ♩!
h

—— Z. 2: Das *dim.* muß schon beim letzten 1/8 von Takt 1 [bar 6]
stehen ! (T. 3. [bar 8] *dim.* 𝄿!)

—— Z. 5. T. 1 [bar 29]: Punkt über ♪ fehlt!

* —— —— T. 5 [bar 33]: ***pp*** (statt ***ppp***)!

p. 11. Z. 2. T. 4 [bar 76]; Punkt über dem 1$^{\underline{sten}}$ Viertel fehlt!

* —— Z. 4. T. 4 [bar 87]: Erstes Viertel Doppelgriff: 𝄞 $^{g}_{es}$) Punkt
darüber!

* —— —— T. 5 [bar 88]: Erstes Viertel einfache Note 𝄞 ^{es} ! (ohne ♭)

—— Z. 7. 1. T. [bar 104] und ⎫
—— Z. 8. T. 1 [bar 105]: ⎭ Punkte beim *pizz.* 𝄿!

* —— st. 4, b. 2 [bar 87]: *Wrong note!* [blue crayon:]
Major error! *B* instead of *A* !

—— st. 8, b. 2 [bar 102]: The 2d ♭ !

*X —— final staff: Instead of 2-bar rest [bars 129–30], in the score:

[blue crayon:]?

* In the fourth bar from the end [bar 131] *poco rit.* is missing!

p. 8, st. 2 [III]. The ═══ must be in the 4th bar [bar 10]!

—— st. 6, b. 5 [bar 33]: ‿‿‿ all the way through to the final eighth
note

—— st. 9, b. 4 [bar 52]: Dot is missing under !

* —— st. 10: Slur is missing in the final two bars [bars 87–88]

14)

Violin II

X p. 9, st. 1: In the score, the slur reaches to the final [bar 98]!

—— st. 3: The ═══ must begin at the 2d eighth note of b. 2 [bar 106]
and end with the 1/8 note *D* of the 3d bar [bar 107]!

—— st. 5 [bars 118–19]: ═══ only up to !

—— st. 6, final bar [bar 127]: slur is missing from *E to A*!

—— st. 7, final bar [bar 133]: ‿‿‿ only up to *D*!

p. 10, st. 1, b. 4 [IV, bar 4]: ♭ is missing before !
B

—— st. 2: The *dim.* must already be at the final 1/8 note of bar 1 [bar
6]! (b. 3 [bar 8] *dim.* !)

—— st. 5, b. 1 [bar 29]: Dot is missing over !

* —— —— b. 5 [bar 33]: *pp* (instead of *ppp*)!

p. 11, st. 2, b. 4 [bar 76]: Dot is missing over the 1st quarter note!

* —— st. 4, b. 4 [bar 87]: First quarter-note *double stop*: $\binom{G}{E\flat}$) *Dot over*
it!

* —— b. 5 [bar 88]: First quarter note a single note *E♭* !
(without ♭)

—— st. 7, final bar [bar 104] and ⎫
—— st. 8, b. 1 [bar 105]: ⎬ *Dot at the pizz.* !

{233}

—— letzte Zeile, Takt 1 [bar 127]: ♩ 𝆕 unter der Note, nicht unter der Pause beginnend!

* p. 12. Z. 4. T. 1 [bar 156]: ♩♪♪ fehlt! — Takt 3 [bar 158]: *più f sempre!*

* —— Z. 10. l. T [bar 174]: ♭ vor d !

p. 13. Z. 2 [bar 194]: *mf legg.*— In demselben Takt (3 u. Punkte noch einmal!)

—— vorl. Z., letzter T [bar 245]: Punkt unter ♪ fehlt!

* —— letzte Z. T. 4 [bar 249]: *mf* statt *f*

* p. 14. Z. 1. T. 1 [bar 258]: <u>*col sordino*</u> über *pizz!* (Punkt hinter *pizz* fehlt!)

—— T. 4. 5 [bars 261, 262]: ⟍ über jede 16tel Gruppe!

—— Z. 3 [bar 267]: <u>*Un poco sostenuto.*</u> (mit Temposchrift <u>obenhin!</u>)

—— Z. 7 [bars 281–284]: (Alle 4 mal ⟍ über die ersten 4 der gebundenen 16tel!)

—— Z. 8: von ♩ im 1sten Takt [bar 285] ab!

* —— Z. 9. letzter T. [bar 291]: <u>*cresc.*</u> oben über die 1/2 Pause!

* —— Z. 10. l. T [bar 296]: *p* zu ♪ fehlt!

Bratsche.

p. 2. Z. 3. T. 4 [I, bar 13]: ' Strichpunkt (Keil) über den *sf*=Accord!

—— Z. 5. T. 2. 3 [bars 21, 22]: ♪ | ♪ Bogen auch unten von *c* zu *es!*

—— Z. 6. T. 4 [bar 27]: Punkt unter das erste 1/4!

X In d. P. gehen die Bogen der beiden letzten Takte [bars 27, 28] bis an das den Achteln folgende Viertel!

* —— Z. 10. [bar 47] *mp espress.* fehlt! (unter ⟨ ⟩!)

—— Z. 11 [bar 53]: statt der 1/2 Pause 2 Viertelpausen!

(15

Bratsche.

p. 3. Z. 1. l. T. [bar 65]: *mf!*

—— Z. 2. T. 1 [bar 66]: Punkte über alle 3 Viertel!

—— T. 3 [bar 68]: *f* über ♪ fehlt!

—— final staff, bar 1 [bar 127]: ♩ beginning under the note, not under the rest!

* p. 12, st. 4, b. 1 [bar 156]: ♩ ♩ ♩ is missing! — Bar 3 [bar 158]: *più f sempre!*

* —— st. 10, final bar [bar 174]: ♭ before *D* !

p. 13, st. 2 [bar 194]: *mf legg.* — In the same bar ♩ (*3* and dots again!)
—— penultimate staff, final bar [bar 245]: Dot is missing under ♪!

* —— final staff, b. 4 [bar 249]: *mf* instead of *f*

* p. 14, st. 1, b. 1 [bar 258]: *col sordino* over *pizz*! (Dot is missing after *pizz*!)
—— b. 4, 5 [bars 261, 262]: ⟩ over each 16th-note group!

—— st. 3 [bar 267]: *Un poco sostenuto.* (*at the top*, in the typeface of the tempo marking!)

—— st. 7 [bars 281–84]: ♫♫ ♫♫ (All 4 times ⟨ over the *first 4* of the slurred 16th notes!)

—— st. 8: from ♩ in the 1st bar [bar 285] on!

* —— st. 9, final bar [bar 291]: *cresc.* above, over the 1/2 rest!

* —— st. 10, final bar [bar 291]: *p* is missing at ♩ !

Viola

p. 2, st. 3, b. 4 [1, bar 13]: ' accent mark (wedge) over the *sf* chord!
—— st. 5, b. 2, 3 [bars 21, 22]: ♪ | ♪ Slur also below, from *C* to *E♭*!

—— st. 6, b. 4 [bar 27]: Dot under the first 1/4 note!
X In the score the slurs in the final two bars [bars 27, 28] extend up to the quarter note following the eighth note!

* —— st. 10 [bar 47]: *mp espress.* is missing! (under ⟨ ⟩!)
—— st. 11 [bar 53]: 2 quarter rests instead of the 1/2 rest!

(15

Viola

p. 3, st. 1, final bar [bar 65]: *mf* !
—— st. 2, b. 1 [bar 66]: Dots over all 3 quarter notes!
—— b. 3 [bar 68]: *f* is missing over ♩ !

—— Z. 5. T. 1. [bar 80] ⌒ fehlt von 🎵 zu 🎵 !

——*ben marc.* erst in den Anfang des 2ten Taktes [bar 81]!

—— Z. 7. ════════ vom letzten 1/4 des 1sten bis Ende des 2ten Taktes [bars 88–89]!

—— Z. 10. T. 2 [bar 100]: *f* ▶═ !

—— Z. 11. T. 1 [bar 104]: ♭ vor das 1ste 8^{tel}! 🎵

* —— Z. 12. *poco rit.*- – – schon in den Anfang des 2ten Taktes [bar 109]!

* p. 4. Z. 1. *rit.* – (ohne *poco*) erst in den <u>letzten</u> Takt [bar 118]!

* —— Z. 2. T. 2 [bar 120]: *f* zum ersten 1/4; das 2te *f* bleibt ebenfalls!

—— Z. 5. T. 2 [bar 134]: *sf* unter das erste Viertel!

*X —— Z. 9. T. 1 [bar 153]: <u>*cresc.*</u> 𝄐! (in den andern Stimmen steht *marc.*, in der Partitur jedoch nicht!)

* —— —— letzter Takt [bar 156]: *mp espress.* (unter ◁ ▷)

* p. 5. Z. 1. l. T. [bar 172]: 🎵 (*cresc.* fehlt! ⌒ nur bis *e*! *f* zum l. 1/4!)

* —— Z. 2. T. 2 [bar 174]: *f* statt *ff*!

—— Z. 3. T. 2 und 3 [bars 179, 180]: > fehlt beidemal über 🎵 [in bars 178, 179]

—— Z. 9. T. 3 [bar 201]: *rf* ◁═ !

—— Z. 10. und 11 🎵 ist bereits geändert in 2 Takte Pause [bars 212–13]!

* p. 6. [II, bars 1ff.] <u>*Andante.*</u> (*con moto* 𝄐)!

—— Z. 2. T. 1. [bar 14] in der P. reicht der untere Bogen bis zum 1/4 *g* [bar 15]!

—— l. T [bar 24]: ◁ unter die 4/16!

—— Z. 3. T. 1 [bar 25]: ════ vorn offen über den ganzen Takt bis *mf* !

X i. d. P. geht <u>ein</u> Bogen über <u>alle</u> Sechzehntel!

—— T. 2 [bar 26]: Das 2te Viertel in 2 Achtel 🎵 ausstechen!

* —— Z. 9. l. T [bar 63]: *mf* st. *mp*!

—— Z. 11. l. T [bar 71]: ◁═ schon vom 4ten Achtel beginnend!

—— Z. 12. T. 1 [bar 72]: ♯ vor das 1ste Achtel *f*! vom 3ten Achtel ♯ 𝄐!

p. 7. Z. 2. T. 3 [bar 81]: Das *dim.* ist bereits eingetragen!

—— Z. 9. T. 1. 2 [bars 105, 106]: Das ◁ ▷ ist bereits entfernt!

—— st. 5, b. 1 [bar 80]: ⌒ is missing from 𝆒 to ♯𝆒 !

—— *ben marc.* not until the beginning of the 2d bar [bar 81]!

—— st. 7: ———————— from the final 1/4 of the 1st bar until the end of the 2d bar [bars 88–89]!

—— st. 10, b. 2 [bar 100]: *f*⟩——!

—— st. 11, b. 1 [bar 104]: ♭ before the 1st 8th note!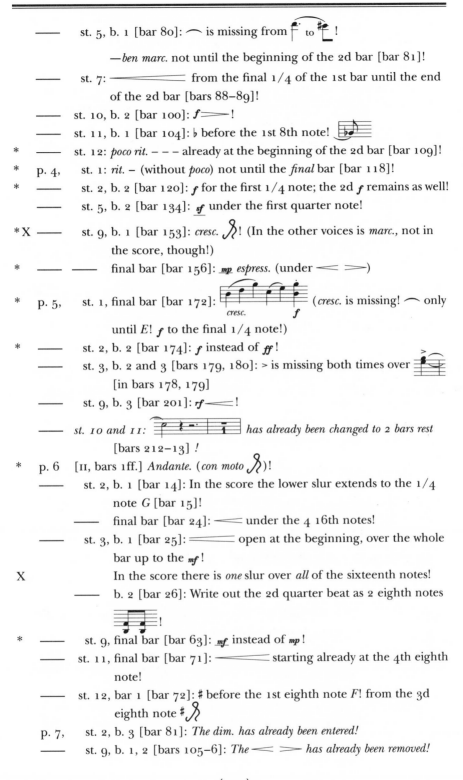

* —— st. 12: *poco rit. - - -* already at the beginning of the 2d bar [bar 109]!

* p. 4, st. 1: *rit. -* (without *poco*) not until the *final* bar [bar 118]!

* —— st. 2, b. 2 [bar 120]: *f* for the first 1/4 note; the 2d *f* remains as well!

—— st. 5, b. 2 [bar 134]: *sf* under the first quarter note!

*X —— st. 9, b. 1 [bar 153]: *cresc.* 𝄐! (In the other voices is *marc.*, not in the score, though!)

* —— —— final bar [bar 156]: *mp espress.* (under ⟨ ⟩)

* p. 5, st. 1, final bar [bar 172]: (cresc. is missing! ⌒ only until *E*! *f* to the final 1/4 note!)

cresc. *f*

* —— st. 2, b. 2 [bar 174]: *f* instead of *ff* !

—— st. 3, b. 2 and 3 [bars 179, 180]: > is missing both times over [in bars 178, 179]

—— st. 9, b. 3 [bar 201]: *rf*⟨——!

—— *st. 10 and 11:* *has already been changed to 2 bars rest* [bars 212–13] !

* p. 6 [II, bars 1ff.] *Andante. (con moto* 𝄐)!

—— st. 2, b. 1 [bar 14]: In the score the lower slur extends to the 1/4 note *G* [bar 15]!

—— final bar [bar 24]: ⟨—— under the 4 16th notes!

—— st. 3, b. 1 [bar 25]: ———————— open at the beginning, over the whole bar up to the *mf* !

X In the score there is *one* slur over *all* of the sixteenth notes!

—— b. 2 [bar 26]: Write out the 2d quarter beat as 2 eighth notes

!

* —— st. 9, final bar [bar 63]: *mf* instead of *mp* !

—— st. 11, final bar [bar 71]: ———————— starting already at the 4th eighth note!

—— st. 12, bar 1 [bar 72]: ♯ before the 1st eighth note *F*! from the 3d eighth note ♯ 𝄐

p. 7, st. 2, b. 3 [bar 81]: *The dim. has already been entered!*

—— st. 9, b. 1, 2 [bars 105–6]: *The* ⟨ ⟩ *has already been removed!*

—— T. 4 [bar 108]: *p cresc. poco a poco* fehlt!

—— letzte Zeile [bar 121]: *dolce* ist bereits eingetragen!

—— Statt 10 T. Pause [bars 123–32] ist zu setzen:

p. 8. Z. 2: Die Zeichen ◁ ▷ [III, bars 8–10] sind bereits verbessert!

Z. 5: Triolen=3 zweimal über das 2ᵗᵉ 16ᵗᵉˡ [bar 21] zu setzen!

Z. 10. T. 1 [bar 51]: fehlt *p*!

—— T. 2 [bar 52]: Das Achtel *g* statt 𝄾 ist bereits eingetragen!

16)

Bratsche.

p. 8. Z. 10. vl. T [bar 63]: *p dolce* (*p* fehlt)!

X p. 9. Z. 2. T. 2. 3 [bars 90, 91]: Der Bogen fängt in der Part. erst beim 1/4 *g* an!

X —— T. 5 [bar 93]: In der Part. steht ein Bogen von ♮*d* bis ♯*f* im vl. T. [bar 97]! Dieser ist bereits eingetragen!

—— Z. 3. T. 2 [bar 99]: fehlt *p*! (*p*◁)

—— Z. 4. Takt 2 [bar 106]: ▷ bis zum vierten 1/16 des folgenden Takts [bar 107] fehlt!

—— Takt 4 [bar 108]: ▷ fehlt!

—— Z. 5. Takt 4 [bar 113]: ◁ Takt 5 [bar 114]: ▷ fehlt!

—— Z. 6. Die 4 fehlenden *pizz.* Takte [bars 118–21] sind bereits eingetragen!

* Hingegen fehlt das Wort *arco* im 1ˢᵗᵉⁿ Takte von **G** [bar 122]!

—— Z. 8. [bar 137] Das *p* ist gemacht!

—— Z. 9. T. 1 [bar 139]: Das *leggiero* ist bereits weggebracht!

—— letzte Z. T. 4 [bar 159]: ⌣ Bogen auch oben!

p. 10. Z. 1. T. 4 [IV, bar 4]: ♭ vor das 1ˢᵗᵉ Achtel *h* fehlt!

—— l. T [bar 5]: ▷ offen unter das letzte Achtel!

—— Z. 2. T. 1 [bar 6]: ▷ unter das 1ˢᵗᵉ Viertel mit Punkt! — *dim.* unter dem letzten Achtel fehlt! Die folgenden *pp legg.* Takte [bars 8ff.] sind nach der Partitur zumeist bereits geändert und das fehlende corrigirt! Sie heißen also jetzt:

[along left margin:] Zeile 2–4

—— b. 4 [bar 108]: *p cresc. poco a poco* is missing!

—— final staff [bar 121]: *dolce has already been entered!*

—— Instead of 10-bar rest [bars 123–32] put in

p. 8, st. 2: *The signs* ≺ ≻ [III, bars 8–10] *have already been corrected!*

st. 5: Triplet *3* has to be put twice over the 2d 16th notes [bar 21]!

st. 10, b. 1 [bar 51]: *p* is missing!

—— b. 2 [bar 52]: *The eighth note G instead of ʼ has already been entered!*

16)

Viola

p. 8, st. 10, penultimate bar [bar 63]: *p dolce* (*p* is missing)!

X p. 9, st. 2, b. 2, 3 [bars 90, 91]: The slur begins in the score only with the 1/4 note *G*!

X —— b. 5 [bar 93]: In the score there is one slur from ♮*D* to ♯*F* in the penultimate bar [bar 97]! *This has already been entered!*

—— st. 3, b. 2 [bar 99]: *p* is missing! (*p*≺)

—— st. 4, bar 2 [bar 106]: ————— through to the fourth 1/16 note of the following measure [bar 107] is missing!

—— bar 4 [bar 108]: ≻———— is missing!

—— st. 5, bar 4 [bar 113]: ≺ bar 5 [bar 114]: ≻ is missing!

—— st. 6: *The 4 missing pizz. measures* [bars 118–21] *have already been entered!*

* However, the word *arco* is missing in the 1st bar of **G** [bar 122]!

—— st. 8 [bar 137]: *The p has already been done!*

—— st. 9, b. 1 [bar 139]: *The leggiero has already been taken out!*

—— final staff, b. 4 [bar 159]: ⌣ slur also above!

p. 10, st. 1, b. 4 [IV, bar 4]: ♭ is missing before the 1st eighth note *B*!

—— final bar [bar 5]: ≻ open under the final eighth note!

—— st. 2, b. 1 [bar 6]: ≻ under the 1st dotted quarter note! — *dim.* is missing under the final eighth note! *The following pp legg. measures* [bars 8ff.] *have already been altered in the score, for the most part, and what was missing has been corrected!* Therefore, they now read:

[along the left margin:] staves 2–4

—— Z. 4. 1. T [bar 17]: ⅔ (statt ♪ ↑)!
g

—— Z. 7. T. 2 [bar 33]: ♭ vor *h*!

—— Z. 8. 1. T [bar 42]: fehlt Punkt über ♮♪ !

—— Z. 9. T. 3 [bar 45]: fehlt Punkt über dem letzten 1/8!

—— Z. 10. T. 5 [bar 53]: | muß Punkt unter dem ersten 1/8 ♫ !

—— Z. 11. T. 3 [bar 57]: | ebenfalls!

p. 11. Z. 3. 1. T [bar 85]: ——♫!

—— Z. 4. T. 1 [bar 86]: ══♫! Im letzten Takt ♮ vor ⌐♫! <u>Punkte</u> über die vier Achtel!

p. 12. Z. 5. 1. T [bar 161]: muß die 2 über der 1/2 P. ♫!

* —— Im 1ͭᵉⁿ Takt [bar 159] fehlt *<u>più f sempre</u>*!

—— Z. 8. T. 1 [bar 169]: fehlt ♮ für die 2ᵗᵉ *Bratsche* ════ !

—— Z. 10. 1. T [bar 181]: fehlt Punkt über dem letzten Achtel!

—— Z. 11. T. 1 [bar 182]: *più f* vor!

p. 13. Z. 1. T. 3 und 4 [bars 194, 195]: Punkte über den einzelnen Achteln ♪♫! *mf <u>legg</u>.* fehlt!

* —— Z. 3. T. 4 [bar 204]: *p* fehlt! (*p*———

(17

Bratsche.

* p. 13. Z. 4. T. 1 [bar 206]: ♮ vor *a* fehlt: ════ [blue crayon:] wichtig!

—— Z. 8. T. 3 [bar 231]: Punkt fehlt über ⸫ !

—— Z. 9. T. 2 [bar 235]: > > über dem 2ᵗᵉⁿ u. 4ᵗᵉⁿ Achtel fehlen!

—— Z. 10. T. 1 [bar 238]: Punkt unter dem 1ˢᵗᵉⁿ Viertel ♫!

—— Z. 11. T. 3 [bar 245]: Punkt unter dem letzten Achtel fehlt!

p. 14. Z. 1. T. 1 [bar 259]: Punkt hinter *pizz.* fehlt!

—— T. 2 [bar 260]: ══ über die 4 Sechzehntel! Auch in den beiden folg. Takten [bars 261–62]! ═► ═► ═► ═►

* —— T. 3 [bar 261]: ♮ vor dem 1ˢᵗᵉⁿ 16ᵗᵉˡ *e* fehlt! letztes 1/16 <u>falsche</u> Note: ════ (*b* st. *f*!)

—— Z. 3 [bar 267]: *Un poco sostenuto.* (mit dicker Temporschrift!)

—— Z. 4. 1. T. [bar 273]: ══ bis ans Ende des Taktes!

—— Z. 5. T. 1 [bar 274]: ══ bis ans Ende des Taktes!

—— Z. 6. T. 1 [bar 278]: *dim.* vor zum <u>letzten</u> Viertel!

—— st. 4, final bar [bar 17]: ⌇ (instead of ♪ ♪)!

—— st. 7, b. 2 [bar 33]: ♭ before *B*!

—— st. 8, final bar [bar 42]: Dot is missing over ♮♪ !

—— st. 9, b. 3 [bar 45]: Dot is missing over the final 1/8 note!

—— st. 10, b. 5 [bar 53]: | Dot should be under the first 1/8 note ♪ !

—— st. 11, b. 3 [bar 57]: | Likewise!

p. 11, st. 3, final bar [bar 85]: ——◁ ♪ !

—— st. 4, b. 1 [bar 86]: ◁ ♪ ! In the final bar ♮ before ⌐♪ ! *Dots* over the four eighth notes!

p. 12, st. 5, final bar [bar 161]: The 2 over the 1/2 rest should be ♪ !

* —— In the 1st measure [bar 159] *più f sempre* is missing!

—— st. 8, b. 1 [bar 169]: ♮ is missing for the 2nd viola 𝄞 !

—— st. 10, final bar [bar 181]: Dot is missing over the final eighth note!

—— st. 11, b. 1 [bar 182]: [Move] *più f* forward!

p. 13, st. 1, b. 3 and 4 [bars 194, 195]: Dots over the single eighth notes ♪ ♪ ! *mf legg.* is missing!

* —— st. 3, b. 4 [bar 204]: *p* is missing! (*p* ◁

(17

Viola

* p. 13, st. 4, b. 1 [bar 206]: ♮ *before A* is missing: 𝄞 [blue crayon:] important!

—— st. 8, b. 3 [bar 231]: Dot is missing over ⸱F !

—— st. 9, b. 2 [bar 235]: > > are missing over the 2d and 4th eighth notes!

—— st. 10, b. 1 [bar 238]: Dot under the 1st quarter note ♪ !

—— st. 11, b. 3 [bar 245]: Dot is missing under the final eighth note!

p. 14, st. 1, b. 1 [bar 259]: Dot is missing after *pizz.* !

—— b. 2 [bar 260]: ▷ over the 4 sixteenth notes! Also in the following two bars [bars 261–62]! ▷ ▷ ▷ ▷

* —— b. 3 [bar 261]: ♮ is missing before the 1st 16th note *E*!

Final 1/16 *wrong note* : 𝄞 (*B♭* instead of *F*!)

—— st. 3 [bar 267]: *Un poco sostenuto.* (with bold script used for tempo indications!)

—— st. 4, final bar [bar 273]: ◁ through to the end of the bar!

—— st. 5, b. 1 [bar 274]: ▷ through to the end of the bar!

—— st. 6, b. 1 [bar 278]: [Move] *dim.* forward to the *final* quarter note!

— Z. 8. Das ⎯⎯⎯⎯⎯ schon vom 1sten Takt ab [bars 285–86]!

* — Z. 9. l. T. [bar 291]: *cresc.* über die 1/2 Pause! unten ⎯⎯ unter die ersten 4/16!

* — Z. 10. T. 1 [bar 292]: ⎯⎯ unter die ersten 4/16! (⎯$\mathcal{S}$)

* — letzte Z. T. 3 [bar 305]: *dim.* fehlt!

Violoncell.

* p. 2. Z. 7. T. 1 [1, bar 36]: *p* fehlt!

— Z. 9. l. T [bar 44]: ungenau:

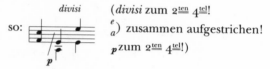

so: *divisi* (*divisi* zum 2ten 4^{tel}!
$^{e}_{a}$) zusammen aufgestrichen!
p zum 2ten 4^{tel}!)

* — Z. 10. vl. T [bar 47]: *mp espress.*!

p. 3. Z. 1. T. 2 [bar 50]: ♯ vor ♩ fehlt!

— Z. 2. vl. T [bar 58]: Punkt fehlt unter dem letzten Viertel ♯*g*!

— Z. 3. T. 1 [bar 60]: Punkt über d. 1sten Viertel fehlt! ♪ ♪ statt 1/2 P.

— T. 3 [bar 62]: *cresc.* vor! unter das letzte Viertel ♮*g*!

— Z. 4. T. 1 [bar 65]: Punkt unter das letzte 1/4!

— T. 2 [bar 66l]: Punkte über das 4te u. 5te Viertel!

— T. 4 [bar 68]: *f* statt *sfz*!

— Z. 5. T. 1 [bar 70]: Punkt unter das 2te Viertel!

* — Z. 7. T. 1 [bar 78]: ⌒ fehlt von [*a zu g*] und T. 3. [bar 80] von [*zu ♯*] !

— T. 4. [bar 81] *ben marc.* vor zu Anfang des letzten Taktes [bar 81]!

*X — Z. 9. l. T [bar 90]: *p* $\mathcal{S}$! (**??**) jedenfalls nicht zum ersten, höchstens zum 2ten Viertel!

* — letzte Zeile T. 3. 4 [bars 98, 99]: Punkt unter jedes Viertel (7 Punkte!)!

— T. 5 [bar 100]: *f* ⎯⎯!

p. 4. Z. 3 [bar 114?]: Das 2te mal *pp sempre* $\mathcal{S}$!

Z. 4 [bar 118]: nur *rit.*– – – – (*poco* $\mathcal{S}$!)

— Takt 3 [bar 120]: *f* unter das 1te Viertel; das 2te *f* bleibt trotzdem!

—   st. 8: The ⟨⟩ already from the 1st beat on [bars 285–86]!

* —   st. 9, final bar [bar 291]: *cresc.* over the 1/2 rest! ⟩ below, under the first 4 16th notes!

* —   st. 10, b. 1 [bar 292]: ⟩ under the first 4 16th notes! (⟨♪⟩)

* —   final staff, b. 3 [bar 305]: *dim.* is missing!

Violoncello

*   p. 2,   st. 7, b. 1 [I, bar 36]: *p* is missing!

—   st. 9, final bar [bar 44]: Imprecise:

like this: (*divisi* on the 2d quarter note!
E⟩ A⟩ together with upward stem!
p on the 2d quarter note!)

* —   st. 10, penultimate bar [bar 47]: *mp espress.* !

p. 3,   st. 1, b. 2 [bar 50]: ♯ is missing before ♩!

—   st. 2, penultimate bar [bar 58]: Dot is missing under the final quarter note ♯*G*!

—   st. 3, b. 1 [bar 60]: Dot is missing over the 1st quarter note! 𝄾 𝄾 instead of 1/2 rest.

—   b. 3 [bar 62]: [Move] *cresc.* forward! under the final quarter note ♮*G*!

—   st. 4, b. 1 [bar 65]: Dot under the final 1/4 note!

—   b. 2 [bar 66]: Dots over the 4th and 5th quarter notes!

—   b. 4 [bar 68]: *f* instead of *sfz*!

—   st. 5, b. 1 [bar 70]: Dot under the 2d quarter note!

* —   st. 7, b. 1 [bar 78]: ⌢ is missing from ♩. ♪ (A to G) and in b. 3 [bar 80] from ♩. to ♯♪ !

—   b. 4 [bar 81]: [Move] *ben marc.* forward to the beginning of the final bar [bar 81]!

*X —   st. 9, final bar [bar 90]: *p* ♪! (? ?) at least not on the first [quarter note]; if at all, on the 2d quarter note!

* —   final staff, b. 3, 4 [bars 98, 99]: Dot under each quarter note (7 dots!)!

—   b. 5 [bar 100]: *f* ⟩!

p. 4,   st. 3 [bar 114?]: The 2d *pp sempre* ♪!

st. 4 [bar 118]: Only *rit.* – – – – (*poco* ♪!)

—   bar 3: [bar 120]: *f* under the 1st quarter note; nevertheless, the 2d *f* remains!

Z. 6. T. 5 [bar 135]: Das ⊐ nicht vor dem Taktstrich beginnen lassen!

—— l. T [bar 137]: ⊏ unter die 1/2 Note mit Punkt! (♩.)

18)

Violoncell.

p. 4.   Z. 7. T. 1 [bar 138]: ♩ ♩ ♩ ♩

offen ⊏⊐ ⊐ fehlt!

X   —— T. 3 [bar 140]: *legg.* unter die 3/8! — In der Part. gehen die Bogen in diesem u. dem folg. Takte bis zum Viertel!

X —— Z. 8. T. 2 [bar 146]: in d. P. fehlt der ⌒ !

* —— Z. 9. T. 3 [bar 153]: *p* unter das 2te Viertel!

*X —— Z. 10. T. 1 [bar 155]: ⊐ fehlt in der Partitur!

* —— T. 2 [bar 156]: *mf espress.*

p. 5.   Z. 1. l. T [bar 169]: 𝄾 𝄾 statt 1/2 Pause!

* —— Z. 2. T. 3 [bar 172]: *f* unter das letzte Viertel!

—— T. 4. [bar 173] ⌒ von *e* zu *e* fehlt!   Punkt unter das 1/4!

* —— T. 5 [bar 174]: *ff sf* 𝄾 !

* —— T. 6 [bar 175]: *mf* 𝄾 !

—— Z. 3. T. 2 [bar 177]: > 𝄾 ! und *fz* 𝄾 !

* —— Z. 6. T. 2 [bar 192]: *cresc.* (obenhin!)

—— Z. 8. vl. T [bar 201]: *rf* ⊏ !

—— Z. 10. [bars 212–13] Die 2 einzelnen Taktpausen zusammenziehen

2

!

X —— Z. 11. T. 2 [bar 219]: Das *f* steht in der P. erst zum 1sten Viertel des folg. Takts [bar 220]!

* —— T. 5 [bar 222]: *p dim.* (*p* fehlt!)

p. 6.   Z. 1. T. 8 [II, bar 8]: so: ⊏ ⊐ länger!

—— Z. 2. l. T [bar 24]: ⊏ unter die 4/16!

—— Z. 3. T. 1 [bar 25]: offen: ⊏⊐

* —— Z. 5. T. 2 [bar 35]: ⊏ ⊐ 𝄾 !

* —— Z. 8. T. 1 [bar 57]: *pp* 𝄾 !

—— T. 4 [bar 60]: ♮ vor *c* (2r Raum)!

st. 6, b. 5 [bar 135]: Do not let the $\Longrightarrow$ begin before the barline!

—— final bar [bar 137]: $\Longleftarrow$ under the dotted 1/2 note! ($\downarrow$.)

18)

Violoncello

p. 4,   st. 7, b. 1 [bar 138]: ♩ ♩ ♩ ♩

open $\Longleftarrow$ $\Longrightarrow$ is missing!

X   —— b. 3 [bar 140]: *legg.* under the 3 8th notes!—In the score the slurs in this and the following bar go up to the quarter note!

X —— st. 8, b. 2 [bar 146]: In the score the $\frown$ is missing!

* —— st. 9, b. 3 [bar 153]: *p* under the 2d quarter note!

*X —— st. 10, b. 1 [bar 155]: $\Longrightarrow$ is missing in the score!

* —— b. 2 [bar 156]: *mf espress.*

p. 5,   st. 1, final bar [bar 169]: ⸮ ⸮ instead of 1/2 rest!

* —— st. 2, b. 3 [bar 172]: *f* under the final quarter note!

—— b. 4 [bar 173]: $\smile$ is missing from *E* to *E*! Dot under the 1/4 note!

* —— b. 5 [bar 174]: *ff sf* ⸮!

* —— b. 6 [bar 175]: *mf* ⸮!

—— st. 3, b. 2 [bar 177]: >⸮! and *fs* ⸮!

* —— st. 6, b. 2 [bar 192]: *cresc.* (above the notes!)

—— st. 8, penultimate bar [bar 201]: *rf* $\Longleftarrow$!

—— st. 10 [bars 212–13]: Add together the 2 single-bar rests !

X —— st. 11, b. 2 [bar 219]: The *f* does not occur in the score until the 1st quarter note of the following measure [bar 220]!

* —— b. 5 [bar 222] *p dim.* (*p* is missing!)

p. 6,   st. 1, b. 8 [II, bar 8]: Like so: $\Longleftarrow$ $\Longrightarrow$ longer!

—— st. 2, final bar [bar 24]: $\Longleftarrow$ under the 4 16th notes!

—— st. 3, b. 1 [bar 25]: Open: $\Longleftarrow$

* —— st. 5, b. 2 [bar 35]: $\Longleftarrow$ $\Longrightarrow$ ⸮!

* —— st. 8, b. 1 [bar 57]: *pp* ⸮!

—— b. 4 [bar 60]: ♮ before *C* (2d space)!

—— Z. 10. l. T [bar 71]: Triolen = 3 zweimal setzen!

* —— Z. 11. vl. T [bar 74]: *cresc.* (*mf* | *cresc.*)

* —— l. T [bar 75]: ⎯< *f* 𝄾 !

* p. 7 Z. 2 Takt 1 [bar 81]: *dim.* unter die 4/16!

* —— Z. 7 Takt 1 [bar 97]: ⎯< 𝄾 !

—— letzte Zeile [bars 130–32]: statt 3 Takte Pause:

poco rit.

p. 8 [III, anacrusis to bar 1] *m. v.* (Punkt hinter *v*!)

*X —— Z. 4. T. 2 [bar 24]: In der Part. geht der Bogen schon vom 1sten 8^{tel} *f* ab!

*X —— Z. 5. T. 2 [bar 31]: " " " " " 1sten 16^{tel} ♮*e* ab!

—— l. T [bar 34]: 2tes ♮ überflüssig! 𝄾 !

* —— Z. 8. l. T [bar 53]: *arco* fehlt!

X p. 9. Z. 1. T. 2. 3 [bar 72, 73]: in der Part. berühren sich die Bogen auf ♮*h*!

—— T. 6 [bar 76]: *dim.* 𝄾 !

—— Das *f* kommt in den Anfang des 4ten Takts [bar 74] zu ♮♩ !

* —— Z. 5. Takt 1 [bar 105]: (*f* 1/16 u. 1/16 P. dahinter!)

(19

Violoncell.

p. 9. Z. 5. Takt 2. 3 [bars 106, 107]: ⎯⎯ bis zum 2ten 8^{tel} des 3ten Takts!

—— T. 4 [bar 108]: ⎯⎯

—— T. 6 [bar 110]: Streichung so!

* —— Z. 6. vl. T [bar 117]: ⅞ genau wie Zeile 5 T. 1. [bar 105] angegeben! (*f* 1/16 u. ⅞ dahinter!)

—— l. T. [bar 118] ⎯<

—— Z. 7. T. 1 [bar 119]: < offen bis zum 2ten Achtel!

—— T. 2 [bar 120]: >⎯

—— Z. 8. T. 2 [bar 130]: *più p* (statt *più dolce*)!

—— Z. 10. T. 2 [bar 147]: Das ⎯< bis *f* !

—— T. 5 [bar 150]: *p* 𝄾 !

—— Z. 11. Das ⎯⎯ fängt schon im 2ten Takt [bar 156] an!

p. 10. Z. 1. T. 4 [IV, bar 4]: ♭ vor *h*!

—— st. 10, final bar [bar 71]: Enter triplet 3s twice!

* —— st. 11, penultimate bar [bar 74]: *cresc.* (*mf* | *cresc.*)

* —— final bar [bar 75]:

* p. 7, st. 2, bar 1 [bar 81]: *dim.* under the 4 16th notes!
* —— st. 7, bar 1 [bar 97]:

—— final staff [bars 130–32]: Instead of a 3-bar rest:

p. 8 [III, anacrusis to bar 1]: *m. v.* (dot after *v* !)

*X —— st. 4, b. 2 [bar 24]: In the score the slur begins already at the 1st 8th note *F*!

*X —— st. 5, b. 2 [bar 31]:   "   "   "   "   " 1st 16th note ♮*E*!

—— final bar [bar 34]: 2d ♮ is superfluous!

* —— st. 8, final bar [bar 53]: *arco* is missing!

X p. 9, st. 1, b. 2, 3 [bars 72, 73]: In the score the slurs touch one another on ♮*B*!

—— b. 6 [bar 76]: *dim.*

—— The *f* goes at the beginning of the 4th bar [bar 74] at !

* —— st. 5, bar 1 [bar 105]: (*F* 1/16 note followed by 1/16 rest!)

(19

Violoncello

p. 9, st. 5, bar 2, 3 [bars 106, 107]: through to the 2d 8th note of the 3d bar!

—— b. 4 [bar 108]:

—— b. 6 [bar 110]: bowing like this!

* —— st. 6, penultimate bar [bar 17]: given exactly like staff 5, bar 1 [bar 105] (*F* 1/16 note followed by ⅞ !)

—— final bar [bar 118]:

—— st. 7, b. 1 [bar 119]: open until the 2d eighth note!

—— b. 2 [bar 120]:

—— st. 8, b. 2 [bar 130]: *più p* (instead of *più dolce*)!

—— st. 10, b. 2 [bar 147]: The until !

—— b. 5 [bar 150]: *p* !

—— st. 11: The starts already in the 2d bar [bar 156]!

p. 10, st. 1, b. 4 [IV, bar 4]: ♭ before *B*!

*   ——   Z.   2. T. 1 [bar 6]: *dim.* zum letzten Achtel!

  ——   T. 3 [bar 8]: ⟩— oben ⟩— unten zu den 4/16!

——   Z.   6. T. 2. 3. und 4 [bars 24, 25, 26] fehlt die Triolen=*3*!
  (nothwendig!)

——   Z.   7. T. 4 [bar 33]: ♭ vor *h*!

——   Z.   8. T. 3. 4 [bar 38, 39]: besser so: ⸜♪♪⸝ als Punkt hinter
  Taktstrich!

X   ——   Z.   9. T. 2 [bar 47]: Das *g* [changed to:] *G* ist wohl besser hier als in
  der Partitur *g*! [red crayon:]?

——   Z. 10. T. 4 [bar 55]: fehlen die beiden Triolen=*3*!

*   ——   T. 5 [bar 56]: *mf* fehlt!

  p. 11. Z.   7 [bar 104] **G:** Die 3 Punkte beim *pizz.* ♪!

* p. 12. Z.   5. T. 1 [bar 159]: *più f sempre* fehlt!

*   ——   Z.   8. T. 5. [bar 174] > > oben ♪! Dafür <u>so wie in den folgenden 3
  Takten</u> unter jedes ♪ Punkt u. *Marcato*zeichen!

  p. 13. Z.   7. l. T [bar 231]: Punkt unter das 1ste Viertel!

——   Z. 10. T. 2 [bar 243]: ♭ vor *h*!

*   ——   Z. 11. T. 4 [bar 249]: *mf* statt *f*!

*XX   Am Ende: <u>*col sord.*</u> steht nicht in der Partitur! [blue crayon:]
  Wenn es gelten soll, muß es pag. 14 oben [bars 253ff.]
  noch einmal stehen!

  p. 14. Z.   1. vl. T [bar 256]: ♯ vor *a* ⸬ und l. T [bar 257]: ♮ vor *d* ⸬
  für das 2te Cello!

  ——   Z.   2. T. 1 [bar 258]: ♯ vor *c* ⸬ ebendeshalb!

    ——   T. 3 [bar 260]: ⟩— zu jeder Sechzehntelgruppe! (⸬)

*   ——   Z.   5. T. 2 [bar 270]: *dim.* fehlt!

——   Z.   7. l. T [bar 291]: *cresc.* (statt ⟨—)!

——   Z.   8. T. 1 [bar 292]: ⟩—♪!

Contrabass.

  p. 3.   Anfang [1, bar 3]: *f sf* (*f* fehlt vor *sf*, es kann auch *f* <u>oben</u> stehen!)

*   Z.   3. l. T [bar 26]: <u>*p*</u> statt *pp*!

      Z.   7. T. 1 [bar 55]: <u>*p*</u> fehlt!

  ——   T. 6 [bar 60]: ♯ vor *g* ♪!

  ——   T. 7. [bar 61] und Z. 8. T. 1 [bar 62]: 𝄾 𝄾 statt d. 1/2 Pause!

* —— st. 2, b. 1 [bar 6]: *dim.* at the final eighth note!

—— b. 3 [bar 8]: ⇒ over, ⇒ under the 4 16th notes!

—— st. 6, b. 2, 3, and 4 [bars 24, 25, 26] are missing the triplet 3s (necessary!)

—— st. 7, b. 4 [bar 33]: ♭ before *B*!

—— st. 8, b. 3, 4 [bar 38, 39]: Better like this: [musical notation] than with the dot after the barline!

X —— st. 9, b. 2 [bar 47]: The *g* [changed to:] *G* is probably better here than the *g* in the score! [red crayon:] ?[†]

—— st. 10, b. 4 [bar 55]: Both triplet 3s are missing!

* —— b. 5 [bar 56]: *mf* is missing!

p. 11, st. 7 [bar 104]: The 3 dots at *pizz.* [musical notation]!

* p. 12, st. 5, b. 1 [bar 159]: *più f sempre* is missing!

* —— st. 8, b. 5 [bar 174]: > > over [musical notation]! Instead, a dot and *marcato* sign under each ♪, *as in the following three bars*!

p. 13, st. 7, final bar [bar 231]: Dot under the 1st quarter note!

—— st. 10, b. 2 [bar 243]: ♭ before *B*!

* —— st. 11, b. 4 [bar 249]: *mf* instead of *f*!

*XX At the end: *col sord. is not in the score*! [blue crayon:] ? If it is correct, it must appear again on p. 14 at the top [bars 253ff.]!

p. 14, st. 1, penultimate bar [bar 256]: ♯ before *A* [musical notation] and final bar [bar 257]: ♮ before *D* [musical notation] for the 2d cello!

—— st. 2, b. 1 [bar 258]: ♯ before *C* [musical notation] for the same reason!

—— b. 3 [bar 260]: ⇒ for each group of sixteenth notes!

([musical notation])

* —— st. 5, b. 2 [bar 270]: *dim.* is missing!

—— st. 7, final bar [bar 291]: *cresc.* (instead of ⟨)!

—— st. 8, b. 1 [bar 292]: ⟨ [musical notation]!

[†]As in original—Ed.

Contrabass

* p. 3, beginning [1, bar 3]: *f sf* (*f* is missing before *sf*; *f* can also be *over* [the notes]!)

* st. 3, final bar [bar 26]: *p* instead of *pp*!

st. 7, b. 1 [bar 55]: *p* is missing!

—— b. 6 [bar 60]: ♯ before *g* [musical notation]!

—— b. 7 [bar 61] and st. 8, b. 1 [bar 62]: 𝄾 𝄾 instead of the 1/2 rest!

{249}

20)

Contrabass.

*   p. 3.   Z. 8. Takt 4 [65]: *mf* fehlt!

*   ——   T. 6 [bar 67]: *sf* fehlt zu ⌐ ⌐! > über d. letzten 1/4 ♪!

*   ——   T. 7 [bar 68]: *p* ♪! > ♪ unter dem ♩ | *forte!*
            [added below:] letzten *f*

——   Z. 9. T. 5 [bar 72]: > fehlt über ♪ !

*X ——   letzte Zeile **F** [bar 90]: Das *p* entweder ♪! oder doch zum 2$^{\underline{ten}}$
            Viertel! [blue crayon:]?

     p. 4.   Z. 1. T. 2 [bar 93]: Punkt über d. 1/4 ♪!

——   Z. 2. T. 4 [bar 100]: *f*——!

*   ——   Z. 3. *poco rit.* – – – – – obenhin und einen Takt früher [bar 109]!!

*   ——   Z. 5. *rit.* – – erst in den 2$^{\underline{ten}}$ Takt [bar 118] und <u>ohne *poco*</u>!

*   ——   T. 2 [bar 118]: unten fehlt *cresc.*!

*   ——   T. 4 [bar 120]: *f* fehlt!

——   Z. 7. Das —— fängt erst beim Taktstrich [bar 135] an!

——   T. 5. 6 [bars 137, 138]: ♩. |♩ ♩ ♩ ♩. |
            so: ——

——   Z. 10. T. 7 [bar 164]: *cresc.* fehlt!

——   Z. 11. Takt 1–3 [bars 169–71]: ⁊ ⁊ statt 1/2 Pause!

*   ——   T. 4 [bar 172]: *f* zum letzten Viertel!

                Takt 6 [bar 174]:

Takt 5 [bar 173]:
                            sf | *f* statt *ff* !

*   ——   Z. 12. T. 3 [bar 177]: *p* ♪! Takt 4 [bar 178]: *sf* ♪!

     p. 5.   Z. 3. l. T [bar 201]: *rf*——— !

——   Z. 6. T. 1 [bar 219]: Das *f* steht in d. Part. erst beim 1$^{\underline{sten}}$ 4$^{\underline{tel}}$ d. 2$^{\underline{ten}}$
            Takts!

*   ——   Z. 10. T. 4 [II, bar 35]: < >♪!

     p. 6.   Z. 1. T. 6 [bar 62]: < > fehlt!

20)

Contrabass

*   p. 3,   st. 8, bar 4 [bar 65]: *mf* is missing!

*   —— b. 6 [bar 67]: *sf* is missing for ⌢ ! > over the final 1/4 note

     !

*   —— b. 7 [bar 68]: *p* ♪ ! > ♪ under the ♩ | *forte* !
            [added below:] final *f*

    —— st. 9, b. 5 [bar 72]: > is missing over ⌢ !

*X —— final staff, **F** [bar 90]: The *p*, either ♪ ! or else at the 2d quarter
          note! [blue crayon:] ?

    p. 4,   st. 1, b. 2 [bar 93]: Dot over the 1/4 note ♪ !

    —— st. 2, b. 4 [bar 100]: *f* —— !

* —— st. 3: *poco rit.* – – – – – placed above and one bar earlier [bar
          109]!! | *poco rit.*

               p   *dim.*

* —— st. 5: *rit.* – – not until the 2d bar [bar 118] and *without poco* !

*   —— b. 2 [bar 118]: *cresc.* is missing below!

*   —— b. 4 [bar 120]: *f* is missing!

    —— st. 7: The ——— does not begin until the barline [bar 135]!

        —— b. 5, 6 [bars 137, 138]: ♩. | ♩ ♩ ♩ ♩. |
                 Like this: ———— ———

    —— st. 10, b. 7 [bar 164]: *cresc.* is missing!

    —— st. 11, bar 1–3 [bars 169–71]: ♪ ♪ instead of 1/2 rest!

*   —— b. 4 [bar 172]: *f* at the final quarter note!

                  Bar 6 [bar 174]:

       Bar 5 [bar 173]:   *sf* | *f* instead of *ff* !

* —— st. 12, b. 3 [bar 177]: *p* ♪ ! Bar 4 [bar 178]: *sf* ♪ !

    p. 5,   st. 3, final bar [bar 201]: *rf* —— !

    —— st. 6, b. 1 [bar 219]: The *f* in the score is not until the 1st quarter
          note of the 2d bar!

* —— st. 10, b. 4 [II, bar 35]: < > ♪ !

    p. 6,   st. 1, b. 6 [bar 62]: < > is missing!

—— Z. 3. vl. T [bar 80]: *ff sfp* (*s* fehlt!)

—— Z. 7. vl. T [bar 115]: *p* fehlt! (⟍— *p*)

—— Z. 9. [bars 130–32] statt der 3 Takte Pause:

* —— Z. 11. T. 1. [III, bar 9]

Zeichen falsch!

* p. 7. Z. 1. T. 2 [changed to:] 3 [bar 21]: — bis *f*! (2$^{\underline{tes}}$ Achtel!)

—— T. 5 [bar 22]: ⟍—! Takt 6 [bar 23]: ⟍—𝄆!

—— Z. 2 [bar 34]: Das genau unter das Achtel! (vor!)

X —— Z. 3. T. 1 [bar 41]: *p* (oder *pp*?) fehlt!

—— Z. 4. vl. u. l. T. [bar 73, 74]:

—— Z. 6. T. 5. 6 [bar 106, 107]: — bis *f*! T. 7 [bar 108]: ⟍—!

—— Z. 7. T. 8–10 [bars 118–20]: ebenso!

—— Z. 10. T. 3–4 [bars 146–47]: — bis *f*!

—— Z. 11. [bars 156–57]

p. 8. Z. 1. T. 4 [IV, bar 4]: ♭ vor *h*! ebenso Z. 6. Takt 4 [bar 33]!

* —— Z. 2. T. 2 [bar 6]: *dim.* zum letzten Achtel!

(21

Contrabass.

X p. 9. Z. 2. [bar 80] statt 1 Takt Pause steht in der Partitur:
  [red crayon:] X

X Die Stimme ist wohl richtig? [blue crayon:]?

—— Z. 6. [bar 104] Die 3 Punkte beim *pizz.* 𝄆!

* p. 10. Z. 2. vl. T [bar 158]: *più f sempre* fehlt!

—— Z. 4. T. 4 [bar 171]: > fehlt! (wie Takt vorher!)

* —— Z. 4. l. T. [bar 175] und Z. 5. T. 1. 2 [bars 176, 177] immer über

das (> und darunter Punkt!)

* p. 11. Z. 5. T. 5 [bar 249]: *mf* statt *f*!

—— st. 3, penultimate bar [bar 80]: **ff sfp** (**s** is missing!)

—— st. 7, penultimate bar [bar 115]: **p** is missing! (⟩—— **p**)

—— st. 9 [bars 130–32]: Instead of the 3 bars rest:

* —— st. 11, b. 1 [III, bar 9]:

B. 1.   2.   3.   4.

[Dynamic] signs wrong!

* p. 7,   st. 1, b. 2 [changed to:] 3 [bar 21]: ⟨—— until *F*! (2nd eighth note!)

—— b. 5 [bar 22]: ——⟩! Bar 6 [bar 23]: ——⟩♪!

—— st. 2 [bar 34]: The ⟨——⟩ exactly under the eighth note! ([move] forward!)

X —— st. 3, b. 1 [bar 41]: **p** (or **pp**?) is missing!

—— st. 4, penultimate and final bars [bars 73, 74]: ⟨—— **f** !

—— st. 6, b. 5, 6 [bars 106, 107]: ⟨—— until *F*! b. 7 [bar 108]: ——⟩!

—— st. 7, b. 8–10 [bars 118–20]: Likewise!

—— st. 10, b. 3–4 [bars 146–47]: ⟨—— until *F*!

—— st. 11 [bars 156–57]: ———— **f** !

p. 8,   st. 1, b. 4 [IV, bar 4]: ♭ before *B* ! Likewise *st. 6, bar 4* [bar 33]!

* —— st. 2, b. 2 [bar 6]: *dim.* at the final eighth note!

(21

Contrabass

X p. 9,   st. 2 [bar 80]: Instead of 1 bar of rest, the score reads:

[red crayon:] X

X   The part is presumably correct? [blue crayon:] ?

—— st. 6 [bar 104]: The 3 dots at *pizz.* ♪!

* p. 10,   st. 2, penultimate bar [bar 158]: *più f sempre* is missing!

—— st. 4, b. 4 [bar 171]: > is missing! (as in previous bar!)

* —— st. 4, final bar [bar 175] and st. 5, b. 1, 2 [bars 176, 177], always over the ♪ (> and dot underneath!)

* p. 11,   st. 5, b. 5 [bar 249]: **mf** instead of **f**!

*   —— Z. 8. vl. T [bar 270]: *dim.* fehlt!

Flöte I.

*   p. 1.   Z.   2. Takt 4 [I, bar 19]: Punkt fehlt hinter der halben Pause!

*X p. 3.   Z.   8. Takt 1 [bar 204]: *f*══ [blue crayon:]? [then:] (fehlt auch i.
 d. P.!)

*   p. 5.   Z.   2 [III, bar 40]: *mp* statt *p*!

*   p. 6.   letzte Zeile Takt [IV, bar 86] falsch! muß heißen: 〔musical notation〕 !!

 p. 7.   Z.   3. T. 2 [bar 111]: ♭ vor ♩!

Flöte II.

*   p. 1.   Z.   3 [I, bar 27]: 〔musical notation〕
 p fehlt!

 p. 2.   Z.   8 [bars 159 ff.]: statt 1/2 Pause 2 Viertelpausen! (wie im darauf
 folgenden Takte!)

 —— Z.   9 [bar 169]: hinter der 2ᵗᵉⁿ 1/2 Pause fehlt der Punkt!

*   p. 3.   Z.   5: T. 1 [bar 204]: *f*══? (fehlt auch i. d. P.!)

*   p. 4.   Z. 2 [II, bar 85]: 〔musical notation〕
 dolce fehlt!

 —— Z.   4. T. 3 [bar 96]: < > fehlt!

 p. 5.   Z.   1. T. 1 [III, bar 99]: *p* fehlt!

Hoboe I.

 p. 1.   Zeile 2 [I, bar 19]: Punkt fehlt über ♩!

*   p. 2.   Z.   7. T. 2 [bar 135]: ══ fehlt!

*   p. 3.   Z.   6 [bar 204]: *f*══!

 p. 4.   Z.   4. l. T [II, bar 101]: ♪ zum [changed to:] vom letzten Viertel
 fehlt!

 —— Z.   6. T. 4 [bar 113]: ♪ ♪ Bogen fehlt!

 —— Z.   9. T. 6 [III, bar 52]: *dolce* unter ♪ fehlt! ebenso Zeile 10 bei **D**
 [bar 61]! 〔musical notation〕
 dolce

 p. 5.   Z.   8. T. 1. 2: [IV, bars 56, 57]: ══ beide mal länger!

 —— Z. 10. T. 1 [bar 67]: Triolen 3 fehlt über der ♩!

* —— st. 8, penultimate bar [bar 270]: *dim.* is missing!

Flute I

* p. 1, st. 2, bar 4 [bar 19]: Dot is missing after the half rest!

*X p. 3, st. 8, b. 1 [bar 204]: *f* [blue crayon:] ? [then:] (also missing in the score!)

* p. 5, st. 2 [III, bar 40]: *mp* instead of *p*!

* p. 6, final staff [IV, bar 86]: Bar *incorrect*! must read: *!!*

p. 7, st. 3, b. 2 [bar 111]: ♭ before ♩!

Flute II

* p. 1, st. 3 [I, bar 27]: *p* is missing!

p. 2, st. 8 [bars 159ff.]: Instead of 1/2 rest, 2 quarter rests! (as in the following bars!)

—— st. 9 [bar 169]: The dot is missing after the 2d 1/2 rest!

* p. 3, st. 5, b. 1 [bar 204]: *f* —? (also missing in the score!)

* p. 4, st. 2 [II, bar 85]: *dolce* is missing!

—— st. 4, b. 3 [bar 96]: < > is missing!

p. 5, st. 1, b. 1 [III, bar 99]: *p* is missing!

Oboe I

p. 1, staff 2 [I, bar 19]: Dot is missing over ♩!

* p. 2, st. 7, b. 2 [bar 135]: is missing!

* p. 3, st. 6 [bar 204]: *f* !

p. 4, st. 4, final bar [II, bar 101]: ♩ to the [changed to:] from the final quarter note is missing!

—— st. 6, b. 4 [bar 113]: ♩ ♩ slur is missing!

—— st. 9, b. 6 [III, bar 52]: *dolce* is missing under ♩ ! likewise, staff 10 at **D** [bar 61]!

p. 5, st. 8, b. 1, 2 [IV, bars 56, 57]: longer both times!

—— st. 10, b. 1 [bar 67]: Triplet *3* is missing over the ♩!

p. 6.   Z.   3. T. 1 [bar 116]: *p* fehlt! — letzter Takt [bar 123]: ♭ vor *h* fehlt!

p. 7.   Z.   1–3 [bars 198–209]: Die ⤛ immer etwas länger! (sieben
　　　　　mal!)

——   Z.   8 [bar 267]: Die Auflösungszeichen nicht in richtiger Ordnung;
　　　　　so: 𝄐

——   Z. 10. T. 8 [bar 294]: ♮ zur Sicherheit vor ♮*e* (1/2 Note)!

22)

Hoboe II.

p. 1.   Z.   5. vl. T [I, bar 54]: 𝄞 (statt ♩')!

*   p. 2.   Z.   3. T. 1 [bar 135]: ⤛ fehlt!

——   Z.   5. T. 3 und 4 [bars 163, 164]: 𝄾 𝄾 statt 1/2 Pause!

——   Z.   9. l. T [bar 187]: ⌐ über die halbe mit Punkt!

——   Z. 10. T. 1 [bar 188]: > über das letzte 1/4 ♭♩ !

*X   ——   letzte Zeile, T. 1 [bar 204]: *f*⤛ (fehlt i. d. P.!)

p. 3.   Z.   6. T. 2 [II, bar 96]: < > fehlt!

——   Z.   7. [bar 113] 𝄞 Bogen fehlt!

——   Z.   8. Stichnoten: Takt 11 [bar 131] das <u>vorletzte Achtel</u> *g* muß 𝄾!

——   Z. 10. T. 1 [III, bar 61]: *dolce* fehlt!

p. 4.   Z.   6. T. 3 [IV, bar 66]: ♮ vor das [changed to:] dem 1$^{\underline{sten}}$ Viertel *g*
　　　　　fehlt!

——   Z.   8. vl. T [bar 89]: ♭ vor *e* 𝄾!

p. 5.   Z.   6. T. 3 [bar 208]: ♮ vor dem 1$^{\underline{sten}}$ Viertel *c* fehlt!

Clarinette I.

p. 1.   Z.   2. T. 7 [I, bar 18]: Punkt über dem 1/4 *g* fehlt!

——   Z.   3. T. 6 [26]: *p dolce* fehlt!

——   Z.   7. l. T [bar 51]: *p leggiero!* (*p* fehlt!)

——   Z.   9. vl. T [bar 60]: 𝄾 𝄾 st. der 1/2 Pause!

——   l. Z. T. 1 [bar 71]: Accent fehlt über *u*! (*più f*!)

*   p. 2.   Z.   1. T. 1 [bar 83]: ♭ vor dem letzten Viertel *g* fehlt! [blue crayon:]
　　　　　wichtig!

*   ——   T. 4 [bar 86]: ♭ vor dem 2$^{\underline{ten}}$ Viertel *e* fehlt! [blue crayon:]
　　　　　wichtig!

p. 6,   st. 3, b. 1 [bar 116]: *p* is missing!—final bar [bar 123]: ♭ is missing before *B*!

p. 7,   st. 1–3 [bars 198–209]: The ⎯◁ always slightly longer! (seven times!)

——   st. 8 [bar 267]: The natural signs not in the correct order; like this:

——   st. 10, b. 8 [bar 294]: A cautionary ♮ before ♮*E* (1/2 note)!

22)

Oboe II

p. 1,   st. 5, penultimate bar [I, bar 54]: (instead of ⌐⁛)!

*   p. 2,   st. 3, b. 1 [bar 135]: ⎯▷ is missing!

——   st. 5, b. 3 and 4 [bars 163, 164]: ⁊ ⁊ instead of 1/2 rest!

——   st. 9, final bar [bar 187]: ⁊ over the dotted half note!

——   st. 10, b. 1 [bar 188]: > over the final 1/4 note !

*X ——   final staff, b. 1 [bar 204]: *f*⎯▷ (missing in the score!)

p. 3,   st. 6, b. 2 [II, bar 96]: ◁ ▷ is missing!

——   st. 7 [bar 113]: slur is missing!

——   st. 8: Cues [for Oboe I]: bar 11 [bar 131], the *penultimate eighth note G* must be !

——   st. 10, b. 1 [III, bar 61]: *dolce* is missing!

p. 4,   st. 6, b. 3 [IV, bar 66]: ♮ is missing before the 1st quarter note *G*!

——   st. 8, penultimate bar [bar 89]: ♭ before *E* !

p. 5,   st. 6, b. 3 [bar 208]: ♮ is missing before the 1st quarter note *C*!

Clarinet I

p. 1,   st. 2, b. 7 [I, bar 18]: Dot is missing over the 1/4 note *G*!

——   st. 3, b. 6 [bar 26]: *p dolce* is missing!

——   st. 7, final bar [bar 51]: *p leggiero*! (*p* is missing!)

——   st. 9, penultimate bar [bar 60]: ⁊ ⁊ instead of the 1/2 rest!

——   final staff, bar 1 [bar 71]: Accent is missing over *u*! (*più f*!)

*   p. 2,   st. 1, b. 1 [bar 83]: ♭ is missing before the final quarter note *G*! [blue crayon:] important!

*   ——   b. 4 [bar 86]: ♭ is missing before the 2d quarter note *E*! [blue crayon:] important!

—— Z. 4. [bar 112] *sostenuto.* (ausstechen!)

* —— Z. 8. T. 2 [bar 141]: ♭ vor *d* fehlt! [blue crayon:] wichtig!

X —— l. T. [bar 149] ══ fehlt in der Partitur!

p. 3. Z. 5. T. 1 [bar 192]: ♭ vor dem 1sten Viertel *e*!

*X —— Z. 6. vl. T [bar 204]: *f* ══ (fehlt auch i. d. P.!)

—— Z. 8. [II, bar 1] Das <u>*semplice*</u> oben ♪ u. hinter *espress.*! (<u>*p espress, semplice*</u>)

—— l. Z. T. 1 [bar 27]: ◠ Bogen vom vorigen Takte herkommend!

p. 4. Z. 2. l. T [bar 54]: ♯ von *c* ♪!

—— Z. 9. T. 3 [bar 110]: ♮ vor dem Achtel *d* fehlt!

p. 5. Z. 5 [III, bar 67–68]: Das letzte ══♪!

—— Z. 8. T. 5 [bar 118]: ══ fehlt!

* p. 6. vl. Z. T. 5 [IV, bar 89]: $\stackrel{\scriptscriptstyle{>}}{\stackrel{a}{\flat}}$ (statt $\stackrel{\scriptscriptstyle{>}}{\stackrel{h}{\flat}}$)! [bue crayon:] sehr wichtig!

p. 7. Z. 2. T. 3 [bar 111]: ♮ vor *c* fehlt!

—— Z. 6. T. 5 [bar 148]: $\stackrel{\cdots}{\flat}$ Punkte über die 1/2 Note, noch besser

ausstechen $\underset{\bullet\,\bullet\,\bullet\,\bullet}{\sqcup\!\sqcup\!\sqcup\!\sqcup}$!

p. 8. Z. 9 [bar 267]: <u>*sostenuto.*</u> (ausstechen!)

(23

Clarinette II.

p. 1. Z. 3. T. 1 [I, bar 18]: Punkt über 1/4 *e*!

—— vl. Z: **E** [bar 77]: *f* ♪!

p. 2. Z. 4. T. 2 [bar 118]: Das 1ste ♭ steht nicht gut auf der 1sten Linie!

p. 3. Z. 4. T. 1 [bar 192]: ♭ vor das erste Viertel *e*!

*X —— Z. 5. vl. T [bar 204]: *f* ══ (fehlt auch i. d. P.!)

p. 4. Z. 6. T. 4 [II, bar 111]: ♮ vor dem 1/8 *a* fehlt!

—— Z. 10 hinter 2 Takt Pause [III, bar 39]: <u>*Solo*</u> obenhin!

p. 5. Z. 1. [bar 98] vor dem ‖ unter $\overset{\frown}{\natural}$

<u>*lunga*</u>!

p. 6. Z. 8. T. 3 [IV, bar 148]: ♯♪ ♪ ♪ ♪ ausstechen!

p. 7. Z. 3. T. 5 [bar 194]: Punkt unter *fis* fehlt!

—— Z. 4. T. 3 [bar 208]: ♮ vor dem 1sten Viertel *d* fehlt!

	——	st. 4 [bar 112]: *sostenuto.* (*engrave in full* !)
*	——	st. 8, b. 2 [bar 141]: ♭ is missing before *D* ! [blue crayon:] important!
X	——	final bar [bar 149]: ⟹ is missing in the score!
	p. 3,	st. 5, b. 1 [bar 192]: ♭ before the 1st quarter note *E* !
*X	——	st. 6, penultimate bar [bar 204]: *f* ⟹ (also missing in the score!)
	——	st. 8 [II, bar 1]: The *semplice* over [the notes] ♪♫ and [place it] after *espress.*! (*p espress. semplice*)
	——	final staff, b. 1 [bar 27]: ⌒ slur coming from the preceding measure!
	p. 4,	st. 2, final bar [bar 54]: ♯ before *C* ♪♫!
	——	st. 9, b. 3 [bar 110]: ♮ is missing before the eighth note *D* !
	p. 5,	st. 5 [III, bars 67–68]: The final ⟹ ♪♫!
	——	st. 8, b. 5 [bar 118]: ⟸ is missing!

* p. 6,   penultimate staff, b. 5 [IV, bar 89]: $\overset{>}{P}$ (instead of $\overset{>}{P}$)! [blue crayon:]

very important!   A   B

	p. 7,	st. 2, b. 3 [bar 111]: ♮ is missing before *C* !
	——	st. 6, b. 5 [bar 148]: P̈ Dots over the 1/2 note, better yet to engrave in full ♪̇♪̇♪̇♪̇!
	p. 8,	st. 9 [bar 267]: *sostenuto.* (*engrave in full*!)

(23

Clarinet II

	p. 1,	st. 3, b. 1 [I, bar 18]: Dot over 1/4 note *E* !
	——	penultimate staff: **E** [bar 77]: *f* ♪♫!
	p. 2,	st. 4, b. 2 [bar 118]: The 1st ♭ is not properly placed on the 1st line!
	p. 3,	st. 4, b. 1 [bar 192]: ♭ before the first quarter note *E* !
*X	——	st. 5, penultimate bar [bar 204]: *f* ⟹ (also missing in the score!)
	p. 4,	st. 6, b. 4 [II, bar 111]: ♮ is missing before the 1/8 note *A* !
	——	st. 10, after 2-bar rest [III, bar 39]: [Place] *Solo* over [the notes]!
	p. 5,	st. 1 [bar 98]: Before the ‖ below ◠𝄽

lunga !

	p. 6,	st. 8, b. 3 [IV, bar 148]: ♯♪̇♪̇♪̇♪̇ engrave in full!
	p. 7,	st. 3, b. 5 [bar 194]: Dot is missing under the *F*♯ !
	——	st. 4, b. 3 [bar 208]: ♮ is missing before the 1st quarter note *D* !

Fagott I.

p. 1. Z. 6. l. T [I, bar 44]: Das 2te # vor [changed to:] ♫! [illegible deletion]

—— Z. 7. l. T [bar 52]: ⌢ nur bis ≣!

—— vl. Z. vl. T [bar 65]: so: [⊔⊔⊔]₄ [⊔⊔⊔⊔⊔]₆ [⊔]₂ Streichung schlecht!

p. 2. Z. 4. T. 2 [bar 91]: Das 2te ♭♫!

    —— l. T [bar 94]: Viertel ♩ undeutlich!

—— Z. 5. l. T [bar 102]: ♩̇ ♩̇⌢ 2 Bogen!

* —— Z. 9. T. 2 [bar 135]: ⟩— fehlt!

* —— Auf Taktstrich zwischen T. 2 und 3 [bars 135 and 136] fehlt der Buchstabe **I**!

—— Z. 10. T. 1 [bar 144]: Punkt hinter 1/2 Pause fehlt!

    —— T. 5 [bar 147]: Die Stichnoten nur <u>abwärts</u>, nicht doppelt gestrichen!

*   *più p* <u>groß</u> dicht vor das ⟩——!

    —— l. T. [bar 149]: *grazioso* (Punkt über dem *i* fehlt!) sehr wichtig!!!

*   —— *p* fehlt (vor *s. v.*)!

p. 3. Z. 1. T. 3 [bar 165]: so: ⊔ [⊔⊔⊔] Streichung schlecht!

—— Z. 3. T. 1 [bar 172]: Punkt über dem 1/4 *e* fehlt!

—— Z. 5. T. 6 [bar 189]: > über ♩̇ ⌢ ! und Takt 7 [bar 190]: > über ♭♩⌢ !

*X —— Z. 7. T. 4 [bar 204]: *f* ⟩—— (fehlt auch i. d. P.!)

* p. 4. Z. 1. T. 4 [II, bar 43]: ⟩—— fehlt über ⟩—— !

—— Z. 6. T. 3 [bar 80]: *sf* fehlt unter *fis*!

—— Z. 10. T. 1 [bar 110]: ♮ fehlt vor ♭♩!

* —— l. Z. T. 6 [bar 130]: *più p* fehlt!

p. 5. Z. 2. am Ende [III, bars 20–21]: | ♪♪♪ | ♪♪♪ | ⟩————— fehlt!

—— Z. 3. T. 1 [bar 22]: ⟩—— fehlt!

—— Z. 4. T. 1 [bar 40]: *p* fehlt!

—— Z. 7 [bars 99–100]: ♩̇ ♮♪ | ♩̂ ‖ ⟨——⟨—— zurück!

Bassoon I

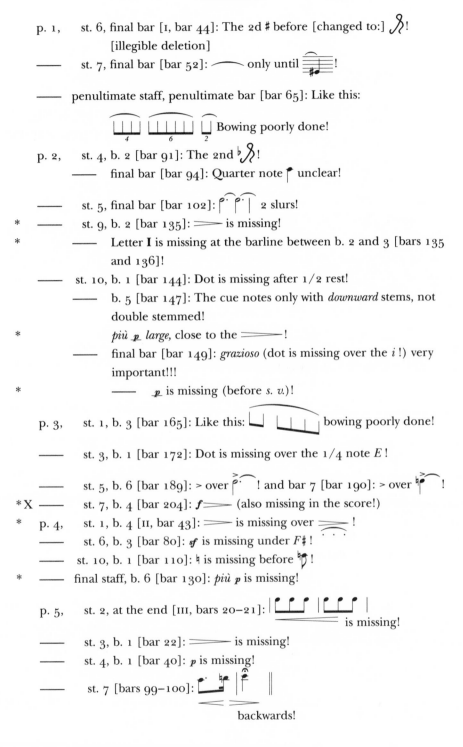

p. 1,   st. 6, final bar [I, bar 44]: The 2d # before [changed to:] ! [illegible deletion]

——   st. 7, final bar [bar 52]: ⌒ only until !

——   penultimate staff, penultimate bar [bar 65]: Like this:

Bowing poorly done!

p. 2,   st. 4, b. 2 [bar 91]: The 2nd ♭!

——   final bar [bar 94]: Quarter note unclear!

——   st. 5, final bar [bar 102]: 2 slurs!

* ——   st. 9, b. 2 [bar 135]: is missing!

* ——   Letter **I** is missing at the barline between b. 2 and 3 [bars 135 and 136]!

——   st. 10, b. 1 [bar 144]: Dot is missing after 1/2 rest!

——   b. 5 [bar 147]: The cue notes only with *downward* stems, not double stemmed!

*   *più p large,* close to the ═══!

——   final bar [bar 149]: *grazioso* (dot is missing over the *i* !) very important!!!

*   ——   *p* is missing (before *s. v.*)!

p. 3,   st. 1, b. 3 [bar 165]: Like this: bowing poorly done!

——   st. 3, b. 1 [bar 172]: Dot is missing over the 1/4 note *E* !

——   st. 5, b. 6 [bar 189]: > over ! and bar 7 [bar 190]: > over !

*X ——   st. 7, b. 4 [bar 204]: *f* (also missing in the score!)

*   p. 4,   st. 1, b. 4 [II, bar 43]: is missing over !

——   st. 6, b. 3 [bar 80]: *sf* is missing under *F*♯ !

——   st. 10, b. 1 [bar 110]: ♮ is missing before !

*   ——   final staff, b. 6 [bar 130]: *più p* is missing!

p. 5,   st. 2, at the end [III, bars 20–21]: is missing!

——   st. 3, b. 1 [bar 22]: is missing!

——   st. 4, b. 1 [bar 40]: *p* is missing!

——   st. 7 [bars 99–100]:

backwards!

24)

Fagott I.

*   p. 5.   Z.   8. T. 9. 10 [bars 119–20]: fehlt!

*   Takt 12 [bar 122]: *dolce* fehlt!

*   —— Z. 9. vl. T [bar 131]: ♮ vor dem letzten Achtel *h* fehlt! (3<u>ter</u> Raum)

      p. 6.   Z.   1. T. 4 [IV, bar 4]: ♭ vor dem 1<u>sten</u> 8<u>tel</u> *h* fehlt! ebenso Zeile 5. Takt 4. [bar 33]!

            —— Z. 9. T. 7 [bar 67]: ♮ vor dem 2<u>ten</u> 4<u>tel</u> *f* fehlt!

            —— l. Z. T. 2 [bar 90]: ♭ vor *a* (5<u>te</u> L.) fehlt!

      p. 7.   Z. 3. T. 2 [bar 111]: ⎫
            —— Z. 4. vl. T [bar 124]: ⎬ ♭ vor dem ersten 1/8 *h* fehlt!

*   —— Drittletzte Zeile Takt 1–4 [bars 174–77]: Unter jedes ♪ (Punkt und >)!

      p. 8.   Z.   6. T. 4 [bar 243]: ♭ vor *h* fehlt!

Fagott II.

      p. 1.   Z.   5. T. 2 [I, bar 50]: ♯ fehlt vor dem letzten 1/4 *c*!

            —— T. 4 [bar 52]: ⎫

            —— Z. 6. T. 4 und 5 [bars 61, 62]: ⎬ immer 𝄽 𝄾 statt der 1/2 Pause!

            —— Z. 7. T. 1 [bar 63]: ⎭

*   —— vl. Z. T. 4 [bar 80]: ♯ vor fehlt!

      p. 2.   Z.   2. T. 2 [bar 97]: Punkt fehlt unter dem ersten 1/4!

*   —— Z. 6. T. 1 [bar 135]: ⟹ fehlt!

            —— Z. 10. T. 1 [bar 164]: *p* fehlt!

            —— Z. 11. T. 2–5 [bars 169–72]: immer 𝄽 𝄾 st. d. 1/2 Pause!

*X   p. 3.   Z. 5. l. T [bar 204]: *f* ⟹ (fehlt auch i. d. P.!)

            —— letzte Z. T. 1 [II, bar 29]: ♮ vor dem 1<u>sten</u> *f* (4<u>te</u> L.)!

      p. 4.   drittletzte Z [bar 114]: *dim.* !

            —— vl. Z [bar 123]: ♮ fehlt vor *a*!

      p. 5.   Z.   3. Takt 2. 3 [III, bars 20–21]: ⟨ bis *f*! T. 4 [bar 22]: ⟹

            —— Z. 6. [bar 57] *p* vor dem ersten ⟹! (*p* ⟹)

*   —— Z. 7. T. 3 [bar 65]: ♭ vor fehlt!

            —— vl. Z. T. 3. 4 [bars 146–47]: ⟨ bis *f*! T. 5 [bar 148]: ⟹

24)

Bassoon I

*   p. 5,   st. 8, b. 9, 10 [bars 119–20]: ♪ ♪ ♪ is missing!

*   Bar 12 [bar 122]: *dolce* is missing?

*   ——   st. 9, penultimate bar [bar 131]: ♮ is missing before the final eighth note *B* ! (3d space)

     p. 6,   st. 1, b. 4 [IV, bar 4]: ♭ is missing before the 1st 8th note *B* ! *likewise, staff 5, bar 4* [bar 33]!

     ——   st. 9, b. 7 [bar 67]: ♮ is missing before the 2d quarter note *F* !

     ——   final staff, b. 2 [bar 90]: ♭ is missing before *A* (5th line)!

     p. 7,   st. 3, b. 2 [bar 111]:   ⎫ ♭ is missing before the first 1/8

     ——   st. 4, penultimate bar [bar 124]: ⎭ note *B* !

*   ——   Third-from-the-last staff, bars 1–4 [bars 174–77]: Under each ♪ (Dot and >)!

     p. 8,   st. 6, b. 4 [bar 243]: ♭ is missing before *B* !

Bassoon II

     p. 1,   st. 5, b. 2 [I, bar 50]: ♯ is missing before the final 1/4 note *C* !

     ——   b. 4 [bar 52]:   ⎫

     ——   st. 6, b. 4 and 5 [bars 61, 62]: ⎬ always 𝄽 𝄽 instead of the 1/2 rest!

     ——   st. 7, b. 1 [bar 63]:   ⎭

*   ——   penultimate staff, b. 4 [bar 80]: ♯ is missing before ♪ !

     p. 2,   st. 2, b. 2 [bar 97]: Dot is missing under the first 1/4 note!

*   ——   st. 6, b. 1 [bar 135]: ⎯⎯ is missing!

     ——   st. 10, b. 1 [bar 164]: *p* is missing!

     ——   st. 11, b. 2–5 [bars 169–72]: Always 𝄽 𝄽 instead of the 1/2 rest!

*X p. 3,   st. 5, final bar [bar 204]: *f* ⎯⎯ (also missing in the score!)

     ——   final staff, b. 1 [II, bar 29]: ♮ before the 1st *F* (4th line)!

     p. 4,   third-from-the-last staff [bar 114]: *dim.* ♪ !

     ——   penultimate staff [bar 123]: ♮ is missing before *A* !

     p. 5,   st. 3, bar 2, 3 [III, bars 20–21]: ⎯< until *F* ! Bar 4 [bar 22]: >⎯

     ——   st. 6 [bar 57]: *p* before the first >⎯ ! (*p* >⎯)

*   ——   st. 7, b. 3 [bar 65]: ♭ is missing before ♪ !

     ——   penultimate staff, b. 3, 4 [bars 146–47]: ⎯< until *f* ! Bar 5 [bar 148]: >⎯

* ——— l. Z. T. 4 [bar 156]: ♭ vor dem Viertel *e* fehlt!

p. 6.   Z.   1. T. 4. [IV, bar 4] und Zeile 5 Takt 4 [bar 33]: ♭ vor *h* fehlt!

———   Z.   4. T. 1 [bar 21]: könnte *d* besser auf der 3ten Linie stehen!

———   Z.   8. T. 1 [bar 51]: Punkt unter dem ersten 1/4 ♪!

* ———   Z.   9. T. 6 [bar 63]: ♮ vor *e*! [blue crayon:] wichtig!

———   Z. 10. T. 2 [bar 68]: ♮ vor *f*!

———   l. Z. l. T [bar 90]: ♭ vor *a* fehlt!

p. 7.   Z.   3. l. T [bar 112]: Pause und Ziffer 5 fehlt!

* ———   Z. 7. T. 5 [bar 157]: ♮ vor *a* fehlt! [blue crayon:] wichtig!

———   Z.   9. T. 1 [bar 168]: ♮ vor *h* fehlt!

* ———   T. 7. 8 und Z. 10 T. 1. 2 [bars 74–77]: unter jedem Achtel

(♪) Punkt und >!

* ———   vl. Z. vl. T [bar 190]: *ff* statt *f*!

p. 8.   Z.   2. vl. T [bar 212]: Punkt fehlt unter dem ersten Viertel! <u>ebenso</u>
             Z. 5. T. 2 [bar 231]!

             Z.   7. T. 3 [bar 243]: ♭ vor *h* fehlt!

(25

Contrafagott.

*   p. 1.   Zeile 1 [I, bar 3]: Anfang *f* entweder vor *sf* oder obenhin!

*X ———   Z. 2. l. T. [bar 21] *sf* steht nicht in der Partitur!

* ———   Z.   4. **G** T. 2 [bar 102]: ♭♩. ♩. Bogen von *des* zu *des* fehlt!

X ———   letzte Zeile [bars 202–24]: Die Stichnoten der *Fl.* können
            veranlassen, daß der *CFag.* 1 Takt zu früh einfällt, weil die *Fl.*
            schon im 17. Takt auf ♩ kommt, daher besser:

p. 2.   Z.   3. Takt 1 [IV, bars 38–39]: besser [notation] als Punkt hinter d.
            Taktstrich!

———   Z. 7. vl. T [bar 90]: ♭ vor *a* fehlt!

p. 3.   Z.   1. l. T. und ganze Zeile 2 [bars 174–80]: <u>Punkte</u> unter jedes
            einzelne <u>Achtel</u>, sowie über alle zusammenhängenden Achtel
            der letzten beiden Takte!

* —— final staff, b. 4 [bar 156]: ♭ is missing before the quarter note *E* !

p. 6,   st. 1, b. 4 [IV, bar 4] and staff 5, bar 4 [bar 33]: ♭ is missing before *B*!

——   st. 4, b. 1 [bar 21]: *D* could be placed better on the 3d line!

——   st. 8, b. 1 [bar 51]: Dot under the first 1/4 note 𝄐!

* ——   st. 9, b. 6 [bar 63]: ♮ before *E* ! [blue crayon:] important!

——   st. 10, b. 2 [bar 68]: ♮ before *F* !

——   final staff, final bar [bar 90]: ♭ is missing before *A* !

p. 7,   st. 3, final bar [bar 112]: Rest and number 5 is missing!

* ——   st. 7, b. 5 [bar 157]: ♮ is missing before *A* ! [blue crayon:] important!

——   st. 9, b. 1 [bar 168]: ♮ is missing before *B* !

*   —— b. 7, 8, and st. 10, b. 1, 2 [bars 74–77]: Under each eighth

note (♪) dot and >!

* —— penultimate staff, penultimate bar [bar 190]: *ff* instead of *f* !

p. 8,   st. 2, penultimate bar [bar 212]: Dot is missing under the first
quarter note! *likewise* st. 5, b. 2 [bar 231]!

st. 7, b. 3 [bar 243]: ♭ is missing before *B* !

(25

Contrabassoon

*   p. 1,   staff 1 [I, bar 3]: Initial *f* either before *sf* or above [the notes]!

*X ——   st. 2, final bar [bar 21]: *sf* is not in the score!

*   ——   st. 4, **G**, b. 2 [bar 102]: ♭♩. ♩. tie is missing from *D♭* to *D♭*!

X —— final staff [bar 202–4]: The cues for the Flute could cause the
Contrabassoon to enter 1 bar too early, since the Flute
already begins in the 17th bar on ♩.; therefore, better:

p. 2,   st. 3, bar 1 [IV, bars 38–39]: Better 🎵 than dot after the
barline!

——   st. 7, penultimate bar [bar 90]: ♭ is missing before *A* !

p. 3,   st. 1, final bar and all of staff 2 [bars 174–80]: *Dots* under each of the
single *eighth notes,* as well as over all of the eighth notes beamed
together in the final two bars!

—— Z. 8. vl. T [bar 238]: Punkt unter das letzte Viertel!

—— Z. 9. l. T [bar 243]: ♭ vor *h* fehlt!

* —— Schlußnote [bar 309]: *pp* fehlt!

Horn I in C.

* p. 1. Z. 5. l. T [I, bar 71b]:  Der Bogen vom 3ten zum
XX 4ten Viertel ist wohl falsch s. Partitur p. 19 Notiz! ebenso bei den 3 andern *Hörnern* an der gleichen Stelle! [line to left of comment in red crayon; to right of comment, in blue crayon:]?

—— { Z. 4. vl. u. l. T [bars 65, 66]:
Z. 5. T. 2 [bar 68]: } immer ⸘ ⸘ st. d. 1/2 Pause!
letzte Z. T. 3. 4. 5 [bars 169, 170, 171]:

* —— drittl. Z. T. 4 [bar 135]: ══ fehlt!

p. 2. Z. 1. T. 1 [bar 177]: *f* fehlt!

*X —— Z. 4. T. 1 [bar 204]: ? *mf* ══ (s. Partitur = Notiz p. 42)

* —— Z. 10 [II, bar 74; 75]. Punkt zu *cresc.* fehlt! *f* statt des letzten *mf*!

—— Z. 11. E [bars 80–85]: wäre besser im 𝄞 zu bleiben:

p. 3. Z. 1. T. 3. 4 [bars 99–100]: ebenso:

* —— Z. 3. T. 2 [bar 118]: fehlt Punkt hinter der 1/2 Note *as:* ♭♩·/ [blue crayon:] wichtig!

*X —— Z. 6. T. 1 ^[III, bar 55]: ? vgl. Frage in der Partitur!
vielleicht
[blue crayon:]?

p. 4. Z. 7. vl. T [IV, bar 97]: ♮ vor 1/2 *d* fehlt!

X p. 5. Z. 2. in den 2 letzten Takten [bar 198, 199]

fehlen die Schweller!

—— Z. 4. T. 1 [bar 212]: Punkt über dem 1/4 fehlt!

* —— Z. 6. T. 2 [bar 229]: ♮ vor *f*! wichtig!

—— st. 8, penultimate bar [bar 238]: Dot under the final quarter note!

—— st. 9, final bar [bar 243]: ♭ is missing before *B* !

* —— final note [bar 309]: ***pp*** is missing!

Horn I in C

*   p. 1,   st. 5, final bar [I, bar 71b]: The tie from the 3d
XX   to the 4th quarter note is probably
wrong; see the score, p. 19, annotation!
Likewise for the 3 other Horns at the
same place! [line to left of comment in
red crayon; to right of comment, in
blue crayon:] ?

—— { st. 4, penultimate and final bars [bars 65, 66]: }   Always ⁏ ⁏ instead
      { st. 5, b. 2 [bar 68]: }   of the 1/2 rest!
      { final staff, b. 3, 4, 5 [bars 169, 170, 171]: }

* —— third-from-the-last staff, b. 4 [bar 135]: ⟍ is missing!

   p. 2,   st. 1, b. 1 [bar 177]: ***f*** is missing!

*X —— st. 4, b. 1 [bar 204]: ? ***mf***⟍ (see annotation in the score, p. 42)

* —— st. 10 [II, bar 74; 75]: Dot is missing for *cresc.*! ***f*** instead of the final
       mf!

—— st. 11, **E** [bars 80–85]: Would be better to remain in 𝄞 :

   p. 3,   st. 1, b. 3, 4 [bars 99–100]: Likewise:

* —— st. 3, b. 2 [bar 118]: Dot is missing after the 1/2 note A♭ / [blue
       crayon:] important!

*X —— st. 6, b. 1 [III, bar 55]: ? cf. *query in the score* ! [blue crayon:] ?
           perhaps

   p. 4,   st. 7, penultimate bar [IV, bar 97] ♮ is missing before the 1/2 note *D* !

X p. 5,   st. 2: In the final 2 bars [bars 198, 199]

 the dynamics are missing!

—— st. 4, b. 1 [bar 212]: Dot is missing over the 1/4 note!

* —— st. 6, b. 2 [bar 229]: ♮ before *F* ! important!

—— Z. 9. [bars 255–59] Die fünf Takte Pause zusammenziehen [♪♪ 5] !

26)

Horn I in C.

p. 5. Z. 10. T. 3 [bar 271]: *p* fehlt!

—— l. Z. T. 5 [bar 300]: Das ♭ vor *d* ♪!

Horn II in C.

p. 1. Z. 2. T. 2 [I, bar 14]: Punkt ♪!

*   —— T. 6 [bar 18]: | - ♩. | *f* fehlt!

*X —— Z. 6. T. 1 [bar 71b]: Bogen vom 3<u>ten</u> zum 4<u>ten</u> Viertel falsch? ⌢ dafür! [blue crayon:]?

* —— Z. 9. l. T [bar 135]: Punkt ♪! =====— fehlt!

—— Z. 4. vl. u. l. T [bars 65, 66]: ♪ ♪ statt d. 1/2 Pause! <u>ebenso p. 2. Z. 2. l. T.</u> [bar 191]!

p. 2. Z. 2. T. 4 [bar 188]: fehlt > über dem letzten Viertel!

* —— vl. Z [II, bar 75]: *f* statt des 2<u>ten</u> *mf*!

p. 3. Z. 1. T. 1 [bar 88]: ⌢ bis zur 1/2 *g*!

—— Z. 2. l. T [bar 106]: *pp* ◁

—— Z. 5. vl. T [III, bar 52]: ♭ besser auf d. 1<u>ste</u> Linie!

*X —— Z. 6. T. 3 [bar 55]: ♪♪ *e* statt ♩? s. Frage in der Partitur! [blue crayon:]??

* —— vor **D** [bar 61]: ♪♪ 1/8 statt 1/4!

* —— vl. Z. Takt vor **I** [bar 149]: *p* st. *pp*!

p. 4. **F** [IV, bar 91]: *sf* statt *sff*!

p. 5. Z. 4. T. 3 [bar 212]: Punkt ♪!

* —— Z. 6. vl. T [bar 232]: ♮ statt ♭ vor *e*! [blue crayon:] wichtig!

—— Z. 10. T. 3 [bar 271]: *p* fehlt!

Horn III in F.

* p. 1. Z. 1. T. 2 [I, bar 2]: ♮ vor dem 2<u>ten</u> *e* ♪!! [blue crayon:] sehr wichtig!

—— st. 9 [bars 255–259]: Add up the five bars of rest ⌐5⌐ !

26)

Horn I in C

p. 5, st. 10, b. 3 [bar 271]: *p* is missing!

—— final staff, b. 5 [bar 300]: The ♭ before *D* ♪!

Horn II in C

p. 1, st. 2, b. 2 [I, bar 14]: Dot ♪!

* —— b. 6 [bar 18]: | ▪· ♩. | *f* is missing!

*X —— st. 6, b. 1 [bar 71b]: Tie from 3d to 4th quarter note incorrect? ⌣ instead! [blue crayon:] ?

* —— st. 9, final bar [bar 135]: Dot ♪! ═══ is missing!

—— st. 4, penultimate and final bars [bars 65, 66]: ⸸ ⸸ instead of the 1/2 rest! *likewise p. 2, st. 2, final bar* [bar 191]!

p. 2, st. 2, b. 4 [bar 188]: > is missing over the final quarter note!

* —— penultimate staff [II, bar 75]: *f* instead of the 2d *mf*!

p. 3, st. 1, b. 1 [bar 88]: ﹀ until the 1/2 note *G*!

—— st. 2, final bar [bar 106]: *pp* ═◁

—— st. 5, penultimate bar [III, bar 52]: ♭ better [positioned] on the 1st line!

*X —— st. 6, b. 3 [bar 55]: [notation] *E* instead of ♩? See query in the score! [blue crayon:] ??

* —— before **D** [bar 61]: [notation] 1/8 note instead of 1/4 note!

* —— penultimate staff, bar before **I** [bar 149]: *p* instead of *pp*!

p. 4, **F** [IV, bar 91]: *sf* instead of *sff*!

p. 5, st. 4, b. 3 [bar 212]: Dot ♪!

* —— st. 6, penultimate bar [bar 232]: ♮ instead of ♭ before *E*! [blue crayon:] important!

—— st. 10, b. 3 [bar 271]: *p* is missing!

Horn III in F

* p. 1, st. 1, b. 2 [I, bar 2]: ♮ before the 2d *E* ♪!! [blue crayon:] very important!

{269}

*X —— Z. 4. T. 1 [bar 31]: besser (sicherer) 𝄞 als *fes*!

—— Z. 6. vl. T [bar 68]: ♩ ♩ st. 1/2 P.!

*X —— Z. 7. T. 4 [bar 71b]: Punkte statt Bogen 3tes u. 4tes Viertel?

p. 2. Z. 3. l. T [bar 191]: ♩ ♩ st. 1/2 P.!

Mitte [II, III]: *tacet* beide mal mit <u>kleinem</u> *t*!

* —— Z. 3. von unten: ⌒ vom vl. zum l. T. [bars 42–43] 𝄐!

—— Z. 2. "   " Punkte über das letzte Viertel *d* [bar 50]!

—— Z. 1. "   " vl. T. [bar 70]: Punkt über 1/4 *c* fehlt!

p. 3. Z. 2. T. 1 [bar 81]: 1/2 *d* besser auf die 4te Linie!

* —— Z. 5 [bars 117–18]: statt 𝄞 welches ein <u>doppelter</u> Fehler

ist, muß es heißen: 𝄞 [blue crayon:] sehr

wichtig! [then in very small script to the right:] Was muß ein
Dirigent für einen Schreck kriegen, wenn das das [!] zum 1sten
mal <u>so</u> geblasen wird!

* —— Z. 8. [bars 167–68] 𝄞 es müssen

beide ⌒ 𝄐!

—— vl. Z. T. 2 [bar 189]: Punkt unter die 2te 4^{tel} Note!

X —— l. Z. [bar 198–99] 𝄞 fehlen

die Schweller!

Horn IV in F.

p. 1. Z. 5. T. 5 [I, bar 63]: Punkt über 1/4 *h*!

—— Z. 5. T. 3 [bar 61] und Zeile 6 T. 3 [bar 68]: ♩ ♩ st. d. 1/2 P.!

* —— Z. 7. T. 1 [bar 71b]: Punkte statt Bogen über das 3te u. 4te Viertel?
[blue crayon:]?

—— Letzte Note auf der Seite [bar 143]: ᵒ⌒ (statt ⟨ ⟩)

p. 2. Z. 5. T. 2 [bar 191]: ♩ ♩ st. 1/2 P.!

* —— Z. 8. T. 2 [bar 214]: *pp* ⟨!

—— Mitte [II, III]: *tacet* beide mal mit <u>kleinem</u> *t*!

*X —— st. 4, b. 1 [bar 31]: Better (safer) 🎵 than F♭ !

—— st. 6, penultimate bar [bar 68]: ↕ ↕ instead of 1/2 rest!

*X —— st. 7, b. 4 [bar 71b]: Dots instead of tie, 3d and 4th quarter notes?

p. 2, st. 3, final bar [bar 191]: ↕ ↕ instead of 1/2 rest!

Middle [movements, II, III]: *tacet* both times with *lowercase t* !

* —— 3d staff from the bottom: ⌢ from the penultimate to the final bar

[bars 42–43] 𝄾 !

—— 2d staff " " " [i.e., from the bottom]: Dots over the final quarter note

D [bar 50]!

—— 1st staff " " " [i.e., from the bottom]: penultimate bar [bar 70]: Dot

is missing over the 1/4 note C !

p. 3, st. 2, b. 1 [bar 81]: 1/2 note D better [positioned] on the 4th line!

* —— st. 5 [bars 117–18]: Instead of 🎵, which is a *double*

mistake, it must read: 🎵 [blue crayon:] very

important! [then, in very small script to the right:] What a shock
it must be for a conductor the first time it is played *like this* !

* —— st. 8 [bars 167–68]: 🎵 both ⌢

must be 𝄾 !

—— penultimate staff, b. 2 [bar 189]: Dot under the 2d 1/4 note!

X —— final staff [bars 198–99]: 🎵

the dynamics are missing!

(27

Horn IV in F

p. 1, st. 5, b. 5 [bar 63]: Dot over 1/4 note B !

—— st. 5, b. 3 [bar 61] and staff 6, b. 3 [bar 68]: ↕ ↕ instead of the 1/2
rest!

* —— st. 7, b. 1 [bar 71b]: Dots instead of tie over the 3d and 4th quarter
notes! [blue crayon:] ?

—— final note on the page [bar 143]: ᵒˑ⸺ (instead of ≺ ≻)

p. 2, st. 5, b. 2 [bar 191]: ↕ ↕ instead of 1/2 rest!

* —— st. 8, b. 2 [bar 214]: *pp* ⸺◁ !

—— Middle [movements, II, III]: *tacet* both times with *lower-case t* !

* —— Z. 3. v. unten, vl. T [IV, bars 34–35]: [notation]. Bogen fehlt!

* —— Z. 2. " " [bars 42–43] Bogen von [notation] zu [notation]!

p. 3. Z. 1. vl. T [bar 70]: Punkt über d. 1/4 *c* fehlt!

* —— Z. 9 [bar 167]: [notation] *ff* (Bogen über 3 [notation]! Punkt unter das 1/4 *g*!

Trompete I.

p. 1. Z. 3 1. T [I, bar 69]: *f* fehlt!

—— drittl. Z. T. 1 [bar 174]: [notation] st. 1/2 P.!

—— 1. Z. T. 2 [bar 199]: Punkt hinter der 1/2 P. fehlt!

unten [II, III]: <u>*tacet*</u> beide mal mit <u>kleinem</u> *t*!

p. 2. Z. 8. T. 3 [IV, bar 167]: *ff* zum 3ten Viertel! (zum 1sten Triolenviertel!)

—— Ende der Zeile [bars 186–87]: [notation] *f* fehlt!

—— Z. 9. T. 1 [bar 188]: *ff* fehlt!

—— 1. Z. nach 7 Takt Pause [bar 299]: fehlt *p* zur ganzen Note *c*!

Trompete II.

p. 1. Z. 1. 1. T [I, bar 13]: Punkt under [notation] fehlt!

—— Z. 3 [bar 69]: [notation] *ff f* (*ff f* fehlt beim ersten [notation] !)

(*f*, nicht *ff*!)

—— Z. 8 [bar 174]: [notation] st. 1/2 P.!

—— Z. 9. Takt 1 [bar 178]: [notation] über das <u>letzte</u> Viertel des 1ten Takts, im

T. 2 [bar 179] [notation]!

unten [II, III]: <u>*tacet*</u> beidemal mit <u>kleinem</u> *t*!

p. 2. Z. 7. T. 11 [IV, bar 162]: ♮ besser auf die 1ste Linie!

—— Z. 8. T. 3 [bar 167]: Punkt über 1/4 *d*! *ff* zum 1sten Triolen Viertel!

—— T. 8 [bar 172]: Punkt unter [notation] fehlt!

—— letzte Takte [bars 186–87]: [notation] fehlt!

f fehlt!

* —— 3d staff from the bottom, penultimate bar [IV, bars 34–35]: ♩♩. Tie are missing!

* —— 2d staff " " " [i.e., from the bottom] [bars 42–43]: Ties from ♩ to ♩♪ !

p. 3, st. 1, penultimate bar [bar 70]: Dot is missing over the 1/4 note *C* !

* —— st. 9 [bar 167]: ♩ ♩ (Slur over the 3 ♪ ! Dot under the 1/4 note *G* !

Trumpet I

p. 1, st. 3, final bar [I, bar 69]: *f* is missing!

—— third-from-the-last staff, b. 1 [bar 174]: ‰ ‰ instead of 1/2 rest!

—— final staff, b. 2 [bar 199]: Dot is missing after the 1/2 rest!

At the bottom [II, III]: *tacet* both times with *lower-case t* !

p. 2, st. 8, b. 3 [IV, bar 167]: *ff* for the 3d quarter note! (for the 1st quarter note of the triplet!)

—— end of the staff [bars 186–87]: ‰ ♩ ♩♩♩ ♩ | *f* ——— is missing!

—— st. 9, b. 1 [bar 188]: *ff* is missing!

—— final staff, after 7-bar rest [bar 299]: *p* is missing for the whole note *C* !

Trumpet II

p. 1, st. 1, final bar [I, bar 13]: Dot is missing under ♩ !

—— st. 3 [bar 69]: ♩♩ | (*ff f* is missing at the first ♩ !) *ff f* (*f*, not *ff* !)

—— st. 8 [bar 174]: ‰ ‰ instead of 1/2 rest!

—— st. 9, bar 1 [bar 178]: ⌐ over the *final* quarter note of the 1st bar, in bar 2 [bar 179] ♪ !

At the bottom [II, III]: *tacet* both times with *lower-case t* !

p. 2, st. 7, b. 11 [IV, bar 162]: ♮ better [positioned] on the 1st line!

—— st. 8, b. 3 [bar 167]: Dot over 1/4 note *D* ! *ff* for the 1st quarter note of the triplet!

—— b. 8 [bar 172]: Dot is missing under ♩ !

—— final bars [bars 186–187]: ——— is missing! ♩ ♩♩♩ ♩ *f* missing!

{273}

—— Z. 9. T. 1 [bar 188]: *ff* fehlt!

—— l. Z. nach 7 Takt Pause [bar 299]: *p* zu ⌣!

Alt-Posaune.

p. 1. <u>unten</u> [III]: *tacet* mit <u>kleinem</u> *t*!

---

28)

Tenor-Posaune.

* p. 1. Z. 7. **L** [I, bar 187]: ♮ fehlt! [blue crayon:] wichtig!

—— <u>unten</u> [III]: *tacet* mit <u>kleinem</u> *t*!

p. 2. Z. 2. l. T [IV, bar 69]: ♭ fehlt!

—— Z. 4 [bar 91]: Das 2$\underline{^{te}}$ ♭ der Vorzeichnung besser auf 5$\underline{^{te}}$ Linie!

—— Z. 9 [bar 233]: nur *sf*! (das >𝄾? [changed to:]!)

Bass-Posaune.

* p. 1. vl. Z. [II, bar 83] so:

dolce

einen Takt vor!

—— <u>unten</u> [III]: *tacet* mit <u>kleinem</u> *t*!

* p. 2. Z. 4. T. 1 [IV, bar 91]: *sf* statt *f*!

* —— Z. 6. T. 4 [bar 167]: (♮*d* st. 1/2 Note nur 1/4, Punkt darüber u. 1/4 P. dahinter!)

* —— Z. 8. [bar 233] *sf* statt *f* und das 𝄾!

Pauken.

p. 1. Z. 1. [I, bar 112] Der Doppelstrich kommt zum Buchst. **H,** vorher 1 facher Taktstrich!

—— st. 9, b. 1 [bar 188]: *ff* is missing!

—— final staff, after 7-bar rest [bar 299]: *p* for ♪ ︶ !

Alto Trombone

p. 1, *at the bottom* [III]: *tacet* with *lowercase t* !

28)

Tenor Trombone

* p. 1, st. 7, **L** [I, bar 187]: ♮ is missing! [blue crayon:] important!

—— *At the bottom* [III]: *tacet* with *lowercase t* !

p. 2, st. 2, final bar [IV, bar 69]: ♭ is missing!

—— st. 4 [bar 91]: The 2d ♭ of the key signature better [positioned] on the 5th line!

—— st. 9 [bar 233]: Only *sf* ! (the > ♪ ? [changed to:] !)

Bass Trombone

* p. 1, penultimate staff [II, bar 83]: Like this: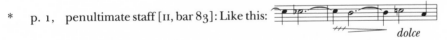

one bar earlier!

—— *At the bottom* [III]: *tacet* with *lowercase t* !

* p. 2, st. 4, b. 1 [IV, bar 91]: *sf* instead of *f*!

* —— st. 6, b. 4 [bar 167]: (♮D instead of 1/2 note, only 1/4 note; dot over it and 1/4 rest after it!)

* —— st. 8 [bar 233]: *sf* instead of *f* and the ══ ♪ !

Timpani

p. 1, st. 1 [I, bar 112]: The double barline occurs at letter **H**, single barlines before that!

—— l. Z. [bar 201–2] 𝄞 *f* statt *rf*! ♭ vor *h*!

Bogen ♪!

unten [II, III]: *tacet* mit kleinem *t*!

p. 2.   Z.   8. T. 1 [IV, bar 223]: *sff sf* statt *ff*!

Ende.

—— final staff [bars 201–2]:

f instead of *rf* !   ♭ before *B* !

ties ♪!

At the bottom [II, III]: *tacet* with lowercase *t* !

p. 2,   st. 8, b. 1 [IV, bar 223]: *sff sf* instead of *ff* !

End

Two Letters from Robert Keller
to Joseph Joachim

1

ROBERT KELLER TO JOSEPH JOACHIM   Berlin, 26 November 1881
(Staatliches Institut für Musikforschung, Preussischer Kulturbesitz, Berlin
West)

26/11 81.

Hochgeehrter Herr Professor!

Anbei sende ich Ihnen Partitur, Principalstimme und Clavierauszug
Ihrer Variationen zur gefälligen baldigen Revision. Die Orchesterstimmen,
(mit deren Durchsicht Sie sich *nicht* zu plagen brauchen,) liegen ebenfalls
bei. Wenn Sie nicht *größere* Correkturen in der Partitur machen (für
welchen Fall ich mir dann Part. u St. zurückerbitten würde) so können
Sie Alles zusammen an Bock schicken. Falls Sie wie ich vermuthe das *g* im
Cello der X.^{ten} Variat. acceptiren, so tragen sie [*sic*] dies wohl freundlichst
in die *Cello* stimme ein.

Sollten Sie im <u>Clavierauszug</u> Aenderungen wünschen, so stehe ich
Ihnen an jedem beliebigen Vormittage bis 1 Uhr zur Disposition für münd-
liche Rücksprache, und brauchen Sie dann nur zu bestimmen, wann ich
kommen soll. Nur <u>morgen</u> habe ich einen Ausflug vor, von dem ich erst
Montag Mittag zurückkomme.

Mit hochachtungsvollem Gruß

Ihr
ergebener
Robert Keller
W. Steglitzerstrasse 1.

26 November 1881

Dear Herr Professor,

I am enclosing the score, principal parts, and piano reduction of your
Variations for you kindly to proofread soon. The orchestral parts (with

whose perusal you need *not* plague yourself) are also enclosed. If you do not make any *large* corrections in the score (in which case I would ask then that you return the score and parts to me), you could send everything altogether to Bock. If you accept the G in the cello of the 10th Variation, as I presume you will, would you then kindly enter it into the cello part.

If you wish to make any changes in the *piano reduction,* I can be at your disposal for discussions any morning until one o'clock, and you need only decide when I should come. Only *tomorrow* will I be on an excursion, from which I will not return until Monday at mid-day.

With respectful greetings,
Yours sincerely,
Robert Keller
W. Steglitzerstrasse 1.

◆

The composition under discussion in this first letter is Joachim's Variations in E Minor for Violin and Orchestra, which Joachim had premiered on 15 February 1881, with Ernst Rudorff conducting, in a concert at the Berlin Hochschule (6:140, n. 1). The work, completed in first draft near the end of 1878 and submitted to Brahms for his comment (see letters of ca. 12 December 1878 and 24 January and 27 August 1879; 6:148, 154, 177), was published in 1882 by Bote & Bock, Berlin.[1] This letter establishes Robert Keller as the arranger of the violin-piano version of the composition and as an editor/arranger working for Bote & Bock.

●◆ 2

ROBERT KELLER TO JOSEPH JOACHIM   Berlin, 7 May 1886 (Staatliches Institut für Musikforschung, Preussischer Kulturbesitz, Berlin West)

7. Mai 1886.

Hochgeehrter Herr Professor!

Es war mir am letzten Quartettabend nicht möglich an Sie heranzukommen, um Ihnen zu sagen, wie wunderbar ergreifend für mich Ihr beseelter und alle Tiefen der Composition erschöpfend wiedergebender Vortrag des *Lento* in dem großen Beethoven gewesen ist. Das war nicht mehr Geigenspiel, das war der Geist der Musik selber, der zu dem Hörer sprach und ihn in das bewegte Meer seiner geheimnißvollsten und erregtesten Stimmungen wieß. Beethovens Athem wehte; hätte er je eine solche Wiedergabe seiner erhabenen Gedanken erleben können! —

So wenig auch diese Worte eines bescheidenen Kunstfreundes Ihrem die Welt erfüllenden Ruhme hinzufügen können: Sie werden die Aufrichtigkeit und Herzlichkeit derselben nicht verkennen und verschmähen. Es hat mir seit jenem unvergeßlichen Abend nicht Ruhe gelassen, so daß ich meiner Begeisterung hierdurch—wenn auch lange *post festum*—noch Luft machen mußte. Auch das Verdienst der Mitwirkende bleibe nicht unerwähnt.

Ihr

ganz ergebener

Robert Keller.

●◇

7 May 1886

Dear Herr Professor,

It was impossible for me to get near you at the last Quartet Evening in order to tell you how wonderfully moving your inspired performance of the Lento of the great Beethoven work had been for me; it fully probed all the depths of the composition. This was not violin playing; it was the spirit of the music itself that spoke to the listener and guided him into the stormy sea of his most mysterious and most agitated moods. Beethoven's breath wafted; if only he could have experienced such a rendering of his sublime thoughts! —

Even though these words of a modest art lover can add little to your world-renowned fame, you will not misconstrue and disdain their candor and sincerity. I have had no peace since that unforgettable evening, so that I had to give vent to my rapture in this way—even if long *post festum*. Also the merits of the other performers shall not go unmentioned.

Yours

very truly,

Robert Keller

◇●

The Beethoven quartet to which Keller refers is probably the String Quartet No. 16 in F Major, Op. 135, which contains a *Lento assai, cantante e tranquillo.* The Joachim Quartet, founded by its leader in 1869 with colleagues from the Berlin Hochschule für Musik, was one of the most celebrated string quartets of the nineteenth century, presenting an annual series of concerts in Berlin and touring Europe. According to Andreas Moser, Joachim's biographer, the ensemble, which played on Stradivari instruments, was noted for its fine shading, unanimity of conception, and astounding blend of voices, with the individual instruments subordinate to the whole.[2] Over the years, the quartet's membership changed; in 1886 the ensemble consisted of Joseph Joachim, Heinrich de Ahna, Emanuel Wirth, and Robert Hausmann.

Robert Keller's Arrangements of Works by Brahms and Others

The information about Keller's arrangements of Brahms's works presented in this appendix is taken from the 1897 edition of the Brahms *Thematisches Verzeichniss* and has been supplemented with information from the Brahms-Keller correspondence and McCorkle, *Brahms Werkverzeichnis* (marked with asterisks).

1

Arrangements of eighty-six solo songs, vocal duets, and choral pieces for solo piano, published in the three *Brahms Albums* issued by N. Simrock in 1883, plate numbers 8353–55 (the numbers in parentheses refer to the volume and the numbers of the arrangements):

Op. 19 Five *Gedichte* (I/1–5)
  20 Three Duets (III/62–64)
  46 Four *Gesänge* (I/6–9)
  47 Five *Lieder* (I/10–14)
  48 Seven *Lieder* (I/15–21)
  49 Five *Lieder* (I/22–26)
  61 Four Duets (III/65–68)
  62 Seven *Lieder* for mixed choir, a capella (III/81–86; I/20)
  66 Five Duets (III/69–73)
  69 Nine *Gesänge* (I/27–35)
  70 Four *Gesänge* (II/36–39)
  71 Five *Gesänge* (II/40–44)
  72 Five *Gesänge* (II/45–49)
  75 Nos. 2 and 3 *Guter Rath* and *So laß uns wandern* (III/74–75)
  84 *Romanzen und Lieder* for one or two voices (III/76–80)
  85 Six *Lieder* (II/50–55)
  86 Six *Lieder* (II/56–61)

2

Arrangements of the *Wiegenlied,* Op. 49 No. 4, "as a 'Paraphrase'" for two-hand piano (1873), four-hand piano (1877), and six-hand piano (1877).

3

Arrangements of piano, chamber, choral, and orchestral works for various forces on one or more pianos:

Op. 8 First Trio for Piano, Violin, and Violoncello (revised version), for four-hand piano (1891)*

12 *Ave Maria,* for four-hand piano (1878)

13 *Begräbnissgesang,* for four-hand piano (1878)

17 *Gesänge* for Women's Choir, for four-hand piano (1876)

18 First Sextet, as a "Sonate . . . in mittelschwerer Spielart" for solo piano (1889)*

21 Variations on an Original Theme, for four-hand piano (1876)

38 Sonata for Piano and Violoncello, for four-hand piano (1875)

40 Trio for Piano, Violin, and Waldhorn, for four-hand piano (1875)

50 *Rinaldo,* for two-hand piano (1874) and for four-hand piano (1874)

52 *Liebeslieder* Waltzes, for six-hand piano (1877)

53 *Rhapsodie,* for four-hand piano (1876)

54 *Schicksalslied,* for two-hand piano and for four-hand piano (both 1874)

56 Variations on a Theme by Haydn, for four-hand piano (1877)

60 Quartet No. 3 for Piano, Violin, Viola, and Violoncello, for four-hand piano (1877)

68 Symphony No. 1, for two-hand piano (1880), for two pianos, eight hands (1878), and for two pianos, four hands (1890)

73 Symphony No. 2, for two-hand piano (1880), for two pianos, eight hands (1879), and for two pianos, four hands (1890)

77 Concerto for Violin, for four-hand piano (1880)

78 Sonata No. 1 for Piano and Violin, for four-hand piano (1880)

80 Academic Festival Overture, for two-hand piano (1882) and for two pianos, eight hands (1882; McCorkle says "1881")

81 Tragic Overture, for two-hand piano (1882) and for two pianos, eight hands (1882; McCorkle says "1881")

83 Concerto No. 2 for Piano, for four-hand piano (1882)

87 Trio No. 2 for Piano, Violin, and Violoncello, for four-hand piano (1883)

89 *Gesang der Parzen,* for two-hand piano and for four-hand piano (both 1883)

90 Symphony No. 3, for two-hand piano, for four-hand piano (movements 1 and 3 revised by Brahms), and for two pianos, eight hands (all 1884)

98 Symphony No. 4, for two-hand piano and for two pianos, eight hands (both 1886)

99 Sonata No. 2 for Piano and Violoncello, for four-hand piano (1887)*

100 Sonata No. 2 for Piano and Violin, for four-hand piano (1887)*

101 Trio No. 3 for Piano, Violin, and Violoncello, for four-hand piano (1887)*

102 Concerto for Violin und Violoncello, for four-hand piano (1889)

108 Sonata No. 3 for Violin and Piano, for four-hand piano (1889)

WoO 1 Hungarian Dances, for simplified two-hand piano (Book 1, 1876; Book 2, 1881), for simplified four-hand piano ("Nach Belieben auch ohne Octavenspannungen zu spielen mit Bezeichnung des Fingersatzes"; Book 1, Nos. 2–4, and Book 2, Nos. 5–7, 1876; Book 3, Nos. 12, 13, 15, 16, and Book 4, Nos. 17, 18, 20, 21, 1881), for six-hand piano (Book 1, Nos. 1, 2, Book 2, Nos. 3–5, Book 3, Nos. 6, 7, 9, and Book 4, Nos. 8, 10, 1877), two pianos, four hands (Nos. 1–8, 13, 15, 17, 18, 20, 21, 1890), and for two pianos, eight hands (Books 1–2, 1874 [McCorkle says "1873"]; Books 3–4, 1881).

The information about Keller's arrangements of the works of other composers has been gleaned from Keller's correspondence with Joseph Joachim (appendix E), Dvořák's letters to Simrock, Franz Pazdírek's *Universal-Handbuch der Musikliteratur,* and Wilhelm Altmann's *Verzeichnis von Werken für Klavier vier- und sechshändig sowie für zwei und mehr Klaviere.* Unless otherwise indicated, the publisher was N. Simrock in Berlin.

1

Song "Paraphrases"

Paraphrase on a Beloved Song *An der Weser*

Two Paraphrases on Beloved Songs: C. G. P. Grädener, *Abendreih'n* ("Guten Abend, lieber Mondenschein!"), Op. 44 No. 6; Hermann Levi, *Der letzte Gruß* ("Ich kam vom Walde hernieder"), Op. 2 No. 6 (Leipzig: J. Rieter-Biedermann)

2

Simplied versions of works for piano

Richard Andersson, *Schwedische Tänze* (1881)

3

Arrangements of piano, chamber, choral, and orchestral works for various forces of one or more pianos:

Eugen d'Albert, Symphony in F, Op. 4, for four-hand piano (Berlin: Bote & Bock, 1888)

Daniel-François-Esprit Auber, Overture to *La muette,* for two pianos, eight hands (1873)

Ludwig van Beethoven, Overture to *Leonore,* No. 2, for two pianos, eight hands (1873)

———, Overture to *Egmont,* Op. 84 (1873), for two pianos, eight hands (1873)

Adrien Boieldieu, Overture to *Le calife de Bagdad,* for two pianos, eight hands (1873)

———, Overture to *La dame blanche,* for two pianos, eight hands (1873)

Max Bruch, *Odysseus,* Op. 41, for four-hand piano (1874)

———, *Das Lied von der Glocke,* Op. 45, for four-hand piano (1882)

———, *Wettspiele zu Ehren des Patroklus aus Achilleus,* Op. 50, for four-hand piano (1885)

Luigi Cherubini, Overture to *Les Abencérages,* for two pianos, eight hands (1873)

———, Overture to *Anacreon,* for two pianos, eight hands (1873)

———, Overture to *Les deux journées,* for two pianos, eight hands (1873)

Antonín Dvořák, Slavonic Dances for Piano, Op. 46, for two pianos, eight hands (1873)

———, Trio for Piano, Violin, and Violoncello, Op. 65, for four-hand piano (1884)

———, Slavonic Dances for Piano, Op. 72, for two pianos, four hands, and for two pianos, eight hands (both 1891)

———, Quintet for Piano, Two Violins, Viola, and Violoncello, Op. 81, for four-hand piano (1888)

———, Quartet for Piano, Violin, Viola, and Violoncello, Op. 87, for four-hand piano (1890)

Christoph Willibald von Gluck, Overture to *Alceste,* for two pianos, eight hands (1873)

———, Overture to *Iphigénie en Aulide,* for two pianos, eight hands (1873)

Maxim Heidrich, Variations on a Little Theme, Op. 1, for four-hand piano (Heilbronn: Schmidt, 1886)

Joseph Joachim, *Dem Andenken des Dichters Heinrich von Kleist* (Overture), Op. 13, for four-hand piano (1878)

————, Variations in E Minor for Violin and Orchestra, for violin and piano (Berlin: Bote & Bock, 1882)

Fritz Kauffmann, Symphony in A Minor, Op. 18, for four-hand piano (Berlin: Carl Paez, 1886)

Felix Mendelssohn, Hebrides Overture, Op. 26, for two pianos, eight hands (1875)

————, *Meeresstille und glückliche Fahrt,* Op. 27, for two pianos, eight hands (1875)

————, Overture to *Athalia,* Op. 74, for two pianos, eight hands (1875)

————, *Die Heimkehr aus der Fremde,* Op. 89, for two pianos, eight hands (1873)

Wolfgang Amadeus Mozart, Overture to *Don Giovanni,* for two pianos, eight hands (1873)

————, Overture to *Le Nozze di Figaro,* for two pianos, eight hands (1873)

————, Overture to *Die Zauberflöte,* for two pianos, eight hands (1873)

Robert Pflughaupt, *Phantasie-Variationen* for Piano, Op. 13, for two pianos, four hands (Berlin: Ries & Erler, 1883)

Karl Gottlieb Reissiger, *Die Felsenmühle von Estalières,* Op. 71, for six-hand piano (1877)

Notes

Preface

1. The manuscript for Op. 3 consists of autographs for songs Nos. 1, 2, and 4–6 and a manuscript copy of No. 3; the manuscript for Op. 6 consists of autographs for songs Nos. 1, 2, 5, and 6 and manuscript copies of Nos. 3 and 4, the first of these in the hand of Julius Otto Grimm. An annotation on the manuscript for Op. 6 establishes that Brahms gave that source to Grimm in December 1853; Brahms very likely presented the manuscript of Op. 3 to him at the same time. At the end of the autograph of Op. 6¹ No. 2 is the date *8ᵗ Sept. [18]52;* this manuscript also contains a copy of the song *Der Überläufer,* Op. 48 No. 2, in Grimm's hand, dated *[18]53.* The manuscripts for WoO 17 and 18 are likewise in Grimm's hand and were prepared from Brahms's autograph manuscript in 1857 (4:51–52, 55). At the turn of the century Florence May reported seeing the manuscripts for Op. 6 and WoO 17 and 18 in the possession of Grimm's daughter Marie (see May, *Brahms,* 148, 198). After that the Grimm collection dropped from sight.

    The one musical autograph in the Massachusetts collection not stemming from Grimm's estate—an *Albumblatt* containing the initial five bars of the vocal quartet *Nein, es ist nicht auszukommen mit den Leuten,* the eleventh of the *Liebeslieder Walzer,* Op. 52, and one of Brahms's favorite musical quotations for autograph seekers—is inscribed *Herrn Landau zu freundlicher Erinnerung,* signed *J. Brahms,* and dated *Wien 1872.*

2. The other group of letters and postcards in the Massachusetts collection comprised seventeen pieces of correspondence from Brahms to Hans and Marie von Bülow, many of which are unpublished.

3. J. A. Stargardt Catalogs 624 (24–25 November 1981) and 626 (8–9 June 1982). The Brahms-Keller letters were item 606 in Catalog 626, in which excerpts from thirteen of the letters and facsimiles of four pages were published (pp. 199–203). For further information on these sources, see Bozarth, " 'New' Brahms Manuscripts"; Biba, ed., *Johannes Brahms: Messe für vier- bis sechsstimmigen gemischten Chor und Continuo (Orgel);* Melamed and Hancock, "Brahms's Kyrie and *Missa canonica*"; and Pascall, "Brahms's *Missa canonica* and Its Recomposition in His Motet 'Warum,' Op. 74 No. 1," and "The Publication of Brahms's Third Symphony."

    In May 1981, a few months before the first Stargardt auction, Sotheby Park Bernet sold two manuscripts with connections to Julius Otto Grimm—the engraver's model, in a scribal hand with Brahms's revisions, for the Piano Sonata in C Major, Op. 1, a work dedicated to Grimm, and a manuscript copy of Brahms's Variations on a Hungarian Song, Op. 21 No. 2, in the hand of Clara Schumann, given to Grimm by Frau Schumann in August 1857 (see May, *Brahms*, 222). These manuscripts, however, seem not to have come from the Massachusetts collection.

4. The vocal part for Opp. 12 and 37 was acquired by G. T. Mandl in Netstal, Switzerland (see McCorkle, *Brahms Werkverzeichnis*, 38, 135); the disposition of the musical *Albumblatt* and the Brahms-Bülow letters is unknown to me.

5. From the contents of the surviving correspondence, it is clear that several letters are missing. Gaps in the two systems that Keller used for numbering the letters—items 1–19 and 32 according to his first system and items 1–2 according to his second (see appendix A)—suggest a correspondence rather more extensive than what has been preserved.

6. Friedlaender, *Brahms Lieder*, 114 (Leese trans., 147).

Introduction

1. Keller's place of birth is registered with the Standesamt Tiergarten in Berlin. Harpersdorf, now called Twardocice, is in the Zlotoryja district of Poland. Keller's date of birth has been calculated on the basis of an entry in the *Todten-Register* of the Zwölf-Apostel-Kirchhof, which lists him as age sixty-three years, five months, and ten days at the time of his death on 16 June 1891.

2. Meyer, "Harpersdorf," in *Das große Conversations-Lexicon*, 15:5.

3. Teuber, *Silesia in Pictures*, 8, 20.

4. Scholz, *Silesia Yesterday and Today*, 32.

5. *Allgemeiner Wohnungs-Anzeiger für Berlin und Umgebungen auf das Jahr 1855*. Also consulted were city directories for the years 1850–54, 1856, 1858–61, 1865, 1868–69, 1873–74, 1876–78, and 1880–91. Directories for the remaining years of Keller's residence in Berlin could not be located. Starting in 1869, the directories took the name *Berliner Adreß-Buch für das Jahr 1869, etc.*

6. Keller's name is missing from the Berlin directory of 1869. The length of his absence from the city cannot be determined, owing to the lack of directories for the years 1870–72.

7. Several maps of nineteenth-century Berlin have been consulted, including D. Reimer, 1850, and Royal Prussian General Staff, 1867–68, with additions in 1874, reprinted in the *Historischer Handatlas von Brandenburg und Berlin*, Lfg. 1 and 21; *Berlin und nähere Umgebung um 1840* and *Plan Monumental von Berlin* (Berlin: Carl Glück Verlag, ca. 1860), published as Beilage 1 and 2 to Zimm, ed., *Berlin und sein Umland.*

8. Hofmann, *Die Erstdrucke der Werke von Johannes Brahms*, xiii–xiv.

9. For an engaging account of life in Berlin at this time, see Masur, *Imperial Berlin*.

10. Zimm, ed., *Berlin und sein Umland*, 34, 63.

11. Masur, *Imperial Berlin*, 43, 73. In 1877 the Simrocks shared the seven-apartment building at Am Carlsbad 3 with a painter, a banker, a businessman, a consul, and two families of private means (one of whom owned the building).

12. Ottendorff-Simrock, *Das Haus Simrock*, 153–56; Wilhelmy, *Der Berliner Salon im 19. Jahrhundert*, 837–38, also 966–69.

13. Between 1855 and 1880, the number of music teachers cited in the Berlin directories nearly doubled, from 268 to 436; during Keller's residence in Berlin, the number of *Korrectoren* rose from a mere 4 in 1855 to 30 in 1891.

14. This letter also contains the first of numerous references in the Brahms-Simrock correspondence to written communications from Keller to Brahms that are no longer extant.

15. Nodnagel, *Gedenkblätter zur Einweihungsfeier der neuen Räume des Stern'schen Konservatoriums der Musik zu Berlin* (unpaginated); and Klatte and Misch, *Das Sternsche Konservatorium der Musik zu Berlin*, 22, 74; see also Eitner, "Stern, Julius." The records of the Stern Conservatory are no longer extant.

16. Three letters from Antonín Dvořák to Balduin Dörffel in 1880 and 1882 establish him as an office employee of Simrock's; in one of these letters, Dvořák asks Dörffel to forward materials to Keller. See *Antonín Dvořák Korrespondenz und Dokumente*, 1:227, 291, 293.

17. *Dvořák Korrespondenz*, 1:390.

18. Simrock's prices, however, were high, a situation about which Brahms complained, threatening to allow C. F. Peters of Leipzig to publish his compositions because Peters would charge less for them. In 1881, for example, Peters sold the orchestral score of Brahms's *Nänie* for Choir and Orchestra, Op. 82 (twenty-nine pages in folio format), for six Marks, while Simrock priced the scores of the Academic Festival and Tragic Overtures, Opp. 80 and 81 (seventy-one pages in octavo format), each at twelve Marks. It needs to be noted, however, that Brahms's honorarium from Peters—three thousand Marks—was considerably less than the forty-five hundred Marks he received from Simrock for each of the overtures.

19. The amounts of these honoraria are taken from Brahms's handwritten *Werkverzeichnis* (Stadt- und Landesbibliothek, Vienna). Typically, Brahms's fee for his arrangements was included in his honorarium for the work; in only a few cases, like Opp. 51 and 55, was a division of the total between original work and arrangement indicated.

20. Bernstein (*Die Geschichte der Berliner Arbeiterbewegung*, 2:272) cites the typical weekly salaries of various types of workers in Berlin in 1888. The average worker in a piano factory, for instance, made 24.55 Marks a week (if paid by the hour) or 27.30 Marks (if paid by the piece); the weekly pay of an engraver was 24.00 or 25.95 Marks, of a cabinetmaker 22.25 or 24.15 Marks, of a hatmaker 20.85 or 23.10 Marks; a baker could expect to make about 20.15 Marks, or 9.90 Marks if room and board were provided by his employer.

21. See Cai, "Was Brahms a Reliable Editor?" and Bozarth, "News and Comment," 10, and "A New Collected Edition for Brahms."

22. This letter, omitted from Litzmann's *Clara Schumann–Johannes Brahms Briefe*, was first published by Roesner in "Brahms's Editions of Schumann," 281.

23. In the 1850s, as part of his study of the music of Robert Schumann, and in response to suggestions from Clara Schumann, Brahms prepared keyboard arrangements of the Piano Quartet, Op. 47 (four hands), and the Scherzo from the Piano Quintet, Op. 44 (two hands). At this time he also arranged three of Joseph Joachim's overtures, *Demetrius* and *Heinrich IV* for two pianos and *Hamlet* for four-hand piano. His later adaptations of Schubert Ländler for two-hand and four-hand piano (D. 366 and 814) were a product of his encounter with unpublished Schubert works in Vienna in the 1860s. On Brahms's keyboard arrangements of his own compositions and the works of others, see Goertzen's comprehensive study "The Piano Transcriptions of Johannes Brahms"; on his Schubert arrangements, see Brodbeck, "Brahms's Edition of Twenty Schubert Ländler."

24. Brahms made piano reductions of the orchestral accompaniments for his two concerti and many of his choral works as well, but here the primary purpose was to facilitate rehearsal.

25. In an earlier letter to Simrock, Brahms had asked whether he might try to improve these arrangements: "I certainly don't want to hurt Keller. Yet, since the arrangement was sent to me *before* printing, I would like to see whether by and by I might permit myself to do this or that with it. May I do that at all?" (5 July 1881; 10:179).

    Hans von Bülow prepared numerous virtuoso piano arrangements of works by his predecessors, including sonatas by Domenico Scarlatti and dances from Gluck's operas. For the arrangements of Theodor Kirchner, who was a member of the Schumann circle and a composer in his own right, Brahms had special words of praise; of his transcriptions of Brahms's two string sextets for piano, violin, and violoncello, Brahms wrote Simrock: "The trios give me extraordinary pleasure! If you had the idea, then I congratulate you, but Kirchner has also executed them superbly" (13 March 1883; 11:18–19). Kirchner, like Keller, adapted numerous Brahms songs for performance by solo piano; three of these arrangements have been reissued in Draheim, ed., *Johannes Brahms und seine Freunde*, 98–107. Kirchner also prepared two-hand, four-hand, and two-piano eight-hand versions of works by Brahms.

26. Compare also Brahms's remarks on the subject to Georg Henschel: "The chief aim of a pianoforte arrangement of orchestral accompaniments must always be to be easily playable. Whether the different parts move correctly, i.e., in strict accordance with the rules of counterpoint, does not matter in the least" (Henschel, *Personal Recollections*, 34).

27. Quoted in Max Broesike-Schoen, "Der moderne Klavierauszug"; also in Goertzen, "The Piano Transcriptions of Brahms," 1. Goertzen (pp. 325–35) has

assessed selected passages from Keller's four-hand arrangement of Brahms's C Minor Piano Quartet, Op. 60, in light of Brahms's usual practices.

28. *Dvořák Korrespondenz*, 1:207, 213, 216, 227, 291, 293, 315, 332–35, 354, 389–90; 2:28, 62, 65, 167, 257, 305, 381, 383; 3:11. Keller's five letters and post-cards to Dvořák (26 May 1879; 25 July 1879; 5 May 1880; 16 July 1881; 13 September 1881) are preserved in the Muzeum České hudby, Prague, and will be published in the *Dvořák Korrespondenz*. I wish to thank Dr. Stanislav Tesař for providing photocopies of this correspondence.

29. *Dvořák Korrespondenz*, 1:332–33.

30. *Dvořák Korrespondenz*, 1:176; translated in Šourek, preface to Antonín Dvořák, *Sextet A Dur op. 48*, p. ix.

31. On Berlin's musical life, see Becker and Green, "Berlin"; and Masur, *Imperial Berlin*, 232–38.

32. Reich, *Clara Schumann*, 175–76.

33. Kahn, "Recollections of Johannes Brahms," 607. Brahms also had personal reasons for not wanting to live in Berlin—to avoid daily contact with one of his oldest friends, Joseph Joachim. As he wrote to Amalie Joachim in December 1880, in the midst of her legal battle with her husband, who believed that she was having an affair with Fritz Simrock:

> You may have noticed that in spite of our friendship of thirty years' standing, in spite of all my love and admiration for Joachim, in spite of all the mutual artistic interests which should bind me to him, I am always very careful in my intercourse with him, so that I rarely associate with him for long or at all intimately, and I have never thought of living in the same town and tying myself down to work with him. Now I hardly need tell you that I knew, even before you did, of the unhappy peculiarity with which Joachim torments himself and others in such an inexcusable way. Friendship and love I must be able to breathe as simply as air. I take alarm when I encounter these beautiful emotions in a complicated and artificial form, and the more so if it has to be maintained and enhanced by painfully morbid excitement. . . . Thus I have saved a small part of my friendship with Joachim by my caution; without this I should have lost all long ago. . . .
>
> I therefore simply want to tell you, explicitly and plainly, as I have told Joachim innumerable times, that it is my opinion and belief that he has done you and Simrock a grievous wrong; and I can but hope that he will abandon his false and terrible delusions. (Quoted in Geiringer, *Brahms*, 143)

In 1869 Brahms had turned down an offer from Joachim to join the faculty of his newly founded Hochschule für Musik in Berlin. After Frau Joachim produced Brahms's letter in court during the divorce proceedings to support her claim of innocence, Joachim broke off all personal relations with Brahms for a number of years. (See also Ethel Smyth's account of this sad episode in "Recollections of Brahms," 554–56.)

34. Information on Brahms's visits to and concerts in Berlin has been gleaned from Hofmann and Hofmann, *Brahms Zeittafel.*

35. Florence May, who was present at these concerts and their rehearsals, provided a firsthand account in her biography of Brahms (*Brahms,* 26–32). The reaction of both public and orchestra to the Second Piano Concerto was tumultuous: "The public applauded wildly, and shouted itself hoarse; the band joined in with its fanfare of trumpet and drum; Brahms and von Bülow were recalled again and again separately and together; and in the moment of the great composer's triumph I saw the . . . Brahms [I had known in the early 1870s] once more standing before me, for, whilst his eyes shone and his face beamed with pleasure, I recognised in his bearing and expression the old familiar look of almost diffident, shy modesty which had been one of his characteristics in former days."

36. Together with this drawing, Menzel sent Brahms a note that read: "We often think of you here, and often enough, comparing notes, we confess our suspicions that on a certain night the Muse itself appeared in person (disguised in the evening dress of the Meiningen Court) for the purpose of executing a certain woodwind part. On this page I have tried to capture the sublime vision" (30 April 1892, quoted in Geiringer, *Brahms,* 178).

37. A number of Brahms's Lieder were also first performed in public in Berlin, by Julius Stockhausen and Amalie Joachim.

38. Letter from Otto Krigar-Menzel to Brahms, 26 April 1892, quoted in Geiringer, *Brahms,* 179. As Geiringer noted, "Brahms and Menzel, who regarded each other as colleagues, each having received the Prussian Order *Pour le mérite* . . . understood each other excellently in their general views of life and the world, and they also shared a peculiar appreciation of the more prosaic joys of life." At Menzel's "mighty banquets . . . they ate, drank, and debated indefatigably; and even after spending as much as seven hours in this fashion, neither the seventy-six-year-old Menzel nor the all but sexagenarian Brahms felt in any degree tired, but positively refreshed."

39. Phenacetin, a drug no longer in use, was prescribed in the late nineteenth century as an analgesic and antipyretic, that is, to relieve pain and fever. Unfortunately, it is toxic to the kidneys and has adverse hematologic effects, causing red blood cells to burst, resulting in anemia. I would like to thank Professor Nelda Murri, director of the Drug Information Center at the University of Washington, for her kind assistance.

40. Professor Keith R. Benson of the Department of Medical History and Ethics of the School of Medicine, University of Washington, has offered two diagnoses for Keller's terminal illness:

> One possible explanation for Keller's condition is a brain tumor. This may have been responsible for the symptoms he suffered [see item 50]

and would account for the treatment he received. Because he lived before the existence of diagnostic tools to diagnose a brain tumor and because there were few operable conditions involving the head, he would have died from the course of the disease and his autopsy may have indicated *cerebral apoplexy.* Another possibility is that Keller suffered from high blood pressure, which was also not well understood. Such a condition could have led to hypertension and could have culminated in a cerebral hemorrhage, again explained as *cerebral apoplexy.*

41. Brahms often recorded his support of friends, members of his family, and colleagues in his pocket calendar books (Stadt- und Landesbibliothek, Vienna), but these documents contain no accounting of his assistance to Keller's sister-in-law.

The First Symphony

1. The extant portion of the autograph score (cited below) bears the inscription *Lichtenthal Sept. [18]76* at the end of the fourth movement.
2. See Newman, "The Slow Movement of Brahms' First Symphony"; Pascall, "Brahms's First Symphony Slow Movement"; Haas, "Die Erstfassung des langsamen Satzes der ersten Sinfonie von Johannes Brahms," which contains a keyboard reconstruction of the first version in piano reduction; McCorkle, "Filling the Gaps in Brahms Source Research," which also describes alterations in the third movement; Pascall, *Brahms's First Symphony Andante,* which attempts to reconstruct a full score of the original Andante; and Brodbeck, review of McCorkle, *Brahms Werkverzeichnis,* 424–26, which discusses sketches for the Andante; see also Gál's *Revisionsbericht* to his edition of this work for the *Brahms Werke,* vol. 1, and McCorkle, "The Role of Trial Performances for Brahms's Orchestral and Large Choral Works," 313–16.
3. A facsimile of this manuscript has been issued by Dover Publications, with an introduction by Margit L. McCorkle.
4. Compare David Epstein, "Brahms and the Mechanisms of Motion," 211–13, and *Beyond Orpheus,* 91–94.
5. Brahms's opposition to "violin" notation was still in evidence in 1886, when he wrote Simrock requesting that Keller standardize the string parts for the Fourth Symphony according to his notation in the score (25 June 1886, 11:124; quoted below in the commentary to item 29). By 1890, however, Brahms seems finally to have become resigned to the string players' manner of designating *portamento.* On 13 December, in a letter to Simrock that accompanied the engraver's models for the revised version of the B Major Piano Trio, Op. 8, and the G Major String Quintet, Op. 111, he noted, "Herr Keller

should be aware that I more frequently mark the score and parts differently! ⌣ ⌣ and ⌢ etc." (12:36).

The Second Symphony

1. Kalbeck, *Brahms,* 3:178.
2. McCorkle, *Brahms Werkverzeichnis,* 310, and "The Role of Trial Performances," 318–19.
3. About the printed parts for the First Symphony, Hans von Bülow complained to Fritz Simrock on 21 November 1887: "If only the orchestral parts were set up a bit more practically! For example, the unlucky violists (*divisi* to boot) have to turn the page in the Finale just six bars before **G** [i.e., at bar 162], and thus the important ticklish passage always comes out badly, stumbling forth with hanging and choking. Naturally the copyist has to help out here. One could register still other inconveniences of this sort" (Hofmann and Fürst, *Johannes Brahms,* 48, revised according to von Bülow's original letter in the collection of the Brahms Institut in Lübeck).
4. Hofmann and Hofmann, *Brahms Zeittafel,* 140.

Songs in Transposed Keys

1. See McCorkle, *Brahms Werkverzeichnis,* 69, 109, 119, 160, 182, 187, 193, 200.
2. In Rieter's transposed editions, all the songs in Opp. 57–59 appeared in lower keys, with the exception of two songs already in a low range: *Schwermuth,* Op. 58 No. 5, was left in E♭ minor, and *Dämm'rung senkte sich von oben,* Op. 59 No. 1, was transposed up a major third into B minor. For the keys of the remaining songs, see McCorkle, *Brahms Werkverzeichnis,* 242, 248, 271.

The Violin Concerto and the Clavierstücke

1. The Library of Congress published a facsimile edition of the autograph manuscript of the full score in 1979, with an introduction by Yehudi Menuhin and a foreword by Jon Newsom. Reviews by Robert Pascall and Linda Correll Roesner have corrected errors in the introduction and foreword and called attention to deficiencies in the photographic reproduction of the manuscript. Roesner's reconstruction of the history of the concerto is particularly thorough and includes a detailed timeline for the genesis of the work from August 1878 through June 1879 (pp. 64–65). See also McCorkle, *Brahms Werkverzeichnis,* 325–28, and "The Role of Trial Performances," 319–20; and Schwarz, "Joseph Joachim and the Genesis of Brahms's Violin Concerto." Schwarz's study, which was prepared for the 1980 International Brahms Congress in Detroit, was revised before publication in 1983, but unfortunately the revision did not take into account the findings presented in Pascall's and Roesner's reviews; it

too contains errors in its commentary on the sources as well as other problems in its readings of the correspondence related to this work.

2. Brahms's alterations in the full score were entered in both red and gray pencil. Roesner (review, pp. 63, 66) has suggested that the annotations in red pencil were made at two different times, some before and some after the gray-pencil revisions, and she has speculated that the first set of red-pencil entries was made in late January 1879, the gray-pencil corrections in mid-April to mid-May, and the final red-pencil markings just before the score was sent to Simrock in late June.

3. Keller's emendations in dark red ink in the autograph score were misidentified as being by Joseph Joachim in the "Color Key" to the Library of Congress facsimile edition (see n. 1, this chapter).

4. The three published *ossia* readings in the first movement occur at bars 241–42, 348–54, and 484–85. The six passages in the Finale for which *ossia* readings were considered but rejected are bars 122–23, 132–33, 195–202, 259–64, 281, and 325–26; in the end, several of the readings originally designated as alternatives were adopted as the final readings, Brahms's initial versions being dropped entirely. When O. Schnirlin prepared a revised edition of the solo violin part for the 1905 Simrock edition of the violin-piano arrangement, he included all these rejected readings as *ossias*, thereby contravening Brahms's express wishes.

Fifty-one Exercises for Piano, Part 1

1. The reference is to the seventeenth-century artist Jacques Callot, who specialized in the rendering of grotesqueries. The nature of the inspiration that Hoffmann drew from Callot is described in the brief essay that prefaces the *Kreisleriana* portion of the *Fantasiestücke*: "May a poet or writer, in whom the figures of everyday life are reflected in his inner romantic spirit-realm, and who then portrays them in the glow by which they are there enveloped, as if in weird and wonderful apparel, may he not justify himself at least by reference to this master and say: He wished to work in the manner of Callot?" (Charlton, ed., *E. T. A. Hoffmann's Musical Writings*, 78).

2. The pair of leaves also contain exercises in Clara Schumann's hand, three of which are identical with or similar to Nos. 12–14 in the 51 Exercises. Another sheet in this miscellany, in Brahms's later handwriting, preserves variants of Nos. 17 and 18, and an additional bifolio contains a fragment of a longer étude.

3. Schumann, *Erinnerungen*, 168 (trans., 141).

4. May, *Brahms*, 8–11.

5. Schumann, *Erinnerungen*, 196–97 (trans., 167); see also December 1878, Schumann, 2:162.

6. Schumann, 2:214–15 (trans., 64–65).

7. Schumann, *Erinnerungen,* 197 (trans., 168). In a letter to Brahms of 7 August 1880, Clara Schumann offered him "a thousand thanks" for his assistance: "I had no idea that I was giving you so much trouble, and only realize it now that I have seen how carefully you must have gone through it in order to do what we wanted" (Schumann, 2:217 [trans., 65–66]). Frau Schumann also depended on Brahms for advice about the pecuniary ramifications of this project: "Shall I do it for nothing, or shall I ask something for it?—The work is quite time consuming, and Cranz will very likely make a profit on it. You are so practical in all such matters and surely will be able to advise me" (8 July 1880; Schumann, 2:215).

8. According to this hypothesis, No. 34 in the 1880 collection, which Keller described as having a "final variant" that "occurs in similar form in Clementi's *Gradus ad Parnassum,*" would be the same as No. 31b in the 1893 collection. But neither this exercise nor any others in the later collection fit Keller's description.

9. Geiringer, *Brahms,* 122.

Therese, *Op. 86 No. 1*

1. The calendar book entry for *Therese,* like those for the other nine songs, gives only poet and key: *Keller D dur.*

2. The same variant readings for *Therese* were preserved in a manuscript copy of the song that Brahms gave to Ottilie Ebner née Hauer, a singer and close friend from his earliest days in Vienna. (No autograph manuscript for the song is extant.) The present location of the Ebner manuscript copy is unknown, but Eusebius Mandyczewski saw it in the early 1920s (in the possession of Frau Ebner's daughter, Ottilie von Balassa of Budapest) and described it in the *Revisionsbericht* for vol. 25 of the *Brahms Werke.* In this source the song was in F major, a third higher than the published version, transposed no doubt for Frau Ebner, who was a soprano. The original readings in this manuscript were the ones eventually published, but they were altered by Brahms to match the readings sent to Keller.

3. Friedlaender, *Brahms Lieder,* 115 (trans., 148). In the revised edition of his poems, Keller changed the crucial final stanza to "Ein leeres Schneckhäusel, / Schau, liegt dort im Gras; / Da halte dein Ohr dran, / Drin brümmelt dir was." This is the version that Hugo Wolf set to music in 1890.

Brahms appropriately employed the alto voice, for the singer of the poem—Gottfried Keller thought of *Therese* as a song, originally placing it as the third piece in his cycle *Von Weibern: Alte Lieder: 1846*—is not a young girl but a mature woman. As the poet explained to Friedlaender: "I originally wished to portray in this series of songs the waxing and waning of the love of a young man for a maturer pampered beauty. In the beginning she dismisses the youthful and inexperienced lover with scorn. Later, however, when she loses a tooth and realizes that she is growing older, she tries to win him back by every means, but it is too late." The poem belonged to the group entitled *Aufsteigende Liebe* (Growing love).

4. Brahms had also thought to change the title of this song. In a letter to Otto Dessoff on 26 June 1878, he expressed intense displeasure with the title *Therese* and suggested that the song be called *schöne* or *schönes Räthsel*. If Dessoff went to Switzerland, Brahms asked that he inquire of Gottfried Keller about the change (16:193). Dessoff wrote back, agreeing to do Brahms this favor, but arguing against the retitling (16:194). In his reply to Dessoff, Brahms revealed the reason why the title went against the grain: "I have known few Thereses and those that I remember from my youth were long and skinny and wore long, skinny lovelocks" (undated; 16:200). Nevertheless, the title *Therese* was retained.

Fifty-one Exercises for Piano, Part 2

1. The engraver's model for the 51 Exercises (Brahms-Archiv, Staats- und Universitätsbibliothek, Hamburg) was prepared by Brahms's regular Viennese copyist William Kupfer. In a second letter, on 17 November 1893, Brahms gave his publisher instructions on details of layout:

> Please add to the remark for No. 1 of the Exercises, as a second paragraph, the following: *Abwechslung in Zeitmaß und Tonstärke bleiben dem Spieler überlassen* [Changes in tempo and dynamics are left to the performer's discretion]. The second remark for No. 3 or 4 (concerning higher and lower octaves) is probably better said: *Nach Belieben in weiteren Oktaven* [In other octaves, as desired]. It is probably troublesome for the layout of the engraving that an exercise must always end on the *right* page—since one cannot turn pages in an exercise. Numbers (instead of notes) in the measure can of course be closely spaced. But the numbers
>
> 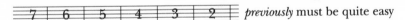 *previously* must be quite easy
>
> to see! Perhaps over the first note (better than over the barline?). We probably must stick with the title *Übungen*. I have given the title *Studien* to pieces already published by Senff, and it would certainly be fine with me if these exercises were the last volume of those studies. (12:109)

The Third Symphony

1. Hofmann and Hofmann, *Brahms Zeittafel*, 176–84; and Pascall, "The Publication of Brahms's Third Symphony," 286–87. The present summary of the process of publishing the Third Symphony is indebted to Pascall's detailed study.

2. In his letter to Simrock of 7 November 1883 (11:38), Brahms wrote of two copyists at work on parts for the Third Symphony. The one he described as "very old and slow" was no doubt Hlavaczek; the other, referred to as "young," would have been Kupfer.

3. For the Vienna premiere Brahms asked Simrock to print nine first-violin, nine second-violin, six viola, five cello, and five bass parts to supplement the manuscript parts.

4. Brahms had already sent Simrock his two-piano arrangement of the symphony, which was released late in March or early in April.

5. Hofmann and Hofmann, *Brahms Zeittafel,* 182. Pascall ("The Publication of Brahms's Third Symphony," 287) notes that there are no references to proofs in the ongoing correspondence between Brahms and Simrock during April and May.

6. Pascall, who was unaware of Keller's cover letter, which is dated "Mid-July 1884," attributed Keller's list of corrections to mid-August ("The Publication of Brahms's Third Symphony," 288).

7. Keller's draft of this letter is owned by the Library of Congress.

8. Pascall, "The Publication of Brahms's Third Symphony," 293.

Thematisches Verzeichniss, *Fourth Symphony, and Piano Trio*

1. The publisher's number for the Brahms catalog is 8607; Brahms's *Vier Lieder,* Op. 96, released by Simrock in March 1886, bears the number 8626.

2. The composition interrupted by the Wagnerians was Saint-Saëns' Piano Concerto No. 4 in C Minor, Op. 44. A review in the *Neue Musik-Zeitung* describes the fiasco:

> With the appearance of the French composer Saint-Saëns in the Philharmonic concert, expressions of displeasure issued from the audience. The weak applause that greeted the guest aroused opposition, which burst forth again during a passage of the piano concerto that contained reminiscences of Wagner. Only later did the auditorium calm down, so that with the second appearance of the composer peace prevailed. Recently a few anti-German remarks by Saint-Saëns, who in earlier years often stayed in Germany and even premiered some of his compositions here, have been circulating. He also participated enthusiastically in the agitation against the *Lohengrin* performance in Paris. (*Neue Musik-Zeitung* 7, no. 3 [1886]: 37)

During Wagner's stay in Paris in 1859, Saint-Saëns had taken part in his Wednesday evening soirees; Saint-Saëns attended the premieres of *Die Walküre* (1870), of the full *Ring* (1876), and of *Parsifal* (1882) at Bayreuth; and in a balanced review of the *Ring* (August 1876) he had defended Wagner against the virulent attacks of the French press, earning the enmity of many a fellow countryman: "To label Wagner an enemy of our country is simply absurd. He was an enemy only to those who were hostile toward his music. They may well be justified in the latter; but they are certainly unjust in labeling the composer of the works they ridicule a monster by birth and lineage. Wagnermania is an excusable error, but Wagnerphobia is a children's disease" ("Bayreuth und der Ring des Nibelungen," 884).

But the publication in 1873 of Wagner's *Eine Capitulation,* a scurrilous farce rejoicing in the suffering of the beseiged and starving Parisians during the Franco-Prussian War (1870–71), described by Saint-Saëns in his review of the *Ring* as "a loathsome parody that no German theater will produce and that can be injurious only to its creator," tested Saint-Saëns's tolerance of Wagner the man. About their final meeting, at Villa Wahnfried in 1876, Saint-Saëns would recall: "I went there very much against my will and with *Eine Capitulation* heavy on my heart, but only because Liszt had wanted me to and I owed him so much that I could refuse him nothing. 'Do you bear me a grudge just because of a joke in bad taste?' Wagner asked me. 'It would have been so easy for you not to make it,' I replied. And he did not answer" (quoted in Harding, *Saint-Saëns and His Circle,* 144–45).

After this episode, Saint-Saëns's writings reflect a more cautious attitude toward Wagner and the influence of German music. In his collection of essays *Harmonie et mélodie,* published in 1885—not long before his appearance in Berlin and in the same year that saw the cancellation of plans to mount the Paris premiere of *Lohengrin* and a political crisis in France accompanied by a marked intensification of anti-Wagner sentiment—Saint-Saëns observed: "What German music brings us is not only music but also German ideas, the German soul." He could accept this when the soul was that of Schiller or Beethoven, but it was not the same with Wagner:

> "Honor your German masters! protect your workers! Send up in smoke the Holy Roman Empire and may holy German art remain to us for evermore." Those are the words which conclude *Die Meistersinger* and which the Patrons of Bayreuth adopted as their motto in 1882. For those who know how to interpret symbols, this is the cry of pan-Germanism and war on the Latin races. . . . Because Beethoven sang of universal brotherhood, because his was the human rather than the narrowly German soul, he remains the greatest, the only truly great. (Quoted in translation in Harding, *Saint-Saëns and His Circle,* 145–46)

For Saint-Saëns the Berlin debacle was only the beginning of his troubles in Germany; one after another his concert engagements were canceled, including Cassel, Bremen, and Dresden (*Neue Musik Zeitung* 7, no. 3 [1886]: 37). Undaunted, he withdrew from the fray and retired to a small Austrian village, where he created his most popular work, *Le Carnaval des animaux.* (On Wagner and the French, see Elaine Brody, *Paris: The Musical Kaleidoscope,* 21–59; and Stegemann, "Camille Saint-Saëns und Deutschland.")

3. There are a number of instances where Brahms's second thoughts about his compositions, while seemingly representing his "final wishes" (*die Fassung letzter Hand*), might better be viewed simply as temporary alternative readings. See Brahms's vacillation over two passages in the song *Therese*, Op. 86 No. 1, discussed earlier, and over alternative readings for the third of the *Magelone* Romances, Op. 33, recounted in Bozarth, "A New Collected Edition for Brahms."

4. Brahms owned copies of both catalogs—the Beethoven catalog in a second edition (1868)—and they are listed in Brahms's fair-copy catalog of his library (see Orel, "Johannes Brahms' Musikbibliothek," 38 [reprint, 159]).

The Gesänge, *the* Lieder, *and a Holiday*

1. The inscription *Manuscript von | Johannes Brahms, Juli 1888 | in Thun* written by Fritz Simrock on the autograph of *Salamander,* Op. 107 No. 2, that was used as the engraver's model for the first edition (see McCorkle, *Brahms Werkverzeichnis,* 433) may establish only the date of the manuscript (or of when Simrock thought the manuscript was prepared), not the date of composition.

2. The Vienna manuscript does have traces of glue along the folded edge, suggesting that it once was bound, but the circumstances under which the binding took place are unknown.

3. The Liepmannssohn catalog described the autograph of the three Op. 106 and 107 songs as a single volume (*Heft*) consisting of "7¼ nine-stave pages."

4. The term *bouquets* (*Lieder-Sträuße*) is one that Brahms himself used when describing his opuses of songs. See Fellinger, "Cyclic Tendencies in Brahms's Song Collections," passim.

5. One of the manuscript copies was prepared by Brahms's copyist William Kupfer, corrected by the composer, and sent to Julius Spengel, conductor of the Hamburg Cäcilien-Verein, in November 1886 (see Spengel, ed., *Johannes Brahms an Julius Spengel,* 29). The other manuscript was copied by Spengel from the Kupfer manuscript in February 1887. In both manuscripts, which are now in the Kurt Hofmann collection in Lübeck, the work is entitled *Der Herbst.*

6. See Hofmann, ed., *Johannes Brahms, Der Herbst—Erste Fassung von 1886, Im Herbst—Zweite Fassung von 1888 für vierstimmigen gemischten Chor a cappella.*

7. Geiringer, *Brahms,* 71.

8. Geiringer, *Brahms,* 153.

9. Friedlaender, *Brahms Lieder,* 145. Elisabet von Herzogenberg took particular exception to Lemcke's poem. Writing Brahms from Nice on 28 October 1888 she remarked:

I ask you whether it is really all our fault if we react with a burst of genuine enthusiasm over the *Kirchhof* song [Op. 105 No. 4], greet three or four others cordially—and can give the rest only a chilly welcome? . . . The *Kirchhof* [is a] *glorious* song in which everything is so distinctive and colorful, words and music coinciding with each other. . . . But one turns the page and the *Mannsbild*, oh the *Mannsbild* [stanza 2 of *Verrat*, Op. 105 No. 5: "Mein Schatz ließ sacht ein Mannsbild raus" ("Cautiously my sweetheart let out a man"); poem also by Lemcke] leaps out and tears one out of all heavens. No, that you could think this poem worthy of being composed by you—I cannot understand, so unattractive, so dry, so cheaply popular with its barren heath; indeed, a barren heath it seems to me. Oh, are all the good poems really so used up that one must latch onto such curdled-milk [*Schlippermilch*] and Lemcke's "cold devils"? How glad I am that I could never stand this Lemcke; now I know even more clearly why. The little *Mädchenlied* by Heyse [Op. 107 No. 5] becomes Goethe by comparison; one suddenly breathes pure, lovely air again. (2:204–6)

String Sextet, Op. 18, "Piano Sonata" Version

1. Hofmann and Hofmann, *Brahms Zeittafel*, 239. Litzmann (*Clara Schumann: Ein Künstlerleben*, 624) first lists this movement as part of Frau Schumann's repertoire in the year 1871.
2. Hofmann and Hofmann, *Brahms Zeittafel*, 96; cited in McCorkle, *Brahms Werkverzeichnis*, 63, as the first public performance.

A Friendly Invitation

1. The anniversary was celebrated early, because Joachim would be on a concert tour in England on the actual date, 17 March, which, however, did not pass unnoticed, as Joachim wrote Philipp Spitta: "Today on the 17th it's nearly as lively here as it was on the 1st. . . . From the Herzogenbergs today, or perhaps yesterday evening, came very dear letters, a violin piece (composed on 8–10 March), and flowers" (see Joachim and Moser, eds., *Briefe von und an Joseph Joachim*, 3:345, 349–50; for the letters from Elisabet and Heinrich von Herzogenberg, written on 14 March 1889, see 3:345–49).
2. Hofmann and Hofmann, *Brahms Zeittafel*, 208.

The Fest- und Gedenksprüche, Op. 109

1. Max Kalbeck (*Brahms*, 4:117) thought it likely that the three works stemmed from the summer of 1888, the last that Brahms spent in Thun. However, in a letter to Eduard Hanslick of 15 March 1888, Theodor Billroth already made

mention of eight-voice choral pieces by Brahms due to receive their premiere on 20 March at the home of Arthur and Bertha Faber in Vienna, and Eusebius Mandyczewski, who conducted the choir on that occasion, reported to Otto Gottlieb-Billroth that he thought he remembered that the pieces were the *Fest- und Gedenksprüche* (Billroth, 425).

2. Geiringer, *Brahms*, 303.

3. Kalbeck, *Brahms*, 4:184. Leipzig Day celebrated the defeat of Napoléon I at the Battle of Leipzig in 1813; Sedan Day commemorated the defeat of Napoléon II at the Battle of Sedan in the Franco-Prussian War of 1870.

4. Brahms knew about his *Ehrenbürgerschaft* at least a week and a half earlier, when Franz Wüllner wrote to congratulate him (11 May 1889; 15:157).

5. Petersen's response, which Karl Geiringer found among the letters in Brahms's estate, reveals a man of humility, a worthy recipient of this dedication: "To me, as a layman, a great honor has been paid. Fortunately, one need not be an expert in order to derive joy from music, and just as I enjoyed this beautiful work at the Exhibition, so I hope often to feel happiness and peace of mind on hearing it in the future. Your work and your name will long outlive mine; so it is pleasant to think that through the medium of your dedication my name will be handed down to posterity" (Geiringer, *Brahms*, 173).

6. For No. 1, bars 38–39 (soprano 2), and No. 3, bars 26 (tenor 2), 28 (tenor 1), 35–36 (bass 1), and 41–42 (alto 1).

7. For No. 1, bars 2 (all voices), 12–15 (all voices), 15–16 (soprano 2, alto 2, tenor 2, bass 2), and 21–23 (all voices). Further lists of revisions, barely readable, appear on the recto page to the right of the first group and below the second group. Very likely, these revisions are a continuation of the first group, since they were not communicated to Keller with the revisions of the second group.

Appendix E

1. Boetticher, "Joachim, Joseph."
2. Oliver, "Joachim Quartet."

Bibliography

Correspondence

Johannes Brahms Briefwechsel. 16 vols. Rev. ed. Berlin: Deutsche Brahms-Gesellschaft, 1912–22. reprint, Tutzing: Hans Schneider, 1974. Neue Folge, 3 vols., Tutzing: Hans Schneider, 1991–95.

Vol. 2. *Johannes Brahms im Briefwechsel mit Heinrich und Elisabet von Herzogenberg.* Edited by Max Kalbeck. 4th, rev. ed. 1921.

Vol. 4. *Johannes Brahms im Briefwechsel mit J. O. Grimm.* Edited by Richard Barth. 1912.

Vols. 9, 10. *Johannes Brahms Briefe an P. J. Simrock und Fritz Simrock.* Edited by Max Kalbeck. 1917.

Vols. 11, 12. *Johannes Brahms Briefe an Fritz Simrock.* Edited by Max Kalbeck. 1919.

Vol. 18. *Johannes Brahms im Briefwechsel mit Julius Stockhausen.* Edited by Renate Hofmann. 1993.

Antonín Dvořák Korrespondenz und Dokumente: Abgesandte Korrespondenz. 3 vols. Prague: Editio Supraphon, 1987–89.

Gottlieb-Billroth, Otto, ed. *Billroth und Brahms im Briefwechsel.* Berlin and Vienna: Urban & Schwarzenberg, 1935.

Joachim, Johannes, and Andreas Moser, eds. *Briefe von und an Joseph Joachim.* 3 vols. Berlin: Julius Bard, 1911–13.

Litzmann, Berthold, ed. *Clara Schumann–Johannes Brahms: Briefe aus den Jahren 1853–1896.* 2 vols. Leipzig: Breitkopf & Härtel, 1927.

Spengel, Annemarie, ed. *Johannes Brahms an Julius Spengel: Unveröffentlichte Briefe aus dem Jahren 1882–1897.* Hamburg: Gesellschaft der Bücherfreunde, 1959.

Stephenson, Kurt, ed. *Johannes Brahms und Fritz Simrock: Weg einer Freundschaft: Briefe des Verlegers an den Komponisten.* Hamburg: J. J. Augustin, 1961.

Wirth, Julia, ed. *Julius Stockhausen: Der Sänger des deutschen Liedes.* Frankfurt am Main: Verlag Englert und Schlosser, 1927.

Books, Articles, and Reviews

Altmann, Wilhelm. *Verzeichnis von Werken für Klavier vier- und sechshändig sowie für zwei und mehr Klaviere.* Leipzig: Friedrich Hofmeister, 1943.

Becker, Heinz, and Richard Green. "Berlin." In *The New Grove Dictionary of Music and Musicians,* ed. Stanley Sadie, 2:565–78. London: Macmillan, 1980.

Bernstein, Eduard. *Die Geschichte der Berliner Arbeiterbewegung.* 3 vols. Berlin: Buchhandlung Vorwärts, 1907–10.

Boetticher, Wolfgang. "Joachim, Joseph." In *Die Musik in Geschichte und Gegenwart,* ed. Friedrich Blume, 7:59. Cassel: Bärenreiter, 1949–68.

Bozarth, George. " 'New' Brahms Manuscripts." *American Brahms Society Newsletter* 1, no. 1 (spring 1983): [4]–[5].

———. "A New Collected Edition for Brahms." In *Brahms 3: Biographical, Documentary and Analytical Studies,* ed. Robert Pascall. Cambridge: Cambridge University Press, in press.

———. "News and Comment." *American Brahms Society Newsletter* 7, no. 1 (spring 1989): 8–10.

Brodbeck, David. "Brahms's Edition of Twenty Schubert Ländler: An Essay in Criticism." In *Brahms Studies: Analytical and Historical Perspectives,* ed. George S. Bozarth, 229–50. Oxford: Clarendon Press, 1990.

———. Review of Margit L. McCorkle, *Johannes Brahms Thematisch-bibliographisches Werkverzeichnis. Journal of the American Musicological Society* 42 (1989): 418–31.

Brody, Elaine. *Paris: The Musical Kaleidoscope, 1870–1925.* New York: George Braziller, 1987.

Broesike-Schoen, Max. "Der moderne Klavierauszug: Eine Rundfrage." *Die Musik* 16 (1923): 97.

Cai, Camilla. "Was Brahms a Reliable Editor? Changes Made in Opuses 116, 117, 118 and 119." *Acta Musicologica* 61 (1989): 83–101.

Charlton, David, ed. *E. T. A. Hoffmann's Musical Writings.* Translated by Martyn Clarke. Cambridge: Cambridge University Press, 1989.

Clapham, John. *Antonín Dvořák: Musician and Craftsman.* London: Faber & Faber, 1966.

———. *Dvořák.* Newton Abbot and London: David & Charles, 1979.

Eitner, Robert. "Stern, Julius." *Allgemeine deutsche Biographie* 36 (1893): 106–7.

Epstein, David. *Beyond Orpheus: Studies in Musical Structure.* Cambridge MA, and London: MIT Press, 1979.

———. "Brahms and the Mechanisms of Motion: The Composition of Performance." In *Brahms Studies: Analytical and Historical Perspectives,* ed. George S. Bozarth, 191–226. Oxford: Clarendon Press, 1990.

Fellinger, Imogen. "Cyclic Tendencies in Brahms's Song Collections." In *Brahms Studies: Analytical and Historical Perspectives,* ed. George S. Bozarth, 379–88. Oxford: Clarendon Press, 1990.

Friedlaender, Max. *Brahms Lieder.* Berlin and Leipzig: N. Simrock, 1922. Translated by C. Leonard Leese as *Brahms's Lieder.* London: Oxford University Press, Humphrey Milford, 1928.

Geiringer, Karl, in collaboration with Irene Geiringer. *Brahms: His Life and Work.* 3d ed. New York: Da Capo Press, 1982.

Goertzen, Valerie Woodring. "The Piano Transcriptions of Johannes Brahms." Ph.D. diss., University of Illinois, 1987.

Grasberger, Franz. *Johannes Brahms: Variationen um sein Wesen.* Vienna: Paul Kaltschmid, 1952.

Haas, Frithjof. "Die Erstfassung des langsamen Satzes der ersten Sinfonie von Johannes Brahms." *Die Musikforschung* 36 (1983): 200–211.

Harding, James. *Saint-Saëns and His Circle.* London: Chapman & Hall, 1965.

Hauptmann, Gerhart. *The Weavers. Hannele. The Beaver Coat.* Translated by Horst Frenz and Miles Waggoner. New York and Toronto: Rinehart & Co., 1951.

Henschel, George. *Personal Recollections of Johannes Brahms.* Boston: Richard G. Badger, Gorham Press, 1907.

Historischer Handatlas von Brandenburg und Berlin. Veröffentlichungen der Historische Kommission zu Berlin, Lfg. 1, 21. Berlin: Walter de Gruyter, 1963.

Hofmann, Kurt. *Die Bibliothek von Johannes Brahms.* Hamburg: Karl Dieter Wagner, 1974.

———. *Die Erstdrucke der Werke von Johannes Brahms.* Tutzing: Hans Schneider, 1975.

Hofmann, Kurt, and Jutta Fürst. *Johannes Brahms: The Man and His Work.* Detroit: Detroit Symphony Orchestra, 1980.

Hofmann, Renate, and Kurt Hofmann. *Johannes Brahms Zeittafel zu Leben und Werk.* Tutzing: Hans Schneider, 1983.

———. *32 Stichvorlagen von Werken Johannes Brahms.* KulturStiftung der Länder–PATRIMONIA, vol. 107. Kiel: KulturStiftung der Länder, 1995.

Kahn, Robert. "Recollections of Johannes Brahms." In Burkhard Laugwitz, "Robert Kahn and Brahms," trans. Reinhard Pauly, *Musical Quarterly* 74 (1990): 601–9.

Kalbeck, Max. *Johannes Brahms.* 4 vols. Rev. ed. Berlin: Deutsche Brahms-Gesellschaft, 1912–21. Reprint Tutzing: Hans Schneider, 1976.

Klatte, Wilhelm, and Ludwig Misch. *Das Sternsche Konservatorium der Musik zu Berlin, 1850–1925: Festschrift zum 75jährigen Jubiläum.* Berlin: Sittenfeld, 1925.

Krammer, Mario. *Berlin im Wandel der Jahrhunderte: Eine Kulturgeschichte der Deutschen Hauptstadt.* 2d ed. Berlin: Rembrandt Verlag, 1956.

Langner, Thomas M. "Stern, Julius." In *Die Musik in Geschichte und Gegenwart,* ed. Friedrich Blume, 12:1278–79. Cassel: Bärenreiter, 1949–68.

Liepmannssohn-Versteigerungs-Katalog 59: Versteigerung am 20. und 21. Mai 1930. Berlin: Leo Liepmannssohn, 1930.

Litzmann, Berthold. *Clara Schumann: Ein Künstlerleben nach Tagebüchern und Briefen.* 3 vols., 8th (vol. 1), 7th (vol. 2), 5th/6th (vol. 3) rev. eds. Leipzig: Breitkopf & Härtel, 1923–25.

Masur, Gerhard. *Imperial Berlin.* New York and London: Basic Books, 1970.

May, Florence. *The Life of Johannes Brahms.* 2d ed., rev. London: William Reeves, n.d.

McCorkle, Margit L. "Filling the Gaps in Brahms Source Research: Several Important Recent Manuscript Discoveries." Paper read at the annual meeting of the American Musicological Society, Ann Arbor MI, 1982.

———. *Johannes Brahms Thematisch-bibliographisches Werkverzeichnis.* Munich: G. Henle Verlag, 1984.

————. "The Role of Trial Performances for Brahms's Orchestral and Large Choral Works: Sources and Circumstances." In *Brahms Studies: Analytical and Historical Perspectives*, ed. George S. Bozarth, 295–327. Oxford: Clarendon Press, 1990.

Melamed, Daniel, and Virginia Hancock. "Brahms's Kyrie and *Missa canonica*." *American Brahms Society Newsletter* 3, no. 1 (spring 1985): [5]–[7].

Meyer, J. *Das große Conversations-Lexicon für die gebildeten Stände*. Hildburghausen: Verlag des Bibliographische Institut, 1850.

Neuer, Adam. "Wroclaw." In *The New Grove Dictionary of Music and Musicians*, ed. Stanley Sadie, 20:542–44. London: Macmillan, 1980.

Newman, Ernest. *The Life of Wagner*. 4 vols. New York: Alfred A. Knopf, 1946.

Newman, S. T. M. "The Slow Movement of Brahms' First Symphony: A Reconstruction of the Version First Performed Prior to Publication." *Music Review* 24 (1948): 4–12.

Nodnagel, Ernst Otto. *Gedenkblätter zur Einweihungsfeier der neuen Räume des Stern'schen Konservatoriums der Musik zu Berlin*. Berlin: n.p., 1899. (Unpaginated.)

Oliver, Robert Thomas. "Joachim Quartet." In *The New Grove Dictionary of Music and Musicians*, ed. Stanley Sadie, 9:654–55. London and New York: Macmillan, 1980.

Orel, Alfred. *Johannes Brahms, 1833–1897: Sein Leben in Bildern*. Leipzig: Bibliographisches Institut, 1937.

————. "Johannes Brahms' Musikbibliothek." *Simrock Jahrbuch* 3 (1930–34): 18–47. Reprinted in Hofmann, *Die Bibliothek von Johannes Brahms*, 139–66.

Ottendorff-Simrock, Walther. *Das Haus Simrock: Ein Beitrag zur Geschichte der kulturtragenden Familien des Rheinlandes*. Ratingen: Aloys Henn Verlag, 1954.

Pascall, Robert. *Brahms's First Symphony Andante—the Initial Performing Version: Commentary and Realisation*. Papers in Musicology, no. 2. Nottingham: Department of Music, University of Nottingham, 1992.

————. "Brahms's First Symphony Slow Movement: The Initial Performing Version." *Musical Times* 112 (1981): 664–67.

————. "Brahms's *Missa canonica* and Its Recomposition in His Motet 'Warum,' Op. 74 No. 1." In *Brahms 2: Biographical, Documentary and Analytical Studies*, ed. Michael Musgrave, 111–36. Cambridge: Cambridge University Press, 1987.

————. "The Publication of Brahms's Third Symphony: A Crisis in Dissemination." In *Brahms Studies: Analytical and Historical Perspectives*, ed. George S. Bozarth, 283–94. Oxford: Clarendon Press, 1990.

————. Review of *Concerto for Violin, Op. 77 by Johannes Brahms: A Facsimile of the Holograph Score*. *Music and Letters* 62 (1980): 95–97.

Pazdírek, Franz. *Universal-Handbuch der Musikliteratur aller Zeiten und Völker*. 34 vols. Vienna: Verlag des Universal-Handbuch der Musikliteratur, Pazdírek & Co., 1904–10.

Reich, Nancy. *Clara Schumann: The Artist and the Woman*. Ithaca and London: Cornell University Press, 1985.

Roesner, Linda Correll. "Brahms's Editions of Schumann." In *Brahms Studies: Analytical and Historical Perspectives,* ed. George S. Bozarth, 251–82. Oxford: Clarendon Press, 1990.

————. Review of *Concerto for Violin, Op. 77 by Johannes Brahms: A Facsimile of the Holograph Score. Current Musicology* 30 (1980): 60–72.

Saint-Saëns, Camille. "Bayreuth und der Ring des Nibelungen." *Die Musik* 2 (1902): 879ff.

————. *Harmonie et mélodie.* Paris: Calmann-Lévy, 1885.

Scholz, Albert A. *Silesia Yesterday and Today.* The Hague: Martinus Nijhoff, 1964.

Schumann, Eugenie. *Erinnerungen.* 2d ed. Stuttgart: J. Engelhorns Nachfolger, 1925. Translated by Marie Busch as *Memoirs of Eugenie Schumann.* London: William Heinemann, 1927. Also translated as *The Schumanns and Johannes Brahms.* New York: L. MacVeagh, Dial Press, 1927. Reprint, Freeport NY: Books for Libraries Press, 1970; Westport CT: Hyperion Press, 1979.

Schwarz, Boris. "Joseph Joachim and the Genesis of Brahms's Violin Concerto." *Musical Quarterly* 69 (1983): 503–26.

Smyth, Ethel. "Recollections of Brahms." *Fortnightly* 139 (o.s. 145; May 1936): 548–58.

Stegemann, Michael. *Camille Saint-Saëns and the French Solo Concerto from 1850 to 1920.* Translated by Ann C. Sherwin. Portland OR: Amadeus Press, 1991.

————. "Camille Saint-Saëns und Deutschland." *Melos/Neue Zeitschrift für Musik* 4 (1976): 267–70.

Teuber, Alfons. *Silesia in Pictures: A Record of Remembrance.* Translated by Margaret D. Senft. Munich: Verlag "Chirist Unterwegs," 1951.

Thematisches Verzeichniss der bisher im Druck erschienenen Werke von Johannes Brahms. Edited by Robert Keller. Berlin: N. Simrock, 1887. Reprinted (and expanded) as *Thematisches Verzeichniss sämmtlicher im Druck erschienenen Werke von Johannes Brahms.* Berlin: N. Simrock, 1897.

Wagner, Richard. *Eine Capitulation.* 1873. Translated by William Ashton Ellis in *Richard Wagner's Prose Works,* 5:3–33. London: Kegan Paul, Trench, Trubner, 1896. Reprint, New York: Broude Brothers, 1966.

Wilhelmy, Petra. *Der Berliner Salon im 19. Jahrhundert (1780–1914).* Veröffentlichungen der Historischen Kommission zu Berlin, vol. 73. Berlin and New York: Walter de Gruyter, 1989.

Zimm, A., ed. *Berlin und sein Umland: Eine geographische Monographie.* Petermanns Geographischen Mitteilungen, vol. 286. Gotha: VEB Hermann Haack, Geographische-Kartographische Anstalt, 1988.

Music

Johannes Brahms, Der Herbst—Erste Fassung von 1886, Im Herbst—Zweite Fassung von 1888 für vierstimmigen gemischten Chor a cappella. Edited by Kurt Hofmann. Leipzig: Deutscher Verlag für Musik, 1983.

Johannes Brahms: Messe für vier- bis sechsstimmigen gemischten Chor und Continuo (Orgel). Edited by Otto Biba. Vienna: Doblinger, 1984.

Johannes Brahms sämtliche Werke. 26 vols. Edited by Eusebius Mandyczewski and Hans Gál. Leipzig: Breitkopf & Härtel, 1926–28.

Johannes Brahms und seine Freunde: Werke für Klavier. Edited by Joachim Draheim. Leipzig: Breitkopf & Härtel, 1983.

Antonín Dvořák, Gipsy Songs Cigánské Melodie Opus 55. Reprint of the original edition by N. Simrock. New York: Associated Music Publishers, n.d.

Antonín Dvořák, Houslovy Koncert Op. 53. Edited by Otakar Šourek. Prague: Státní Nakladatelství, 1955.

Anton Dvořák, Quartet für 2 Violinen, Bratsche und Violoncell, Op. 51. Berlin: N. Simrock, 1879.

Antonín Dvořák, Sextet A Dur op. 48. Edited by Antonín Čubr and Otakar Šourek. Prague: Státní Nakladatelství, 1957.

Facsimiles (Arranged by Opus Number)

Johannes Brahms. Opus 24. Opus 23. Opus 18. Opus 90. New York: Robert Owen Lehman Foundation, 1967.

Johannes Brahms, Symphony No. 1 in C Minor, Op. 68: The Autograph Score. Pierpont Morgan Library Music Manuscript Reprint Series, ed. Stanley Appelbaum and J. Rigbie Turner. With an introduction by Margit L. McCorkle. New York: Dover Publications, 1986.

Concerto for Violin, Op. 77 by Johannes Brahms: A Facsimile of the Holograph Score. With an introduction by Yehudi Menuhin and a foreword by Jon Newsom. Washington DC: Library of Congress, 1979.

Johannes Brahms: 4. Symphonie in E-moll Op. 98: Faksimile des autographen Manuskripts aus dem Besitz der Allgemeinen Musikgesellschaft Zürich. With an introduction by Günter Birkner. Adliswil-Zurich: Edition Eulenberg, 1974.

General Index

Index of Brahms's Compositions